# Windows 8

BARRIE SOSINSKY

Peachpit Press

Visual QuickStart Guide
# Windows 8
Barrie Sosinsky

Peachpit Press
1249 Eighth Street
Berkeley, CA 94710
510/524-2178
510/524-2221 (fax)

Find us on the Web at: www.peachpit.com
To report errors, please send a note to errata@peachpit.com.
Peachpit Press is a division of Pearson Education.



Editor: Clifford Colby
Production editor: Robyn G. Thomas
Production editor: Danielle Foster
Copyeditor: Scout Festa
Tech editor: Marcus Perry
Indexer: Valerie Haynes Perry
Cover design: RHDG / Riezebos Holzbaur Design Group, Peachpit Press
Interior design: Peachpit Press
Logo design: MINE™ www.minesf.com



ISBN-13: 978-0-321-88895-2
ISBN-10:     0-321-88895-2

9 8 7 6 5 4 3 2 1

Printed and bound in the United States of America

## Dedication

To Allie and Joe, the lights of my life

## Acknowledgments

I would like to thank the many people who contributed to the making of this book. The first is my literary agent and long-time friend, Matt Wagner of Fresh Books (www.fresh-books.com), for keeping me in mind for this project and pitching me to Peachpit. Thanks also to Cliff Colby, who as the acquisition editor, has the ultimate responsibility for delivering a quality product; I appreciate his taking a chance on me and his professionalism all the way through.

The editorial team I worked with was really first class. Robyn Thomas and Scout Festa were the two editors responsible for keeping the content on track and accurate. Countless times they made suggestions that improved the quality of the book. They made sure that the book you are holding is appropriately *Peachpit wacky*, and not *Barrie wacky*, something I'm sure I'll be happy about as this book ages. I also want to thank my friend Marcus Perry for serving as tech editor on this project. Marcus and I share a love of building computers and putting new operating systems through their paces.

As with most projects, there were countless behind-the-scenes people who worked silently to bring this book from concept to reality: Danielle Foster, compositor; Valerie Perry, indexer; and many more. I thank you for doing what you do with the devotion you do it.

As always, I learned a lot while writing this book. Windows 8 will keep Microsoft humming along and relevant in the years to come. With this book to press, I'm looking forward to more long runs, some extra time at the gym, playing with my cats (Stormy, Shadow, Smokey, Scamper, Slate, and Spats), and—oh yes, more sleep!

# Table of Contents

# Introduction

Windows 8 represents the most radical departure from previous versions of Windows since the introduction of Windows 95. Windows 95 made Windows come alive by adding the Internet. Windows 8 pays homage to an increasingly mobile world by adding a new application model and a touch-oriented interface. This might come as a shock to many users of previous Windows versions, but Windows 8 is easy to use, and in many ways it is a more refined version of what has gone before. Gone is the Start menu; enter the Start screen Ⓐ.

The new Windows 8-style apps have no windowing system, run in a much smaller memory footprint, and save their contents from memory when you are not using them. Thus, your laptop, tablet, and cell phone will have longer battery life, be more stable, and be less susceptible to crashes. And a lot of behind-the-scenes work has gone into making connecting to networks seamless and pervasive.

When you think about it, an operating system that can use the same basic code to run on devices as diverse as PCs and cell phones is a considerable achievement. No other vendor offers such an operating system. What this means to you is that your applications will be available on—and will behave nearly identically on—all of your devices. When a device doesn't have a particular feature, the application simply doesn't implement it. For developers, this means that the expensive up-front development costs of a Windows application may be amortized by having their application run across the entire Windows 8 universe.

The Windows 7-style Desktop has not gone away in Windows 8 Ⓑ. You can access the Desktop from a tile on the Start screen, and you can move from the Start screen to the Desktop by pressing the ⊞ key. Little of the functionality found in Windows 7's Desktop and its related management applications and control panels has been removed, but Microsoft has duplicated control panel functionality in new, touch-enabled panes called *bars*.

**A** The Start screen features Live Tiles, which launch programs and display relevant information.

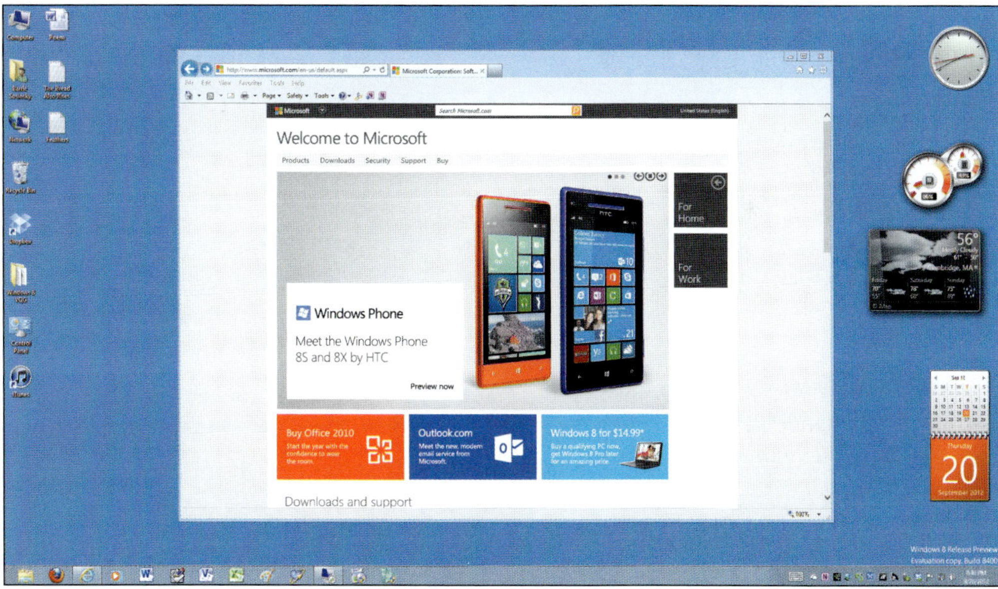

**B** The Desktop and its windowing environment have been carried over from Windows 7 to Windows 8. Shown are the familiar taskbar, the windowed version of Internet Explorer 10, and gadgets.

(C) is an example of how a touch-oriented interface is implemented. Compare Internet Explorer running in the new, tile-based style (C) to the same browser on the Desktop (B). Gone are complex menus; they are replaced by buttons, bars, and very simple pop-up menus. This new type of application, which we will refer to in this book as an app, is simple to learn and simple to use. It will take you a little while to learn all the ins and outs of these apps, but hopefully this book will help you get up and running quickly.

In the new, touch-oriented interface, corners and edges have actions associated with them. Swipe in from the right and you see the Charms bar (D), another of Windows 8's most notable new features. If you select the Settings charm and then click the *Change PC settings* link, you display the touch-oriented version of the Control Panel. This gives you some idea of how these new features are implemented. But if you don't have a phone, tablet, or touch screen and want to work with Windows 8 on a PC, don't worry. Everything you can do with touch gestures, you can do with a mouse and keyboard. This book will show you how.

## Is This Book for You?

This book assumes no prior knowledge of the Windows operating system. Perhaps this is your first Windows book—if so, you will learn enough about Windows 8 to perform the most important operations that users must perform in their daily work.

As a Visual QuickStart Guide, this book is meant to help you learn about a feature quickly and perform the task you need with minimum effort. This book doesn't tell you everything there is to know about a topic and doesn't delve much into theory, but it does tell you a lot.

### What's in a Name?

These new apps and the tile-based Start screen interface were developed under the code name "Metro." Unfortunately, just as Windows 8 was coming to market Microsoft learned that the name Metro is the trademarked property of Metro AG, a giant wholesale/retail chain with properties across Europe and Asia. To avoid a costly lawsuit, Microsoft dropped the name Metro from its product literature and website.

The *Windows 8 styled* name for the Start screen interface itself is still unclear. For the sake of simplicity and clarity, this book calls the new Windows 8 Start screen interface *the tiled-based interface* and the new style of apps *tile-based apps*.

The older desktop interface that Windows 7 users are accustomed to is referred to as the Desktop, and the applications built to run in a windowed environment—such as Quicken, Adobe Photoshop, and the Microsoft Office suite—are referred to as legacy applications or Desktop applications.

It's not pretty folks—but I'm sure you will find that Windows 8 *is* pretty.

Indeed, the Desktop cannot go away any time soon because billions of dollars of applications run in that environment. But over time, many of these applications will be rebuilt as smaller, more modular apps.

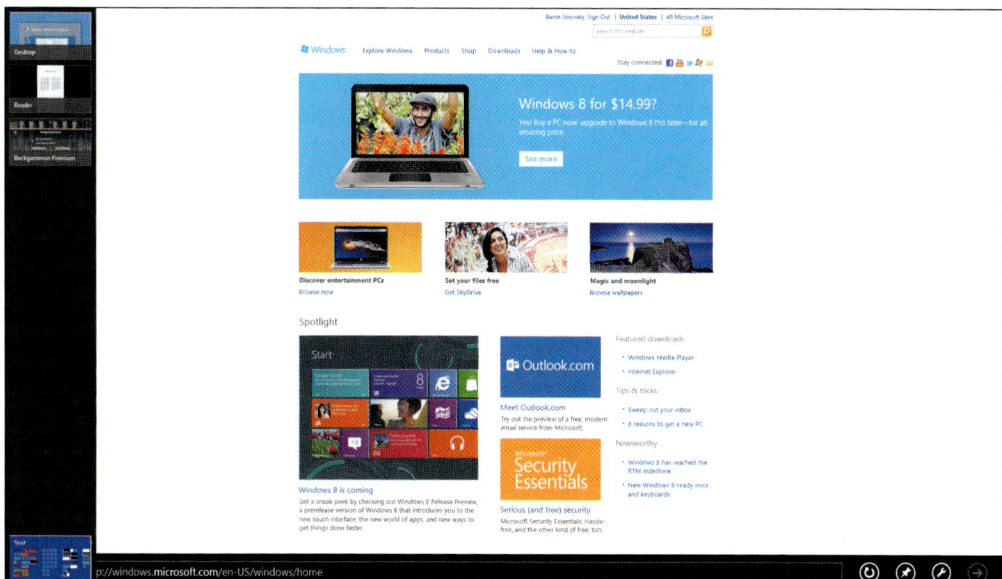

**C** The tile-based Internet Explorer app consumes the entire screen. A bar on the left shows open apps, but this sliding feature isn't usually shown.

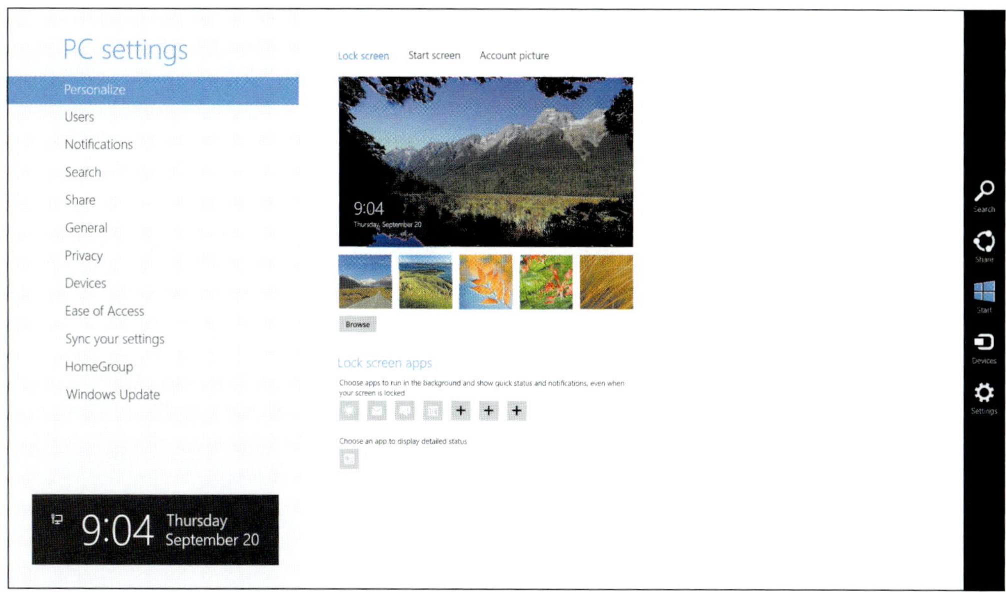

**D** The Charms bar (on the right) and the PC settings screen

It would be nice if you had the time to read this book sequentially from cover to cover, but it isn't essential. Some chapters build on earlier chapters, but most chapters and many of the topics are self-contained. You can jump into this book wherever you need to.

## What This Book Will Teach You

There are 17 chapters in this book, each on a separate topic. Here's a short summary of what you will find in each chapter:

- **Chapter 1**, "Getting Started," tells you about the different versions of Windows 8, the features they contain, and how to install and upgrade the operating system.

- **Chapter 2**, "The Start Screen," introduces you to the Start screen, Live Tiles, the Charms bar, the Apps bar, and the other touch-based interface features you need to know to work with the new apps.

- **Chapter 3**, "Touch and Gestures," tells you how to navigate using touch and, when touch isn't available, with a mouse and keyboard.

- **Chapter 4**, "The Classic Interface," is an introduction to the Desktop interface. You will learn about personalizing the screen, using the taskbar, and how windowed applications work.

- **Chapter 5**, "Settings and Customization," explains how to use control panels and settings to manage your computing environment. This chapter also describes the powerful new search function and the options available to you from the Charms bar.

- **Chapter 6**, "Applications," describes how to open applications, switch between applications, and organize and modify apps in both Windows 8 interfaces.

- **Chapter 7**, "Windows 8 Tile-Based Apps," describes the new apps that ship with Windows 8. These apps are cloud-connected to web services and include all manner of people, places, and things. You'll find a calendar, an address book, media content organizers, and many more apps that have many unique features.

- **Chapter 8**, "Managing Content," contains an introduction to how data is stored and accessed on your computer. You'll learn here about file types, the Clipboard, drag and drop, libraries, media lists, and many other topics.

- **Chapter 9**, "Printers and Devices," describes the different devices that you can connect to a Windows 8 system, and how to configure them so that they work properly. The tile-based interface has a simplified print routine that is described in this chapter.

- **Chapter 10**, "Windows Explorer," tells you about the main tool that you use to manage files in the file system. Windows Explorer has long been a mainstay in Windows, and Windows 8 makes it more powerful and adds a ribbon interface and some interesting new tools to it.

- **Chapter 11**, "Diagnosis and Recovery," describes how to solve problems and learn more about how your system is working. This chapter contains information about troubleshooting Windows 8 with new Refresh and Restart commands, how to use the new, much more powerful Task Manager, and much more.

- **Chapter 12**, "Disks and Storage Devices," tells you about the different types of disks and storage types you can use with Windows 8 and how to prepare them for use. You will learn about disks, volumes, partitions, and more. New features such as Storage Spaces are described in this chapter.

- **Chapter 13**, "Networking," describes how to connect to networks of all types. Windows 8 relies very heavily on an Internet connection, and a lot of work has gone into making connectivity easier, faster, and more reliable. This is plumbing, but it's an essential topic. You'll learn about what's new in networking in this chapter.

- **Chapter 14**, "Internet Explorer 10," describes Microsoft's new web browser. IE10 is one application, but it comes in two forms: one on the Desktop (windowed), and the second in the tile-based interface (where it is full screen). There are many new features in IE10 that enhance security, make browsing easier, and provide faster and smoother performance.

- **Chapter 15**, "Mobile Computing," describes the features in Windows 8 that support tablets and cell phones. Windows Phone 8 is a significant phone operating system. Some Windows 8 tablets are full-fledged Windows 8 computers, while others—running Windows RT—use only the new, tile-based apps.

- **Chapter 16**, "Security," is an important chapter because with an Internet-connected device you are always vulnerable. This chapter describes the basic rules you need to follow to be secure, presents Windows 8's built-in security tools, and explains how you should use them. Read this chapter and you will find out what you can do to avoid intrusions.

- **Chapter 17**, "Cloud Connections," rounds out this book by describing how Windows 8 leverages a wide variety of Microsoft services on the Internet to add great power to your Windows 8 device. Through the cloud, you can back up your data and settings and synchronize them across many devices. You'll want to know more about these services, because they make Windows 8 much more powerful and fun to work with. This chapter also presents the new Windows Store, which is where you will get your new-styled apps.

# What's Not in This Book

Windows 8 is a consumer-based operating system in which you start up in the Start screen and the new tile-based interface. That's fine for devices built for Windows 8, but it presents an issue for Windows 8's adoption into the corporate world. Windows 8 contains all of the corporate features found in Windows 7; that is, you can join a domain, have domain security, and use group policies. This book does not address Windows 8 in a business context. There's little discussion of how Windows 8 will be used in a corporate setting. The rationale for this omission is that Windows 8 is built for a world based on BYOD, or Bring Your Own Device, and the corporate world is not there yet.

You also won't find a lot of computer theory in this book. We don't tell you about how the Windows 8 operating system runs on hardware and operating system modules, how CPUs operate, or how software instructions are processed through threading.

Virtual machine technology is an advanced topic and is not included in this book, but it is an important new feature in Windows 8 that many advanced users will find useful.

It would really take two books to explain how to use Windows 8 as well as how Windows 8 works (its internals).

There are other worthy topics that didn't make it into this edition of the book. Some of them aren't yet fully developed in Windows 8; this is a new operating system, after all. Other topics, such as gaming, Xbox integration, and in-depth descriptions of individual apps, were dropped to keep the book length reasonable. Applications that are central to Windows 8, such as Internet Explorer and Windows Explorer, are included.

## How This Book Works

Each chapter is organized around a topic, and each section is generally organized around a task or related set of tasks. In a section, you get a short introduction to the topic, followed by step-by-step instructions on how to perform the tasks. This book tries to cherry-pick the most important task, and when there is a large set of related tasks, the task that is either most important or most representative of the set is included.

You'll find that the instructions come with graphic icons, screens, and operations that are keyed with circled letters, such as A, B, C, and so on. These figures allow you to stay oriented as you perform these operations, which will allow you to be more successful and accurate.

This version of Windows contains two different interfaces, so as a general rule there is always more than one way to perform an action. Whenever possible, this book tells you how to do things in multiple ways. It's our belief that the more ways you learn

how to perform an action, the greater the chances are that you will remember one of them and get your task done successfully.

Finally, each section ends with a tip that will expand your knowledge of the topic. We hope you will find these tips useful and that your curiosity will lead you to use them to learn more about Windows 8.

## Conventions Used in This Book

In this book we make it a point to describe a feature not only by its name but by its type as well. For example, a control panel called Devices and Printers is referred to as the Devices and Printers control panel. For menus and commands, we will tell you to, for example, "select the Exit command from the File menu."

This isn't a programming book, so there isn't a lot of code, but when it does appear, it's in **a unique font**. When you have to enter text into a field or dialog box, you will see it displayed in **bold**. The names of links appear in *italics*.

Acronyms and initialisms—such as PnP, which stands for Plug and Play—are defined when they first appear. Most terms are in the index, if you need to look them up.

One more thing—if you purchased this book, you are entitled to download its electronic version. Peachpit has also recorded to video many of the common operations described in this book for you to use as you need them. People learn in many different ways. A book is one way, but demonstrations in the form of videos are also a powerful way to learn. So please make use of these resources.

# Getting Started

Windows 8 arrives in a computing world that is very different from that in which previous versions of Windows were installed. Each of the previous seven major releases was destined to run on an Intel architecture x86 PC. Today there is a cell phone for nearly every person on the planet, and tablets outsell PCs roughly six to one. For Microsoft to stay relevant in this world, it needed an operating system like Windows 8 to compete with Apple's iOS and Google's Android.

Windows 8 presents the user with a unified code base that allows apps to run across a wide range of devices (PCs, tablets, and phones) and to carry the same apps and data from one to the other via Microsoft's cloud-based properties. No other vendor has that. To do this, Microsoft has developed a new style of application based on a new programming model. Microsoft refers to these new apps as Windows Store apps, but the name I'll use throughout this book is *tile-based apps*.

## In This Chapter

The most dramatic change is that Windows 8 boots up into a tile-based interface called the Start screen, which conserves video and memory resources. The Start screen **A** is Windows' new face to the world. The new apps look different, and behave differently, with less overhead and fewer controls.

**A** The Start screen is designed to run on displays as small as a cell phone.

In the center panel of **B** is the new News application. The left pane shows legacy applications running in the Desktop, and on the right is the Charms bar for performing searches, sharing content across apps, working with devices, and altering a variety of settings. Although designed for touch, this new interface works equally well with a mouse and keyboard.

Gone in Windows 8 are resource hogs like the Aero interface; gone too are familiar metaphors such as the Start menu. What is not gone is the Windows 7 Desktop and windowing system, because hundreds of thousands of apps have been written for the windowing system that is part of the Desktop interface. Those legacy applications are not going away any time soon, but new apps will eventually adopt the new programming style for the same reason that Microsoft created it: It gives developers access to a much broader audience across a range of devices.

If you are a Windows 7 user migrating to Windows 8, the new interface may come as a bit of a shock. Windows 8 needs touch-enabled devices to be fully appreciated, and there are new techniques to learn and old techniques to unlearn. There's a lot in Windows 8 to like. Microsoft has dramatically improved the performance of the operating system. Apps are faster, batteries last longer, searches are more powerful, there are more connection options, startup can be nearly instantaneous, and recovery from system faults is more graceful. So keep an open mind. Windows 8 is Microsoft's future, and there are many things in it to embrace.

 News is an example of the tile-based apps. The operating system maintains the Windows 7-styled Desktop (left) but also has touch-oriented control functions, as exemplified by the Charms bar (right).

# Windows 8 Versions

Windows 8 comes in four different versions for four different audiences:

- Windows 8 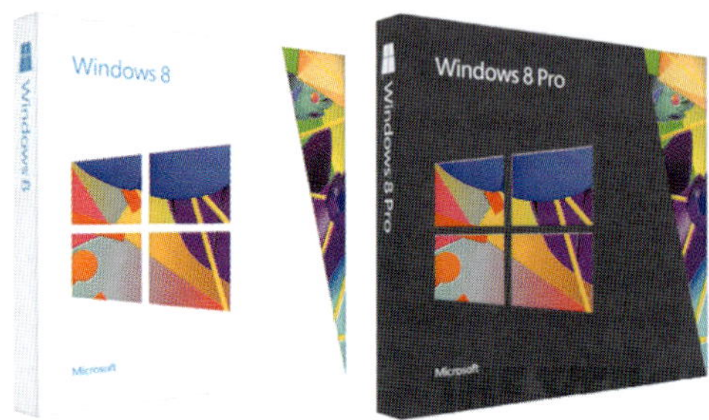 is for home users. It is a basic version for Intel x86-32 and x86-64 systems. This version comes with the Start screen and Desktop, Microsoft accounts, Live Tiles, semantic zoom, the Windows Store, Internet Explorer 10, and the other features the majority of users will want.



**A** Windows 8 (left) and Windows 8 Pro (right) retail packaging

- Windows 8 Pro **A** (the box shown on the right) is for business and professional users. Pro adds domain support (Windows security groups), the encrypted file system, Hyper-V, virtual hard disk booting, group policy support, and BitLocker. Users will be able to add Windows Media Center as a free add-on to Pro, which is the most compelling reason for the average PC user to want this version of the product.

- Windows 8 RT is for mobile users running devices with ARM processors and is not sold separately to the public. Windows 8 RT will support tile-based apps with no Desktop support but comes with touch support and special touch-centric versions of the Microsoft Office suite.

- Windows 8 Enterprise is sold to businesses that buy desktops in bulk. The Enterprise edition adds to Windows 8 Pro additional network security features, more virtualization tools, and mobility options. Neither Windows 8 RT nor Enterprise come in retail packaging.

Individual users will most likely be interested in either Windows 8 or Windows 8 Pro, depending on whether they need features such as file system encryption, domain support, or virtual machine technology.

**TIP** Microsoft allows you try Windows and Office products free for 90 days before you must purchase them. If you want to give Windows 8 and Office 2013 a try, you will find links for trials on each product's home page: www.microsoft.com/windows and www.microsoft.com/office.

# Features by Version

Windows 8 has a number of new features, but not all features appear in every version of the operating system. Use **Table 1.1** to determine if the version you are interested in has the features you need.

**TABLE 1.1** Windows 8 Features

| Features | Windows RT | Windows 8 | Windows 8 Pro | Windows Enterprise |
| --- | --- | --- | --- | --- |
| Packaging | Installed on devices | Retail | Retail | Volume Licenses |
| Processor | ARM (32-bit) | Intel architecture x86 32- or 64-bit | Intel architecture x86 32- or 64-bit | Intel architecture x86 32- or 64-bit |
| Desktop | Partial | ✔ | ✔ | ✔ |
| Legacy applications | ✘ | ✔ | ✔ | ✔ |
| Start screen/tile interface | ✔ | ✔ | ✔ | ✔ |
| Touch interface/virtual keyboard | ✔ | ✔ | ✔ | ✔ |
| Touch apps[1] | ✔ | ✔ | ✔ | ✔ |
| Office applications | Touch version | Separate | Separate | Separate |
| Exchange ActiveSync | ✔ | ✔ | ✔ | ✔ |
| Internet Explorer 10 | ✔ | ✔ | ✔ | ✔ |
| Windows Store | ✔ | ✔ | ✔ | ✔ |
| Microsoft Account | ✔ | ✔ | ✔ | ✔ |
| Xbox Live | ✔ | ✔ | ✔ | ✔ |
| VPN | ✔ | ✔ | ✔ | ✔ |
| Remote Desktop | Client | Client | Client/Host | Client/Host |
| Mobile broadband | ✔ | ✔ | ✔ | ✔ |
| Windows Media Player | ✘ | ✔ | ✔ | ✔ |
| Windows Media Center | ✘ | ✘ | Free download | ✘ |
| Storage Spaces | ✘ | ✔ | ✔ | ✔ |
| Domain support | ✘ | ✘ | ✔ | ✔ |
| Group policy | ✘ | ✘ | ✔ | ✔ |
| Hyper-V[2] | ✘ | ✘ | ✔ | ✔ |
| AppLocker | ✘ | ✘ | ✘ | ✔ |
| Windows-To-Go[3] | ✘ | ✘ | ✘ | ✔ |
| Improved Task Manager | ✔ | ✔ | ✔ | ✔ |
| Refresh and Reset | ✔ | ✔ | ✔ | ✔ |
| File History | ✔ | ✔ | ✔ | ✔ |
| Windows Update/Defender | ✔ | ✔ | ✔ | ✔ |
| Trusted Boot | ✔ | ✔ | ✔ | ✔ |
| Encryption[4] | Device encryption | ✘ | BitLocker/EFS | BitLocker/EFS |

1. Calendar, Mail, Messaging, Music, People, Photo, Reader, SkyDrive, and Video
2. Requires 64-bit version and a motherboard/CPU with SLAT (Second Level Address Translation) support.
3. Windows-To-Go creates a bootable Windows 8 installation on a USB flash drive.
4. EFS = Encrypted File System

# System Requirements

What does it take to run Windows 8? If you purchase a PC, tablet, or phone with Windows 8 already installed, you won't have to ask this question. But for those of you upgrading a device, Microsoft's official position is that Windows 8 will run on any device that is capable of running Windows 7. In fact, Windows 8 may run better than Windows 7 on older devices because it makes fewer hardware demands. The minimum system requirements to run Windows 8 are the following:

- **CPU:** 1 GHz or faster.

  Note that only tile-based apps will work well at this clock speed. Any dual-core processor running at 1.4 GHz or higher would be a better choice for Desktop applications.

- **RAM:** 1 GB for the 32-bit version of Windows 8; 2 GB for the 64-bit version of Windows 8.

- **Graphics:** A card capable of running Microsoft's DirectX 9 rendering library with WDDM 1.0 support. Tile-based applications require at least 1024 x 768 screen resolution, with 1366 x 768 required to use the snap feature.

  WDDM is the Windows Display Driver Model graphics driver architecture. A better choice would be an AMD (ATI) Radeon 2000 or NVIDIA GeForce 8 series video card or better.

- **Disk space:** 16 GB for the 32-bit version of Windows 8; 20 GB for the 64-bit version of Windows 8.

  This recommendation is for the base operating system. If you plan to add applications and data to your system, you will need more disk space. A more realistic expectation is that a boot disk with Microsoft Office and a game or two will require a minimum of 80 GB.

There are some other requirements you may want to consider in choosing a Windows 8 device:

- **UEFI BIOS.** If you want to use the Secure Boot feature, you will need a motherboard with a Unified Extensible Firmware Interface (UEFI) BIOS.

  UEFI is a software interface that is embedded in your motherboard's startup logic and can be used to control the operating system before it starts up.

  The Microsoft Secure Boot feature uses UEFI to prevent other operating systems and software from loading before the Windows startup sequence begins. This feature, which is mandated with new Intel x86 and ARM PCs, will be indicated by a Windows 8 sticker on the case. Secure Boot is somewhat controversial as there are concerns that this feature will disable operating systems like Linux from booting on Windows systems. However, what Secure Boot was really designed to do is prevent malware like rootkits from capturing your computer. The UEFI stores a Microsoft certificate and checks that there is a matching certificate in the operating system before it allows the boot loader to start up the OS. A more detailed description of the pre-OS environment and UEFI may be found at `blogs.msdn.com/b/b8/archive/2011/09/22/protecting-the-pre-os-environment-with-uefi.aspx`.

- **Trusted Platform Module (TPM).** If you want to use the BitLocker feature (particularly on a USB flash drive), this feature on your motherboard will make it easier.

  TPM is a secure computing standard implemented in a specialized secure computing chip that calculates and stores security keys to protect data contained on the computer.

- **Hyper-V Virtualization.** To run Hyper-V you will need to install the 64-bit version of Windows 8 and enable virtualization in your motherboard's BIOS.

  Virtualization creates memory partitions that are configured to run as independent separate computers, emulating a physical computer. This can be useful because it allows you to run applications or services for safety, testing, and myriad other purposes.

Use the System control panel to determine if your system can run Windows 8. That control panel lists all of your system components and gives a Windows Experience Index, which is a measure of how powerful (fast) your equipment feels. As a general rule, the Windows Experience Index is limited by the slowest component you have. For example, if your lowest-rated component is a graphics board that is rated as 4.2, then that is the rating your system is given. This rating is a general guideline, but it can be useful when you are deciding which component to upgrade to improve performance.

## To view the System control panel:

1. Press ▦+X or right-click the lower-left corner of your display to view the Computer Management menu; then select the Control Panel command.

2. Tap or click the *System and Security* link (the first group on the home page).

3. Tap or click the *System* link to view the System control panel **A**.

**TIP** If you intend to game on your PC, consider purchasing a graphics board that can run DirectX 10. Also, always download the latest graphics drivers from the manufacturer's website.

**TIP** It is a good idea to update your motherboard's BIOS and install any updated system drivers for your computer when they become available. Don't rely on Windows Update to give you the latest and greatest versions of critical hardware system software.

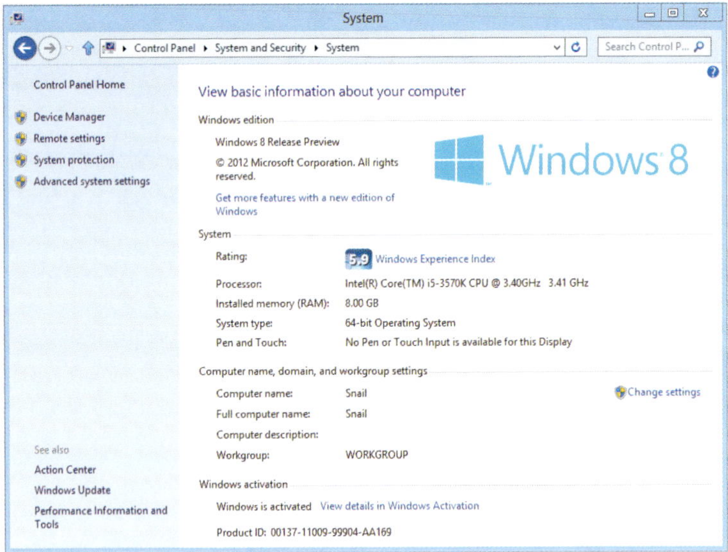


**A** The System control panel lists your operating system details, your hardware, and the Windows Experience Index.

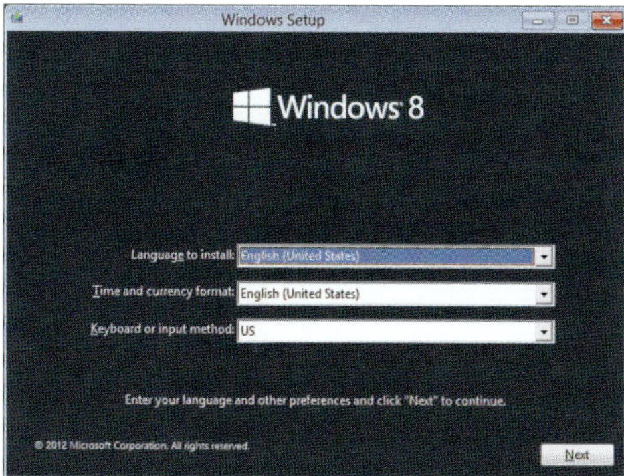

**A** The Windows Setup dialog box begins the installation process.

# Installing Windows 8

The method you use to install Windows 8 will depend on which type of installation you are performing:

- Clean installation
- Upgrade installation
- Virtual machine installation
- USB flash drive installation

A *clean install* is when you install an operating system on a storage device that has been totally erased. When you get a new computer, you should receive it as a clean install. In the case of a previously used computer, the clean install option removes all settings and data from the system.

When you have a serious virus or want to return your system back to a "new" state, you will sometimes want to perform a clean install—but rarely. Usually you perform a clean install only once: when you first get Windows 8.

## To perform a clean install of Windows 8:

1. If you have downloaded Windows 8 as an ISO file, burn that file to a disc.

   The section "Optical Discs" in Chapter 12 describes how to burn a disc.

2. If you have an installation disc from a retail package (or from step 1), insert it in your optical drive and start your computer.

3. In the Windows Setup dialog box **A**, select the language, the time and currency format, and the keyboard type; then tap or click Next.

*continues on next page*

4. Tap or click Install Now to initiate the installation.

5. Enter the product key from the packaging or from your sales source 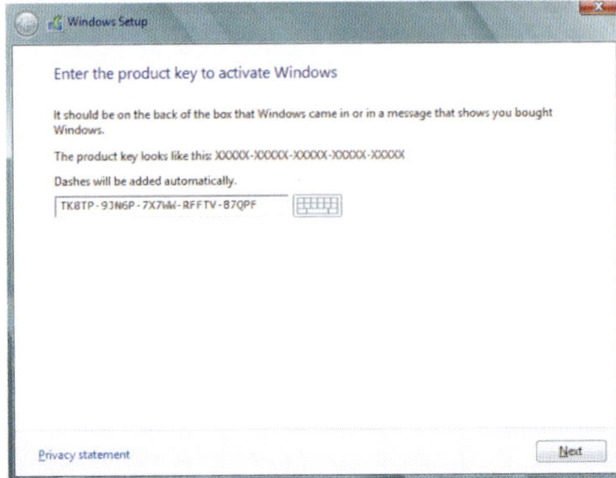, then tap or click Next.

6. Accept the End User License Agreement (EULA) by selecting the "I accept the license terms" check box. Tap or click Next **C**.

7. Double-click or double-tap the Custom Install button to perform a clean install **D**.

   The Custom Install lets you create partitions and a multi-boot setup (if desired) and can allow you to keep your old version of Windows along with Windows 8. A boot menu at system startup will allow you to choose between different operating systems installed on your computer.

**B** Enter the product key in the text box.

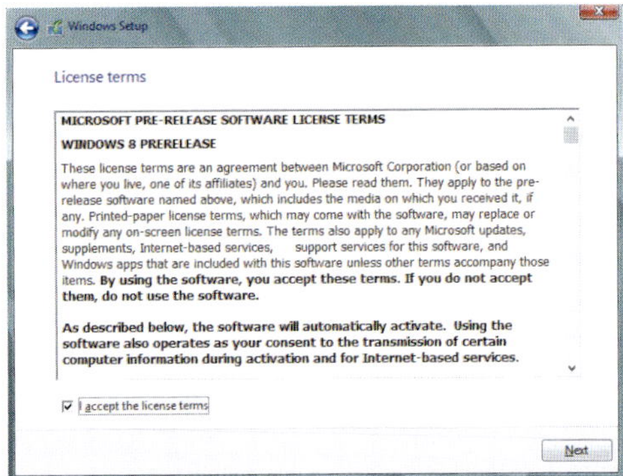

**C** Accept the EULA.

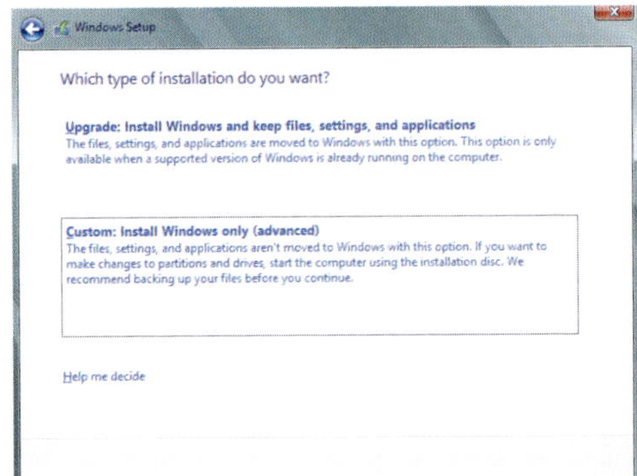

**D** For a clean install, select the Custom Install button.

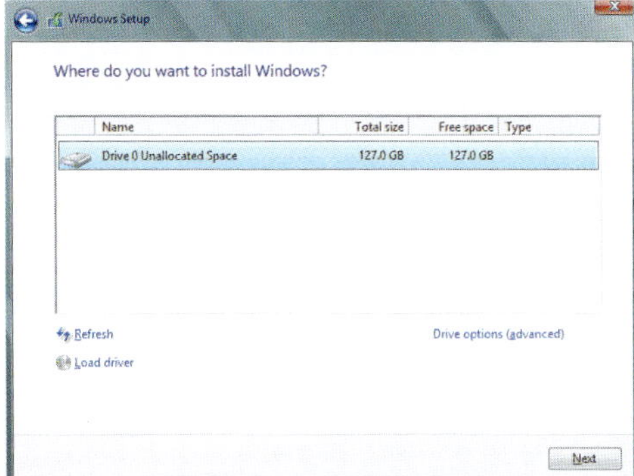

**E** Installing on the default boot disk

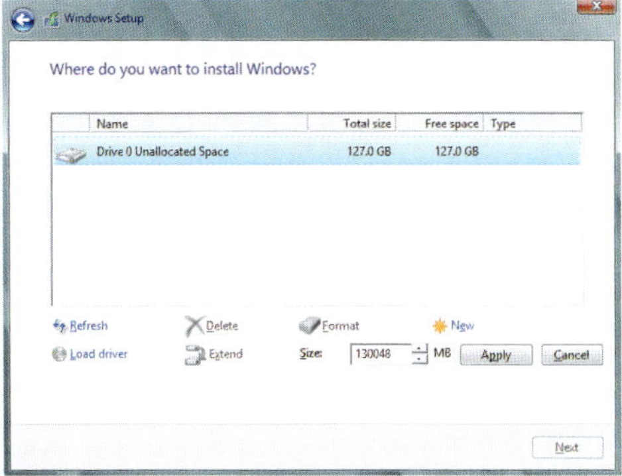

**F** This step lets you prepare a partition for installation.

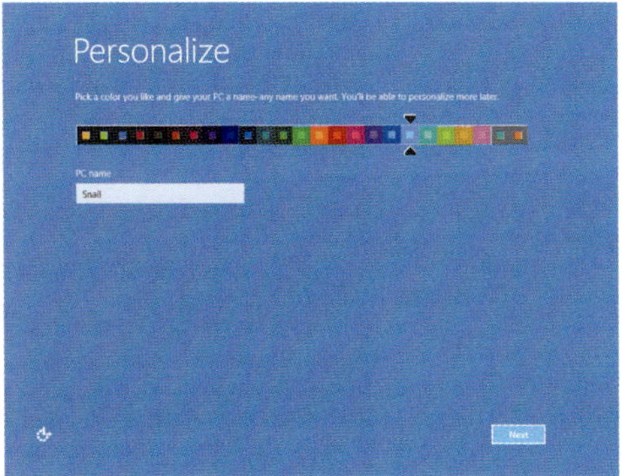


**G** Name your computer and select a color scheme.

8. In the "Where do you want to install Windows" step, you will need to select a disk partition to install Windows 8 onto; that is your boot partition. For a virtual machine installation or on a new computer, you will need to create a partition. Tap or click Drive Options (advanced) **E**.

   If your mass storage device doesn't appear in the list, you may need to install a driver for it. Obtain the driver from the manufacturer, and click the *Load driver* link to select the driver file to install.

9. Tap or click New **F**, select the storage device, enter the disk size you desire, tap or click the Apply button, and tap or click Next.

   Windows formats the partition you select (if necessary). If you select a partition size less than your disk size, Windows Setup will post an alert box stating that additional partitions may be created for system files. Click OK to close this alert box and continue.

10. After Windows 8 copies all the files to your machine, it restarts and displays the Personalize screen **G**. Enter your computer name, pick a color scheme (you can change it later), and tap or click Next.

*continues on next page*

**11.** Review the Settings screen **H**, and tap or click the Use Express Settings button.

**12.** On the Sign In To Your PC screen **I**, enter the user name for the account(s) you wish to create; then tap or click Finish.

The clean installation completes, and the Start screen displays **J**.

**TIP** With the exception of the product key, all of the settings that you enter during the installation can be altered from within the Windows 8 interface.

**TIP** Windows Media Center is not included in the installation. If you have the Pro edition you can go to the Add Features to Windows wizard, enter your product key, and then select Media Center from there. Media Center appears as a tile on the Start screen.

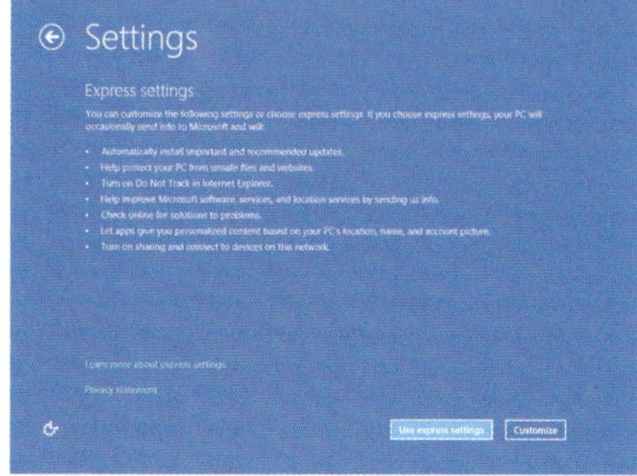

**H** The Express Settings screen

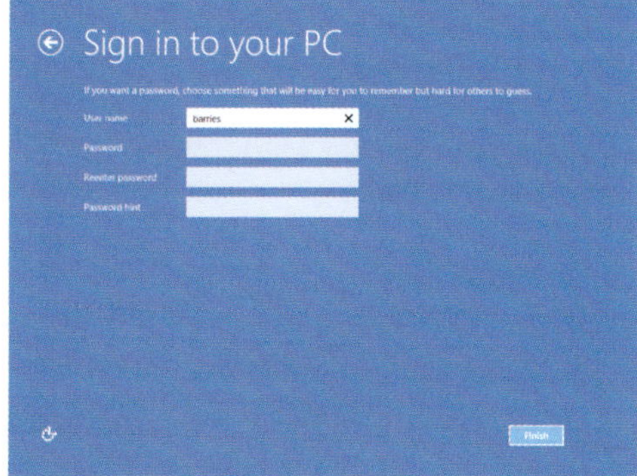

**I** Create one or more user accounts that you will use to access your system.

**J** The Start screen after a clean install

# Upgrading to Windows 8

Operationally, a Windows 8 upgrade installation is almost entirely the same as a clean install. The difference is that in an upgrade you leave in place all of your system data, the file system, and as many system settings as Windows 8 can possibly retain. This will prove useful when you need to do an in-place upgrade of a previous Windows 8 installation or when you want to continue using what you've been working with in Windows 7.

Although many experts say that operating system upgrades are less stable than clean installs, Microsoft usually does a very good job of ensuring that compatible settings are retained and that non-compatible settings are discarded.

Not all Windows 8 upgrades are allowed, however. **Table 1.2** shows the kinds of upgrades from Windows 7 that Microsoft allows.

**TABLE 1.2**  Upgrades Allowed from Windows 7 to Windows 8

| Windows 7 Version | Upgrade to Windows 8 Enterprise | Upgrade to Windows 8 Pro | Upgrade to Windows 8 | Upgrade to Windows RT |
| --- | --- | --- | --- | --- |
| Starter | ✗ | ✔ | ✔ | ✗ |
| Home Basic | ✗ | ✔ | ✔ | ✗ |
| Home Premium | ✗ | ✔ | ✔ | ✗ |
| Professional | ✔ | ✔ | ✗ | ✗ |
| Ultimate | ✗ | ✔ | ✗ | ✗ |
| Enterprise | ✔ | ✗ | ✗ | ✗ |

The upgrade install differs from a clean install in several ways:

- Your computer already has a name, so you won't be prompted for a new one.

- The user accounts already exist, so you won't be prompted to create new ones.

- Your applications should still be installed and should retain their settings.

- Many of your system settings remain intact.

- Your data should be intact in folders that you created.

You can upgrade Windows 7 and leave your personal data, settings, and apps in place. The upgrade can be applied to Windows XP and Vista, but with those operating systems you can only retain your personal data; everything else is lost. Also, and most importantly you can only upgrade a 32-bit OS to 32-bit Windows 8, and a 64-bit OS to 64-bit Windows 8.

## To upgrade to Windows 8:

1. Insert the Windows 8 installation disc into the optical drive of your computer and start up from your optical drive.

   *or*

   Double-tap or double-click the Windows 8 ISO file or use the Notification box to open the disk and launch the ISO file.

2. Follow steps 3–6 in the previous section. On the "Which type of installation do you want" screen, click the Upgrade button **A**.

   If you log in to Windows 8 and begin an installation, the installer assumes you want to upgrade your installation if it finds an existing Windows installation on your system, and you will go directly to step 4.

3. Select the boot partition that contains your Windows 7 (or 8) operating system, and then tap or click Next.

4. On the screen titled Choose What to Keep, select one of the following three radio buttons:

   ▸ **Keep Windows settings, personal files, and apps.** This can be selected when upgrading Windows 7 to Windows 8.

   ▸ **Keep personal files only.** This option applies to any version of Windows from Windows XP on.

   ▸ **Nothing.** This option is available for any version of Windows from Windows XP on.

5. Tap or click the Next button.

6. Complete steps 10–12 from the previous section.

**TIP** It is always a good idea to back up your system before you upgrade to a new operating system. To be really safe, many experts recommend that you back up your system twice, to two different types of media. Things can go wrong during an upgrade, so take some precautions.

**Upgrade: Install Windows and keep files, settings, and applications**
The files, settings, and applications are moved to Windows with this option. This option is only available when a supported version of Windows is already running on the computer.

**A** The upgrade installation option overwrites your system files and leaves your data and settings intact.

# Sleep, Shut Down, and Restart

One of the oddities of Windows 8 is that it is missing the power down options that were so prominently displayed as part of the Start menu in Windows 7. That menu is now on the Settings bar, which is accessed from the Settings charm. You can also shut down Windows from the Desktop by pressing Alt+F4, or from anywhere in the operating system by pressing Ctrl+Alt+Del.

Microsoft designed the tile-based apps so that you don't need to shut down Windows to save power, nor do you need to close those apps when you switch away from them. On a tablet or phone, the sleep function may be sufficient for most of your needs. To conserve resources, the tile-based apps save themselves to disk and remove themselves from memory when you switch away from them.

Each device that runs Windows 8 also comes with a physical Power button, and some come with a physical Sleep button as well. You also invoke the sleep function when you close the lid on a laptop or tablet. The Power Options control panel in Windows 8 contains a setting **A** that allows you to modify the function of the Power and Sleep buttons.

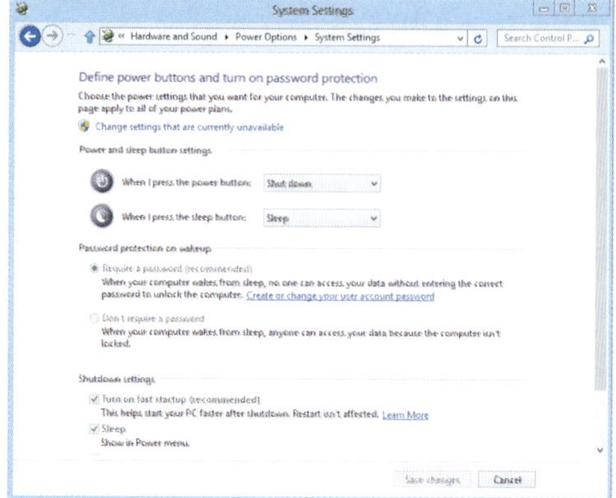

**A** The Power Options control panel lets you set the behavior of buttons on your Windows 8 device.

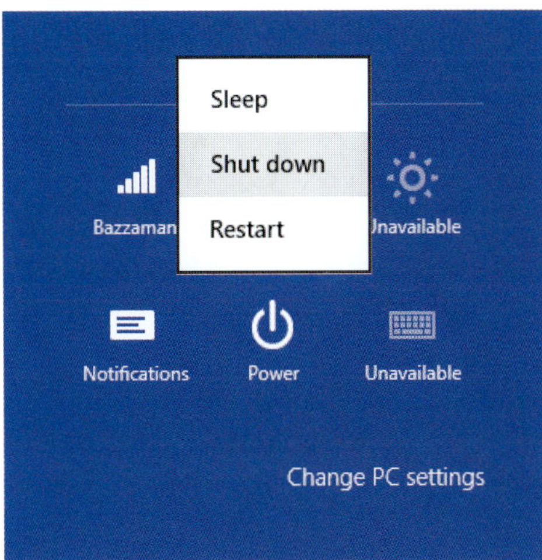



**B** The Power Down menu as accessed from the Settings Charm

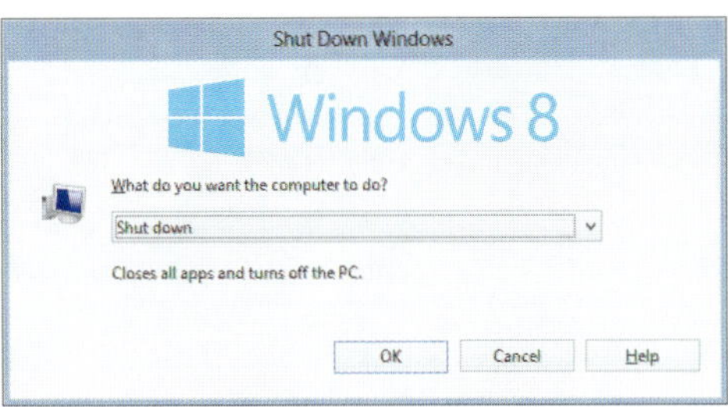



**C** From the Desktop, display the Shut Down Windows dialog box by pressing Alt+F4.

## To access the Power Down menu from the Charms bar:

1. To open the Charms bar, swipe from the right edge of your display or press ⊞+C.

2. Tap or click the Settings charm.

3. Tap or click the Power icon, and select Sleep, Shut down, or Restart from the pop-up menu **B**.

If you access the Power Down menu by pressing Ctrl+Alt+Del, you will see the same Power icon and menu in the lower-right corner of the display.

## To shut down Windows 8 from the Desktop:

1. Tap or click the Desktop to make it active.

   *or*

   Click the Show Desktop button at the far right of the taskbar to minimize all windows and make the Desktop active.

2. Press Alt+F4 to open the Shut Down Windows dialog box **C**.

3. Select the action you wish to take from the drop-down list: Switch user, Sign out, Sleep, Shut down, or Restart.

4. Tap or click OK to complete the action.

**TIP** Alt+F4 is the equivalent of the Exit command that is commonly placed at the bottom of an application's File menu. You can use this keystroke to close out almost all Windows applications—often, even troublesome ones that appear frozen.

**TIP** The System Settings area of the Power Options control panel contains settings that allow you to control when a device automatically goes to sleep or shuts down.

# Getting Help

Getting help in Windows 7 was easy: Click the Start menu and choose the Getting Started command to open the Windows 7 Help system. Guess what—Windows 8 is just as easy, but you have to look in a different place. The key to getting help in Windows 8 is to access the Search function and enter the topic for which you want help. Windows 8 Help is just as extensive as ever, and with the improved Search function you can get help much more quickly.

## To access the Help home page:

1. To open the Charms bar, swipe from the right edge of your display or press ⊞+C.

2. Tap or click the Search charm.

3. Enter **help** into the Search box, and then click the Help and Support app Ⓐ.

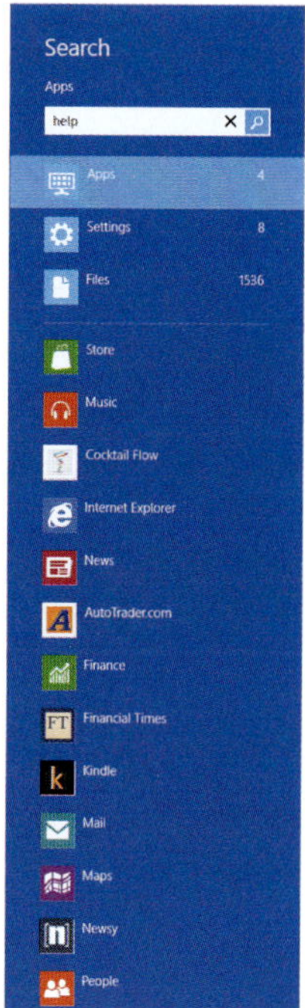

Ⓐ Use the Search function to access the Windows 8 Help system.

4. On the Windows Help and Support home page **B**, enter the topic you want help for and tap or click the Search icon.

*or*

Click any of the buttons to open the Help system for that topic.

To access help on a specific topic, feature, or application, enter a search string appropriate to that item within the Help system. For example, you could enter the term **lock screen** or **gestures**. The menu in the lower-left corner of the Help app indicates that it is connected to online content.

**TIP** Press the F1 key to summon help on the Desktop and in most Windows programs. Although it doesn't work on the Start screen or in the tile-based apps, it does work in most legacy applications.

**TIP** Help shows the answers to only the most common problems. The links under the More to Explore section take you to the Windows website and to Microsoft Answers, where you can view online content and go to support forums.

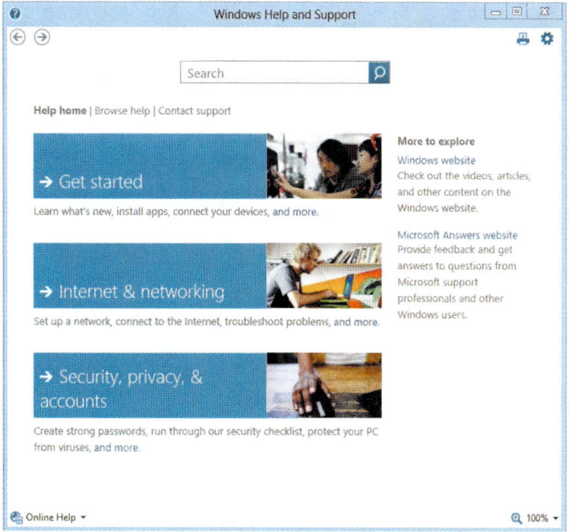


**B** The home page for the Windows 8 Help system

# Putting It All Together

- Windows 8 introduces a new touch-based tile interface with a new style of apps.

- Windows 8 runs on a wide range of devices—including personal computers, tablets, and cell phones—using a single, unified operating system.

- In three of the four versions of Windows 8, Desktop legacy applications will run with all of the important features found in Windows 7.

- There are four versions of Windows 8: Windows 8 RT, Windows 8, Windows 8 Pro, and Windows 8 Enterprise.

- Windows 8 has very modest system requirements, particularly for the new, tile-based apps.

- You can upgrade some versions of Windows 7 to Windows 8 and retain your data, your applications, and many of your system settings and personalizations.

- Windows 8 Help is extensive and can be accessed through the Search function or by pressing the F1 key on the Desktop.

# The Start Screen

The tile-based interface's new Start screen is what you see when you log in to Windows 8. This screen, as well as the tile-based model of applications, was developed to use minimal system resources, be informative, and be single-focused—thus the flat icons, single-task procedures, and one-window-at-a-time approach. The tile-based interface is meant to be the kind of glance-and-go experience that phone users need, carried over to the tablet and the PC. Like it or not, this is the future of Windows.

In this chapter, you'll see how Windows handles screen locking and sign-in for your user accounts. There are some new ways to log in to Windows besides passwords—gesture-based picture passwords and a PIN login are now supported. Those features are great for a phone, but you may like them on your other Windows devices too.

The Start screen is the default user interface in Windows 8. It is a tile-based user interface, where each tile launches an experience: an app, a website, a service, or the Windows Desktop. Tiles are visual and can display live information, notifications, or badges.

## In This Chapter

# The Lock Screen

The Windows 8 Lock screen is a feature that is borrowed from smartphones of all types: the iPhone, the Android, and, yes, the Windows 7 phone. The idea is that when a certain period of inactivity is detected, your device locks up and waits for you to do something to unlock it.

The Lock screen is not just a pretty picture—it can be your pretty picture. In Windows 8, the Lock screen also displays the date and time, system settings (like the current power or network status), and, optionally, notifications (like the number of mail messages). When you first start, boot up, or wake your system from sleep, the Lock screen is the first thing you see.

The Lock screen is useful on a phone, less so on a tablet, and not so much on a PC. You can make several modifications to the Lock screen.

### To display the Lock screen on your device:

In either the tile-based or Desktop interface, press ⊞+L (for Lock).

### To close the Lock screen:

- Swipe up from the bottom edge of the display.
- Press any key on your keyboard.
- Click your mouse button.

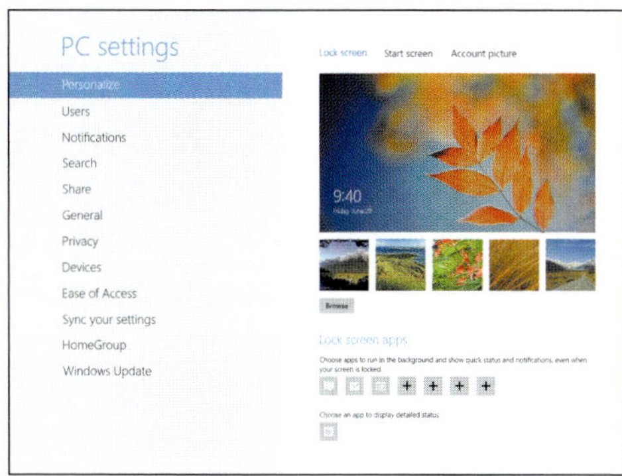

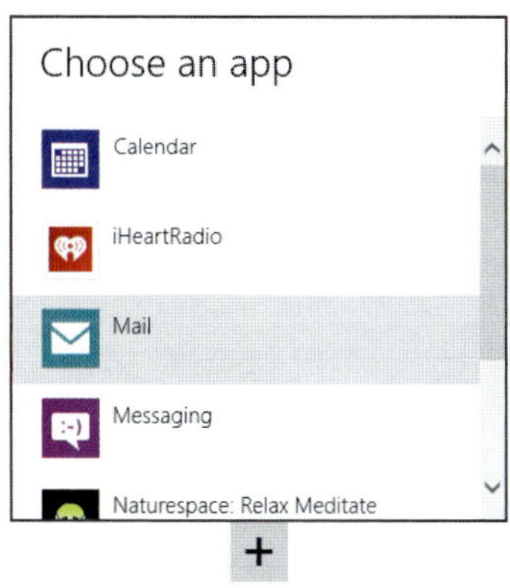


**A** The Lock screen

**B** The app notification pop-up menu

## To change the Lock screen:

1. Press ⊞+C (for Charms), and tap or click the Settings icon.

2. Tap or click Change PC Settings at the bottom of the Charms bar (the bar that appears on the right side of the screen).

3. Tap or click the *Lock Screen* link (if necessary, since it's the default) to go to the PC Settings Personalize page **A**.

4. To change your Lock screen picture, click any of the picture thumbnails.

   *or*

   Click the Browse button, navigate to a picture of your choosing, and select that picture.

5. To have an app show its detailed status on the Lock screen, click the icon in the Choose An App To Display Detailed Status section, and then select that app. **A** shows the Calendar app selected (the default).

6. To have apps run in the background and show notifications (when they have any), click the plus (+) button in the Choose Apps To Run In The Background section and select the app from the pop-up menu **B**.

   To enable an app to show notifications, turn this feature on in the Notifications section of PC Settings.

**TIP** For a better effect, try to match the screen resolution of the Lock screen picture to the resolution of your display.

# Sign In

The Sign In (or Log In) screen is where you authorize a user to gain access to Windows 8. When you dismiss the Lock screen, you see the Sign In screen Ⓐ.

The Sign In screen lets you do the following:

- Turn on ease of access tools. Click the Ease of Access button to view a menu that lets you select the different ease of access tools.

  These tools help impaired users work with Windows by substituting other functions for sight, touch, and sound. Narrator reads the screen options aloud. On-Screen Keyboard lets you perform keyboard entry with your mouse. Magnifier gives you a zoomed-in view of the screen. StickyKeys allows you to activate the Ctrl, Alt, and Delete keys one at a time. High Contrast turns your screen black and white. Filter Keys

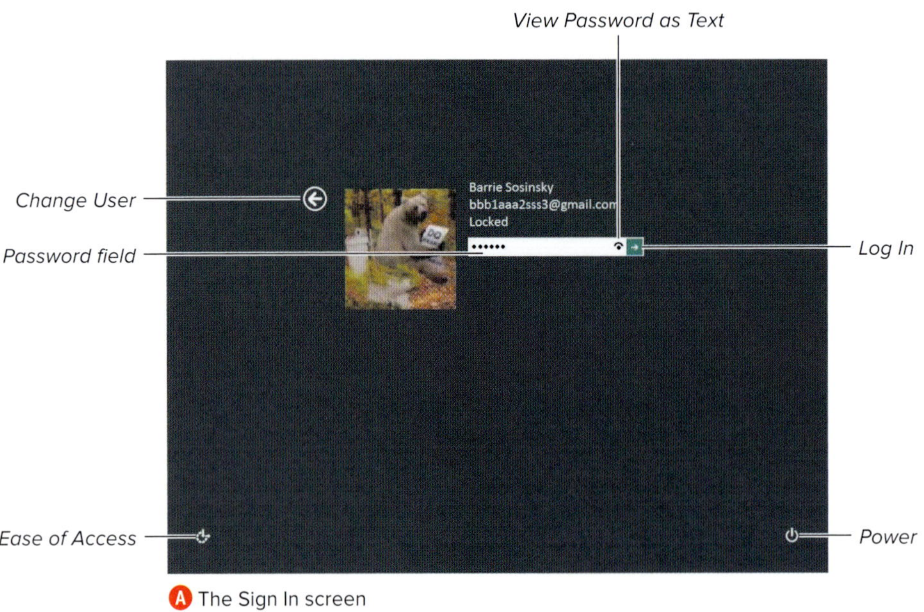



Ⓐ The Sign In screen

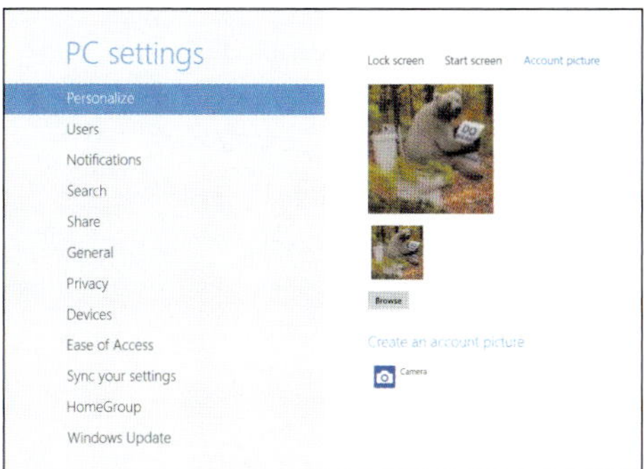

**B** The Account Picture screen lets you personalize your avatar.

lets you ignore or slow down brief or repeated keystrokes and adjust keyboard repeat rates.

- Access the power functions. Press the Power button to view a menu where you put your system to sleep, shut it down, or restart it.

- Click the Change User button to go to an account screen where you can switch to a different user account.

  You see the Change User button only when two or more accounts are activated.

- Press the View Password as Text (eye icon) button to view your entered password as clear text.

- Press the Log In button to open the tile-based interface Start screen.

## To change the Account picture:

1. Open the PC Settings Personalize screen (see previous section).

2. Click the *Account Picture* link **B**.

3. Use the Browse button to select a photo, or use the Camera button to import a picture from a device.

**TIP** You can also find these functions in the **Make The Keyboard Easier To Use** control panel.

# Passwords, Picture Passwords, and PINs

Most users are accustomed to supplying alphanumeric passwords to gain entry to PCs. When you install Windows 8, it asks you to supply a password, and you use the Sign In screen described in the previous section to enter your password. Changing your password is easy to do.

If you want to boot directly to the tile-based interface Start screen without logging in to your account, Windows 8 makes this easy; it's a setting on the User Account screen.

The *Can't Access Your Account* link lets you reset your password through your Microsoft account, a feature that is new to Windows 8. It takes you to the Microsoft account reset password feature. If you've set up the Microsoft account login, you can regain access through this mechanism. You need to set this feature up, and later in this chapter you learn how. Consider it password insurance.

Password access can be cumbersome on a touch-based device like a phone or tablet. Windows 8 has a new method for gaining access to your system or logging in: the "picture password." It's fast to use and simple to set up. You provide a picture and then define a set of gestures that you perform over the picture to provide entry to Windows 8. Gestures can be taps, swipes (lines), and enclosures (circles).

A PIN is a Personal Identification Number, a four-digit number that you can use to log in to Windows 8, if you so choose.

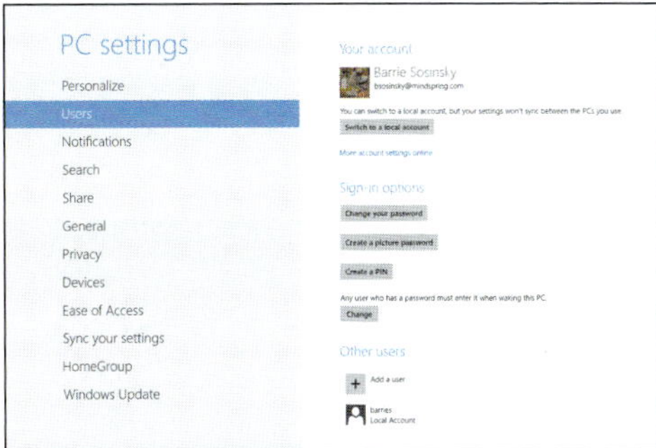

**A** The Users settings let you change your password, create a picture password, create a PIN login, and even boot into your computer without logging in at all.

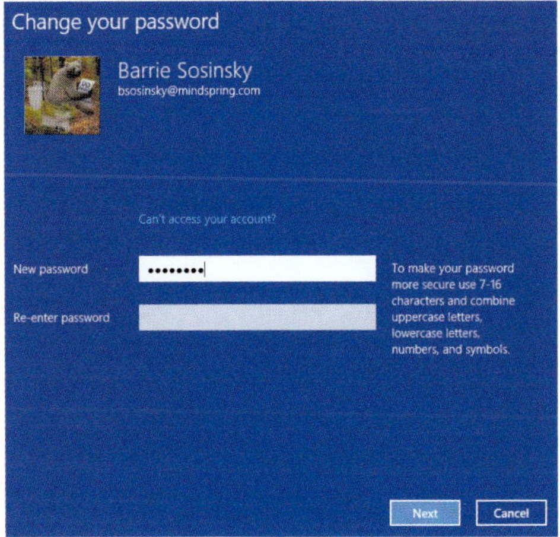


**B** The Change Password dialog box

## To change your current password:

1. Press ⊞+C to open the Charms bar, and tap or click the Settings icon.

2. Tap or click Change PC Settings, and then tap or click the *Users* link to view your account **A**.

3. Tap the Change Password button, and then enter your old password and your new password (twice to confirm) into the Change Password dialog box **B**. Click Next.

## To boot into Windows 8 without a password:

Enable the feature by clicking the Any User Who Has A Password Must Enter It When Waking This PC section and then clicking the Change button **C**.

You should use this feature only when you are the only person who uses this PC, because it removes your system's security.

## To set up and use a picture password:

1. In the tile-based interface or on the Desktop, press ⊞+C or swipe from the right edge to open the Charms bar.

2. Tap or click the Settings charm, tap or click Change PC Settings, and tap or click the *Users* link to view the Your Account screen **A**.

3. Click the Create A Picture Password button, and then enter your account password into the Create A Picture Password dialog box **D**.

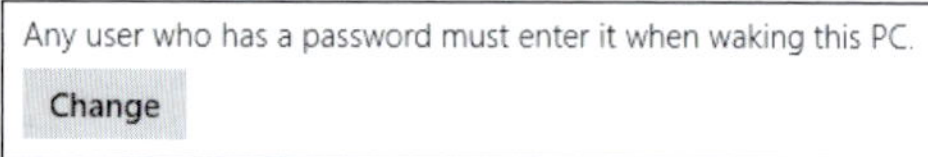


**C** The direct boot with no login option

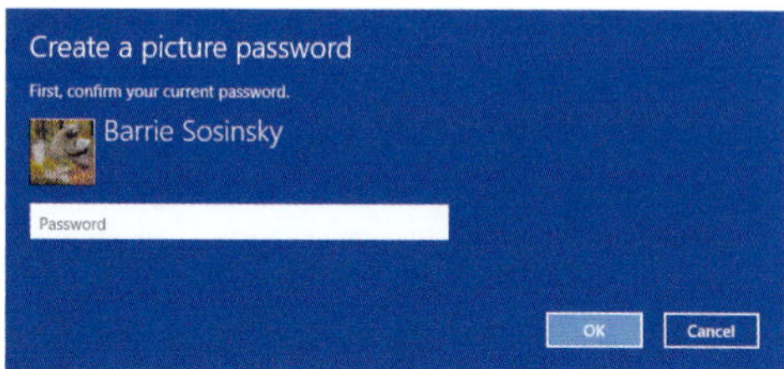


**D** Enter your account password to begin creating a picture password.

4. On the Welcome To Picture Password screen, tap or click the Choose Picture button to open a file picker. Select the picture you want to use, and then click Use This Picture.

5. With the picture selected **E**, perform three gestures (tap, line, or circle).

6. Confirm your entry by repeating the three gestures, and then click Finish.

   On your next login, the picture appears and you can perform your gestures to gain entry to your system.

   Or you can click the Switch To Password button to use the standard Sign In screen.

## To create a PIN login:

1. On the Your Account screen **A**, click Create a PIN.

2. Log in to your account in the Create a PIN dialog box.

3. Enter the PIN twice in the Create a PIN dialog box, then click Finish.

   If you decide to remove either your picture password or your PIN, click the Remove button and that login is canceled.

**TIP** **If you make a mistake when you gesture using the picture password login, click the Start Over button and try again. You get five chances before Windows 8 switches back to the alphanumeric password login.**

**E** Perform your gesture twice to set the picture password.

# Start Screen

The tile-based interface Start screen is Windows 8's most noticeable feature. It's Microsoft's glance-and-go interface. You see it when you log in to Windows 8, and even if you use Desktop on a PC for most things, you'll find that you transit through the Start screen often. As tile-based apps become more prevalent, Desktop users will find themselves increasingly spending time inside the tile-based interface. And of course, if you are using Windows 8 on a tablet or phone, then the tile-based interface is your friend.

The interface is organized around a tile-based flat wall of icons. A scrollable wall of icons has been used by many operating systems and data visualization shells and is very useful in browsing a lot of items quickly through visualization. Let's start our visit to the tile-based interface by looking at its main features, and then we'll take a look at some of the small customizations that are possible with the Start screen.

Most of the functionality of the Start screen is hidden, and much of what you do on the Start screen is associated with tiles, which we will get to in a moment. You can't customize the Start screen very much in this version of Windows.

Windows 8 uses the Charms bar to display some of the central settings that were once found on the Start menu and in various control panels. The Charms bar is also available to you when you are on the Desktop.

The Apps bar appears at the bottom of the screen and offers you options that relate to what an app is doing at the moment. Think of the Apps bar as the equivalent of a right-click or context menu on the Desktop (the Desktop doesn't have an Apps bar). Since the main thing that the tile-based interface does is work with tiles, most of the buttons on the Apps bar relate to tiles, particularly when a tile is selected. In many instances, Apps bar buttons will display a pop-up menu of commands when you tap or click them.

There's not much you can customize in tile-based interface, but you can select a new background design and color from a limited number of choices; and you can move tiles around and create new groupings.

The customization features of the Start screen are clearly a work in progress. Future versions of Windows 8 will undoubtedly give you a fancier display. And if Microsoft doesn't do it, you can count on third-party utilities to offer better features.

It's obvious that the tile-based user interface was built with touch in mind.

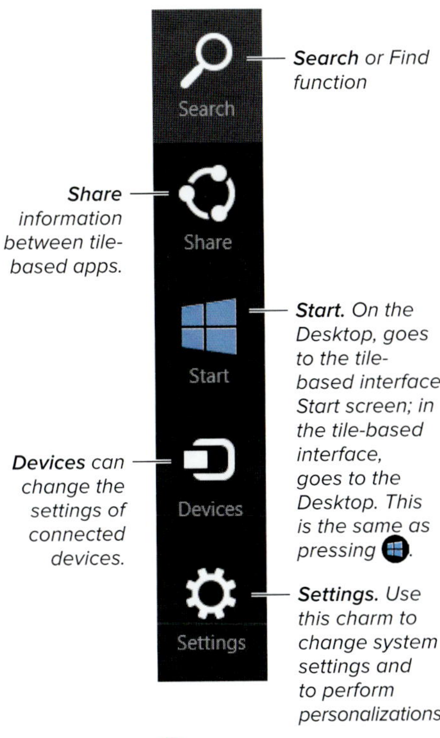



*Search or Find* function

*Share* information between tile-based apps.

*Start.* On the Desktop, goes to the tile-based interface Start screen; in the tile-based interface, goes to the Desktop. This is the same as pressing ⊞.

*Devices* can change the settings of connected devices.

*Settings.* Use this charm to change system settings and to perform personalizations.

**A** The Charms bar is available from both the tile-based interface Start screen and the Desktop.

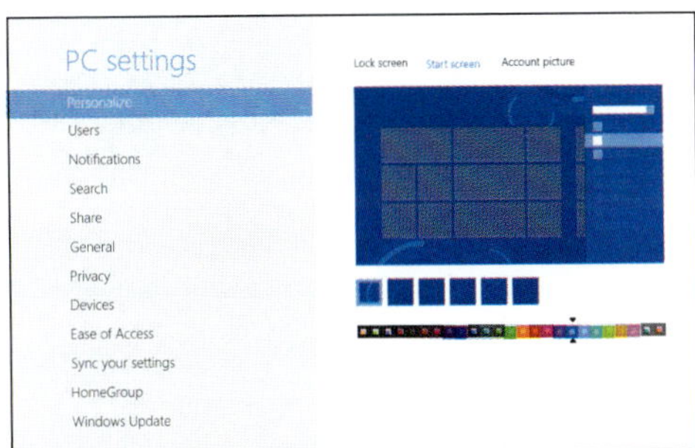



**B** You can personalize the Start screen by changing its color and design.

## To open the tile-based interface Start screen:

- Log in to Windows.

- On the Desktop, press ⊞. (Press the key again to return to the Desktop.)

- Tap or click the lower-left corner of your display. Windows 8 shows a thumbnail of the Start screen on a PC. On a tablet, you don't see the thumbnail, but you when you click the lower-left corner, you switch between the Desktop and the Start screen.

## To move your view of Start screen content:

- Swipe right or left.

- Use the scroll bar to move left or right.

- Use your mouse's scroll wheel to move left or right.

- Move the cursor to the left edge of the display to scroll all the way to the left, or to the right edge to scroll all the way to the right.

## To view the Charms bar:

- Press ⊞+C.

- Swipe from the right edge.

- Hold your cursor on the upper-right corner of the display **A**.

## To change the Start screen colors and background:

1. Open the PC Settings Personalize screen, then click the *Start screen* link **B**.

2. Click one of the six patterns in the top row of boxes or one of the 25 different colors.

## To customize the tile-based interface using the corners and edges:

- Tap, or move the cursor to, the lower-left corner to view a thumbnail of the Desktop that you can click to move. On the Desktop, this corner shows the Start screen thumbnail, which you can click to move to the Start screen.

- Tap, or move the cursor to, the upper-left corner to view the next open app in the tab order. Click to cycle through the tab order from one open app to another. Drag down to view a pane with all of your open apps.

- Tap, or move the cursor to, the upper-right corner to view the Charms bar. Drag down to open the Charms bar.

- Tap, or move the cursor to, the lower-right corner to view the Charms bar. Drag up to open the Charms bar.

- Tap and hold, or click, the lower-right corner to see a reduced-tile-size view of the tile-based interface screen **C**. You can select groups of tiles here and move them left or right. Swipe from the left edge on the Start screen to move to the next app in the tab order.

- Swipe up from the bottom edge or down from the top edge to view the Apps bar.

- Swipe in from the right edge to view the Charms bar.

**TIP** If you start to type a text string on the Start screen, you are automatically taken to the Search function and matches are displayed.

**C** This reduced tile-based view can be used to select groups of tiles and move them left or right.

# Tiles

Tiles are really what this new interface is about. A tile can be a tile-based app, a Desktop app, a website, a library or other special folder (like Desktop, Control Panel, and so on) a script or macro, or some other experience. The tile-based interface comes populated with a set of tiles, and as you install programs, their tiles are added to the interface. You can find additional features and add them to the Start screen, group them logically, and perform other actions. This section tells you how.

With tiles selected, the Start screen displays the Apps bar **A**, which contains tool buttons for altering the properties of your selected tiles **B**.

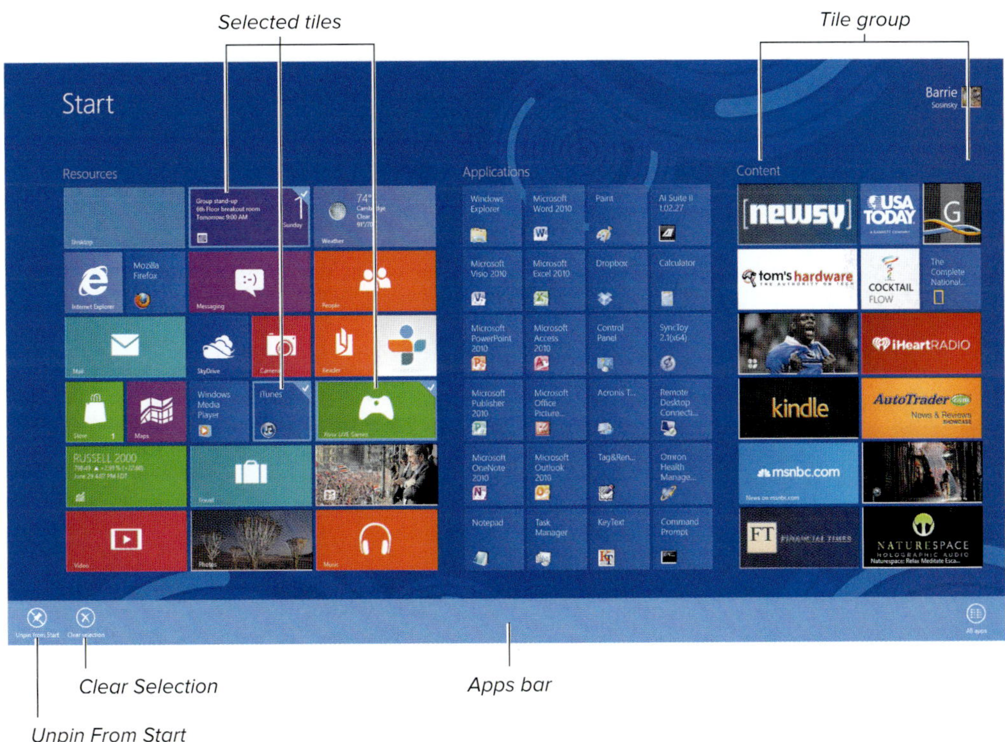



**A** The Start screen, with three selected tiles and the Apps bar

The All Apps button allows you to toggle between the Start screen and the All Apps screen 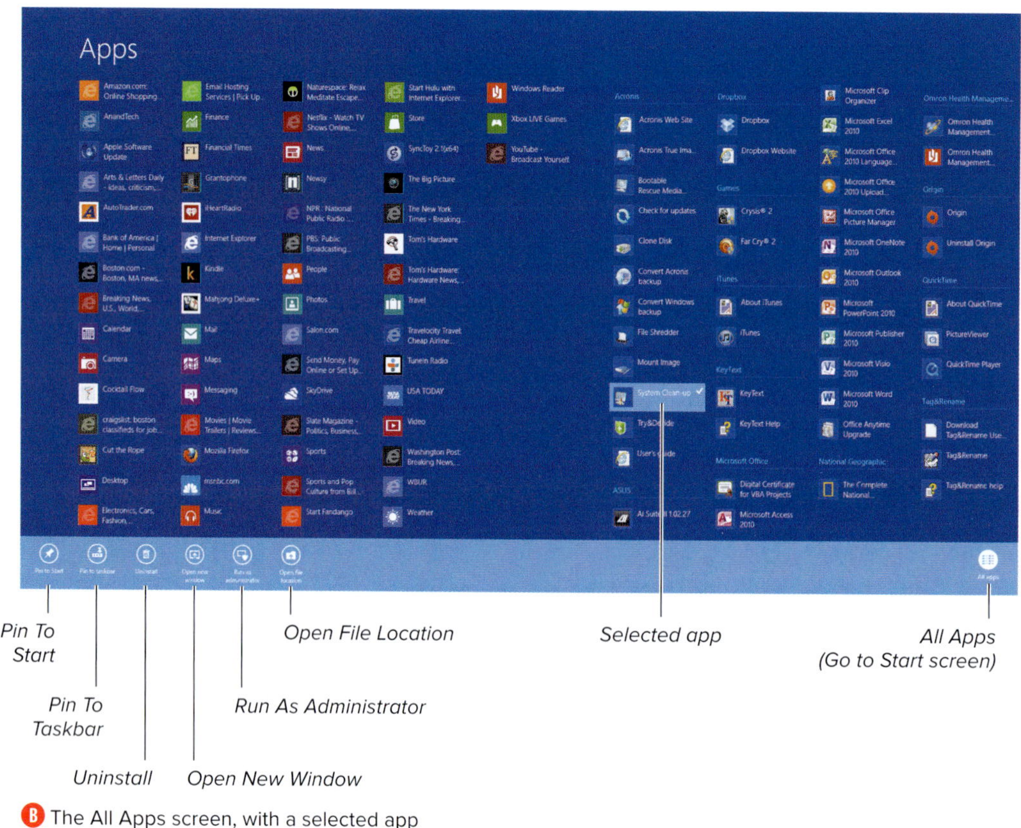. When you select an app on the All Apps screen, buttons on the Apps bar allow you to perform tasks specific to a selected app:

- **All Apps.** Takes you back to the tile-based interface Start screen.

- **Open File Location.** Goes to the folder that contains the program, executable file, folder, or other object.

- **Run As Administrator.** Runs the program with elevated privileges, which may be required to install a program, for a program to run, or to use particular features.

- **Open New Window.** Opens the object in a new window, the program in a new instance, and so forth.

- **Uninstall.** Opens the Programs And Features dialog box for a legacy application so that you can remove the program. For a tile-based program, the program is simply deleted.

- **Pin To Taskbar.** Places a shortcut to the object on the Desktop taskbar. This button changes to Unpin From Taskbar when the object is already in the taskbar.

- **Pin To Start.** Adds the tile to the Start screen. This button changes to Unpin From Start when the object is already in the Start screen.



**B** The All Apps screen, with a selected app

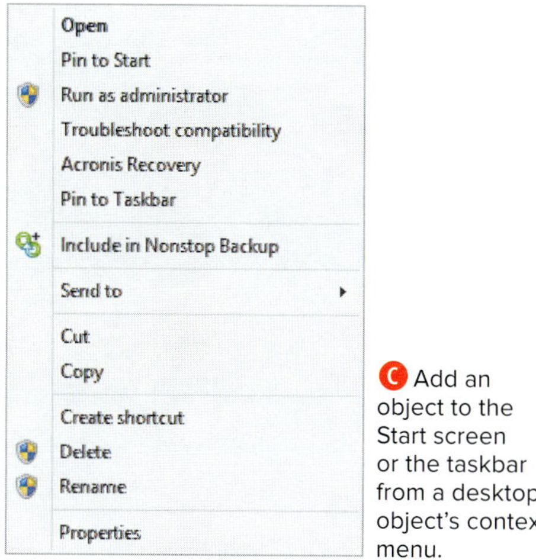



**C** Add an object to the Start screen or the taskbar from a desktop object's context menu.

You can also add items to the Start screen (and Taskbar) from a desktop icon's context menu or from an icon inside Windows Explorer (see Chapter 10). Nearly all objects in Explorer have this feature **C**.

## To launch a tile:

- Tap or click it.

- If the tile is already selected, it will have a white border around it; press Enter to launch that tile.

- With no tile selected, press Enter to open the upper-left tile in the left tile group.

## To select a tile:

- Use the arrow keys to move your selection left, right, up, or down.

- Use the Home and Page Up keys to move to the upper-left tile in the left tile group; use the End and Page Down keys to move to the upper-right tile in the right tile group.

- Right-click the tile to select it; that tile displays a check mark in its upper-right corner.

- To select more than one tile, hold the Ctrl key and either click or right-click additional tiles.

## To move a tile to a new location:

Tap or click the tile and drag it where you want it.

## To remove a tile or tiles
## from the Start screen:

- Select the tile or tiles and tap or click
  the Unpin From Start button.

- Select the tile or tiles and press Delete.

- Click the Unpin From Start button, as
  described in the next section.

## To add an app tile to
## the Start screen:

1. Right-click the Start screen to display
   the All Apps button.

2. Click All Apps, find the app you want,
   and select it Ⓑ.

3. Click the Pin To Start button in the Apps
   bar to add the tile to the right side of
   the Start screen.

4. To add this app to the Desktop taskbar,
   click the Add To Taskbar button.

**TIP** **Shortcuts are pointers that activate the object that they point to. Shortcuts can be tiles on the Start menu. Doing this gives you an opportunity to name the tile anything you wish. Choose the New command on a context menu to create a shortcut. You can also use a drag-and-drop copy operation (hold down the Ctrl key while you drag and drop) to create shortcuts.**

# Tile Groups

A tile group is a collection of tiles. The default tile-based interface screen has groups of tiles organized haphazardly. In the main group on the left are tile-based apps that Microsoft wants to highlight, such as Mail, Calendar, and Weather (you'll learn about those apps in Chapter 7). One of your first orders of business when you start working in the tile-based interface is to create a set of tile groups that are meaningful to you and that let you find what you want in a hurry.

A tile group can be a 6 x 6 set of small tiles or a 3 x 6 set of large tiles. In the larger view you can have four rows of icons, which allows for a display of 6 x 8 small tiles or 3 x 8 large tiles.

Tile groups don't have names by default. You have to name them.

## To create a new tile group:

- Install a new app or program, or add a new object to the Start screen; the tile-based interface adds the tile all the way to the right, in its own new tile group.

- Tap or click a tile and drag it all the way to the right until you see a separation bar appear to the left of the tile, then release Ⓐ.

## To resize a tile or tiles:

- Select a large tile or tiles, and tap or click the Smaller button on the Apps bar.

- With a small tile or tiles selected, click the Larger button on the Apps bar.

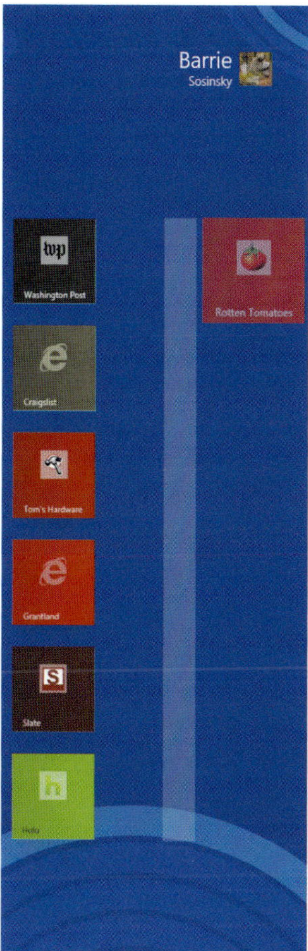

Ⓐ Drag a tile to the right to create a new tile group.

## To name a tile group:

1. Tap or click the lower-right corner of the Start screen to view the Apps Overview display **B**.

2. Tap and hold, or right-click, the group you want to name.

   If you tap or click the group, you go back to the Start screen.

3. Tap or click the Name button on the left side of the Apps bar.

4. Enter the name you want, and click the Name button.

   You are returned to the Start screen, and the group displays the name you assigned to it.

## To move a tile group:

Select the tile group and drag it left or right.

**TIP** Tile-based apps have a secondary tiles feature. In an app like People, you can add the tiles for individual contacts directly to your Start screen. When the People tile is live, at a glance you can see what every Tom, Dick, and Harry is up to.

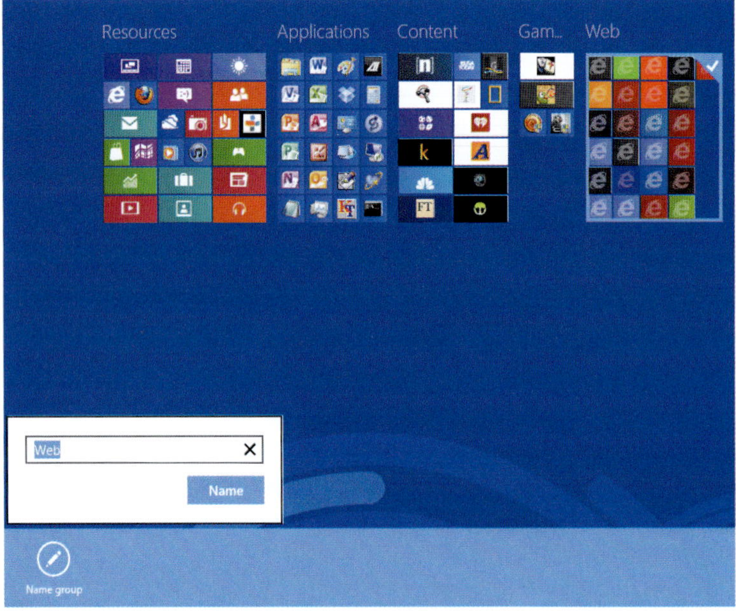

**B** Add a name to a tile group.

# Live Tiles

In Windows 7 and earlier, icons were static objects that developers adorned with all sorts of non-standard accoutrements to show a message or state. That's still true on the Desktop in Windows 8, but it is no longer the case in the tile-based interface. A carryover from the Windows Phone interface, Live Tiles can convey messages and states and display pictures and picture shows.

Live Tiles are a feature of tile-based apps; don't expect to find them in legacy applications. To see a Live Tile in action, you need to turn the feature on.

Live Tiles are somewhat inconsistently implemented in early versions of Windows 8. Some apps, like Mail and Calendar, are live and you don't get a choice. Other apps require you to turn the app on to get the feature working. Many apps don't offer the feature at all. And, of course, what a Live Tile does is completely up to the developer Ⓐ.

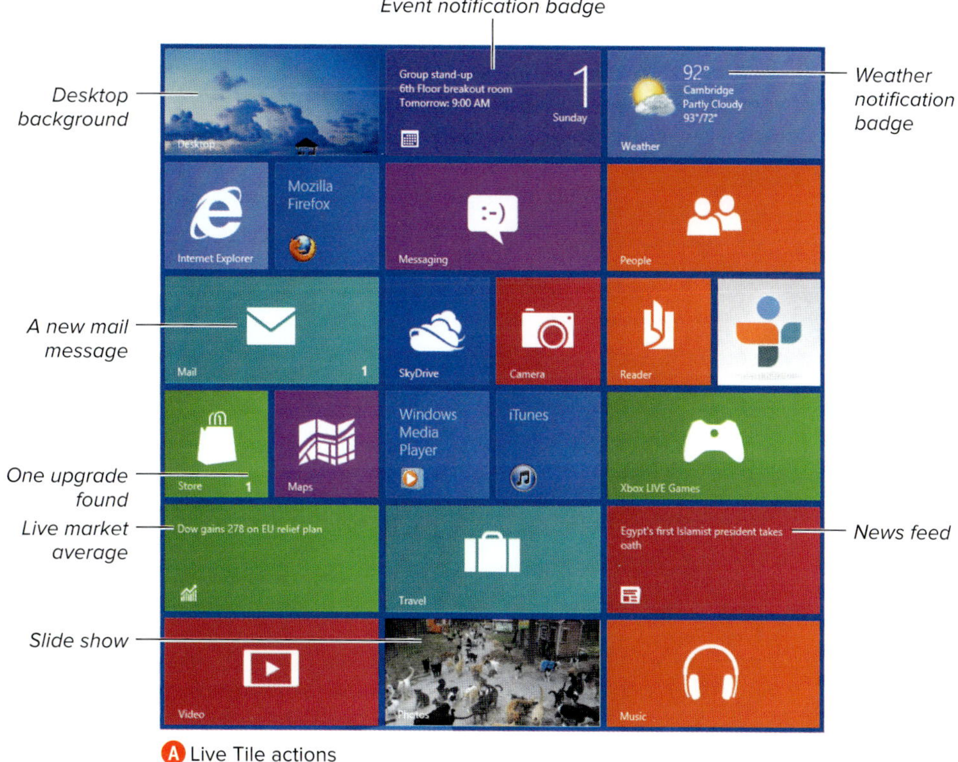


Ⓐ Live Tile actions

Live Tiles are used by the following apps:

- Weather, to list temperature and conditions
- Desktop, to show a thumbnail image of your current Desktop (including its background)
- People, to list postings to connected social accounts
- Calendar, to list appointments
- News, to list a news feed
- Photos, to present a slide show
- Mail, to list the number of unread messages and more.

The information displayed in a Live Tile is called a *badge*. To show badges, you have to enable the app so that it is allowed to communicate with you in this fashion.

If the app needs to know your geolocation, you need to turn presence on for that app.

## To turn a Live Tile on or off:

- Select the tile on the Start screen, and tap or click the Turn Live Tile On button **B**.
- Select the Live Tile on the Start screen, and tap or click the Turn Live Tile Off button **C**.

**B** The Turn Live Tile On button

**C** The Turn Live Tile Off button

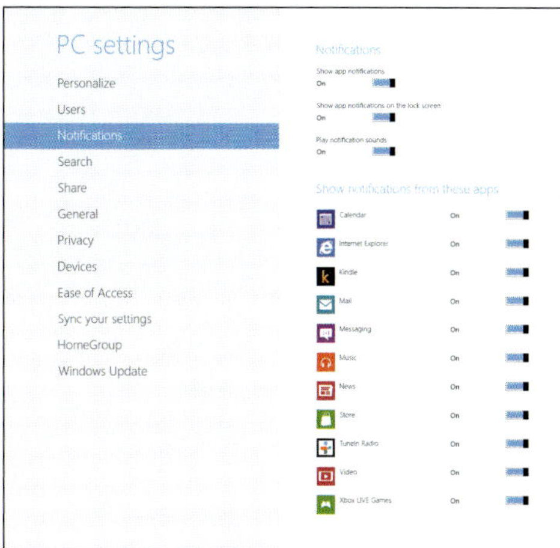



**D** The Notifications screen

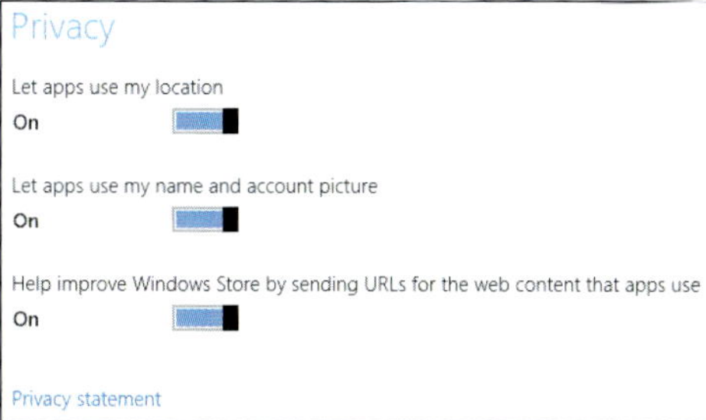



**E** The presence feature in the Privacy settings allows your location to be used by an app for notifications and other purposes.

## To enable an app's notifications:

1. Press ⊞+C or swipe from the right edge to display the Charms bar.

2. Tap or click Settings, tap or click Change PC Settings, and tap or click Notifications to view the Notifications screen **D**.

3. Move the Show App Notifications slider to On to enable notifications globally.

   You can also enable notification sounds and the notification displays on the Lock screen on this page.

   *or*

   Move the slider for an individual app to On to enable that app to send you notifications.

## To turn on presence:

1. Click the *Privacy* link to open the Privacy settings.

2. Enable the Let Apps Use My Location setting **E**.

**TIP** Secondary tiles can also be Live Tiles. If the developer went to the trouble to use the secondary tiles feature, they likely did so to enable Live Tiles. For example, Calendar lets you pin multiple locations to your Start screen, with notifications for each; People does this with individual contacts; and Mail with individual accounts. Search may bring up multiple tiles for an app, and you can pin those tiles to the Start screen to see if they are live. Experiment!

**TIP** Unfortunately, in Windows 8 the presence feature is a global setting. It would be better if it were assigned by the app (as it is in the iPhone)—but so be it.

# Putting It All Together

- The Lock screen appears after a period of inactivity when your system goes to sleep or when you lock your system.

- The Sign In screen is where you log in to a user account.

- Depending on your preference, you can sign in with a password, picture password and gesture, or PIN.

- The tile-based Start screen is a tile-based graphical user interface, or shell.

- The Charms bar and Apps bar provide tools for modifying your system or current app.

- Each corner and edge of the tile-based display is active and can provide shortcuts through gestures and keyboard entries.

- Tiles represent a feature that provides an experience: launch an app, view a website, open a control panel, and more.

- To launch a tile, tap or click it.

- To modify a tile, select it and then use the tools in the Apps bar to make changes.

- Tiles can be organized into groups and rearranged into sets.

- Tiles can be live and can display messages and notifications, among other things.

- For Live Tiles to function, you may need to turn on notifications for individual apps and allow your geolocation to be used (presence).

# Touch and Gestures

Although some interface navigation commands were included in Windows 7, in Windows 8 touch navigation has been greatly enhanced and refined.

Touch gestures are valuable on tablet devices and cell phones, but they work on personal computers just as well. New generations of input devices—such as touch screens (digitizing monitors), input tablets, touch-enabled mice, and a variety of other devices—will be introduced over the next few years to make touch navigation on a PC more viable. Until then, any touch gesture you might use has a corresponding mouse action or keyboard shortcut.

When you're learning Windows 8, experiment with the actions associated with the display corners and edges. Each corner and edge exposes navigational features essential to working in Windows 8. In this chapter, you'll learn about those features and get up to speed navigating the Windows 8 interface.

## In This Chapter

# Touch Navigation

Windows 8 comes with a touch "language" that is used throughout the operating system—not just on the Start screen or in tile-based apps but on the Desktop as well.

These are the six basic gestures **A** in Windows 8:

- Tap (and, less frequently, double-tap)
- Tap and hold
- Swipe (tap and drag)
- Pinch
- Expand
- Rotate

Microsoft publishes guidance for developers on the design principles that apply to the touch interface. Here are some key principles:

- Adopt the Windows 8 touch language in your applications (of course).
- Use fingers for large targets that support direct manipulation, such as tiles.
- Use finger pinch and expand for semantic zoom.
- Swipe for pans.
- Provide user feedback for touch interactions such as moves.
- Provide for an undo feature.
- Provide multi-touch features for custom application commands.

  Windows 8 supports up to eight points of finger interaction.

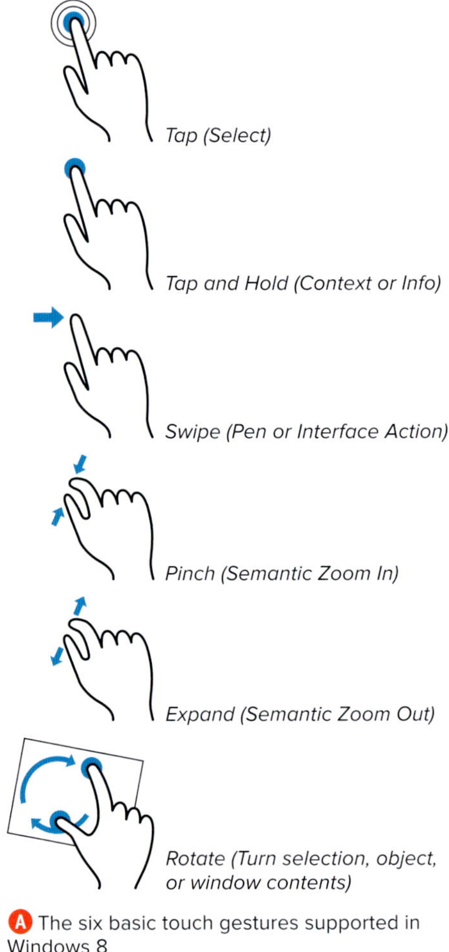



**A** The six basic touch gestures supported in Windows 8

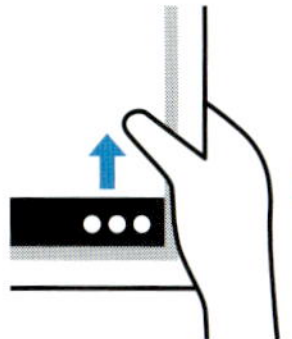

**B** Swipe from the bottom or top edge of your display to view application commands and toolbars.

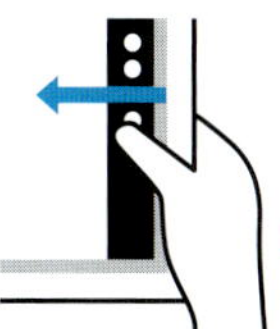

**C** Swipe from the right or left edge of your display to view system commands and toolbars.

## Semantic Zoom

A semantic zoom is more than a simple enlargement. In a normal zoom, you drill in to view the same information expanded in size. A semantic zoom changes what you see based on the current size of the object.

For example, consider the back of a baseball card. At a far zoom, where the object is small, you might see only the baseball player's name. Zoom in closer to a medium level and not only does the name appear, but also the team and position. At a close zoom, you can see the entire card, with the player's picture, year and lifetime statistics, and other information.

Semantic zoom is a much more powerful way to manipulate objects on small displays when you have only gross manipulations, such as pinch or expand, available to you.

- Touch interactions such as double-tap or tap and hold should be untimed because they are difficult to perform with fingers.

- Tap is for primary action (launching and opening); slide is for movement or panning; and swipe selects, commands, or moves objects.

- Tap and hold should display context information or help.

- Swipe from the top or bottom edge is for app commands **B**, and swipe from the left or right edge is for system commands **C**.

If this is the guidance that Microsoft gives developers, then you should anticipate that more and more of these types of actions will be available to you as a user of Windows 8-compatible applications. You should experiment to see which ones are currently supported. These touch interface guidelines require not only application support but also digitizing surfaces and new sets of device drivers. So the eventual range of interactions will take some time to develop.

**TIP** Depending on the type of digitizing surface that you use, you may find that using a pen or stylus device instead of a finger will give you more precision.

**TIP** All finger actions have corresponding mouse actions, although they aren't intuitive. A tap is the same as a left-click on the mouse, but a tap and hold correlates to a right-click.

# Corner Hotspots

The key to navigating quickly between the tile-based Start screen and the Desktop is to realize that each corner and edge has a specific action associated with it. Taps and clicks are associated with corners. Swipes and drags are associated with edges.

When you're using a mouse in Windows 8, it is worth taking some time to see what happens when you move your mouse cursor to a corner and right- or left-click. You should also experiment by tapping or clicking each corner.

## To use the actions available at the lower-left corner of your display:

- To view a thumbnail of the Desktop or Start screen, tap or click the lower-left corner of the display or press ⊞. Click the thumbnail to switch between the Start screen and the Desktop Ⓐ. On a tablet, you don't see the thumbnail in the lower-left corner of the display, but when you click the lower-left corner, you switch from the Desktop to the Start screen and vice versa.

- Right-click the lower-left corner to view the Computer Management menu Ⓑ. You can also use ⊞+X to open the Computer Management menu.

  The Computer Management menu allows you to access system tools and utilities that are part of the Desktop interface. It is a stripped-down version of Windows 7's Start menu. Some of the commands, particularly settings and searches, are contained in the Charms bar, as described in the "Edge Gestures" section. In a touch-based interface, most users will prefer to change settings and perform searches using the contents of the Charms bar.

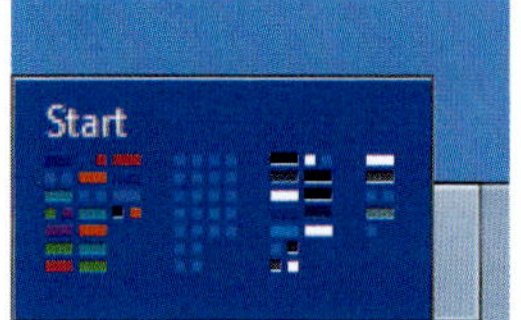


Ⓐ Click the Start screen thumbnail or the Desktop thumbnail to switch between the two interfaces.

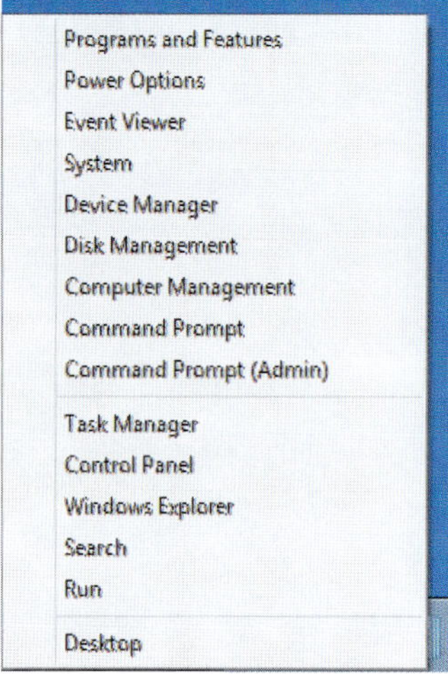


Ⓑ The Computer Management menu is available from the lower-left corner of either the Start screen or the Desktop.

**C** The next open app in the tab order is displayed in the upper-left corner of your display.

**D** All open apps displayed as a bar

## To use the actions available at the upper-left corner of your display:

- To view a thumbnail of the next application open in the tab order, click the upper-left corner of the Desktop **C**.

- To view a menu that lets you switch to or close the next application, right-click the upper-left corner of the Desktop.

- To view all open applications in a bar, tap or click the upper-left corner of the Desktop and drag or swipe down **D**.

- With the tab order open, you can click an application to open it.

- Swipe from the left edge to move to the next app in the tab order. Tap and hold the upper-left corner of the Start screen to display the Apps bar at the lower edge of the screen.

## To use the actions available at the upper-right corner of your display:

- Tap or click the upper-right corner and you will see no action. This is to not interfere with functions such as clicking the X button to close a window.

- To view a highlight of the Charms bar, move the mouse cursor to the upper-right corner; to display the Charms bar for use, drag the cursor or your finger down.

  Press ⊞+C to open the Charms bar directly.

## To use the actions available at the lower-right corner of your display:

- To view the Charms bar, tap or click the lower-right corner of the display on the Desktop.

- To view the app groups in miniature, tap or click the minus (-) just to the left of the lower-right corner of the display on the Start screen **E**.

- To minimize all windows and show the Desktop, tap or click just to the left of the lower-right corner of the display on the Desktop; click again to restore all minimized windows.

**TIP** If you are using a multi-monitor setup, the hot corners are found only on the primary display. Even if you extend the desktop onto a second (or third) screen, your gestures are still confined to a single monitor. This means that you can use a touch screen as your primary monitor and get the full benefit from that display type.

**E** App groups are displayed from the lower-right corner of the Start screen.

**A** The Charms bar is exposed by clicking the upper-right corner of the display or swiping from the right edge of the display.

**B** All the open apps in the order bar

# Edge Gestures

Edges are activated by swipes. The top and bottom edges are reserved for application toolbars or elements. The left and right edges are used for system toolbars— notably the Charms bar.

Think of the Charms bar as a version of the Windows 7 Start menu's greatest hits, optimized for touch and gestures. From top to bottom, the Charms bar **A** exposes Windows 8's powerful Search function, application data sharing through the Share charm, your current location (in **A** it is the Start screen), the Devices charm for managing and installing devices (such as printers), and a Settings function—all in the tile-based style. Settings captures the most important control panel options. (The Charms bar was covered in detail in Chapter 2.)

## To use the actions available at the left edge of your display:

Swipe from the left edge to view the tab order bar for apps **B**, then tap the app you wish to switch to. On a tablet when you swipe from the left edge, you change to the next app in the tab order.

Press ⊞+Tab to move forward in the tab order; press ⊞+Shift+Tab to move backward in the tab order.

## To use the actions available at the right edge of your display:

Swipe from the right edge to view the Charms bar on both the Start screen and the Desktop Ⓐ.

## To use the actions available at the bottom edge of your display:

In tile-based apps in the app itself or on the Start screen, swipe from the bottom edge to view an app toolbar.

## To use the actions available at the top edge of your display:

- To display an application toolbar or menu, swipe from the top edge.

- Drag the top edge to resize a window and move it to one side of the screen or the other, a procedure called snapping.

**TIP** **The new generation of touch mice and keyboards will allow you to emulate touch gestures in place of clicks and drags.**

# Touch Keyboards

To support alphanumeric entries using touch, Windows 8 comes with a greatly enhanced touch keyboard. In previous versions of Windows, this feature was primarily used as an Ease of Access tool and was referred to as the on-screen keyboard. In Windows 8, the touch keyboard comes in three basic flavors, two of which are much more useful when you're working with your fingers:

- The QWERTY keyboard, in either a docked or floating form

- A split keyboard that is primarily useful when holding a tablet or cell phone with both hands, because it allows for thumb input

- A pen input keypad that is useful when you are using a tablet that comes with a stylus or digital pen

When you are working on a tablet or phone, chances are that the current application will automatically display the split keyboard when you need it. You can work with all the types of touch keyboards on the Desktop. However, there are no commands on the Computer Management menu for the touch keyboards, nor does the tile-based Start screen come with a tile that activates it. So the quickest way to work with the touch keyboard is to enable the touch keyboard toolbar that lives on the Desktop taskbar.

## To open the touch keyboard:

1.  Right-click the Desktop taskbar, select the Toolbars command, and then select Touch Keyboard from the submenu 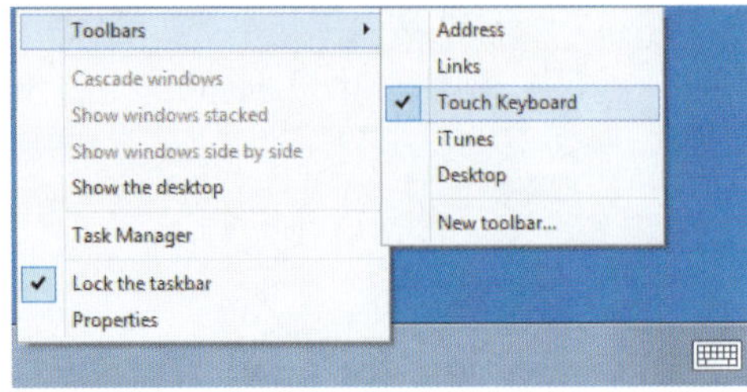.

2.  Tap or click the touch keyboard icon to display the touch keyboard in the state that it was in when you last opened it.

    **B** shows the touch keyboard fully maximized across the bottom of the screen.



**A** When you select Toolbars > Touch Keyboard, the touch keyboard icon appears at the bottom right.

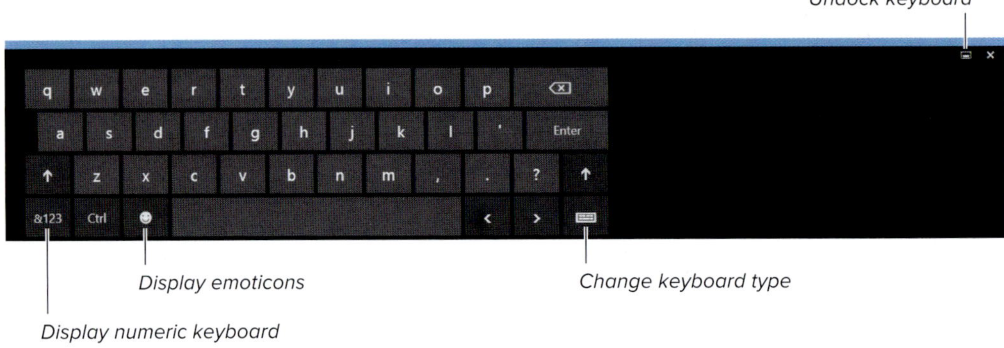



**B** The touch keyboard toolbar in its QWERTY form and docked

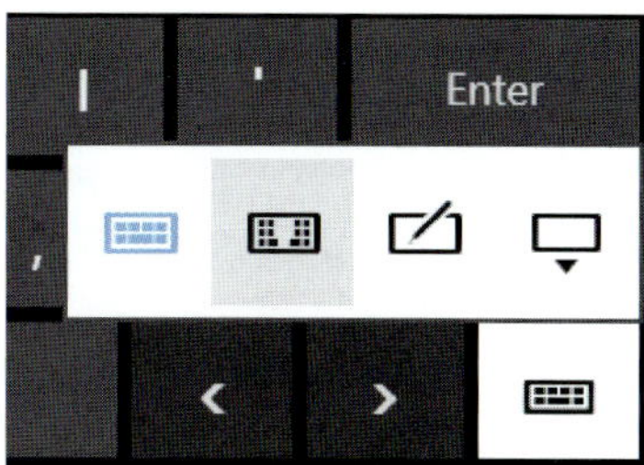



**C** The Change Keyboard Type menu with the split keyboard icon selected

## To display the split keyboard:

Tap or click the Change Keyboard Type button, and then click the split keyboard icon **C**. The split keyboard displays **D**.

The split keyboard is particularly useful on a tablet because you can use your thumbs to type on it.

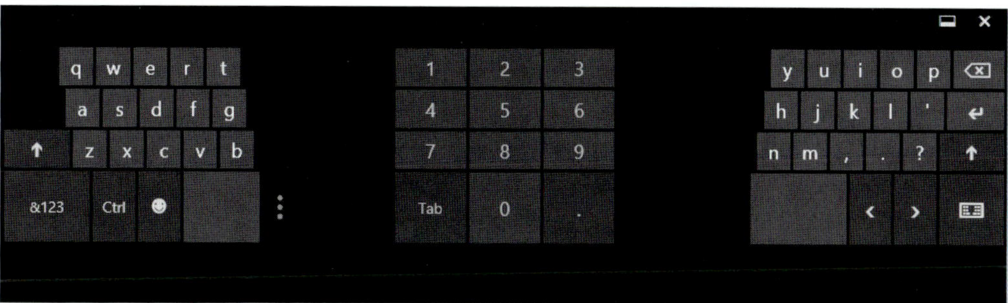



**D** The split keyboard in its undocked state

In **C**, the two icons to the right of the split keyboard icon are the Pen Input panel icon and the minimize keyboard icon. The minimize keyboard icon removes the touch keyboard from view. The Pen Input panel converts your pen (or finger) input into characters **E**.

**TIP** Windows 8 ships with a speech recognition feature as part of the Ease of Access toolset. To open and use this feature, enter "speech recognition" into the Search function and open the Speech Recognition control panel. Speech is useful for screen navigation, voice commands, and many other functions, but not for speech dictation. For that function you will need to use a program such as Dragon NaturallySpeaking.

**E** The Pen Input panel takes your handwriting and automatically converts it into alphanumeric keyboard entries.

# Touch Mice

To really appreciate the Windows 8 touch interface, you need input devices that allow you to perform gestures. For a phone or a tablet, the input device is the screen. Touch monitors already exist, and Windows 8 will undoubtedly make them more popular. It is also highly likely that we will see a new generation of touchpads in the form of graphics tablets, which have been popular with engineers and digital artists for years now.

To lead the way, Microsoft is releasing a new generation of touch mice and touch keyboards. The company has three different models of touch mice that have built-in drivers in Windows 8:

- Microsoft Touch Mouse

- Microsoft Explorer Mouse, which is similar in function to the Touch Mouse

- Microsoft Wedge Mouse, which is small and looks a lot like a doorstop

A new set of gestures has been developed that emphasizes the tile-based interface's qualities and removes some of the touch gestures that were aimed at controlling Desktop features in Windows 7.

An application called Device Center allows you to customize a touch mouse Ⓐ. In Device Center, you can control the rate of movement, turn the thumb gesture on or off, and assign app-specific actions.

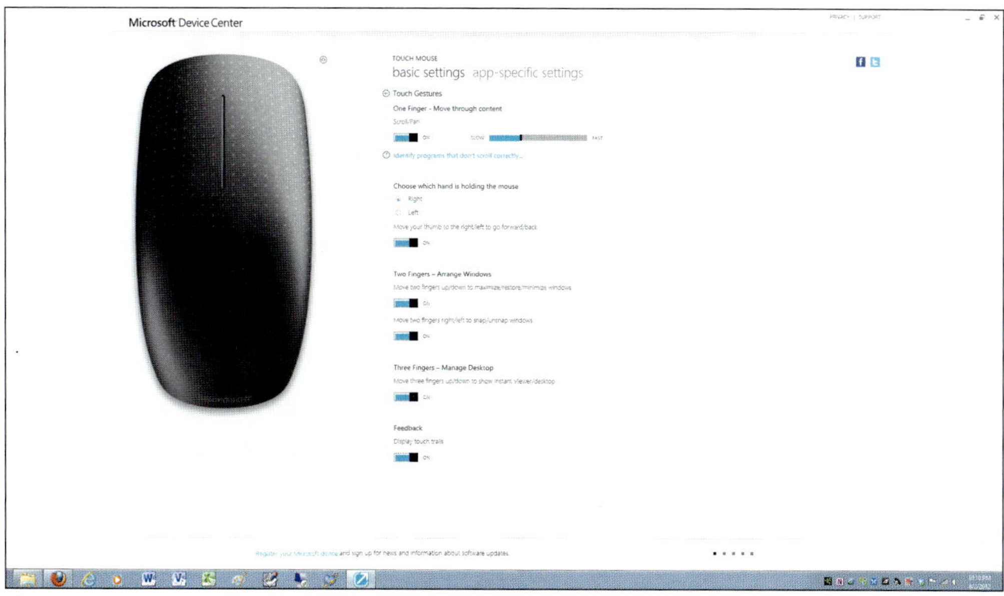

Ⓐ Touch gestures with basic settings

## To shift content with one-finger gestures:

- Slide your finger in any direction to scroll your screen in that direction.

- Flick your finger to scroll quickly in the direction of the flick.

- Move your thumb right or left to move forward or backward, respectively, through open applications (this is the same as pressing Alt+⊞ and Alt+Shift+⊞).

## To manage applications with two-finger gestures:

- Swipe two fingers to the right to toggle between open applications, as you would do by pressing ⊞+Tab.

- Swipe two fingers to the left to open the Charms bar, which is the equivalent of pressing ⊞+C.

- Swipe two fingers upward to perform an application-specific action, such as opening a browser to show the address bar or toggling a window state from full to restore.

## To perform a zoom with three-finger gestures on a touch mouse:

- To zoom in, slide three fingers forward on the top of the mouse.

- To zoom out, slide three fingers backward on the top of the mouse.

Since Windows users will expect third-party mice to perform the same gestures, you should expect to see these touch semantics widely used in the industry.

## To modify a touch mouse's gestures:

1. Press ⊞+Q to open Search.

2. Enter **Device Center** in the Search field, then tap or click the Microsoft Device Center icon.

3. In the Device Center screen, tap or click the *Touch Gestures* link.

4. Modify the basic settings as desired, altering or disabling any one-, two-, or three-finger gestures Ⓐ.

5. Tap or click the *app-specific settings* link to assign a mouse button or gesture to a program Ⓑ.

**TIP** Device Center provides access to the *Healthy Computing Guide*, which contains tips on how to work more comfortably with your computer.

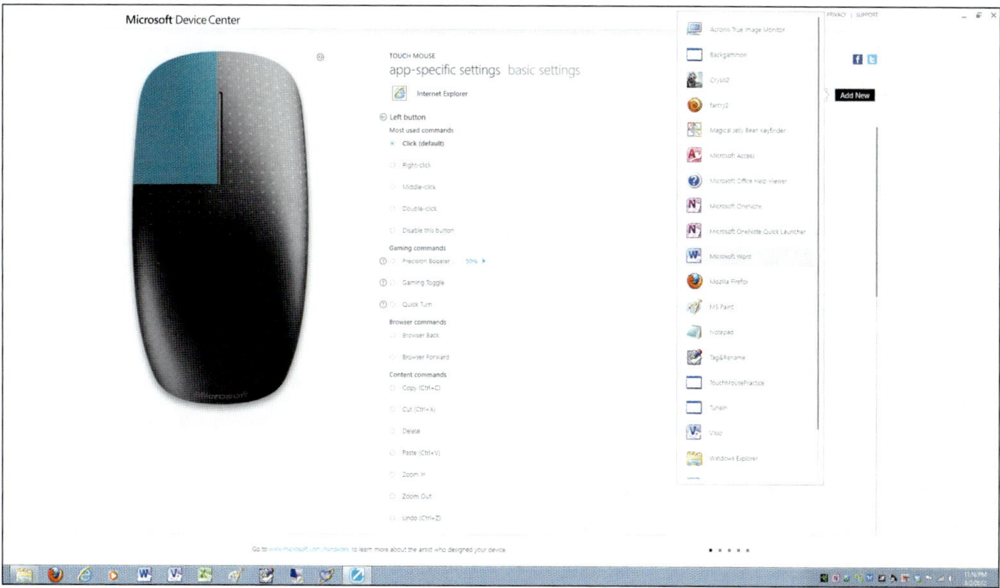

Ⓑ You can assign buttons and gestures to specific applications.

# Putting It All Together

- Windows 8 supports a multi-touch interface capable of complex manipulations.

- There are six basic gestures associated with touch: tap, tap and hold, swipe, pinch, expand, and rotate.

- Microsoft's touch interface guidelines should begin to be adopted by apps over time.

- Semantic zoom displays different levels of information for an object, depending on the size at which the object is displayed.

- Each corner of the display is a hotspot that provides a navigational feature.

- The left and right edges are activated by swipes and display system toolbars like the app tab order and the Charms bar.

- The top and bottom edges are activated by swipes and display application-specific toolbars.

- Windows 8 comes with a variety of soft, or virtual, keyboards, including a QWERTY keyboard and a split keyboard.

- You can display the Pen Input panel to enter characters using your fingers or pen.

- Microsoft touch mice are a good way of adding touch capability to a PC.

# The Classic Interface

For most users, Windows is defined by the Desktop, the Start menu, and the windowing system (I always look at a window to see what operating system a device is running). In the tile-based interface, there's no Start menu and there are no windows.

The Start menu, which was introduced in Windows 95 to the strains of the Rolling Stones' "Start Me Up," is gone. But pretty much everything else you've grown accustomed to about the Desktop is still there, with a few improvements. It's a good thing too, because the tens of thousands of applications that depend on the Microsoft windowing system—such as Microsoft Office, Adobe Acrobat, and Intuit Quicken—still require the Desktop to run correctly.

If you long for the days of yesteryear and want to live on the Desktop, this chapter tells you how. For this chapter at least, bid the tile-based interface adieu, don your Mouseketeer hat, and whip out your clicky keyboard.

## In This Chapter

# Start Me Up

The tile-based interface starts by default when you install Windows 8. This is by design, because the tile-based interface works best on mobile devices, and the world of computing looks increasingly mobile. But the Desktop, which is the classic Windows interface, is only a click or two away.

## To launch the Desktop:

- If there are open windows, press ⊞+D (for Desktop) to close the windows and show only the Desktop. Press ⊞+D a second time to see the Desktop with all open windows restored.

  Press ⊞ to toggle between the Start screen interface and the Desktop.

- On the Start screen, tap or click the Desktop tile Ⓐ.

- On the Start screen, tap or click a tile for a legacy application or web page; that item opens on the Desktop.

- On the Start screen, tap or click the lower-left corner of the screen to toggle between the tile-based interface and the Desktop.

- On the Start screen, tap or click the upper-left corner of the display, and cycle through the icons until you can tap or click the Desktop icon.

You might think that the Desktop is an application, because it launches from a tile in the tile-based interface, but it is not. The Desktop is a shell—specifically, a graphical user interface (GUI). In that regard, it is the same thing that the tile-based interface is.

When you install Windows 8, the Desktop tile is placed in another group lower down the screen than is shown in . In Ⓐ, the tile has been moved to the upper-left position, which leads me to one of my favorite tips: To move a tile, tap and hold it, and then drag it to a new position; or with the mouse, just drag it.

**TIP** **Press Enter in the tile-based interface to open the upper-left tile Ⓐ.**

*Tap or click here to toggle through open apps to reach the Desktop.*

*Tap or click the Desktop tile to go directly to the Desktop.*



*Tap or click here to toggle between the Desktop and tile-based interfaces.*

Ⓐ Places in the tile-based interface that take you to the Desktop

# Desktop Elements

The Desktop contains many of the common elements that you've grown to know and love: a taskbar, viewable toolbars, icons, and so on **(A)**. Let's take a look at what these features do.

- **Icons** represent objects in the file system; you will generally put special folders or program icons on the Desktop.

- **Desktop wallpaper** is a graphic—for show, of course.

- **Gadgets** are little tools or utilities that you add to the Desktop for additional functionality.

- **The Desktop switch** is a button in the lower-right corner that switches from the tile-based interface to the Desktop. (You see the button only when your mouse button is down.)

- **The Notification area** shows icons of various utilities (usually system utilities); it was once called the Status tray.

- **Toolbars** contain related commands or objects that you can place on the taskbar.

- **The taskbar** is a container for toolbars and the Notifications area.

**TIP** In **(A)**, you see that the taskbar can be minimized into a hierarchical menu display. This mode mimics a lot of what the Start menu did.

**TIP** Most desktop elements are turned on using the context menu that appears when you either right-click or tap and hold an object.

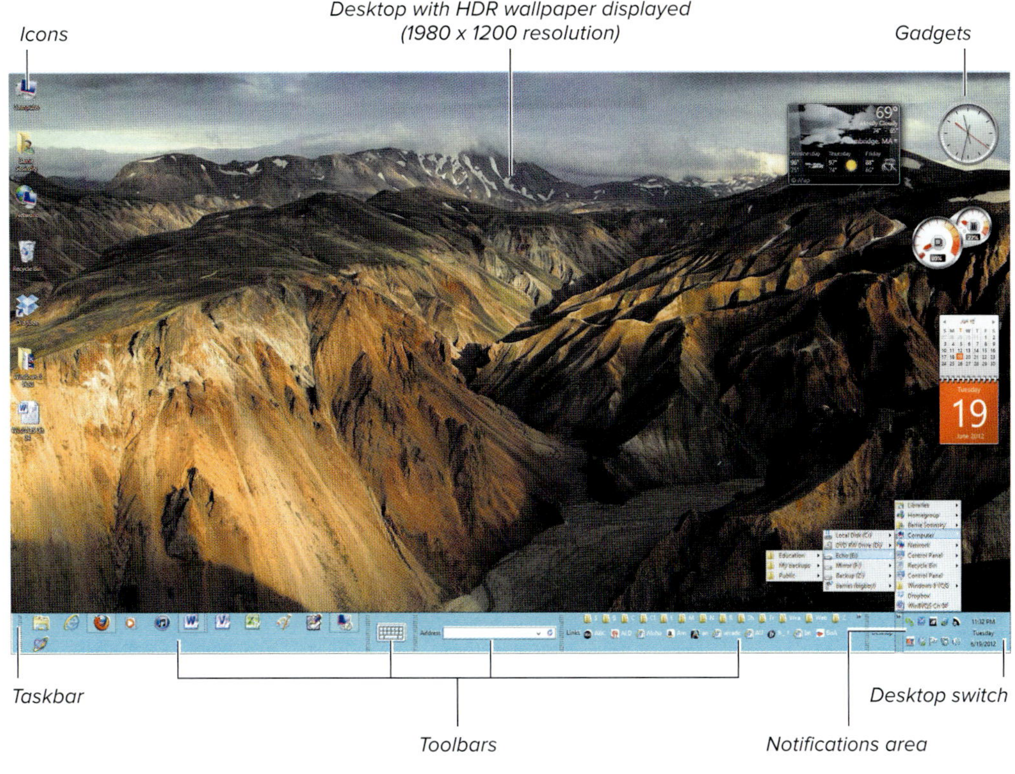


Ⓐ The Desktop

## The Desktop Management Menu

Although the Start menu is gone (sigh), Windows 8 does come with the Desktop Management menu Ⓑ.

To open the Desktop Management menu:

- Right-click the lower-right corner of the Desktop.

The top section of this menu is a list of a few important control panels you will want to open frequently: Programs and Features, Power Options, and Systems— as well as Control Panel itself, which lists the control panels by type.

Other choices open dialog boxes based on an extensible framework called the Microsoft Management Console (MMC), including Device Manager, Disk Management, and Computer Management. Toss in a few important commands like Run (⊞+R), Search (⊞+F), and Windows Explorer (⊞+E), and you have what is essentially a stripped-down Start menu.

Ⓑ The Desktop Management menu contains many of the important commands once found on the Start menu in Windows 7.

# The Taskbar

The taskbar offers many shortcuts that can greatly speed up your work. Let's start by exploring the taskbar's context menu, because you can use that to open the various toolbars and options.

### To view toolbars:

1. Right-click, or tap and hold, the taskbar to view the Taskbar menu .

2. Select from the Toolbars submenu to display one or all of the toolbars.

### To change the height of the taskbar:

1. Deselect the Lock The Taskbar command Ⓐ to disable it (remove its check mark).

2. Drag the top edge of the taskbar up or down as desired.

Notice that with the taskbar unlocked, each toolbar has a resize edge that you can drag. When you lock the taskbar, toolbars are frozen in position. Ⓐ in the "Desktop Elements" section shows the toolbars with the taskbar unlocked.

### To pin a program icon, folder, or other object to the taskbar:

- Tap and hold, or right-click, the tile for the object in the tile-based interface, and then tap or click the Pin To Taskbar button in the bottom bar Ⓑ.

- You can also drag an object from the Desktop—a program, a folder, a drive, and so on—onto the taskbar to anchor it there.

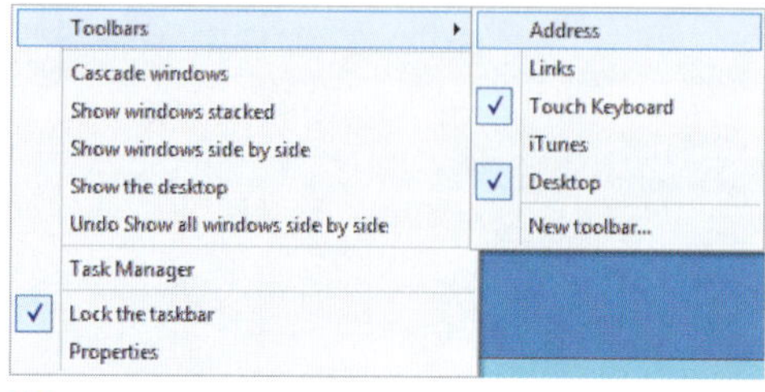

Ⓐ The Taskbar menu

Ⓑ The Pin To Taskbar button in the tile-based interface

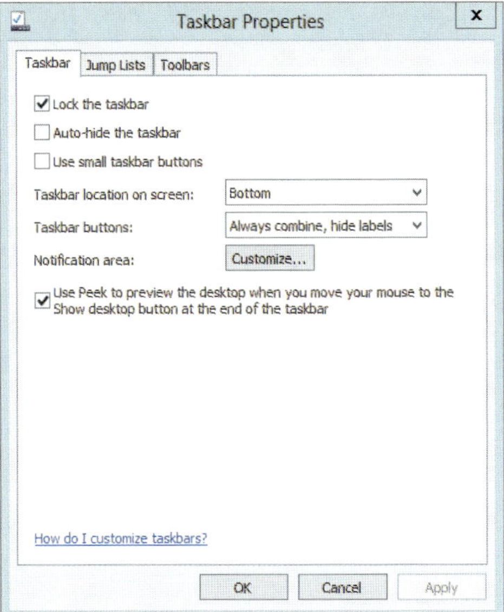

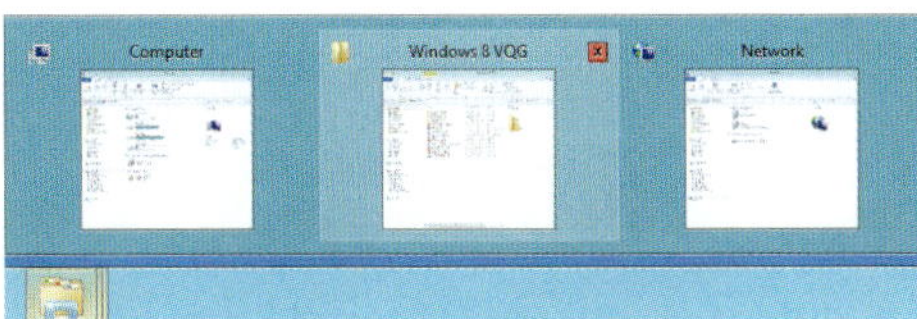

**C** The Taskbar Properties dialog box

**D** Three Windows Explorer windows in thumbnail view

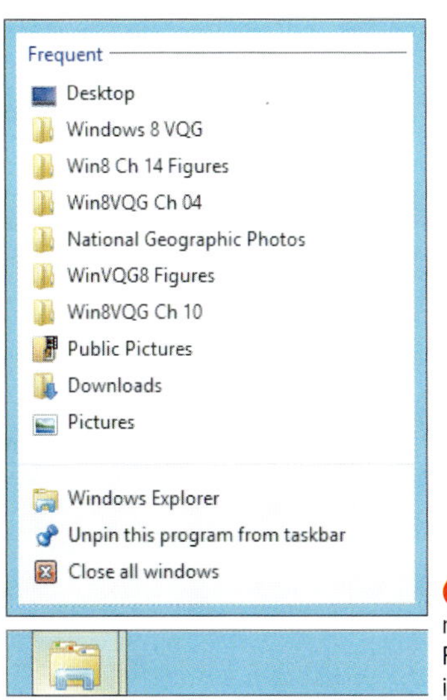

**E** The jump menu for Frequent items

# To set taskbar options:

Several important options for taskbar icons are set in the Taskbar Properties dialog box **C**. Its command is the bottommost one in the menu shown in **A**.

- Select the Auto-hide The Taskbar check box to hide the taskbar automatically when it is not in use; tap or click the bottom edge of the screen to restore the taskbar.

- Select the Use Small Taskbar Buttons check box to reduce the size of the icons, which is valuable for work on a smaller screen.

- Select an option from the Taskbar Location On Screen drop-down menu to move the taskbar to different edges of your display.

- Select an option from the Taskbar Buttons drop-down menu to control how multiple instances of open like objects are displayed. (I like to combine them.)

- Select the Use Peek To check box to show a Desktop thumbnail on the Show Desktop button.

- Click the Apply button to enforce the settings you select but continue working in the dialog box.

- Click the OK button to enforce the settings you select and close the dialog box.

Experiment with these options to find the ones you like.

When you hover your cursor over a taskbar icon, it will display thumbnails of windows that you can switch to or close (click the X) **D**. When you right-click a taskbar icon, the context menu offers you several options, including a jump list of Frequent items **E**.

**TIP** To create a new instance of a program or window, hold the Shift key and click its taskbar icon.

# Notifications

The Customize button in the Taskbar tab of the Taskbar Properties dialog box opens the Notification Area Icons dialog box **A**, which allows you to modify the Notification area. You can choose to do the following for all or some tools:

- Show icons and notifications
- Hide icons and notifications
- Show only notifications

The Only Show Notifications option displays the status icon only when there is a message or condition that the program wants you to know about.

The Notification Area Icons dialog box is a control panel. Notification area icon menus typically contain commands that open utilities and control panels. The Date/Time icon is a good example of this behavior.

## To change the date or time:

1. Tap, or move your cursor over, the Date/Time icon (at the far right of the taskbar).

2. In the Date/Time pop-up window that appears **B**, click the *Change date and time settings* link.

   This opens the Date And Time control panel.

3. Make your changes, and then close the control panel.

There are many other ways to get to control panels. For example, you can use the search function in Windows 8 to find a control panel by its name. But using a Notification area icon to launch control panels is one of the easiest methods.

**TIP** Press ⊞+X to open the Desktop Management menu.

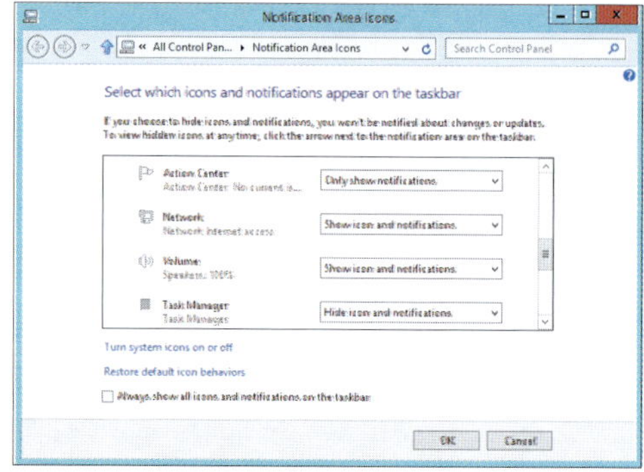

**A** The Notification Area Icons dialog box allows you to alter the behavior of Notification icons on the taskbar.

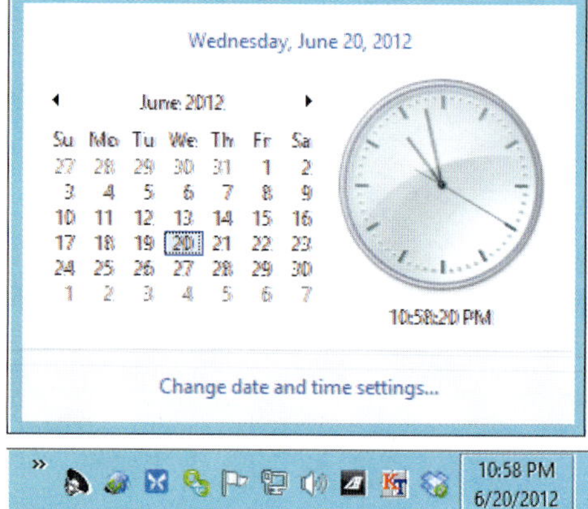

**B** The Date/Time icon can be used to view and modify the system date and time.

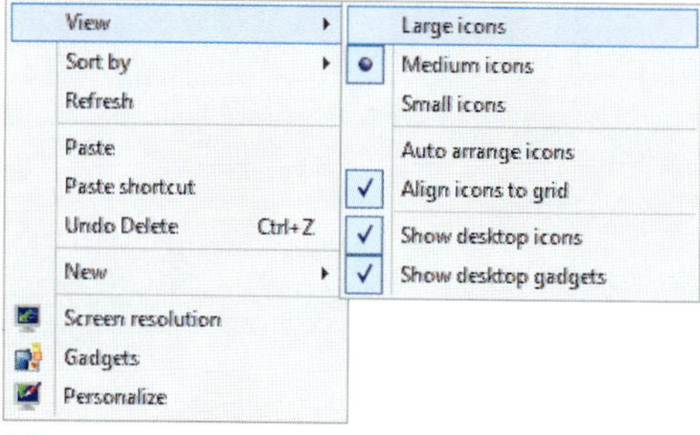



**A** The top three commands in the Desktop context menu demonstrate its container nature.

# Desktop Operations

The Desktop survives. Once it was plain; for a while, it was "active." It has been adorned by screen savers, gadget bars, picture shows, themes, and wallpapers—things that were pretty, things that were mesmerizing, things that were useful, and things that went bump in the night. But the Desktop remains.

The Desktop is a container object, just as a folder is. However, the Desktop is a special container because it can not only show files, folders, and object icons, it can contain the taskbar, which you have just seen.

But by far the Desktop's most important function is as a container of "windows." Windows are content containers that are controlled by a piece of system software called the Window Manager. Windows are the whole point of the Desktop's existence. Without windows (lowercase, please), Windows is just another tile-based life form. Let's start by looking at the Desktop context menu.

### To view the Desktop context menu:

Right-click an empty area of the Desktop **A**.

The View and Sort By submenus contain commands that are typical of folders. Refresh (F5) updates the Desktop manually.

### To select something on the Desktop (or in a window):

- Click the object.

- Drag a selection area around a contiguous range of objects.

- Click at the beginning of a contiguous range of objects, hold the Shift key, and click the end of the range.

- Click the first object in a noncontiguous range, hold the Ctrl key, and click the other objects you want in the range.

## To perform window actions on a selection using the Clipboard:

- Press Ctrl+X to delete the object and copy it to the Clipboard system memory.

- Press Ctrl+C to leave the object but place a copy on the Clipboard.

- Press Ctrl+V to paste a copy of the object at your current location.

## To perform window actions on a selection using drag and drop:

- Drag selected objects to move them from folder to folder.

- Drag selected objects from one disk to another to make a copy of your selection.

- Hold the Ctrl key while dragging selected objects to make a copy of the objects even if the default action is to move them.

- Hold the Alt key while dragging selected objects to create a shortcut to the objects.

- Press the Delete key to remove any selections and place them in the Recycle bin.

- Drag and drop items into the Recycle bin to delete them.

- Press Ctrl+Z to undo the last action if you make a mistake.

The expanded New command for the Desktop context menu 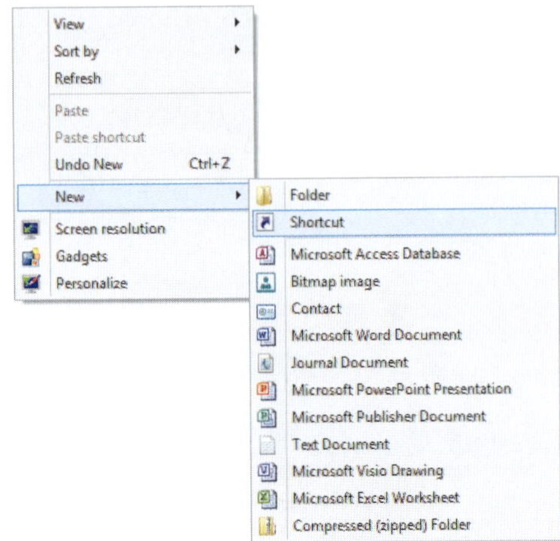 allows you to create files and shortcuts of various types. As you install programs in Windows, additional file types are added. The New Shortcut command opens a wizard that lets you create a shortcut or pointer (what Unix and Linux call a symbolic link) to objects in other locations.

**B** Use the New command to create objects and files quickly.

**TIP** When you delete something, it is not dead. That is, in Windows there are different levels of dead. You can double-click the Recycle bin and use the Restore command to return items to their previous locations. If you've emptied the Recycle bin, then you will need a special third-party undelete program to restore that object. Even then, the object is still on disk until Windows needs to overwrite its location on disk, after which its return is beyond the reach of mere mortals.

**TIP** Windows gives you visual indicators during the operation to keep you informed.

# Personalization

There are many things to play with in the Personalization control panel, and you can have hours of self-indulgent fun there. But let's highlight a few of its more practical features.

## To add Desktop icons:

1.  Right-click the Desktop and select Personalize from the context menu to view the Personalization control panel Ⓐ.

*continues on next page*

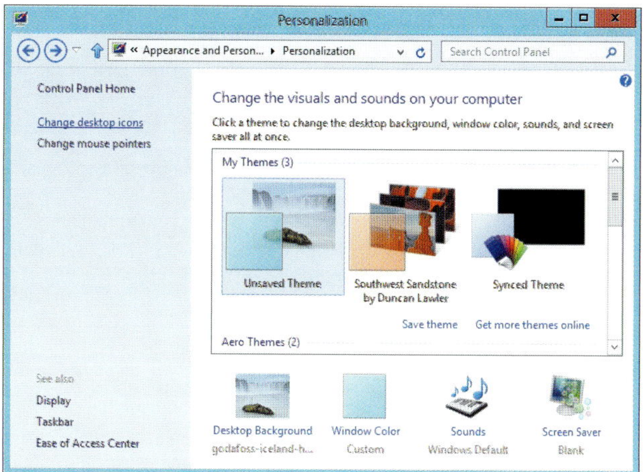

Ⓐ The Personalization control panel allows you to change the appearance of the Desktop.

**2.** Click the *Change desktop icons* link to view the Desktop Icon Settings dialog box **B**.

**3.** Make your selections, and then click OK.

Desktop backgrounds are more commonly known as "wallpapers," and for reasons that escape me, people are truly passionate about them.

## To change the Desktop background:

**1.** In the Personalization dialog box, click the Desktop Background icon to view the Desktop Background dialog box **C**.

**2.** Click the Picture Location drop-down menu, and make a selection from a solid color palette, your Pictures library, or another folder that you designate.

**3.** Select an option from the Picture Position drop-down menu to fill, fit, stretch, tile, or center the picture.

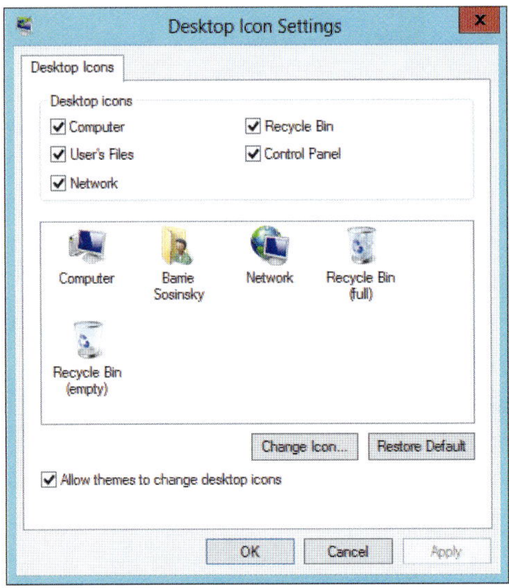

**B** In the Desktop Icon Settings control panel, you can add special folders and places to the Desktop.

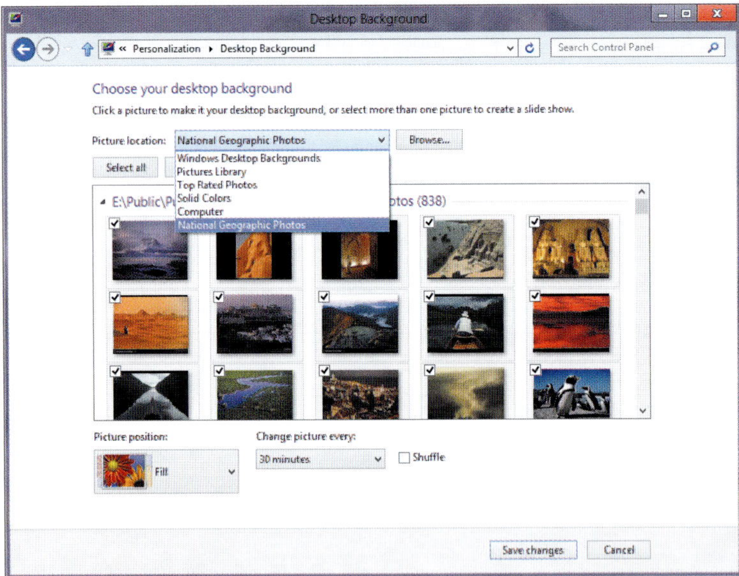

**C** The Desktop Background dialog box

4. For a slideshow, select a time period from the Change Picture Every drop-down menu. Select the Shuffle check box, if desired.

5. Click the Save Changes button to display your new background.

## To change your theme:

A theme is a collection of Desktop backgrounds, Windows color and font styles, system sounds, and other elements all bundled up as a package and applied at once.

- Scroll the central window (marked My Themes in Ⓐ) and select a new theme.

- Click the *Get more themes online* link, and find one on Microsoft's website.

You may want to explore the Change Mouse Pointers and Sound dialog boxes. Click the *Change mouse pointers* link Ⓐ to open that dialog box. The Sounds dialog box is opened with the Sounds icon Ⓐ. Sounds and mouse pointers are part of a theme, along with fonts, window styles, and colors. Mouse pointers are cursor sets that you can apply; several cursor sets are good for the visually impaired, some are helpful on laptops, and a few are simply amusing. Sounds are short clips that play after various window events; changing sound sets has never appealed much to me, but other people like customized sounds.

Themes can apply sets of cursors and sounds, but you can also do this independently, and it does add personality to a system. You can download many more themes from the Microsoft website.

## To add a gadget:

Gadgets used to be constained to the Gadget bar, but now they have been set free to float above your desktop.

1. Right-click the Desktop and select the Gadgets command from the context menu.

   The Gadget gallery appears 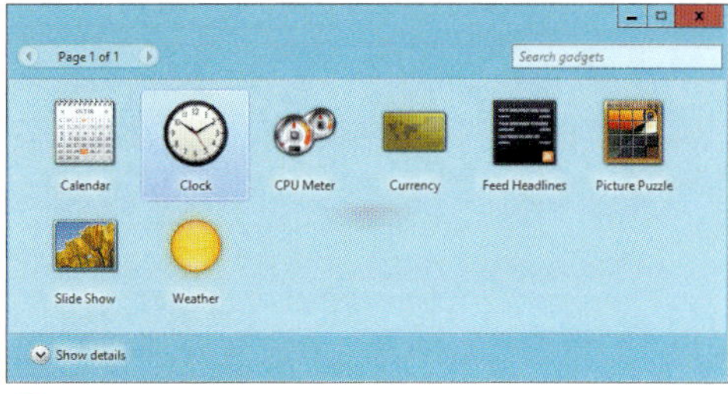.

2. Drag a gadget to your desktop.

**TIP** Visually impaired users can use the Ease of Access Center to turn on a magnifier, have the Desktop narrated, turn on an onscreen keyboard, and set up a high-contrast display. Click the *Ease of Access Center* link on the Personalization control panel.

**D** The Gadget gallery

# Windowing

As noted, a window is a content container. Desktop windows are of two basic types: modal and non-modal. A non-modal window is one that you can switch out of and then switch back to. A modal window is one that requires you to perform an action before it allows you to do something else. An alert box is an example of a modal window something you must deal with before you can do other work.

In **(A)**, a non-modal application window is shown with some of its window interface elements identified. Here you can work in more than one window at the same time. The application is Microsoft Publisher, and the document is an origami crane.

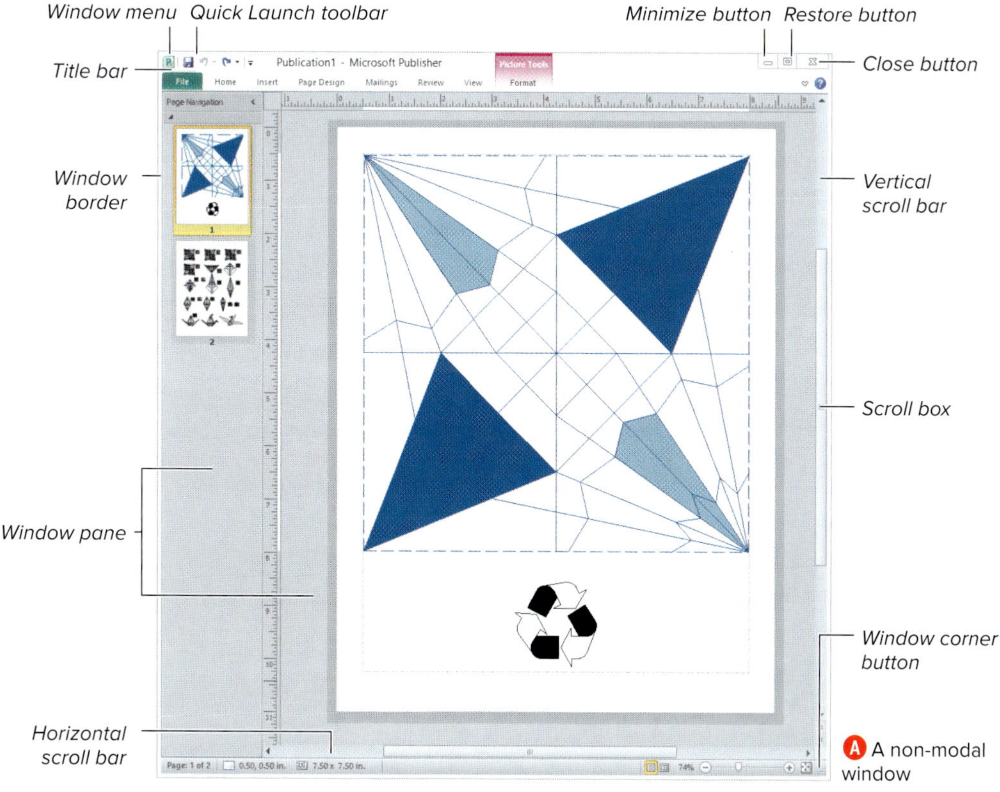

Windows were designed to work with both your mouse and your keyboard. You won't use touch to use windows of this type.

Here's a brief description of the important window elements:

- **Title bar.** This bar contains the window name and, usually, the name of the application that is responsible for it. Drag the title bar to move the window from place to place.

  When a title bar has focus, its window is the active window and can be acted upon.

- **Window menu.** The application icon is actually the Window menu, put there to allow you to perform window actions with your keyboard. Click the icon or press Alt+spacebar to reveal commands that allow you to restore, move, size, minimize, maximize, and close (Alt+F4) the window **B**.

  Note that the Window menu and the Quick Launch toolbar shown in **A** are application-specific features (Microsoft Office). Here the application is Publisher, so that icon shows.

- **Restore command.** This command **B** toggles a maximized window back to its previous size.

- **Move command.** This command **B** selects the window and allows you to use the arrow keys or your mouse cursor to move the window in any direction.

- **Size command.** This command **B** allows you to use the arrow keys or your mouse cursor to resize your window.

- **Minimize.** Click this button on the toolbar or select this command **B** to reduce a window to an icon.

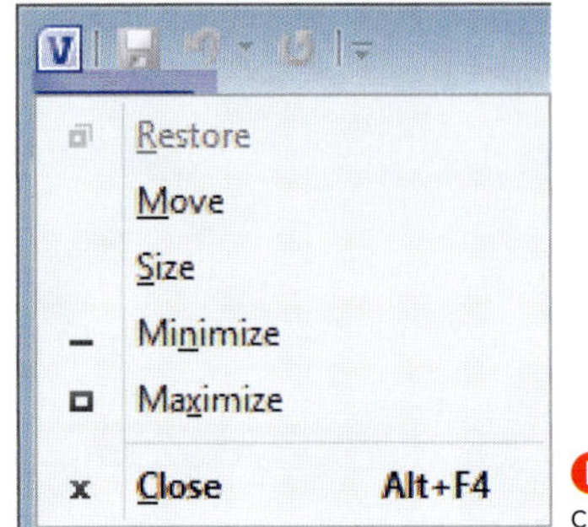

**B** Window commands

- **Maximize.** Click this button on the toolbar or select this command Ⓑ to display a window full screen.

- **Restore.** Click this button on the toolbar or select this command Ⓑ to return the window to its former size (before you minimized or maximized it).

- **Close button.** Click this button or press Alt+F4 to close a window. The application should prompt you to save any changes, if necessary.

  Note that you can press Alt+spacebar to open the Window menu, and then press the underlined key to execute the command. This is a general Windows feature. For example, Alt+N minimizes the window.

- **Window border.** Drag a window border to resize the window in one direction. Use the window corner to resize the window in two directions.

- **Scroll bars.** The scroll bars are used as a visual indicator for your horizontal or vertical position inside the window. Click a scroll bar arrow to move one increment in that direction. Click the scroll bar to move one screen page in that direction. Drag the scroll box (slider) to move the view of the window contents as far as you like.

There are many keystrokes that move your window view. Use Home to move to the top of the window; End to move to the bottom; and Page Up or Page Down to move up or down one full page or screen. These keystrokes support the vertical toolbar.

To switch between windows on the Desktop, click a window to make it active or use the Task Switcher.

Sometimes a window can be both modal and non-modal. A modal window is one that requires an action before you can close it or that forces you to act before you can do anything else. Modal windows illustrate some important general window navigation features. **C** shows a Save dialog box. It is both non-modal and modal at the same time. You can do things in programs other than Word; but it is a modal window for Word because you can't do anything else in Word until you dismiss it.

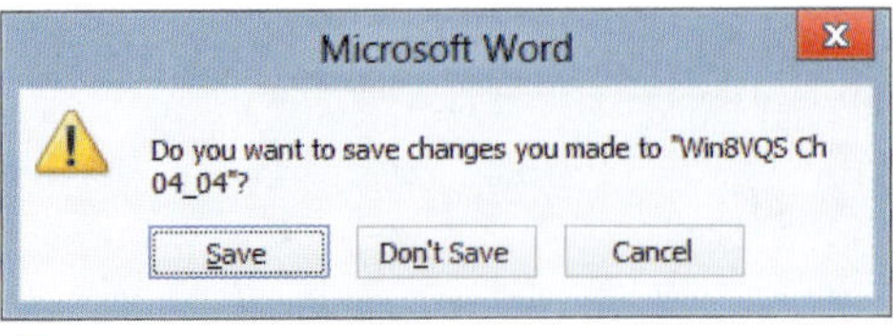

**C** A Save dialog box

Non-modal windows have the following features:

- **A Default action.** This button is usually drawn with a bold button frame and can be activated by pressing Enter. **D** shows the Save button bordered with a blue dotted frame.

- **A Cancel or Escape action.** This removes the dialog box without making changes. Press the Esc key or click the Cancel button to perform this action.

- **A Tab order.** Press the Tab key to move from button to button in the tab order, or press Alt+Tab to move backward in that order.

- **Shortcuts.** Dialog boxes and alert boxes have keystroke equivalents for buttons, fields, and other items. They are usually indicated by underlined letters. Here, you press the S key to perform the Save action.

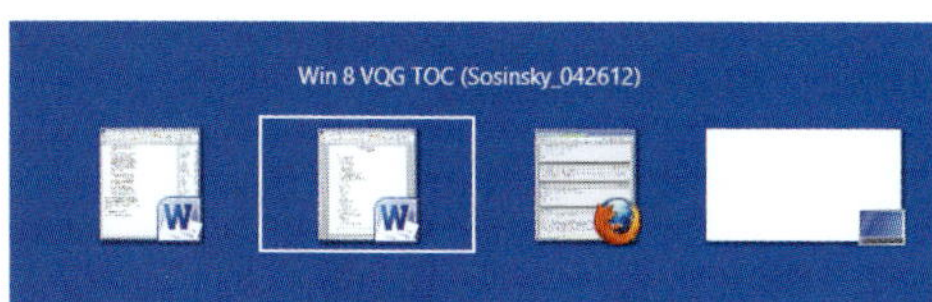


**D** The Task Switcher lets you switch quickly between open windows. It also works in Metro.

## To use the Task Switcher:

1. Press Alt+Tab to view the Task Switcher **D**.

2. Hold the Alt key down and press the Tab key repeatedly to cycle through all the open windows until the one you want is highlighted.

3. Release the Alt key. You can use Shift+Alt+Tab to move backward through the Tab order.

**TIP** Devices such as the Microsoft Intelli-Mouse and apps such as Move Mouse provide options for manipulating windows—even the elusive scroll right and left functionality.

# Putting It All Together

- The Windows Desktop is a graphical user interface required by legacy programs.

- There are many ways to switch between the tile-based interface and the classic Windows Desktop interface.

- The Desktop is a container for various objects, including file system objects, devices, and utilities such as the task-bar and gadgets.

- The taskbar is highly configurable through its Properties dialog box, and you can add toolbars and Notification area icons to it.

- Many Desktop icons provide customization through control panels. A few are found on the Desktop Management menu.

- The Desktop supports standard window-selection techniques, as well as drag-and-drop technology and the Clipboard.

- Among the many personalization features that the Desktop supports are Desktop icons, backgrounds, themes, cursor sets, and system sound sets.

- The Desktop is a container for windows, and windows are a container for content.

- A window contains standard interface elements controlled by the Windows Manager software.

- Non-modal windows allow you to switch out of and then back into them and can be moved or resized.

- Modal windows force you to perform an action before you can close them, or they force you to close them before you can do anything else.

# Settings and Customization

Windows 8 has thousands of settings for your system and for individual users. When you install additional programs, devices, and services, you add even more. Windows 8 comes with a number of methods for managing, storing, and modifying these settings.

The most common settings are exposed through a control panel applet. Control panels are small programs displayed within the Control Panel framework. From the System Management menu, you can access control panels in the form in which they appeared in previous versions of Windows. You can also access a subset of control panel settings using the Settings bar.

Settings are stored in the Windows Registry, which is a database used to organize and manage settings by type. You can manipulate values in the Registry to solve problems and customize your system.

In this chapter, you will learn how to turn Windows features on and off, as well as how to modify a system's startup behavior by turning startup programs and services on and off.

## In This Chapter

# Control Panels

The Control Panel is a collection of *applets*, or small programs, that modify different aspects of your Windows 8 system, including hardware, software setup, security, configuration, and user account management. The Control Panel is a special folder that contains pointers to these .cpl applets. Every version of Windows since 1.0 has had a Control Panel.

You can think of the Control Panel home screen 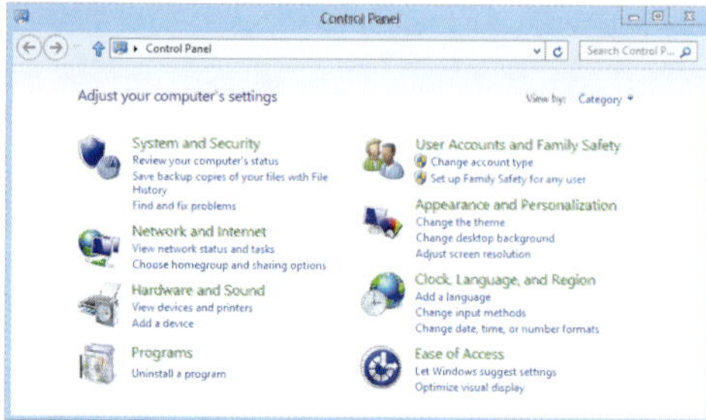 as a "table of contents," where each link opens either a control panel applet (known as a control panel item) or another category screen. The search box allows you to search the control panels by name, keyword, or function. If you open the drop-down menu, you can replace the category view with an icon view 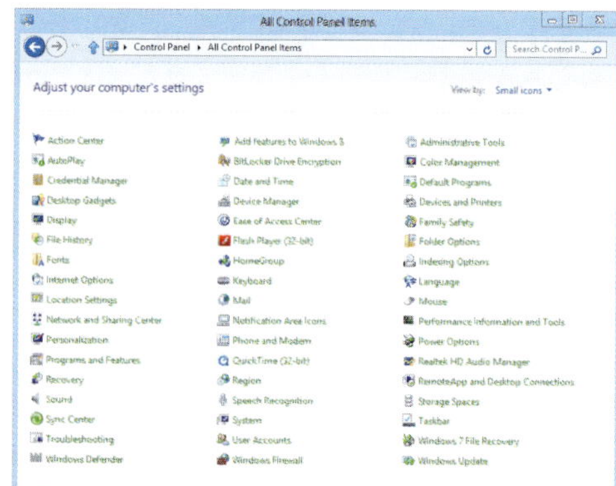. You can access all the control panels from this interface, whereas only a subset of the more important control panel settings are exposed in the tile-based interface Settings screens.

Control panels are opened via from a variety of interface actions. For example, you can select the Personalization command from the Desktop's context menu to open the Personalization control panel. Control panels are extensible, so you will find third-party control panels from other vendors either as stand-alone panels or as add-in tabs in existing control panels. A very common example of a third-party control panel is the extensions that mouse vendors create. The groupings that you see in the Control Panel home page are category pages. From a category page you can open multiple control panels.

**A** The Desktop Control Panel home page gives you access to all Control Panel functions.

**B** The icon view of the Control Panel

"

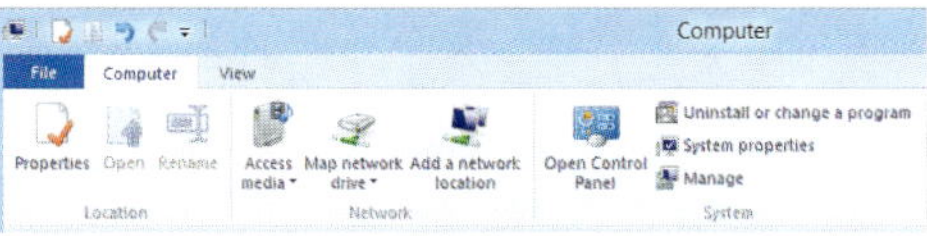

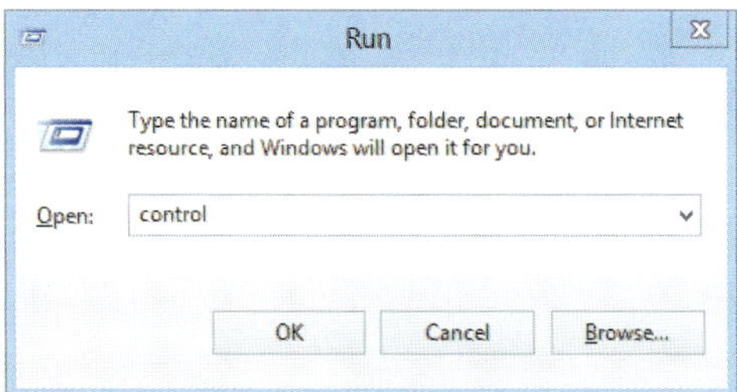



**C** The Control Panel command



**D** Click the Open Control Panel icon in the ribbon to view the Control Panel.



**E** Enter **control** into the Run dialog box to open the Control Panel.

Control panels allow you to set literally thousands of settings, too many to fully document here. The best way to figure out how to use a control panel feature is to use Windows 8's excellent Search function.

## To open the Control Panel:

- Right-click the lower-left corner of your display or press ⊞+X, and select Control Panel from the Management menu **C**.

- Press ⊞+E to open Windows Explorer. Click the Open Control Panel icon in the Computer ribbon **D**.

- Press ⊞+R to open the Run dialog box, enter **control**, and tap or click OK **E**.

*continues on next page*

- Press ⊞+C to open the Charms bar  **F**; tap or click the Settings charm. The Settings menu displays a Control Panel link just under the category heading **G**.

- In the tile-based interface, start typing the word **control**. Search will highlight the Control Panel as its default match.

## To search for a Control Panel feature:

1. Press ⊞+W to open Search for Settings.

2. Type in the function you wish to change—**screen resolution**, for example.

   There's a good chance that Windows will display a match for the control panel that adjusts that setting.

> **TIP** .cpl files are stored in the `Windows\System32` folder, among other locations. Unless you show hidden file extensions, you can't search for or see these programs. When you double-click these program files, the Control Panel interface appears. Type `control` *<control panel name>* into the Run dialog box to open that control panel.



**F** Use the Settings charm to access the Control Panel.

**G** The Control Panel command inside the tile-based interface Settings pane

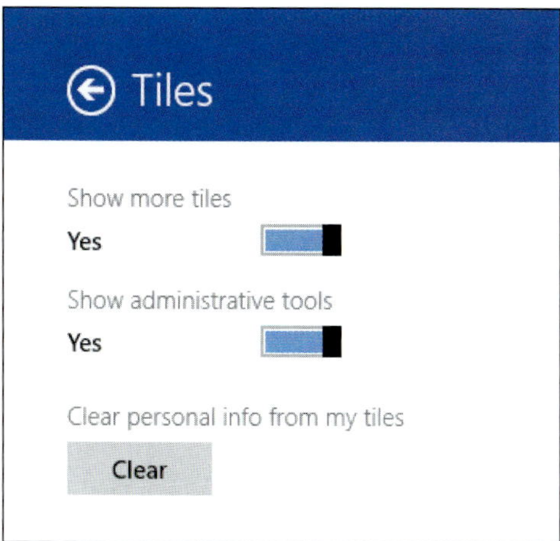



**A** The Tiles settings for the tile-based interface

# Settings

Settings are accessed via the Settings bar. Think of the Settings bar as the "Control Panel's greatest hits." Microsoft has grouped the customizations and personalizations they think you will use the most into categories. These settings are meant to set you free from the clickety-clack of keyboards—fingers rule.

The first disabled link underneath the Settings bar title tells you where you accessed the Settings bar from. In the tile-based interface, you get just a few settings to play with. The tile-based interface is supposed to be simple, so there's very little to change here.

The Tiles settings **A** allow you to show more tiles, up to a display that is 6 x 8. The extra two rows of tiles are quite useful on the large displays typically used on PCs but not useful on phones or tablets.

The Desktop has many more settings that are useful to you. The Control Panel and Personalization categories were covered in detail in the previous chapter, so you are already familiar with many of them.

The icons in the Settings bar perform simple but essential system functions. Depending on the type of device you are using, you may find some of the icons grayed out.

- **Network.** Tap this icon to view the status of your network connection.

- **Volume.** Tap this icon for a slider that adjusts your system volume.

- **Brightness.** Tap this icon for a slider that adjusts your display brightness.

- **Notifications.** Tap this icon for a pop-up menu that lets you hide notifications for 1, 3, or 8 hours.

- **Power.** Tap this icon for a pop-up menu that lets you put your device to sleep, shut it down, or restart it.

- **Keyboard.** Tap this icon to show or hide the virtual onscreen keyboard.

The Power icon's placement does make me wonder. Microsoft has hidden away your system's on/off button inside a secondary toolbar, and you have to ask yourself why. I suspect it's because Microsoft believes that most of the devices of the future (phones and tablets) will simply go to sleep when they aren't in use, and users won't be using the Power button much.

## To show a group of utilities that manage Windows 8:

Tap or click the Show Administrative Tools slider to turn it on **B**.

## To reset the tile-based interface to its default values:

Tap the Default button.

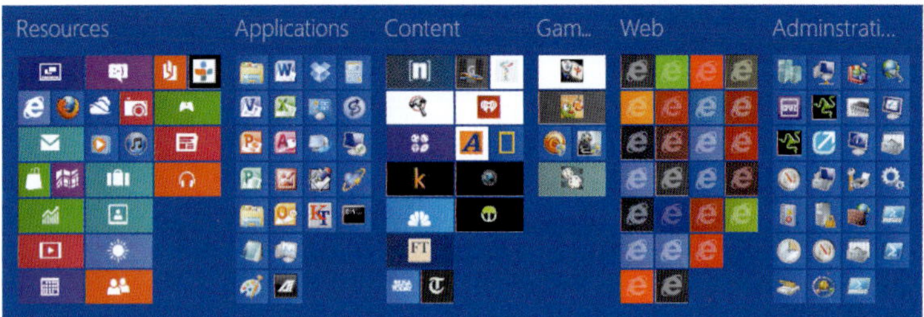


**B** The Show Administrative Tools setting adds the tile group on the right to the tile-based interface.

**C** The Settings charm gives access to the Settings bar.

## To access the Settings bar:

- Swipe in from the right edge of your display, press **⊞**+C to open the Charms bar **C**, and tap or click the Settings charm. The settings bar appears **D**.

- Move the cursor into the upper-right corner of your display and then move down to view the Charms bar **C**. Tap or click the Settings charm **D**.

- Press **⊞**+I.

**TIP** There are other places from which you can shut down your system: Use the Lock screen's Power icon, or make the Desktop active and press Alt+F4. Laptop and tablet users can use the Power Options control panel to enable the physical Power button on the device.

**TIP** The Help link leads you to the Windows Help and Support system.

*The tile-based interface Settings bar*

*Desktop Settings bar*

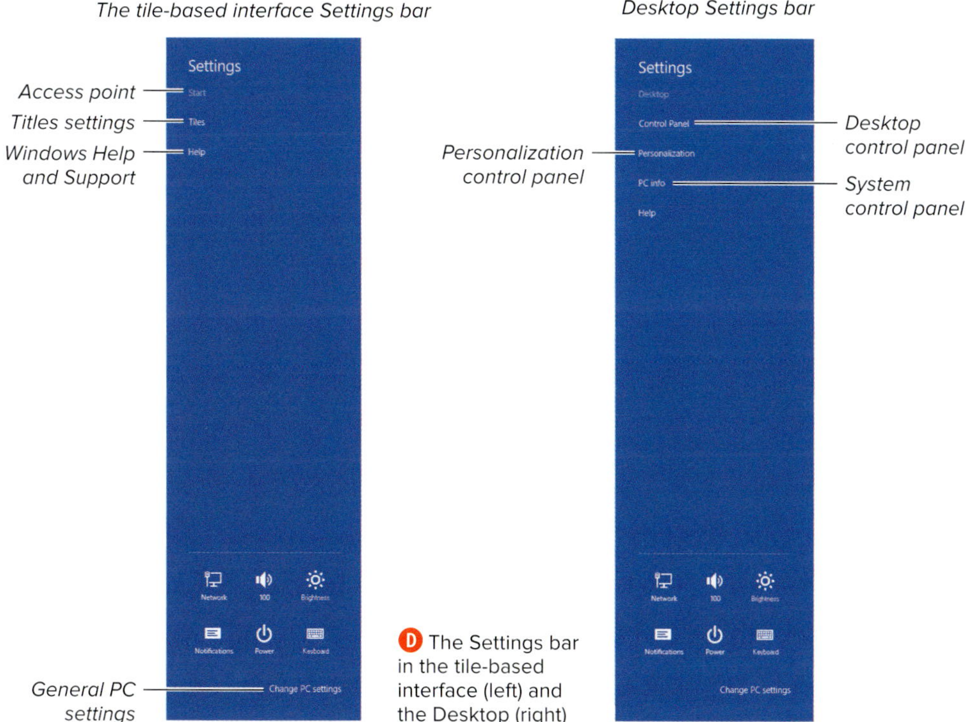


Access point

Titles settings

Windows Help and Support

Personalization control panel

Desktop control panel

System control panel

General PC settings

**D** The Settings bar in the tile-based interface (left) and the Desktop (right)

# Windows Features

A "feature" is a Windows program, application, utility, or service. Some features are installed and operational right out of the box for Windows 8, such as Internet Explorer. Other features require that you turn them on before they are available to use. In the past, users were forced to install features in the same way as they did a program, which meant that they were required to uninstall them when they didn't need them—which few users did. So systems grew more and more bloated over time.

To make it easier for users to turn features on and off, Microsoft has added something called Windows Features. In it, you can enable Internet Information Services (IIS, a personal web server), Media Features, Network Projection, and more. Since there are some attractive features that are not on by default, it's a good idea to poke around in this dialog box from time to time.

### To turn Windows Features on or off:

1. Press ⊞+W, and enter the search string **features**.

   *or*

   Open Search from the Charms bar, and tap the Settings function.

2. Tap or click the *Turn Windows features on or off* link to view the Windows Features dialog box **Ⓐ**.

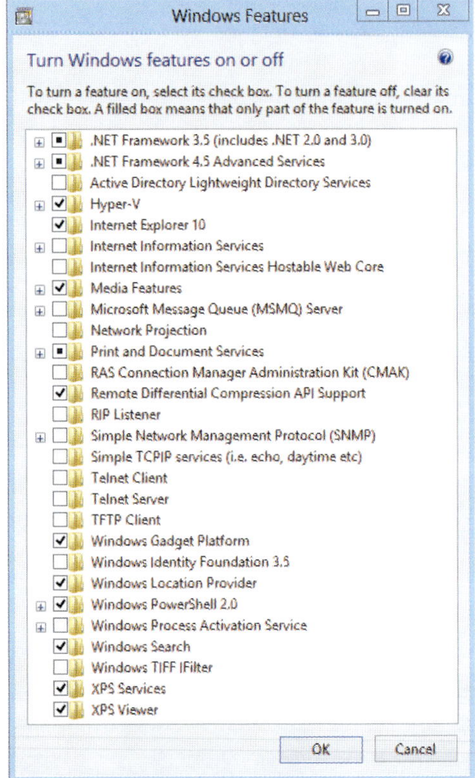

**Ⓐ** The Windows Features dialog box

3. In the Administration Privileges dialog box, either supply your admin password or click OK to elevate your privileges.

4. Click a feature's check box to either enable or disable the feature.

   A feature that is dimmed or partially checked may contain an item within it that is disabled. Double-tap or double-click the folder to view all the contained features. Or, click the + (plus sign) to open the folder.

5. Click OK.

   Windows displays a progress bar and will post a dialog box informing you that it has completed the requested changes.

6. Tap or click either Restart Now or Don't Restart.

**TIP** Turning a feature off does not delete the feature from your system; it simply disables it.

**TIP** As a general rule, features that enable security aspects of Windows 8 will require a reboot before they are activated; many features, such as utilities, do not need a system reboot to function.

**TIP** An alternative method for opening Windows Features is to go to the Control Panel home page, tap or click Programs and Features, and then click the *Turn Windows features on or off* link.

# Modifying Startup Programs and Services

In Windows 7, it was easy to add or remove a startup program. There was a Startup folder on the Start menu that you added program shortcuts to or deleted program shortcuts from. It was simple, but it was incomplete because a lot of things that started up never showed up in the Startup folder. So knowledgeable users paid a visit to the System Configuration (**MSCONFIG**) utility. That utility still exists in Windows 8, and you can use it to disable services you no longer need or want.

## To disable startup programs:

1. Press ⊞+R to open the Run dialog box, and type **msconfig**. Tap or click OK.

   The System Configuration utility opens to the General tab 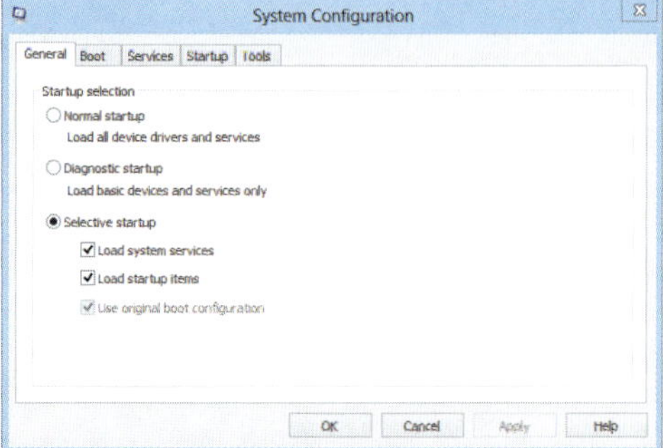. **Normal startup** loads everything; **Diagnostic startup** places you into Safe Mode so that you can fix broken drivers and other problems; and **Selective startup** lets you turn programs and features on and off.

2. Leave the Selective Startup radio button enabled, and tap or click the Services tab **B**.

   CAUTION: When you disable a service, be careful that you aren't disabling something that is essential for Windows operations. You can read a description of the service, what it does, and its dependencies in the Services control panel.

**A** The General tab of the System Configuration dialog box lets you set the type of startup configuration your system will use.

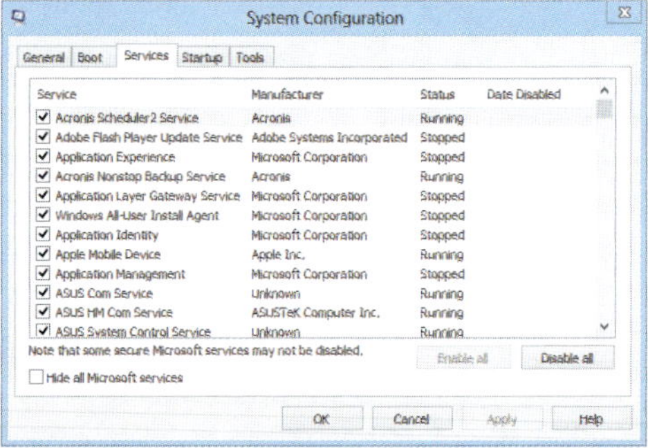

**B** The Services tab lets you see which services are in use.

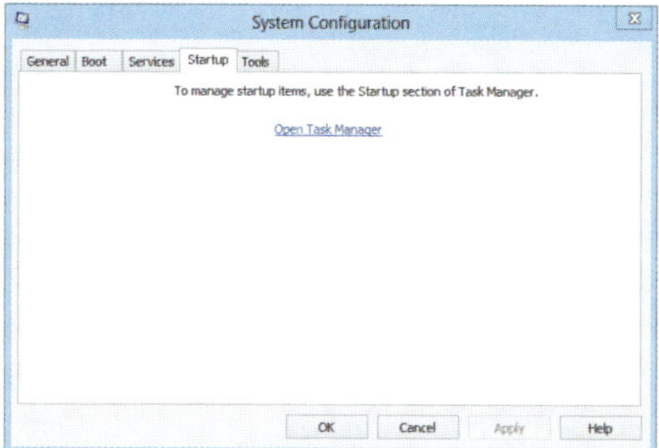

**C** The Startup tab leads you to the Task Manager.

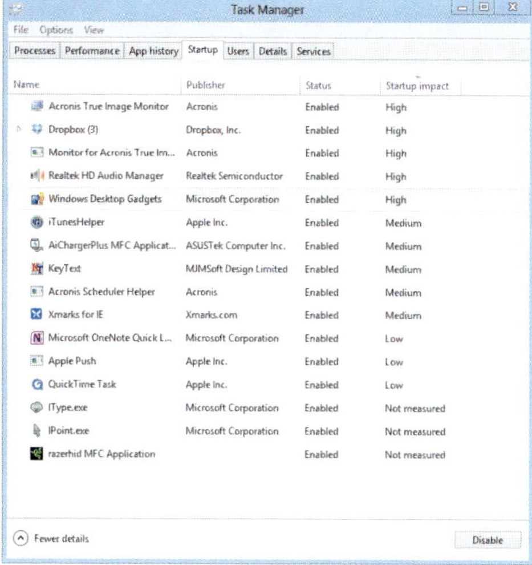

**D** The Startup tab of the Task Manager shows the effect that startup programs have on Windows 8.

3. The Services tab lets you see what services are currently running on your system and allows you to disable any of them by deselecting their check boxes.

4. Click the Startup tab, and then click the *Open Task Manager* link **C**. Task Manager opens.

5. To disable a startup application, tap or click its name and then tap or click the Disable button **D**.

**TIP** Although the Startup folder no longer appears on the Start menu, it hasn't disappeared. To view it, press ⊞+R to open the Run dialog box, and type in %appdata%. The Startup folder is called Roaming and is stored in your user profile. In Windows Explorer (⊞+E), you can enter the path %appdata% or C:\Users\<username>\AppData\Roaming to view this folder.

# The Registry

Most books consider the Registry an advanced topic, and it is. But the Registry is the heart and soul of Windows, and it is essentially what makes Windows what it is. The Registry is a hierarchical database of settings for components—services, the kernel, device drivers, hardware, the Security Accounts Manager, software, the graphical user interface, you name it.

When you change things in Windows, you write a value or set of values to one or more places in the Registry. When you install a component, it registers itself in the Registry. The main branches in the Registry are called *hives*, and each contains a set of branches. Branches contain a set of folder-like structures called *keys*, and within the keys you find locations that contain name/value pairs where data is stored.

Application developers use the Registry to read settings that already exist and to write their own. The Registry is extensible, but it is also optional, and developers aren't required to use it. Game developers, makers of portable applications, and certain Windows components write their settings to files within their own folders.

The Registry replaces the initialization files that were used in early versions of Windows. The Registry is why you can't simply copy files over to a system folder and have Windows work.

You should exercise caution when you make any changes to the Registry, because a careless change to the wrong key can make your system unbootable and will require Windows to refresh itself. However, there will be times when your system doesn't behave properly. In those cases, consult the Windows Knowledge Base for specific instructions, where you may find information on how to resolve issues by modifying the Registry.

### To alter a value in the Registry;

1. Press ⊞+R, and type **regedit**. Press Enter.

2. The User Access Control dialog box opens and asks you to elevate your privileges; click OK.

   The Registry Editor opens **A**.

3. Navigate to the key you wish to modify by double-clicking or double-tapping the key or by clicking or tapping the + (plus sign) to the left of the key.

4. Double-click or double-tap the key itself to open the Edit String dialog box.

5. Make your changes, and click OK.

**TIP** The Registry can become fragmented just like any other file can. There are Registry defraggers as well as optimization tools that remove unused Registry keys (uninstalled programs are supposed to remove their keys, but many don't). But I don't find that these programs make any discernible difference in performance.

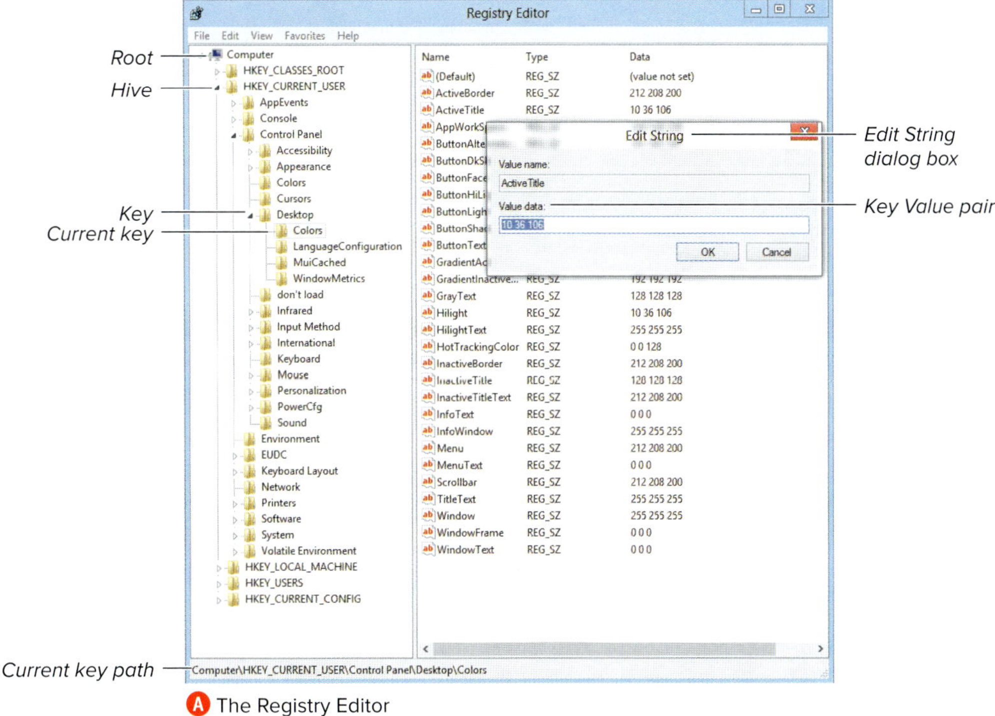

**A** The Registry Editor

# Policies

A *policy* is a method for enforcing Registry settings and making sure that users can't change those settings. Policy settings are most often enforced for a group of users, thus the term "group policy" is used.

Policy settings can be applied to a single computer by using **GPEDIT.MSC**, or to a group of computers by using **GPMC.MSC**. The MSC extension indicates that this is a Microsoft Management Console Snap-in application. It appears inside the Computer Management application, which you can open from the Management menu on Windows 8.

There are hundreds of policies that you can set for Windows 8, although many more settings are available to network administrators than to a user who is an administrator on a local Windows device. You can turn system menus on or off; control how the Desktop looks; manage access to programs, to the network, to storage, and to browser settings; run startup, shutdown, and logoff scripts; and more. Policy settings create a special policy file (**POLICY.POL**) that can be merged into the Registry and thereby block access to keys.

The Local Group Policy Editor can be used to set a policy for all users on a system. However, most common policies are available as settings in the control panels.

## To view the Local Group Policy Editor:

1. Press ⊞+R, and type **gpedit.msc**. Press Enter.

2. The User Access Control dialog box opens and asks you to elevate your privileges; click OK.

   The Local Group Policy Editor appears **A**.

3. Tap or click the Action menu, and select the Filter Options command.

4. Select the Enable Requirements Filters check box, and click OK.

   The Local Group Policy Editor shows you all policies associated with Windows 8.

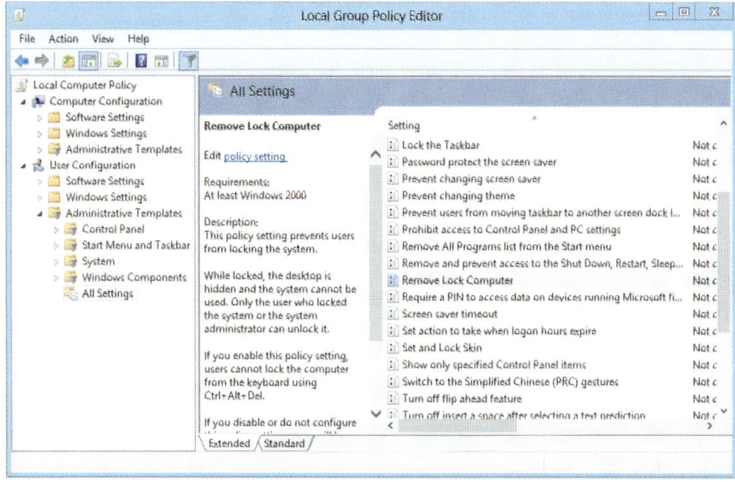

**A** The Local Group Policy Editor displays a setting that lets you disable the Ctrl+Alt+Delete keystroke and thus deny access to the Lock screen.

# Putting It All Together

- The Control Panel is a set of applets that allow you to customize and personalize your system.

- In the tile-based interface, you can access a small number of settings from the Settings charm's Settings bar.

- When you access control panels from the System Management menu, you see the classic Control Panel home screen organized by category type. You can use the search function in this dialog box or in Windows 8 Search to figure out which control panel you need.

- A set of icons in the lower part of the Settings bar lets you alter system functions such as sound volume and display brightness, but most importantly it lets you power your system off.

- Not all features in Windows 8 are installed by default. You can use the Windows Features utilities to turn additional features on and off.

- Use the Task Manager's Startup tab to turn startup programs on and off; use the System Configuration utility's Services tab to turn startup services on and off.

- The Windows 8 Registry is used to store system and user settings.

- You can use the Local Group Policy Editor to turn Windows features and settings on and off.

# 6

# Applications

Windows 8 has two different styles of applications: the tile-based interface and legacy. Tile-based applications are immersive and are meant to be viewed full screen using touch and gestures. They typically use less memory, and when you move to another application, you can leave them saved in memory.

Tile-based programs are usually referred to as *apps* and are found in the Windows Store. The Windows Store handles the details of installing, updating, tracking, and removing tile-based apps, just as the Apple App Store and Google Play do for their apps (iPhone/iPad and Android devices, respectively).

Legacy programs require the Desktop windowing system to function. When you launch a legacy application, the Desktop opens and your program and its window appear. Programs on the Desktop are larger, consume more memory, and use the Windows Installer for installing and uninstalling. I wouldn't call them apps—they are too large. I would call them applications. The vast majority of the programs currently available are legacy applications. But over time, that will change.

## In This Chapter

# Launching an Application

There are a number of ways to launch an application, depending on whether you are on the Start screen or the Desktop. This section covers the most accessible ones.

Some applications are "pinned" to the Start screen by default when you first install Windows 8.

Most applications are not represented by a tile on the Start screen. You can still launch an application using a tile, but you may need to switch to the All Apps screen to do so.

Windows builds the list of programs you see on the All Apps screen from the user programs folder at **C:\Users\\<User Name>\ AppData\Roaming\Microsoft\Windows\ Start Menu\Programs** and from the common programs folder at **C:\ProgramData\ Microsoft\Windows\Start Menu\Programs**. You can get to these folders by entering **shell:programs** or **shell:common programs** into the Windows Explorer address bar. (The Explorer address bar is described in detail in Chapter 10.) Removing or renaming shortcuts, or consolidating items into folders, changes what you see on the All Apps screen.

If there is an application that you use frequently, you can add it to your Start screen and to the taskbar of the Desktop, which is a great time saver.

## To find an application:

1. Display the tile-based interface Start screen (or the Search screen).

2. Start typing the name of the application.

3. When the application appears on the Find screen, click its name **A**.

## To launch an application from the Start screen:

- Find the application tile on the Start screen and tap or click it.

- Click the taskbar icon on the Desktop.

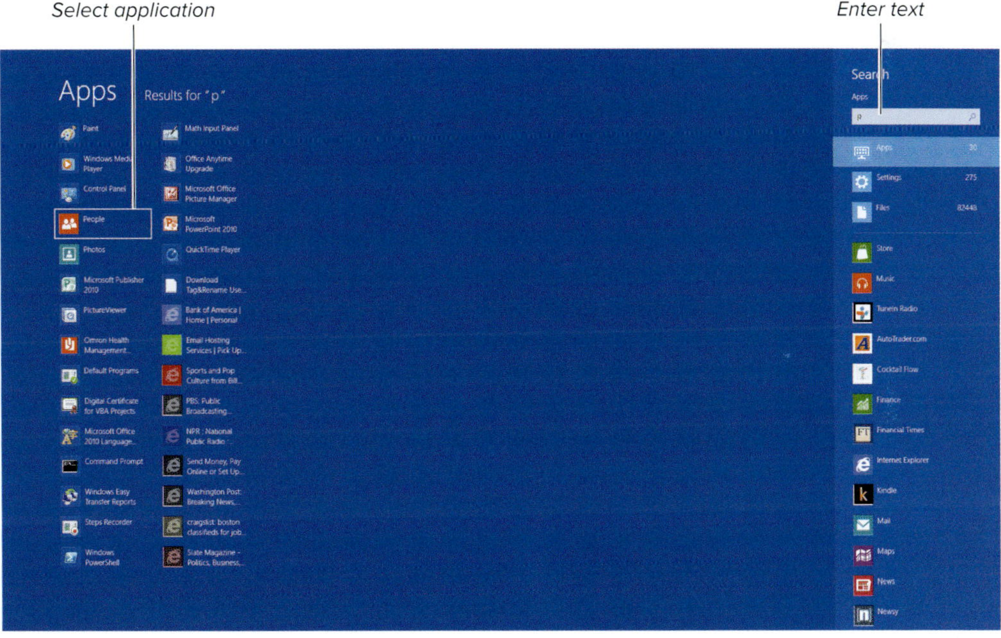


**A** Launching an application from the Search screen

## To launch an application
## from the All Apps screen:

1. Swipe from the bottom edge, right-click the Start screen, or press ⊞+Z.

2. Click the All Apps button in the Apps bar. (The Apps bar appears across the lower portion of your screen.)

3. Click the tile in the All Apps screen for the application you want to launch .



**B** Launching an application from the All Apps screen

## To add or remove an application tile or Desktop taskbar icon:

1. Display the Start or All Apps screen.

2. Right-click the application tile to select it. The tile shows a check mark in the upper-right corner **C**.

3. Click the Pin To Start button to add the application's tile to the Start screen; click the Unpin From Start button to remove the application's tile from the Start screen.

4. Click the Pin To Taskbar button to add a taskbar icon for that application to the Desktop taskbar; click the Unpin From Taskbar button to remove that application's taskbar icon from the Desktop taskbar.

**TIP** **You can drag and drop a program icon from the Desktop or Explorer to the Desktop taskbar to pin it there.**

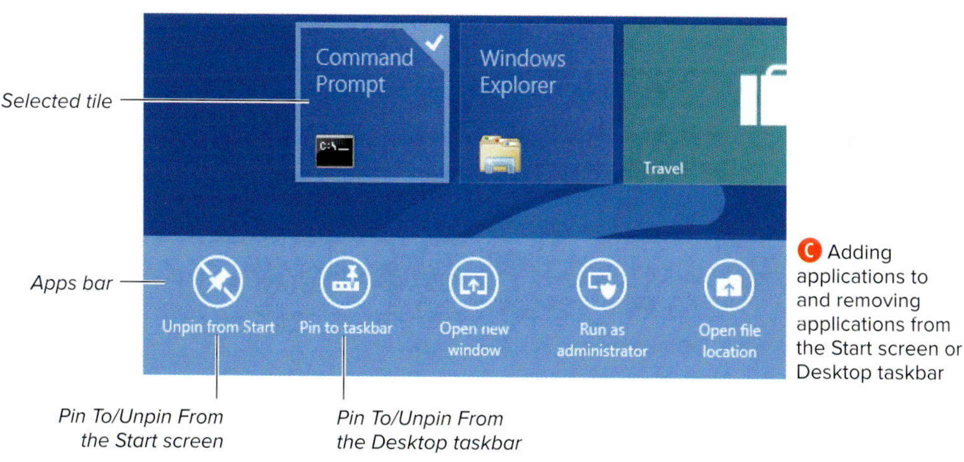


*Selected tile*

*Apps bar*

*Pin To/Unpin From the Start screen*

*Pin To/Unpin From the Desktop taskbar*

**C** Adding applications to and removing applications from the Start screen or Desktop taskbar

# Program Shortcuts and Compatibility

Since the Command Prompt is actually a program, we can use its shortcut and Properties dialog box to illustrate how shortcuts work. In the Properties dialog box, you can create a keyboard shortcut for a program, find the executable file that is referenced by the shortcut, or open the program in a compatibility box (which is valuable for making older programs work inside Windows 8).

Many programs, particularly games and utilities, may not work correctly in Windows 8. However, all is not lost. If you open the Properties dialog box and click the Compatibility tab, you can choose to run the program in emulation inside an older version of Windows 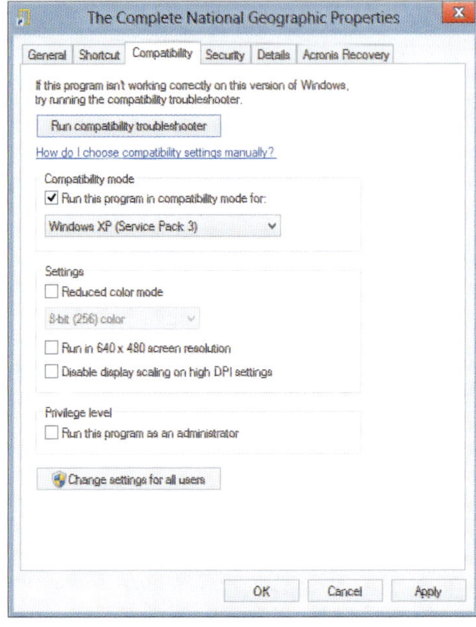. Click the Run Compatibility Troubleshooter button to get suggestions, or select the Run This Program In Compatibility Mode For check box and select the version of Windows from the drop-down menu. Other valuable options alter runtime settings.

Not all programs offer a compatibility box. You may find that additional options and tabs appear in the Properties dialog box for other programs as you install them. It's worth poking around here to learn more about the customizations that are possible.

Ⓐ Use the Compatibility tab to run older programs that don't work correctly in Windows 8.

## About Command Prompt

Command Prompt is a Windows shell, but not a graphical one. Command Prompt (**CMD.EXE**) is an MS DOS emulator, into which you can enter DOS commands. You can also use CMD to perform PowerShell (Windows' advanced scripting language) commands. The General tab of the Properties dialog box for a program offers some additional options, such as Open File Location, which takes you either to a shortcut that opens the program (executable) file in Windows Explorer or to the program itself (depending on whether the shortcut is a shortcut to a shortcut or a shortcut to the program file itself).

**B** The Open File Location button

## To launch a program using a custom keystroke:

1. Right-click the Command Prompt tile on the tile-based interface Start screen.

2. Click the Open File Location button **B** in the Apps bar.

3. Right-click the application shortcut and select Properties from the context menu **C**.

4. Click the Shortcut tab. Click in the Shortcut Key text box and enter a single key, such as C. Windows creates the Ctrl+Alt+C keystroke shortcut for the Command Prompt.

**TIP** Click the Open File Location button **A** to locate the program file. Click the Change Icon button in the General tab of the Properties dialog box to apply a custom icon to that shortcut. You can also apply a shortcut to a file through its Properties dialog box.

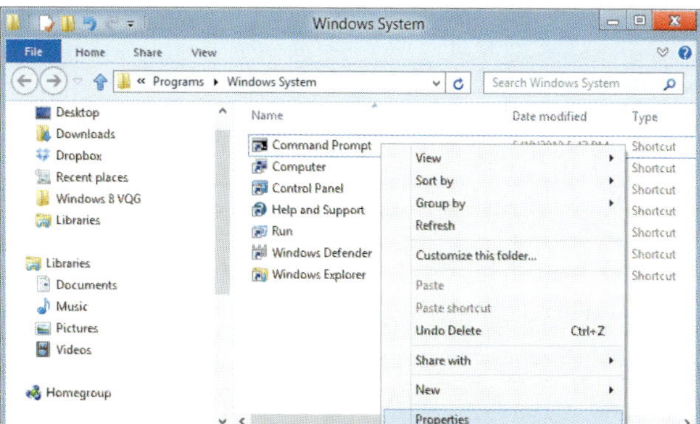

**C** Use the context menu to open an icon's Properties dialog box.

# Installing or Removing a Program

Windows 8 has two very different types of installers. One installer is associated with the tile-based interface, and the other is associated with the Desktop.

When you install a program on your Desktop, you use the Windows Installer. The exact details for an installation vary from program to program, but usually the installation starts when you double-click the **Setup.exe** (executable) file. That file sometimes takes the program name.

You remove a legacy program using the Programs and Features control panel.

### To install a program in the tile-based interface:

1. Tap or click the Store tile.

2. Find the program you want to install, and tap or click its tile.

3. On the app's description screen **A**, click the Install button.

   The app will be silently installed and its tile added to your Start screen.

### To install a program from the web:

1. Go to the web page, and click the Download button for the program.

2. A dialog box above the Apps bar **B** will prompt you to run, save, or cancel the operation.

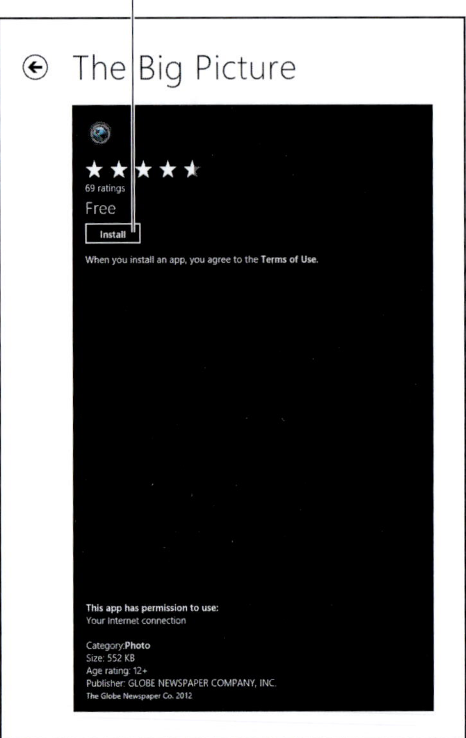


**A** Installing an app in the tile-based interface from the Windows Store

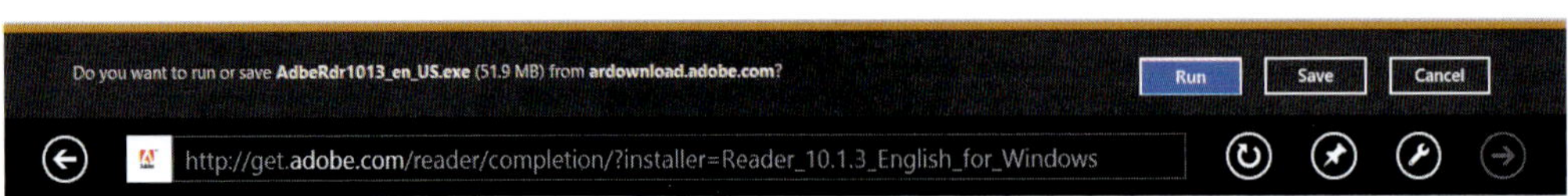


**B** Installing a program from a download in the tile-based interface version of Internet Explorer

**C** The disk insertion notice

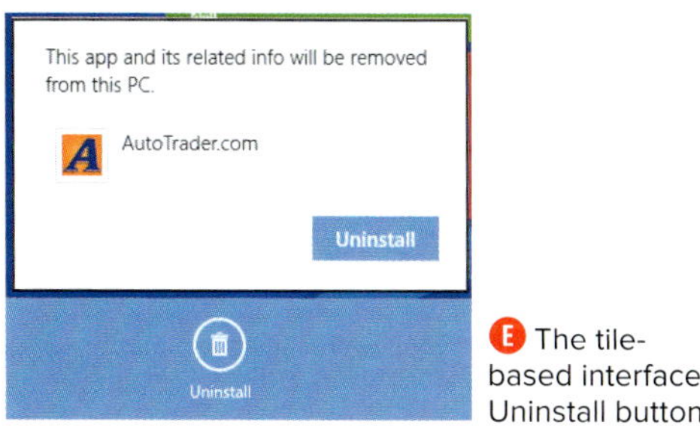



**D** The installer options



**E** The tile-based interface Uninstall button

3. Click the Save button to download the file to your Download folder or to a folder you specify.

4. Open the folder with the installer. Then double-tap or double-click the installer program to start the installation.

*or*

Click the Run button.

The installation proceeds.

## To install from media:

1. Insert the disk; Windows posts a notification box **C** allowing you to choose what action to take.

2. Tap or click the notice, and then click the Run option **D**.

## To remove a tile-based app:

1. Tap and hold, or right-click, the app tile on the Start screen to select that app.

2. Tap or click the Uninstall button on the Apps bar, then tap or click the Uninstall button **E**.

The tile-based interface silently removes the app from your system.

## To remove a legacy program using the Programs and Features control panel:

1. In the tile-based interface, right-click the program tile to select it, and then click the Uninstall button on the Apps bar  **F**.

   *or*

   On the Desktop, right-click the lower-left corner, and select Control Panel from the menu. Then click the *Uninstall a program* link in the Programs section of the control panel **G**.

2. Find the program you want to delete, and click or tap to select it.

3. Click or tap the Uninstall button to launch the program's installer program **H**.

4. Click or tap the Uninstall button to remove the program, and follow the program's instructions.

**F** Apps bar Uninstall button

**G** The *Uninstall a program* link to the Programs and Features control panel

**TIP** If you apply an update to a program that causes problems, you can use the Programs and Features control panel to remove it after the fact. Click the *View installed updates* link **H**, select the update, and click the Uninstall button.

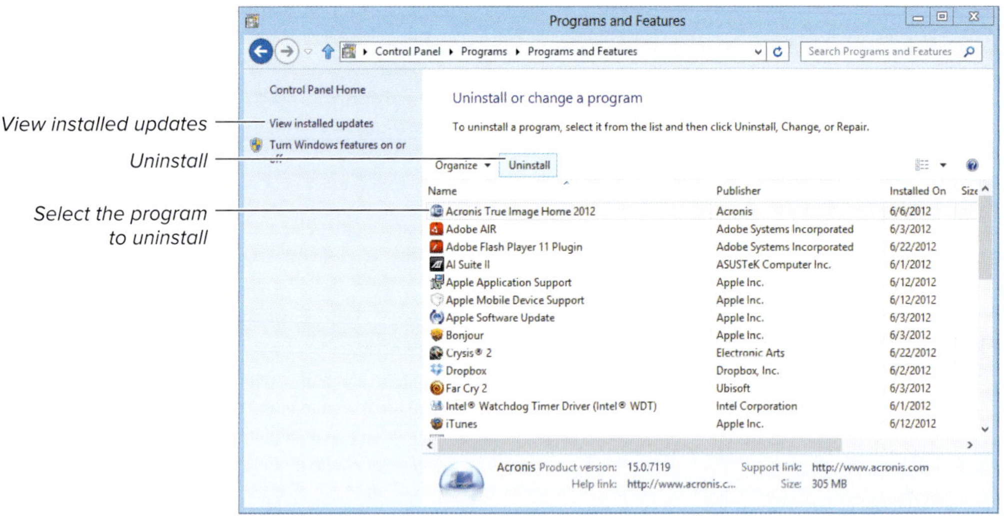

**H** Use the Programs and Features control panel to uninstall legacy programs

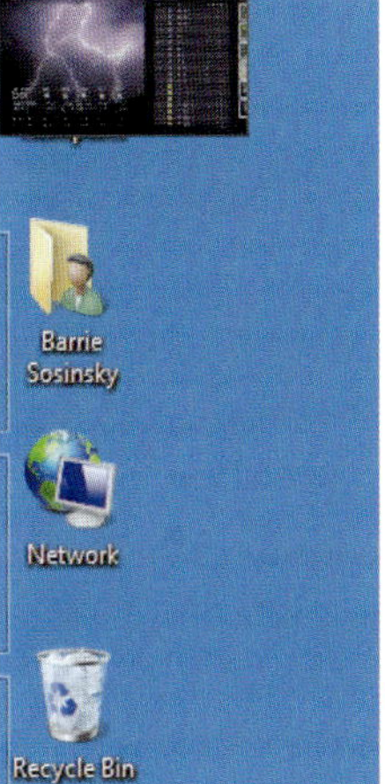

A Click an application thumbnail to switch to that application.

# Switching Apps

When you work in the tile-based interface, you work on one application at a time. If you switch applications in the tile-based interface, Windows puts the program to sleep. You don't need to close an application to open another one in the tile-based interface, provided you have enough memory in your device. Windows 8 treats the Desktop as if it were just another the tile-based program.

## To switch apps using thumbnails:

1. Tap or click the upper-left corner of your screen to see a thumbnail of an open program; click it to open it A.

2. Tap or click the open thumbnail again to see the next open app, and then click that app to open it.

3. Tap the upper-left corner and drag down, or right-click and drag down and then up again, to show the Switch list B. Tap or click the application you want to switch to.

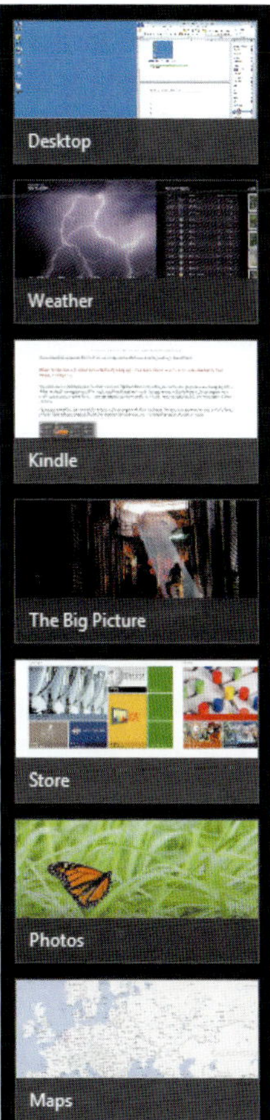

B The Switch list allows you to click the program thumbnail you want to switch to.

## To switch apps with the Task Switcher:

1. Press Alt+Tab to view the Task Switcher **C**.

2. Press Tab again until you highlight the application you want to switch to, and then release all pressed keys.

When you have multiple applications open in the sidebar, you can use ⊞+Tab to move between the programs in the sidebar from top to bottom. ⊞+Shift +Tab moves you between applications from the bottom to the top.

## To switch apps on the Desktop:

- Click the application icon on the taskbar.

- If there are two or more open documents (windows), hover over an icon and click the file thumbnail for the app you want to select.

**TIP** **If a program freezes and you can't switch out of it, press Ctrl+Shift+Esc to open the Task Manager. You can then use the Task Manager to close the non-responsive program as well as switch to another program.**

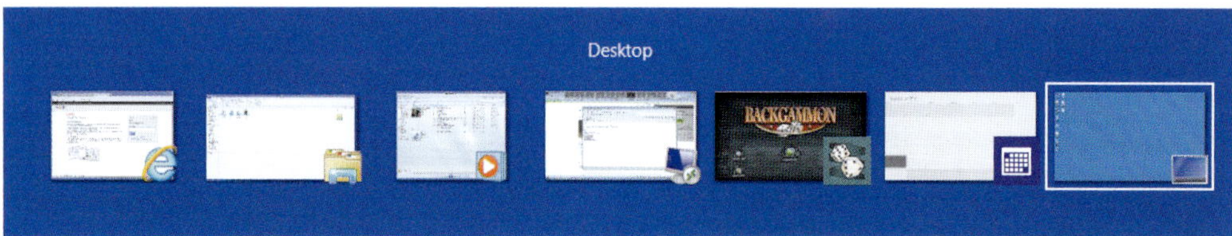


**C** The Task Switcher is activated by pressing the Alt+Tab keystroke/.

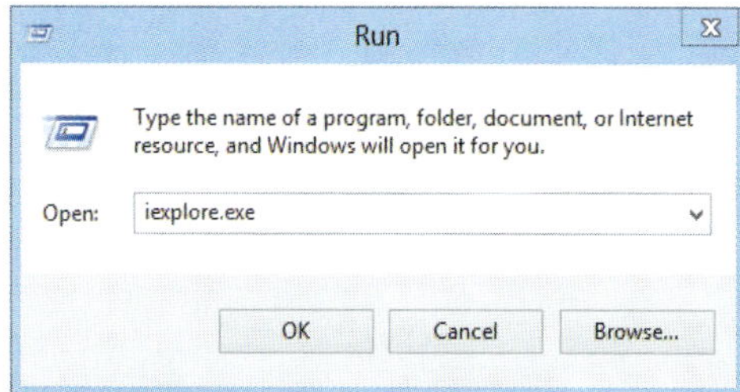



**A** The Run dialog box is a single-line command processor.

# The Run Dialog Box

The Run dialog box has been around since Windows 95. Think of it as a graphical representation of the Run command, which is a single-line command processor.

The Run dialog box is not the same thing as the Command Prompt, although it shares similar functionality.

This dialog box takes all manner of commands, and offers users an incredibly powerful tool.

### To open the Run dialog box:

- Press ⊞+R.

- Right-click or tap the lower-left corner of the Desktop, and select Run from the Desktop menu **A**.

### To run commands in the Run dialog box:

Enter a command, and press the OK button or the Enter key to execute the command.

### Use the Run dialog box to:

- Open control panels by name. Type `timedate.cpl` to open the Date and Time control panel.

- Open a program by name. Type `iexplore.exe` to open Internet Explorer, type `tskmgr.exe` to open the Task Manager, or browse to find the program you want to open.

- Open the Command Prompt. Type `cmd`.

- Open a folder by entering a path. Type `C:/Users/<User Name>/Desktop` to view your Desktop.

- Open a network share. Type `\\<Computer Name>\<Shared Folder Name>`.

- View or change your IP address. Type `ipconfig /all`.

**TIP** The Run command stores a history of previous commands in the Open drop-down menu.

**TIP** If you need to have administrator privileges to perform a command, you will need to open the Command Prompt as an administrator; Run does not support this function. Right-click the lower-left corner of the Desktop, and select Command Prompt (Admin) from the menu.

# Snapping

If you have multiple applications open in the tile-based interface and on the Desktop, you will want to explore a feature in Windows 8 called snapping. Snapping is a convenient way to switch applications and view content in one application while working in another. Here's how it works.

**A** shows the Desktop apps snapped right, with the Map app on the left.

When the Desktop is snapped right or left, Windows creates a Switch list from open Desktop windows, providing an excellent graphical way to switch Desktop applications.

**A** The Desktop snapped into a Switch list

## To snap with your mouse:

- Tap or click the top edge of the app and drag it to the left or right side of your screen **B**.

*continues on next page*

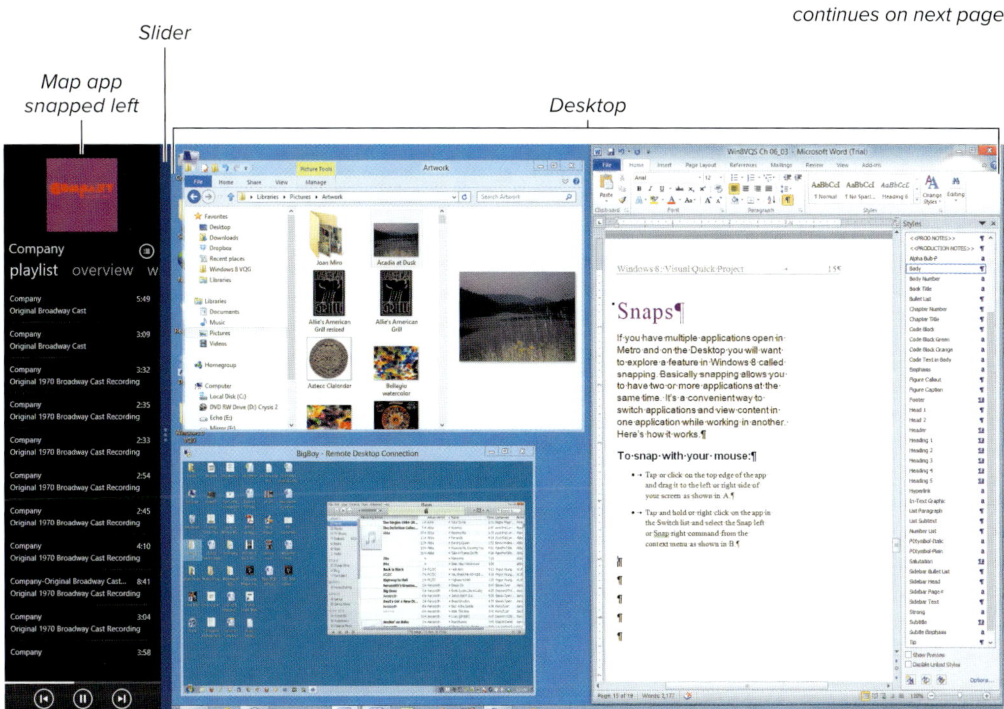

Slider

Map app snapped left

Desktop

**B** A snapped application

- Tap and hold, or right-click, the app in the Switch list, and select the Snap Left or Snap Right command from the context menu 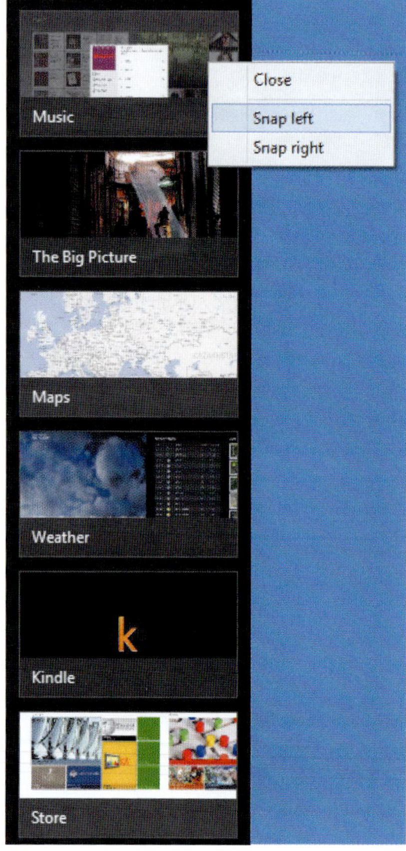.

## To resize or close a snapped application:

- To resize the snapped application, tap and drag (or click and drag) the slider.

- To close the app, tap and drag (or click and drag) the slider to one edge.

**TIP** Press ⊞+. (period) to move a snapped app through the following cycle: snap left, three-quarter screen left, full screen, and snap right.



C An app's context menu in the Switch list

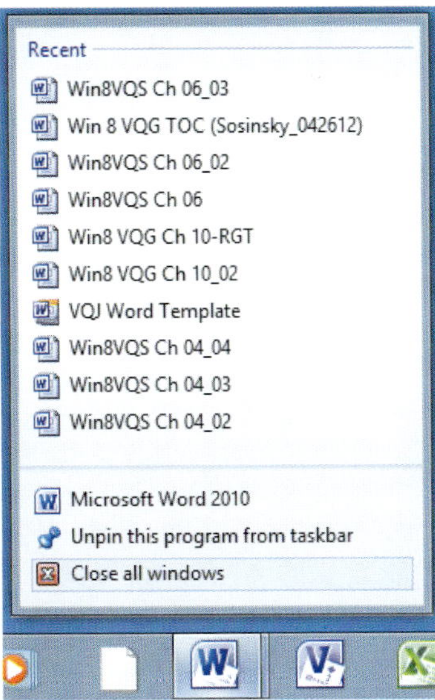



**A** A taskbar application icon's Close All Windows command

# Closing a Program

In the tile-based interface, you don't need to close programs when you move to another program unless Windows informs you that you are running short of memory.

Desktop programs consume more memory, so it's more likely that you will want to close a program on the Desktop when you are finished using it.

## To close a tile-based app:

Tap and hold, or right-click, any tile-based (or Desktop) app thumbnail, then select the Close command from the context menu.

## To close an application on the Desktop:

1. Right-click the application icon on the taskbar to view the context menu **A**.

2. Select the Close All Windows command.

    *or*

    Click the Close box in the title bar of all application windows.

    *or*

    Use the Close command on the Window menu (press Alt+spacebar to see it).

    When the last window is closed, the application is released from memory.

## To close any app from the keyboard:

Make the application your current application, and then press Alt+F4.

**TIP** Most legacy programs contain an Exit command on their File menu; you can use the Exit command to close a program. If there is any open window with unsaved work, the program will ask if you wish to save it.

# Putting It All Together

- There are two types of programs running on Windows: tile-based applications and legacy applications.

- You can launch programs from tiles on the Start screen, from taskbar icons, by using the Search function, or by using the Program file.

- You can use the All Apps screen to add program tiles to the Start screen or to the taskbar.

- A program's Properties dialog box has a feature that allows you to create a keyboard shortcut to launch it.

- If a program doesn't operate correctly, try running it inside a compatibility box.

- Tile-based apps are installed silently from the Windows Store and are uninstalled from the program's Apps bar Uninstall button.

- Legacy programs use the Windows Installer to install themselves, and they register their installation in the Programs and Features control panel.

- To uninstall a legacy program, use the Programs and Features control panel's uninstall option.

- Thumbnails are a great way to switch between programs, and the snap feature allows you to view tile-based apps and the Desktop side by side.

- The Run dialog box is a convenient and powerful single-line command processor.

- Tile-based programs are designed to have a small memory footprint and don't really need to be closed when you are not using them.

# Windows 8
# Tile-Based Apps

Windows 8 brings to your phone, tablet, and desktop a new set of immersive apps that allow you to centrally organize your content inside the tile-based environment:

- **People** is a unified visual contact database. It stores all your "who" information, along with pictures of your contacts. It organizes contacts in a manner that will be familiar to smartphone users.

- **Calendar** stores all your events and reminders. Events are your "whens."

- **Mail** is a POP3 client that can display your mail from services such as Gmail, Hotmail, and Yahoo.

- **Messaging** is a real-time instant messaging application that can work with a variety of services.

- **Photos**, **Music**, and **Video** show and play content that is on your local device or on systems you connect to. The contents of these apps are your "whats."

- **Reader** is an immersive eReader in the tile-based interface.

## In This Chapter

- **Maps** helps you locate places and, when coupled with presence, allows other applications to tailor their services to your current location. Maps are the "where."

Who, what, when, and where are what you need on a smartphone or tablet, and indeed, these apps are the next generation of apps from the Windows Phone 7. They are cloud connected to a collection of web services that were formerly branded as Windows Live. In recasting these apps for Windows 8, Microsoft has tried to solve two very difficult problems:

- How do you make an app work successfully on devices across a range of display resolutions and capabilities?

- How do you centralize the data stored in multiple systems?

Microsoft calls these "service-connected apps." Let's take a look at how well Windows 8 has done in this area.

# People

The People app is a flat file contact database—a rich address book that can draw information from multiple sources (called accounts), consolidating contact data from your email and from sites such as Facebook, Twitter, and LinkedIn. People creates a unified contact card for each person you know and helps you keep track of activities associated with those people.

People is really too rich to fully explore here, so consider this just a taste of what is possible.

## To add a contact to People:

1. Tap or click the People tile on the Start screen .

2. Swipe from the bottom or right-click, and tap or click the New button on the right side of the Apps bar **B**.

3. On the New Contact screen, enter all appropriate information **C**.

*continues on next page*

**A** The People tile

**B** The New button

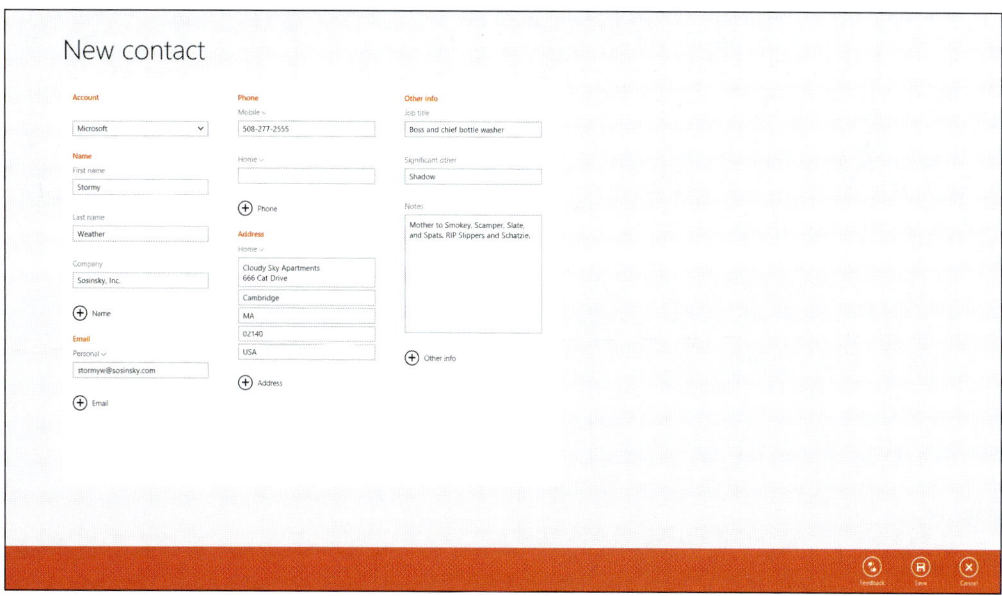

**C** The New Contact screen and the Apps bar

4. Click the plus (+) buttons to expand additional fields as needed.

5. Swipe from the bottom or right-click, then tap or click the Save button in the Apps bar.

6. In the People picker, tap or click a letter **D**, then click a person to view their contact card **E**.

7. Tap or click the Send Email button to open the Mail app with a message already started.

8. Tap the Map Address button to open the Maps app and see the location of the contact's address.

9. Tap the View Profile button to see complete contact information **C**.

**TIP** The People app can use the tile-based interface secondary tiles feature. Select a person's tile in People and use the **Pin To Start** button to place that tile on your **Start** screen. The tile is live and displays information like incoming emails and newly posted photos. One click takes you to that person's contact card; a second click lets you view their photos or send them an email.

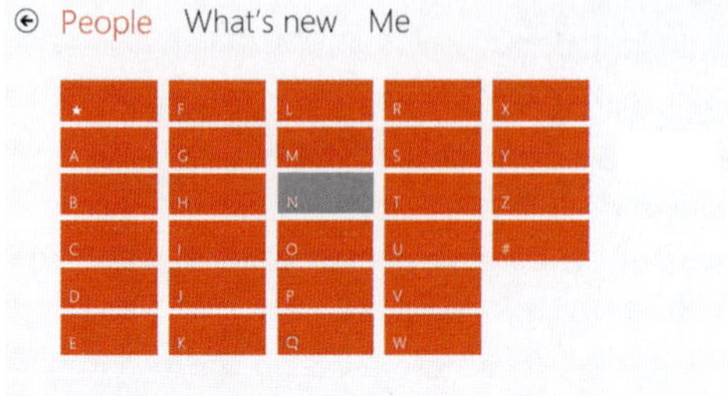

**D** The People picker lets you open names by selecting letters.

**E** The People picker lets you send email, map the address for a contact, and maintain the contact's information.

**A** The Settings button

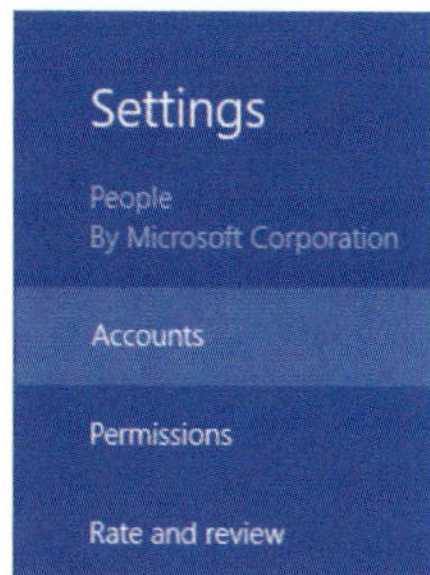

**B** The Settings bar *Accounts* link

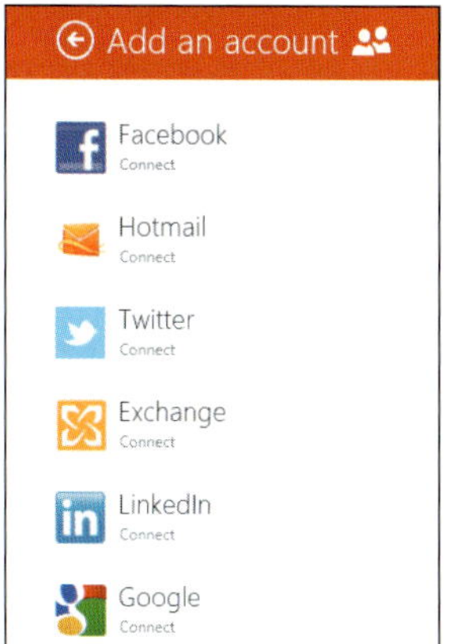

**C** Add An Account options

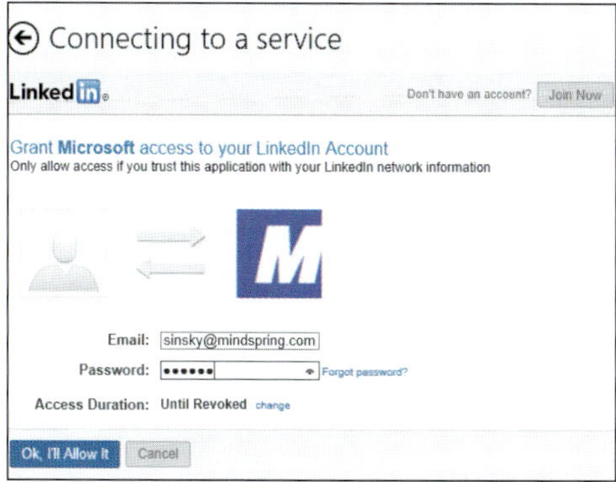

**D** Enter your login information.

# Cloud Service Connections

When you add a cloud service to People, you get real-time notifications when your contacts post new photos, comments, and tweets. Each cloud service is configuarable as part of a "contract" that determines what information you share and who can connect to you. When you unfriend some-one or delete a contact in a cloud service, People is smart enough to pick up on that.

## To add an account to People:

1. With People open, tap and drag from the right edge (or move the mouse to the upper-left corner) and select Set-tings **A** from the Charms bar.

2. Click Accounts on the Settings bar **B**; then click the *Accounts* link to view the available services.

3. Tap or click the service you wish to add **C**, and enter your account login information **D**.

   When you connect to a service, your friends appear in your contacts.

**TIP** Once you are connected to a service, you can turn on various Sharing properties for all your Windows 8 apps.

# Calendar

Calender stores your events, lets you view events in various day and time formats, and provides reminders when you require them. There are options to color different categories of items and to hide or show events. Calendar is fully touch enabled; it's easy to move around between events and to switch views.

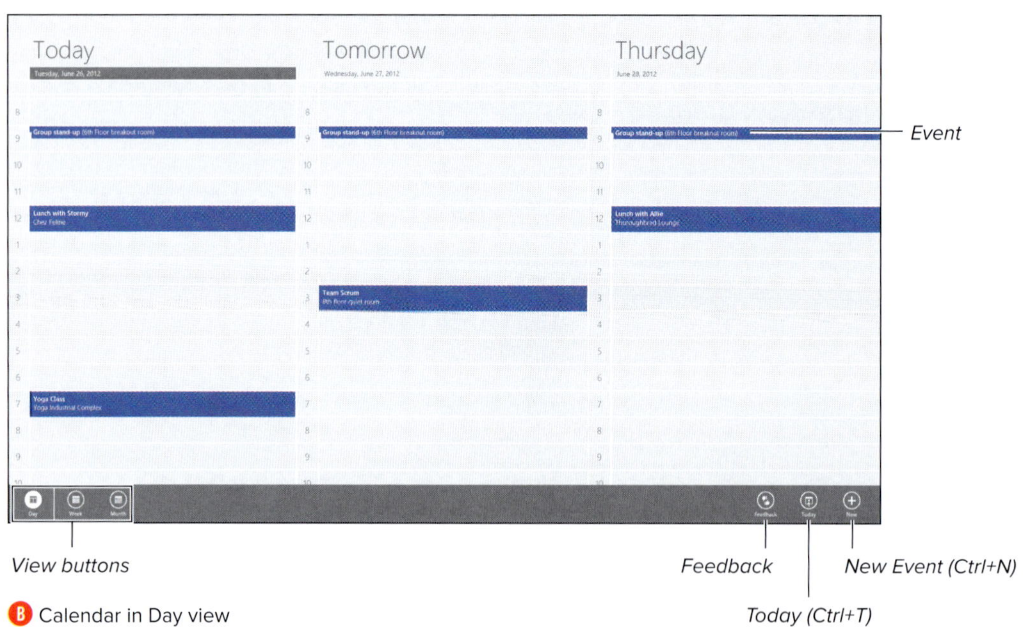

**A** The Calendar tile

## To add an event to Calendar:

1. Tap or click the Calendar tile **A** to open the Calendar app.

   The last Calendar view you had open appears on your screen.

2. To open the New Event/Edit Event page, swipe from the bottom edge or right-click to see the Calendar toolbar, then tap or click the New Event button **B**.

   *or*

   Tap or click the time period of an event.



Event

View buttons

Feedback

New Event (Ctrl+N)

**B** Calendar in Day view

Today (Ctrl+T)

3. In the Details section, enter the event's title, duration, and frequency, along with whatever reminder you need **C**, then tap or click the Save button in the upper-right corner.

When you create an event, Calendar sends a reminder to the email address that you used to register the service.

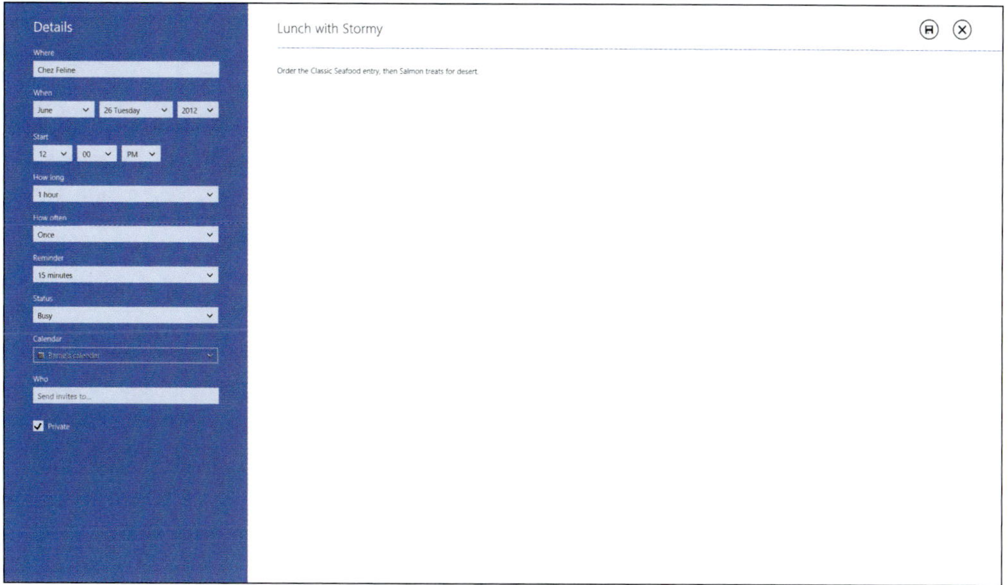


**C** The New Event/Edit Event screen

## To modify an event:

1.  Tap or click the event.

2.  If it is a recurring event, tap or click the
    Change One or Change All button in
    the dialog box 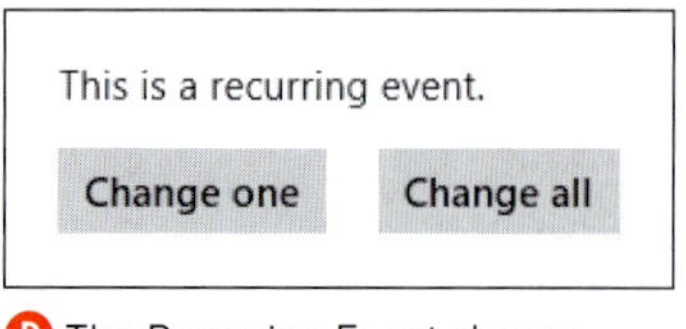.



**D** The Recurring Event change
dialog box

## To create multiple calendars:

1.  Display the Charms bar, then click the
    Settings button.

2.  Click Options **E**. Choose whether to
    Show or Hide the calendar, and select
    a color.

## To move forward or
## backward in time:

-   Move forward days, weeks, or months
    by swiping left, pressing the Page Down
    key, or tapping or clicking the Forward
    button.

-   Move backward by swiping right, press-
    ing the Page Up key, or tapping or click-
    ing the Back button.

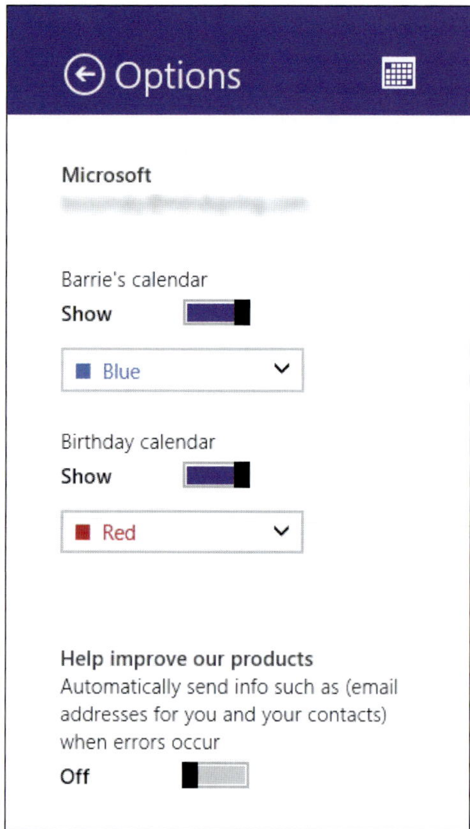



**E** The Options bar lets you show or hide
calendars and give them colors.

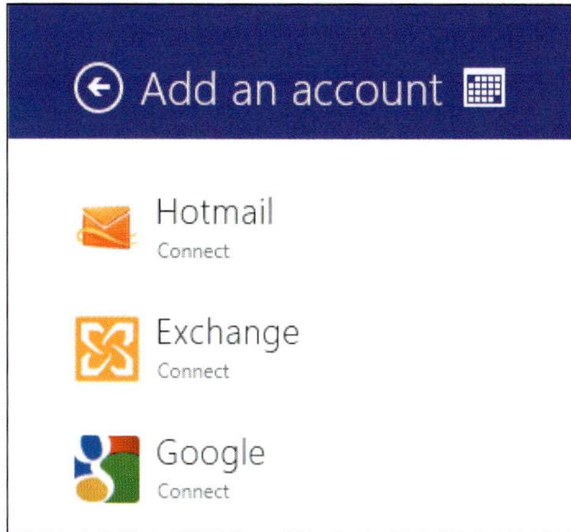



**F** The Account Selection dialog box

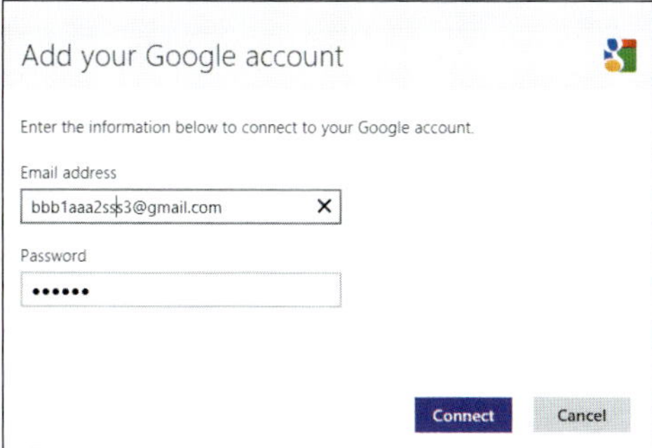



**G** Enter your email address and password.

## To add calendars from other cloud services:

1. Tap or click Settings in the Charms bar.

2. Tap or click Accounts, then click the *Add an account* link.

3. Tap or click the service you want to add **F**.

4. Enter the email account and password associated with your cloud service **G**. This will ensure that Calendar can access that service's events.

5. Tap or click the Connect button.

   When you create an event, Calendar sends reminders to your email at the times you requested in the event details **C**. Calendar also posts a reminder notice in the upper-right corner of your device display.

**TIP** Press Ctrl+1 to view the Day calendar, Ctrl+2 to view the Week calendar, and Ctrl+3 to view the Month calendar. Calendar is also well suited to be snapped to the side of your display so that it is always viewable while you work.

# Mail and Messaging

Mail is designed to be easy to use, work with mutliple email accounts, and offer a real-time mail experience. Mail emphasizes the display of content and assumes that the user won't do a lot of filtering or organizing into nested levels of folders. Mail isn't Eudora or Outlook, but what it lacks in power it makes up for in ease of use.

Mail was designed to look good in a snap position. You can share content with Mail using the Share charm and print a message in Mail using Print in the Devices charm. The Mail tile rotates through the five most recent unseen messages.

To start working with Mail, you need to add an account; the procedure is identical to the one for adding an account to the People app. (See "To add an account to People" in "Cloud Service Connections.") Mail supports Exchange ActiveSync (EAS) and IMAP, and it should support POP3 in upcoming versions. Once you add the account, Mail populates itself with all the content it finds on your Mail server **A**.

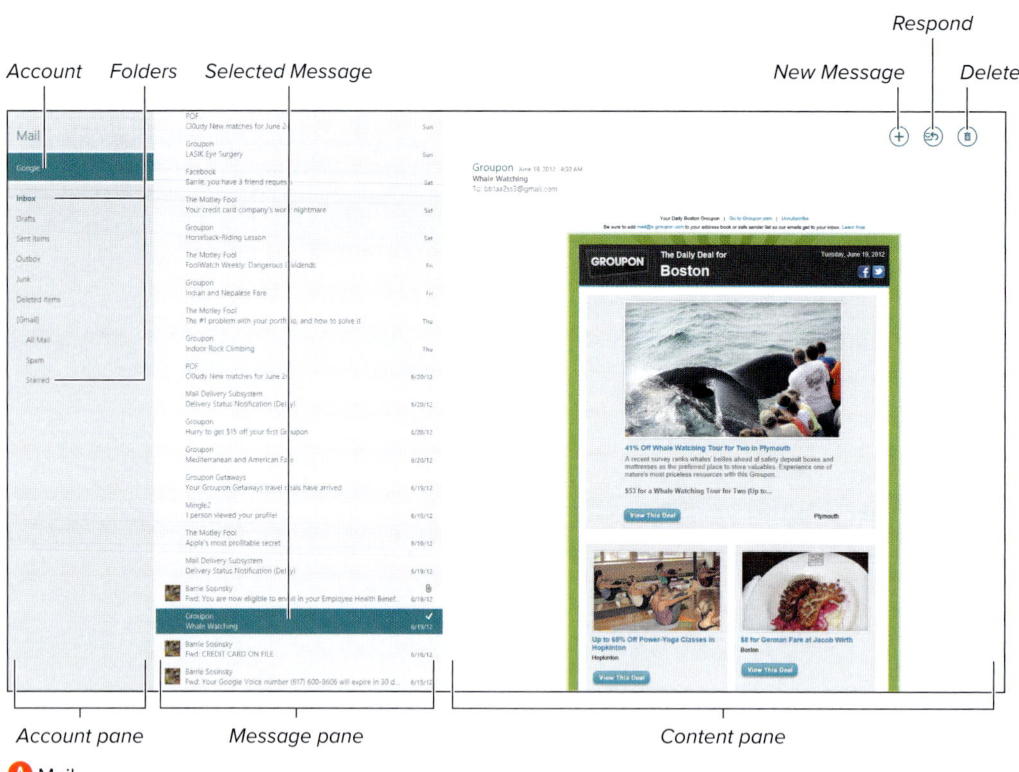



**A** Mail

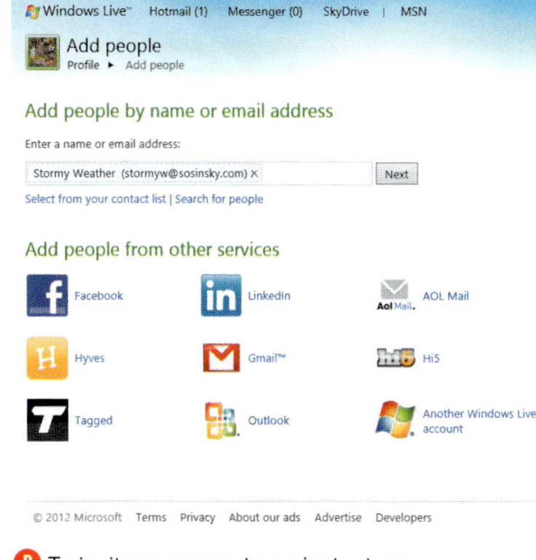


**B** To invite someone to an instant message, open Windows Live and connect to them there.

**C** The Mail tile

If you add two or more accounts, they are listed individually; select an account to see its emails. Email appears as it arrives, but you can set an interval that you wish to wait. When an email shows up, Mail posts a notification box.

The Messaging app provides real-time instant messaging to social networks such as Facebook, LinkedIn, and others. You use the People app to add the accounts and people you want message with. When you want to invite a friend to message, the Invite button on the left of the Apps bar takes you to Windows Live, where you can connect to them at the various services **B**.

## To view your new emails:

1. Tap or click the Mail tile **C** on the Start screen.

2. Add an email account or accounts using the procedure described in the section "To add an account to People" in the "Cloud Service Connections" section. Mail populates itself with messages it finds on your sever.

3. Click the folder that contains the messages you wish to see (your Inbox usually).

## To create a new email:

1. Tap or click the New Message button Ⓐ.

2. Fill in the fields; right-click the message to view the format buttons Ⓓ.

   If you have a tablet or phone, you'll see the onscreen keyboard appear.

3. Attach any pictures using the *Attachments* link and the Picture picker that appears.

4. Click the Send button in the upper-right corner to send the message.

5. You can tap or click the Cancel button to either discard your email or save a draft.

**TIP** If you are using Mail on a phone or tablet, use Windows 8's metered Internet account function to minimize your downloads. Only portions of the message are downloaded— mainly the header information. You can download the bulk of a message's content when you are connected to your LAN.

**TIP** Mail makes good use of the secondary tiles feature. You can not only use the Pin To Start button to show tiles of individual accounts, but you can also place secondary tiles on the Lock screen.

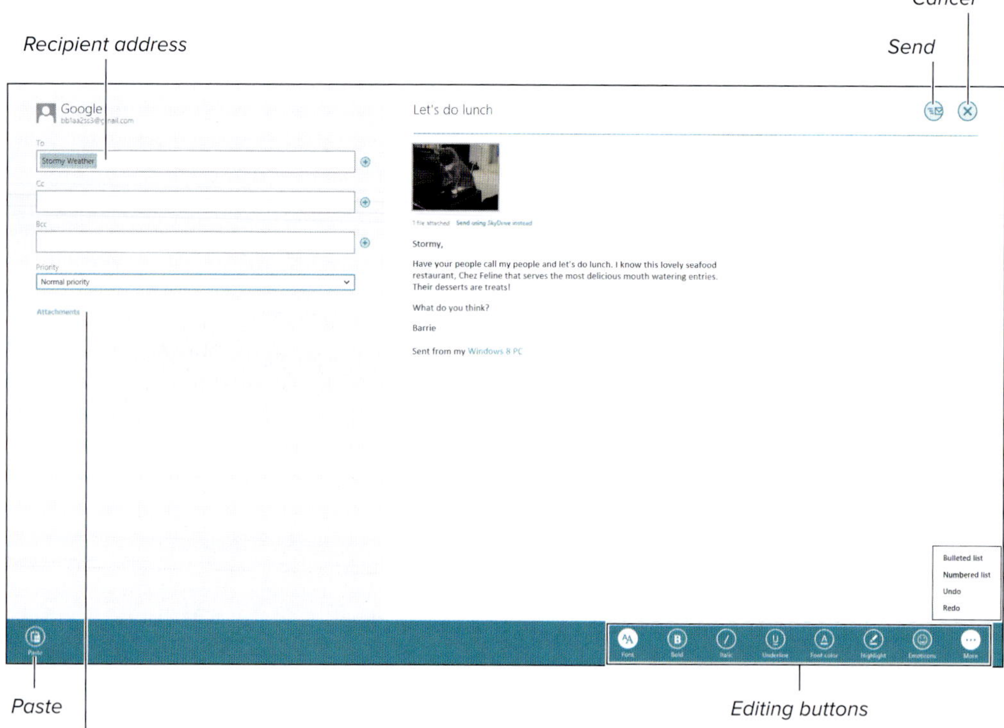


Paste

Attachments link

Ⓓ A message screen and its Apps bar

**A** The Photos tile as it looks with Live Tiles turned off or with no connected content or services yet configured

**B** Photos app Start screen

# Photos

Photos begins our discussion of Windows 8's rich-content tile-based apps. Photos can display photos from your connected devices and your libraries. You can also add accounts of services like Flickr and view any albums you created there. Through Windows Live, Photo will pick up SkyDrive photos. If you've connected Live to other photo services, then Photos will show those too. All in a simple to navigate interface.

## To access your photos:

1. Tap or click the Photos tile on the Start screen **A**.

2. The Photos app displays a Start screen that shows you content from your libraries, devices, and online services **B**.

3. Tap or click the tile of the collection you want to see; Photos displays your artwork as thumbnails **C**.

*continues on next page*

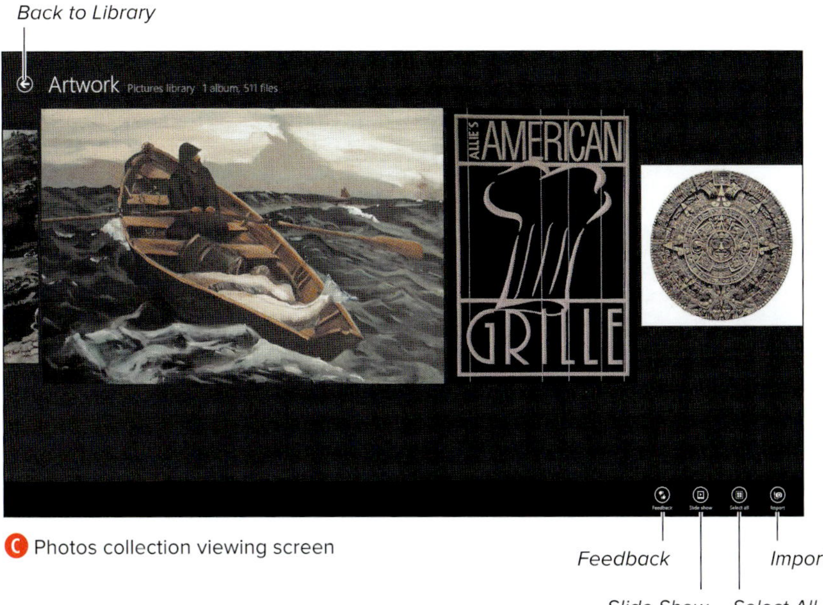


**C** Photos collection viewing screen

**4.** Tap or click the photo you want to see; Photo displays it full screen **D**.

## To navigate between albums or photos:

- To view the previous or next photo or album, swipe left or right, press the left or right arrow key, click the Back or Forward button, or use the scroll wheel on your mouse.

- Press the Home or End key to move to the first or last album or photo.

- To move one full screen left or right, press the Page Up or Page Down button, or click the page arrow buttons on the left and right sides of the screen **D**.

- Click the Slide Show button **C** to view your photos in a slide show.

## To add photos from your phone, camera, or other device:

Click Import **C** to import photos from a connected device.

**D** A photo displayed full screen

**E** The Turn Live Tile On button

**F** A live tile

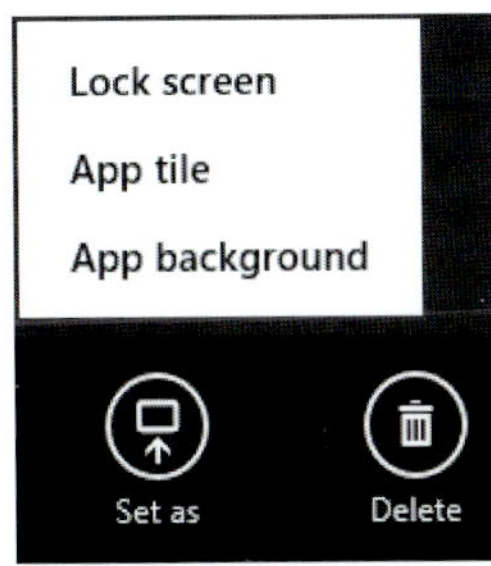


**G** The Save As button menu

## To make Photos a live tile:

1. Tap and hold, or right-click, to select the Photos tile on the Start screen.

2. On the Apps bar, click the Turn Live Tile On button **E**.

   The Photos tile shows pictures from your currently selected album and rotates the picture every five seconds **F**.

## To make a background image:

1. Select a picture in Photos that you want to use.

2. Swipe from the bottom edge or right-click to view the Apps bar.

3. Tap or click the Save As button to view its menu **G**.

4. Select the Lock Screen command to have the picture appear on your Lock screen.

5. Select the App Tile command to have the picture appear on the Start screen Photos tile.

6. Select the App Background command to have the photo appear as the background on the Photos screen.

7. Click the Slide Show button on the Apps bar if you want Photos to display the current album as a slide show.

   Press the Esc key or tap the screen to end the slide show.

**TIP** When you double-click an image in Windows Explorer, the tile-based Photos app opens. If you don't want this app to open, use the Set Default Programs control panel to choose a different program as a viewer.

# Music

The Music app is a touch-oriented music player, a music browser, and a music content store. From Music, you can preview new music and add it to your collection. For a phone or tablet, this is great, though on desktop computers you may prefer to use Windows Media Player, which still ships with Windows 8. Let's put Music through its paces.

**A** The Music app tile

## To play a song:

1. Tap or click the Music tile on the Start screen **A**.

   Music appears with tile groups **B**.

   All the group titles are links to more content, categorized by genre.

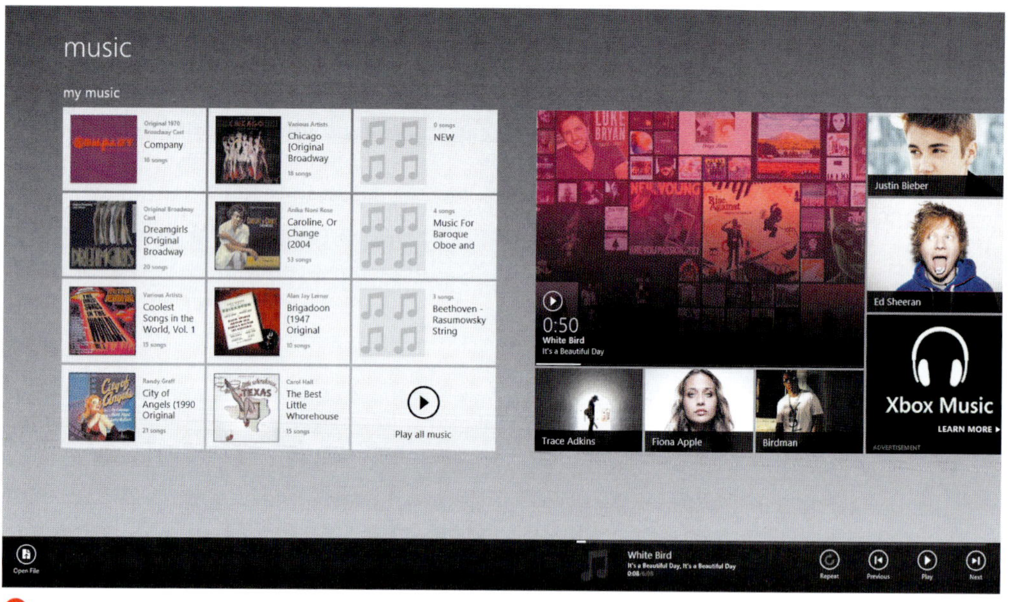



**B** The Music app main screen

**2.** Click the *my music* link to view your current album or folder.

*or*

Swipe from the bottom or right-click, and then tap or click the Open Files button to open the File picker **C**.

*continues on next page*

**C** The File picker

3. Navigate the file system to locate the song or album you want to play, then tap or click to select an item. You can select multiple items, and you can move to additional folders to select items to build a playlist .

The Files screen with selections from different folders forming a playlist

4. Click the Open button to play your selection.

The basic Music player then plays your song **E** and diplays a set of player buttons.

The Music app builds a cool background composed of your album art and content Windows 8 selects for you.



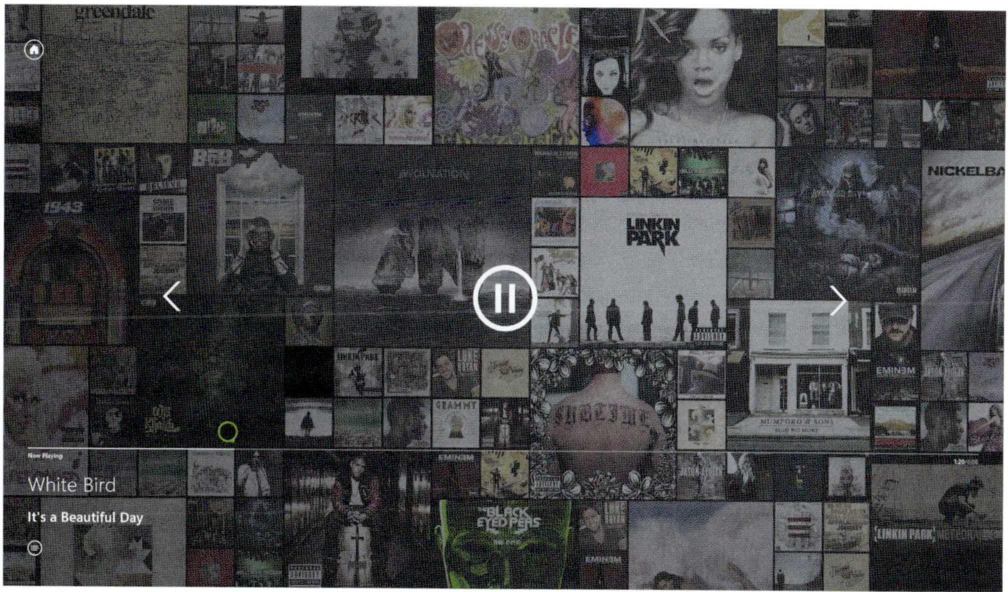 The Music app player

## To create and save a playlist:

1. On the Music main screen, click the *my music* link to view your music by categories **F**.

2. Click the plus (+) button next to the *Playlist* link.

3. Enter a name for the playlist in the pop-up menu, then click Save.

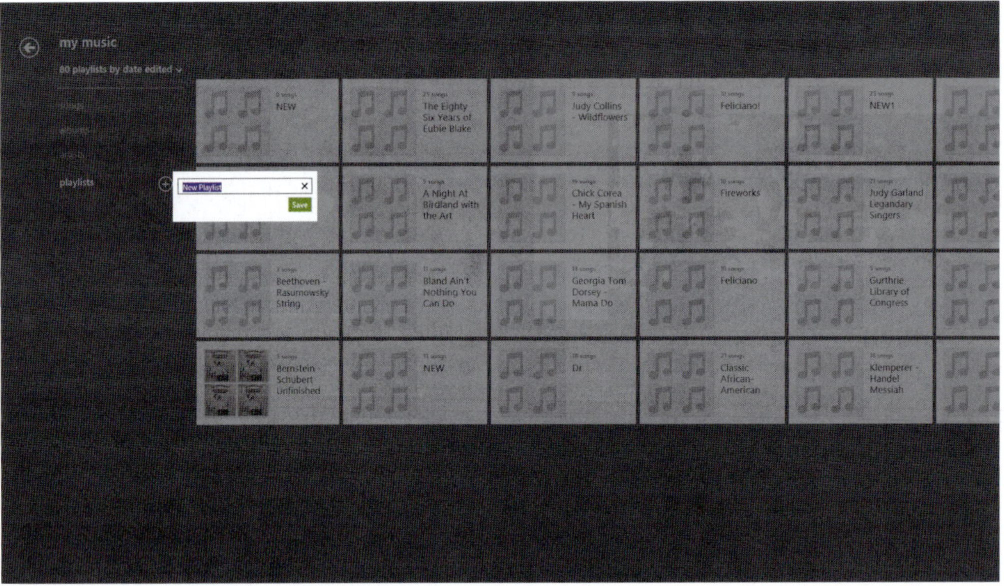

**F** You create a new playlist on the Music category screen.

## To add songs to a playlist:

1. Click the *Songs* or *Albums* link.

2. Select the songs or albums you wish to add to your playlist.

3. When you have selected all the songs and albums you want on your playlist, click the Add To Playlist button on the Apps bar **G**.

continues on next page

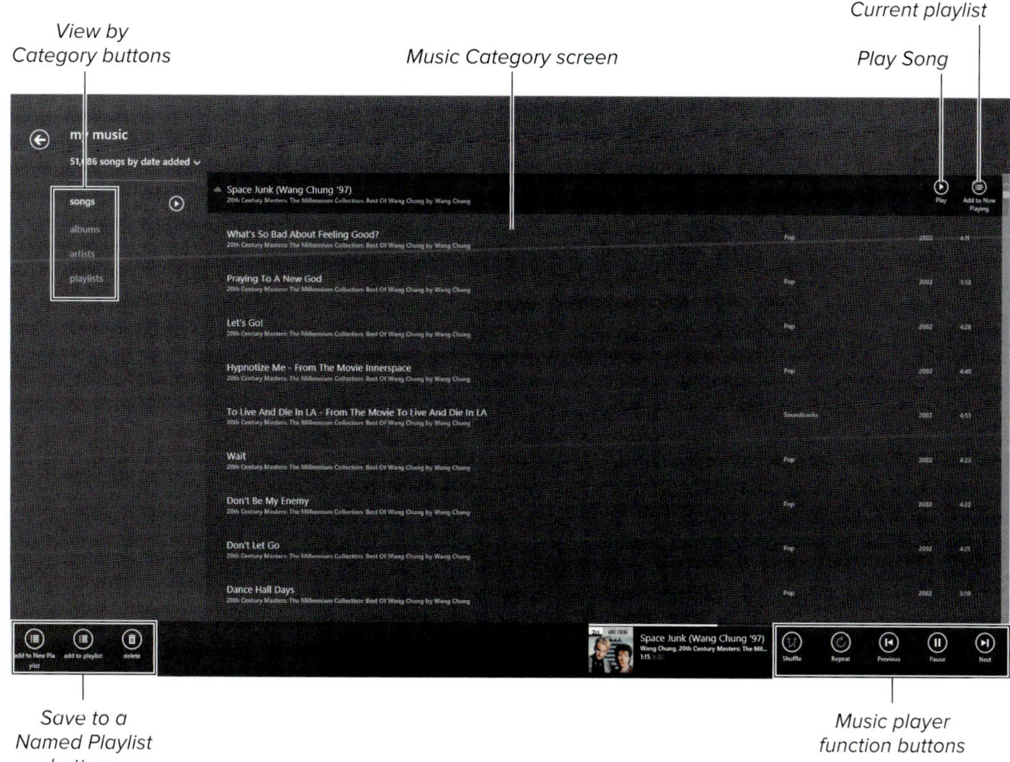



**G** Select songs and albums for your playlist, then click the Add To Playlist button to add them as a group to the list.

**4.** Click the playlist name in the scrolling
window **H**.

**TIP** **To quickly search for a song or album in
Music, press ⊞+Q and start to type the name.**



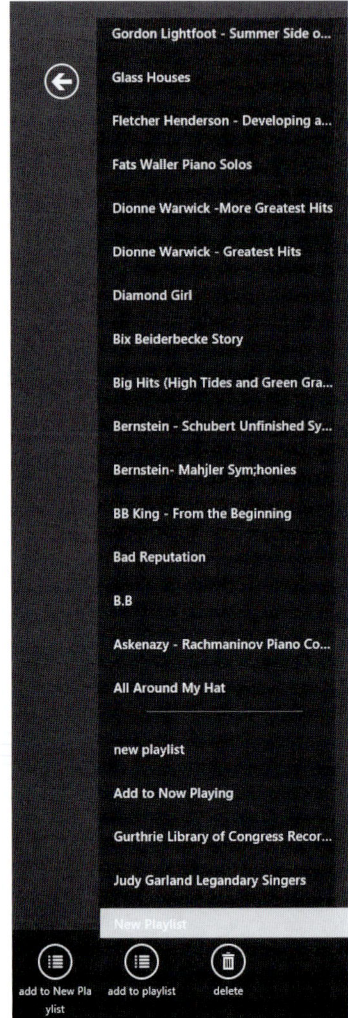 Select the playlist to add your
songs to here.

**A** The Video app tile

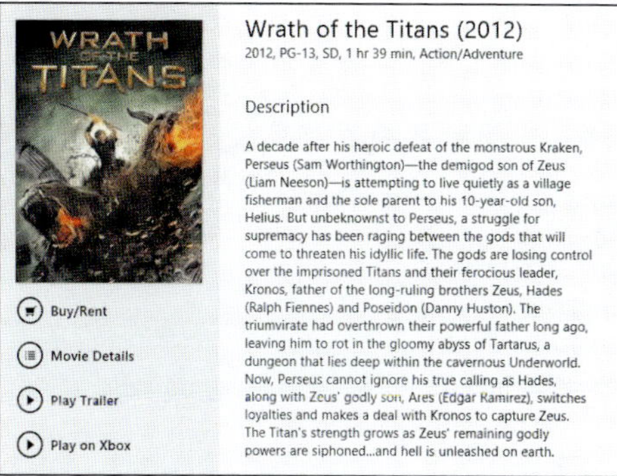

Wrath of the Titans (2012)
2012, PG-13, SD, 1 hr 39 min, Action/Adventure

Description

A decade after his heroic defeat of the monstrous Kraken, Perseus (Sam Worthington)—the demigod son of Zeus (Liam Neeson)—is attempting to live quietly as a village fisherman and the sole parent to his 10-year-old son, Helius. But unbeknownst to Perseus, a struggle for supremacy has been raging between the gods that will come to threaten his idyllic life. The gods are losing control over the imprisoned Titans and their ferocious leader, Kronos, father of the long-ruling brothers Zeus, Hades (Ralph Fiennes) and Poseidon (Danny Huston). The triumvirate had overthrown their powerful father long ago, leaving him to rot in the gloomy abyss of Tartarus, a dungeon that lies deep within the cavernous Underworld. Now, Perseus cannot ignore his true calling as Hades, along with Zeus' godly son, Ares (Edgar Ramirez), switches loyalties and makes a deal with Kronos to capture Zeus. The Titan's strength grows as Zeus' remaining godly powers are siphoned...and hell is unleashed on earth.

Buy/Rent

Movie Details

Play Trailer

Play on Xbox

**B** Selecting a movie tile in the content section opens a description box with purchase and viewing options.

**C** *Lawrence of Arabia* playing in the Video player

# Video

The Video app is organized along the same lines as the Music app. It shows your local content, content associated with your Xbox account, and video content that Microsoft thinks you will be interested in—movies, TV shows, and more. If you want video content from your Netflix, Hulu, or other online account, then you will need to download that company's tile-based app from the Windows Store. Let's take a brief look at Video to see how it's organized.

## To view a movie:

1. Tap or click the Video tile **A** to open the app. The Video home screen displays **B**.

2. Tap or click a movie tile; a description appears, as well as buttons to buy the movie or play it on your Xbox.

3. When you click the tile of a movie that's currently in theaters, your browser opens and you can purchase tickets from a site like Fandango.

4. Tap or click a movie to play it **C**.

   *or*

   Tap or click the Movie tile group title to open the File picker, and select your movie there.

**TIP** Windows 8 comes with the Camera app, but you will need a webcam to see it show up on your Start screen. (You can add it later.) You can use the Camera app to record and play back video.

# Reader

Reader is a very basic PDF reader that you can use as an alternative to Adobe Reader. Windows Reader is simple to use, immersive, and very fast, so it may have some appeal to you when you are on the go.

Ⓐ shows Reader displaying a chapter of this book, which was saved from Microsoft Office as a PDF file.

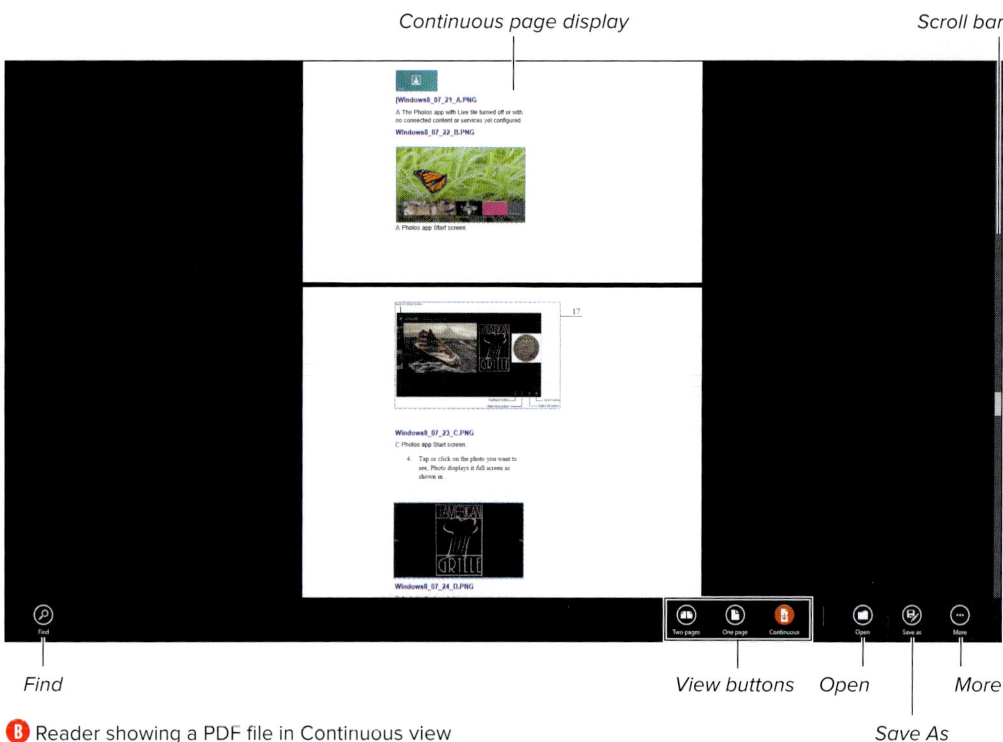



Ⓑ Reader showing a PDF file in Continuous view

Reader

 The Reader tile

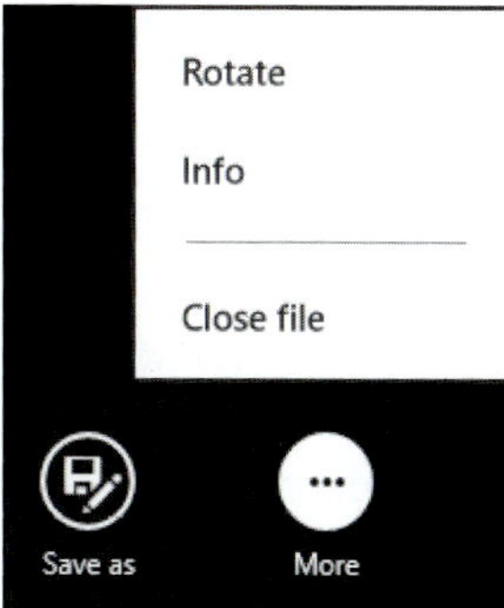

Rotate

Info

Close file

Save as    More



**C** The More button menu

## To open a book or file:

- Tap or double-click a PDF file.

- Tap or click the Reader tile **B** on the Start menu; Reader opens to the last book or file page you were viewing.

## To use Reader options:

- Tap or click the Find button to search for a string in the document.

- Tap or click the Two Pages, One Page, or Continuous View buttons to alter the display type.

- Tap or click the Open button to open another file.

- Tap or click the Save As button to save the document as a PDF file with a name and location you choose.

- Tap or click the More button to view its menu **C**. You can rotate the page 90 degrees, or view the file's Info page (properties and permissions).

- To move up and down through the pages, swipe up or down, use the scroll bar, or use your mouse's scroll button. Page Up, Page Down, the arrow keys, Home, and End work in Reader the same as they do in all scrollable windows.

- You can select text and copy it or save it to a PDF file. With a digital pen (like you find on the Microsoft Surface), you can add ink-based notes.

- To print, press Ctrl+P. Or press ⊞+C, and select your printer in the Devices charm.

**TIP** To zoom in, press Ctrl++ (plus); to zoom out, press Ctrl+– (minus). You can also use the pinch in or pinch out gesture to zoom.

# Maps

Microsoft has had a strong mapping function ever since it developed the Streets application many years ago. There's some discussion about whether Maps will eventually be replaced by something else, but it is a simple and useful application nonetheless. Other apps can use Maps to search for an address, you can use it to get directions, and you can view your current location as a road map or in a satellite view that zooms down to house level.

**A** The Maps tile

## To view a map:

**1.** On the Start screen, tap or click the Maps tile **A**.

Maps opens **B**. When the Apps bar is showing, the Zoom buttons are hidden.

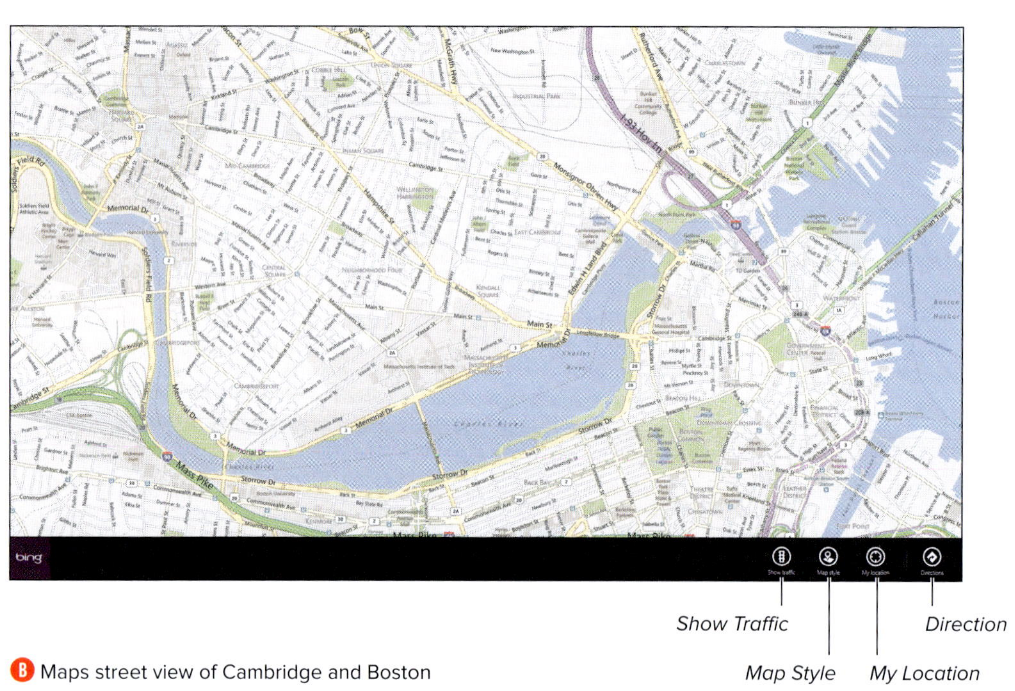



**B** Maps street view of Cambridge and Boston

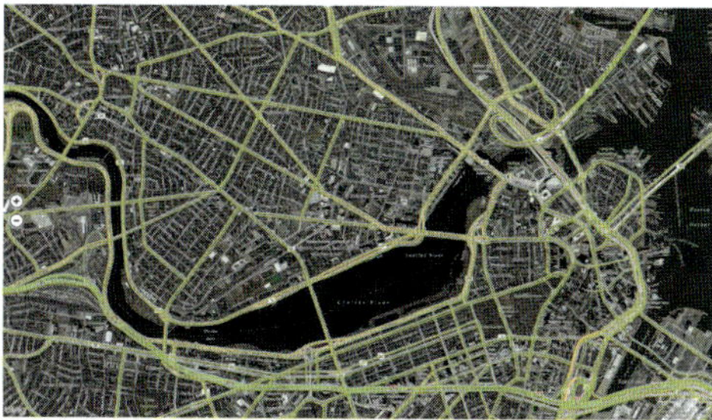

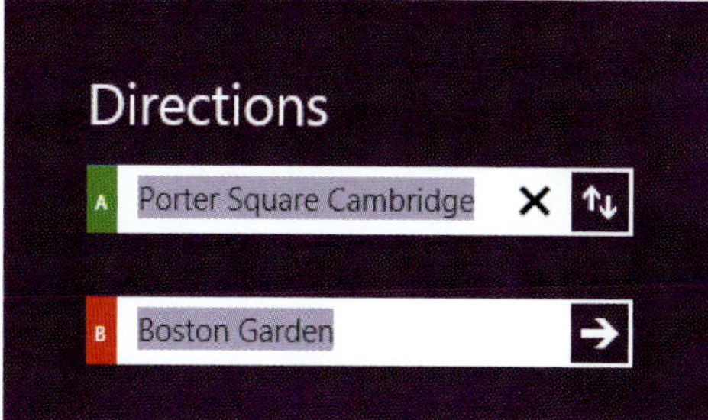

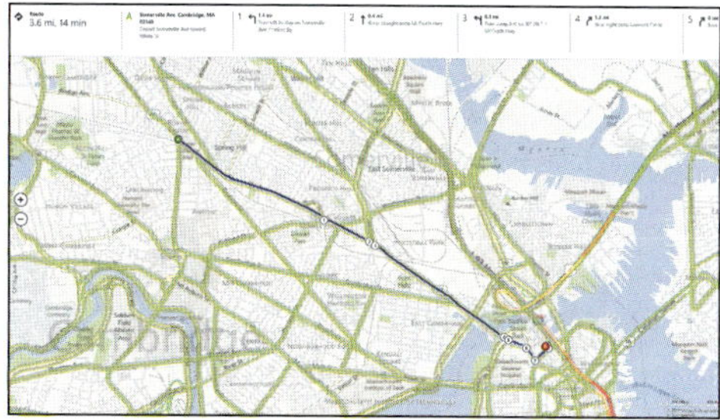

**C** Aerial view of Cambridge and Boston

**D** The Directions text boxes

**E** A mapped set of directions

2. Click the Zoom In (+) or Zoom Out buttons.

   *or*

   Press Ctrl++ (plus) or Ctrl+− (minus), respectively, to perform the same functions.

3. To view traffic overlaid on the roads, click the Show Traffic button.

4. To change to a satellite view **C**, click the Map Style button and select Aerial.

## To view your current location:

Tap or click the My Location button.

## To get directions:

1. Click the Directions button **B**.

2. Enter addresses in the A and B text boxes **D**, then press the arrow key in the B box.

   Press the double arrows to swap the A and B locations.

   **E** shows the result of this search.

3. The Waypoint bar displays directions and mileages to each waypoint of your route. Swipe or scroll left or right to see more waypoints.

**TIP** The Directions text boxes accept not only addresses but also places and concepts. For example, if you typed "airport" as your destination, this map would route you to Logan International Airport, which is the closest major airport to my location.

**TIP** For current location to work, you need to go to the Settings charm, click Permissions, and turn the Location slider to On. Allowing an application to use your geolocation is a feature called *presence*, and many applications require it for additional functionality.

# Putting It All Together

- Windows 8 provides you with a very comprehensive set of touch- and gesture-oriented applications.

- These apps are effective but not as powerful as applications you can use on the Desktop.

- People is a flat file contact database that can aggregate your contacts from different social media services.

- Photos can show images from the Picture library, SkyDrive (cloud storage), and cloud-based services such as Flickr and Facebook.

- The Music app allows you to view and play music, connect to other sources to view content you own, and view and purchase music from the Microsoft Store.

- The Video app shows and plays video files. Video provides content you can purchase online, as well as a method for buying tickets to currently playing movies.

- Reader is a simple but effective PDF viewer.

- With Maps, you can get directions, view your current location, and view maps in Road view or Aerial view.

# Managing Content

Managing content is one of the main reasons that computers exist. Your computer may have hundreds of apps and videos, it may store thousands of pictures and songs, and its overall file count may number in the hundreds of thousands. That's not atypical for Windows users. The challenge is how to manage this content, find what you need, arrange it so that you can find it next time, and share your information with other people. Windows 8 offers some new tools in this area that are presented in this chapter.

Files are the atomic building block of modern operating systems. Files have a file type, a default app that can open that type, and *properties* (information about the file). Properties are metadata, and they are used to manage content. You can search for objects by type and by property.

The tile-based interface comes with a new Search function that is simple to use but powerful. It is one of Windows 8's best features. There is also a new touch-oriented file selector called the Picker. Both are discussed in this chapter.

## In This Chapter

Libraries are special folder types that can point to other folders. Windows organizes libraries around file types: documents, music, photos, and videos. You can also create custom libraries. Libraries are a great way to manage content. You can share libraries using a feature called HomeGroup (introduced in Windows 7), which allows other users to access your libraries from other computers. Home-Group can also stream content and share devices like printers.

Windows also has a new interapplication sharing feature called Share. With Share, two apps can agree on what they will share and how the content can be used—an agreement called a contract. You'll see an example of how to use the Photos app with the Mail app in a moment.

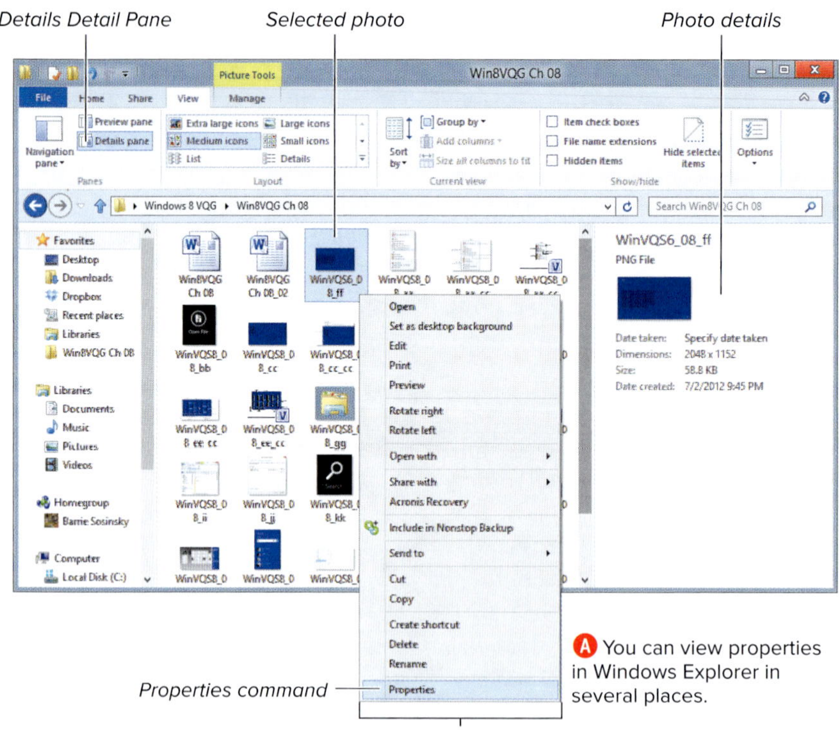


A You can view properties in Windows Explorer in several places.

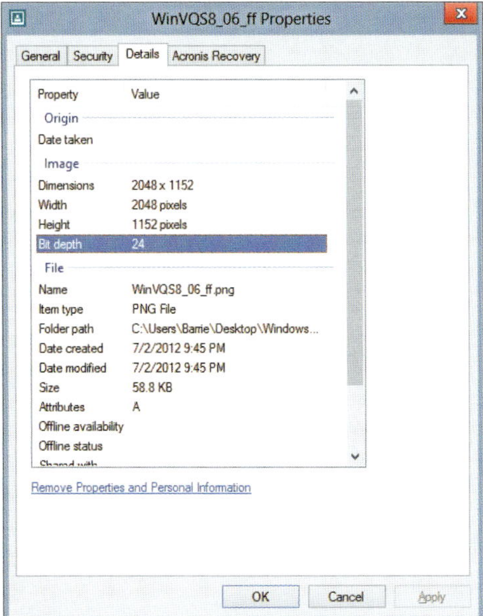

**B** A file's properties (also called attributes or metadata) are shown (and can sometimes be altered) in the Properties dialog box.

# Media Types

To manage content, you manage files. A file is a container object that has information and data in it that programs can work with. Some files are programs themselves—they are executable, and when you "open" them the program runs. Some files contain data, such as text, music, photos, or video.

To differentiate one type of file from another, files are given a three-letter file extension. For example, a program uses the .exe file extension. Each extension is assigned a default application that opens that file. File extensions are hidden by default in Windows 8, but it is the extension that determines the icon type you see.

When you do a search in Windows for a file with the word *love* in it, then all file types with *love* in the name appear. Change the search string to *love.mp3*, and you get songs of only that type. Windows Search is organized by file type, and you can use apps, files, settings, and application-specific searches to isolate the content you want. Libraries are collections of files of a certain type.

In **A**, Windows Explorer has a picture file selected. A thumbnail and details are shown in the Preview pane (on the right), and the Properties command is shown on the context menu. The Properties dialog box for the selected photo is shown in **B**.

Properties are labels that can be applied to files, and different file types allow for different property types. For example, the property called "Bit depth" Ⓑ is the number of colors that each pixel can choose from. The number 24 indicates a palette of $2^{24}$, or 16.8 million, colors. That property can't be changed, but the filename, date taken, and other properties can be altered. The set of properties is called a file's metadata; metadata is data about data. Metadata is used to manage content by apps in all sorts of ways. These properties are what you use every day to make your content meaningful.

## To view a file, folder, or object's properties:

- On the Desktop or in Windows Explorer, move the cursor over an object so that it gains focus; Windows displays an informational box about the object.

- In Windows Explorer, tap or click an object to view properties in the Details pane. (Use the View menu to turn this feature on, if necessary.)

- Tap and hold or right-click an object, and select the Properties command from the context menu.

**TIP** System folders and files are hidden in Windows by default, as are the three-letter file extensions. Sometimes you need to see them, but Windows considers this an advanced feature. To change these defaults, open Windows Explorer, tap or click the View tab, then tap or click the Options button. The Hidden Files And Folders setting allows you to display hidden files. Deselect the Hide Extensions For Known File Types setting to display file extensions. Note that when you change a file extension, the program assigned to open it will no longer work. Be cautious when using this feature.

Ⓐ The Open File button opens the Picker in the tile-based interface.

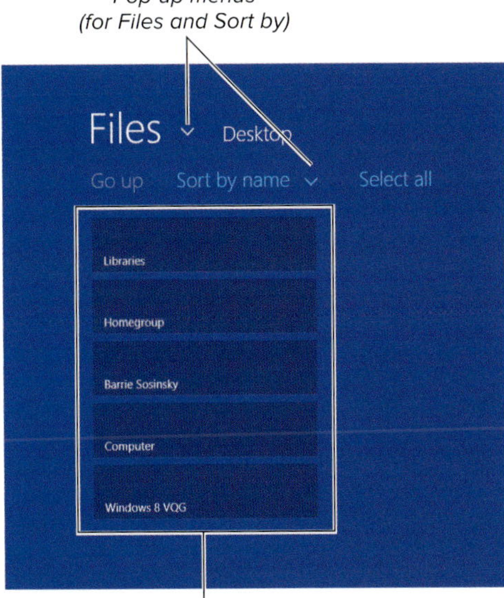



*Folder buttons*

Ⓑ The Desktop folder in the Picker

# The Picker

The Windows 8 Picker is a touch-oriented control for selecting files in the tile-based interface. You might think of the Picker as a dumbed-down version of Windows Explorer (covered in Chapter 10)—but I like to think of it as a "thumbed-down" version of Explorer. You saw the Picker when we explored the Photos and Music apps in Chapter 7; they both use this control for the same purpose. Since the Picker is a standard item, you'll see it in more and more apps going forward, and it will likely become more developed than what you see here, which is version 1.0. The Picker is very simple to use—and given that it's meant to be part of the glance-and-go interface on a phone or tablet, it has to be.

The Picker allows you to view your folders by name (descending alphabetical order) or by date (most recent first).

## To select a file in the Picker:

1. In a tile-based app, tap or click a button in the Apps bar with a function similar to the Open File button Ⓐ. (The name of the button may vary slightly depending on the app; for example, it might be titled "Open.")

   The Picker opens to the same location in the file system that you last exited it from.

2. Click the *Go up* link until you see the Desktop folder Ⓑ, the top level of the file system.

3. Each folder is represented by a button. Tap or click a folder's button to open it.

## To navigate the Picker:

- Tap or click a folder to open it.

- Tap or click Files to open the Files menu **C**. Select a category, and the Picker takes you to the top level of that item.

  Documents, Downloads, Desktop, Homegroup, and Network take you to those special folders. Pictures, Music, and Videos take you to the top level of those libraries. Computer shows you all your disks and other connected devices. SkyDrive is your cloud-connected storage.

## To open a file or files:

1. Tap or click through the folder hierarchy until you find the file or files you want to open.

2. Tap or click the file or files.

3. Tap or click the Open button.

   The file or files open in whatever app is the default tile-based app for that file type. In **D**, it is the Music app.

   **D** shows a selection of songs (with check marks), and an info box that appears when you move the cursor over an item.

## To select a file or files:

- Tap or click the file or files to select them.

- Tap or click the *Select All* link to select all items in the folder.

- Tap or click a selected file to deselect it.

- Tap or click Clear Selected to deselect all selected files.

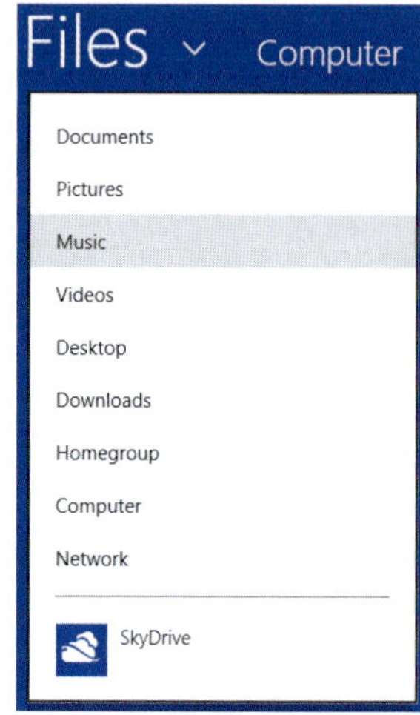



**C** Use the Files menu to quickly navigate your libraries, special folders, and disks, as well as your cloud storage on SkyDrive.

## To view an alphabetical directory of your folders:

Click one of the lettered Folder or Directory buttons **E**.

**TIP** Use the Home and End buttons to go to the first and last items in a folder, respectively, and use the Up and Down arrow keys to move up or down the list.

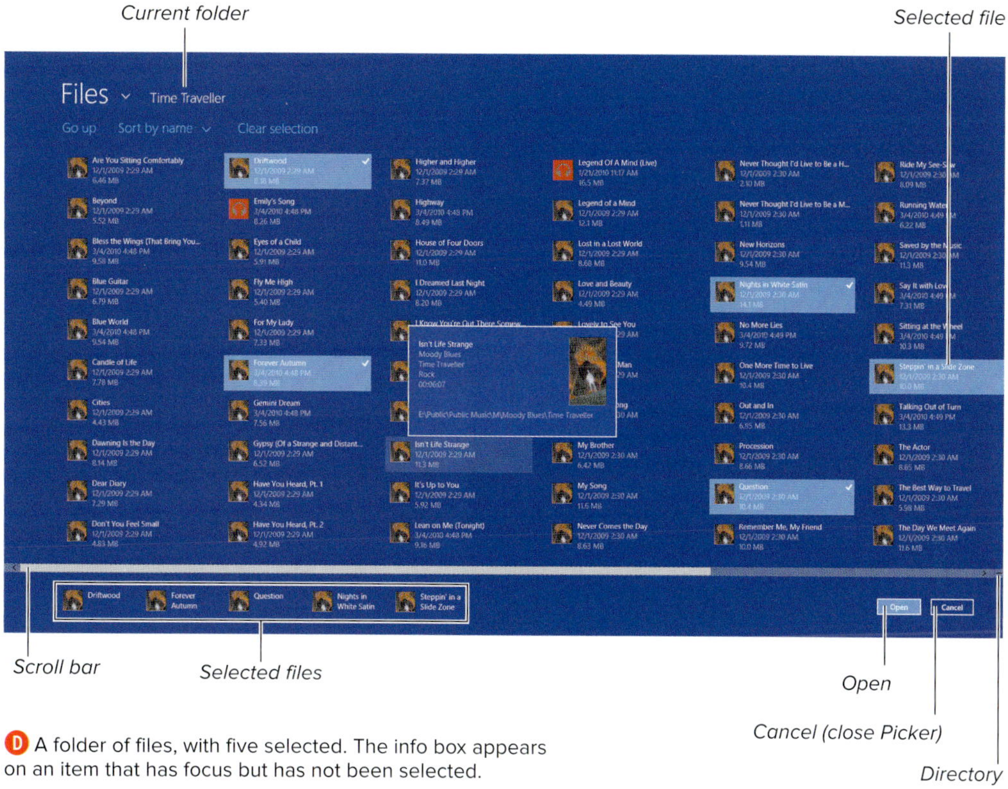

**D** A folder of files, with five selected. The info box appears on an item that has focus but has not been selected.

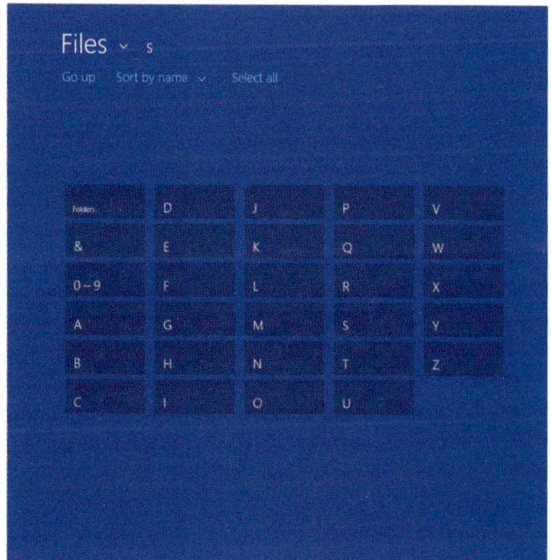


**E** This directory takes you to folders that start with the letter you select.

# Libraries

Libraries were introduced in Windows 7 and have carried over to Windows 8. Libraries are special folders that you can use to present a unified view of content, even when the files are stored in different locations. The default library folders are found at **C:\Users\<User Name>**, and a public folder is found at **C:\Users\Public**.

Libraries are containers for managed shortcuts to folders that are stored locally, on attached disks, in shared network storage, or even using SkyDrive. If you can use Windows Explorer to add a folder to the library, you can include and manage that content centrally. Libraries take some getting used to, but they can make everyday tasks easier.

There are four standard libraries built into Windows 8: Documents, Music, Pictures, and Videos. You see these libraries not only in Explorer, but also in the standard file system Save (PUT) and Open (GET) dialog boxes. You can also create custom libraries of your own.

The Libraries tile on the Start screen takes you to Explorer **A**.

To modify the contents and view of a library, you work with the Library Tools ribbon in Windows Explorer, which becomes available to you when you select a library.

## To open and view your libraries:

- Tap or click the Windows Explorer icon **B** on the Desktop taskbar.

- Press **⊞**+E to open Windows Explorer, then click the Libraries icon in the Navigation pane **A**.

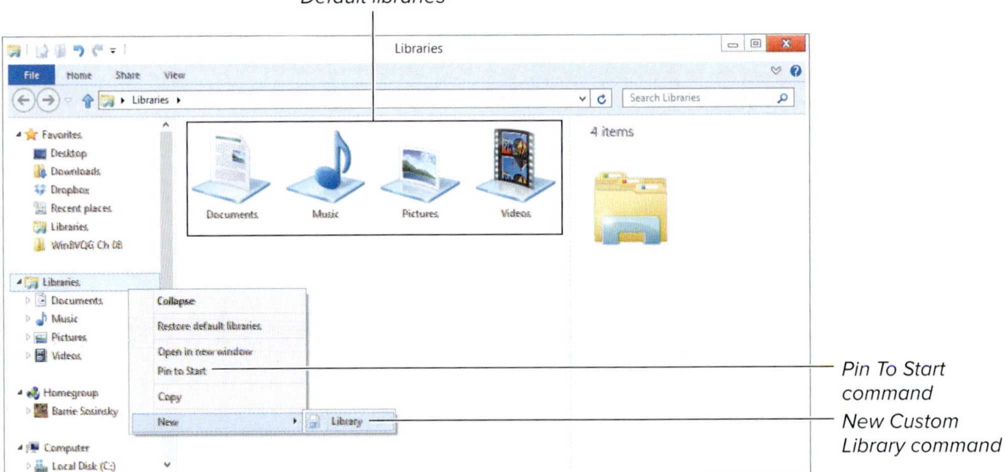



**A** Windows Explorer with the default library folders showing. You can also create custom libraries using the New command as shown here.

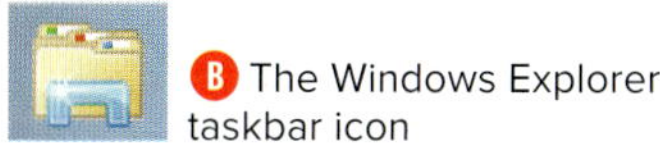 **B** The Windows Explorer taskbar icon

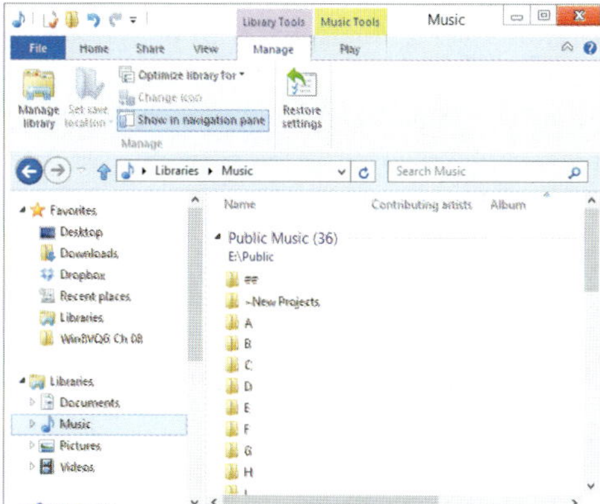

**C** Manage your library using the Library Tools ribbon.

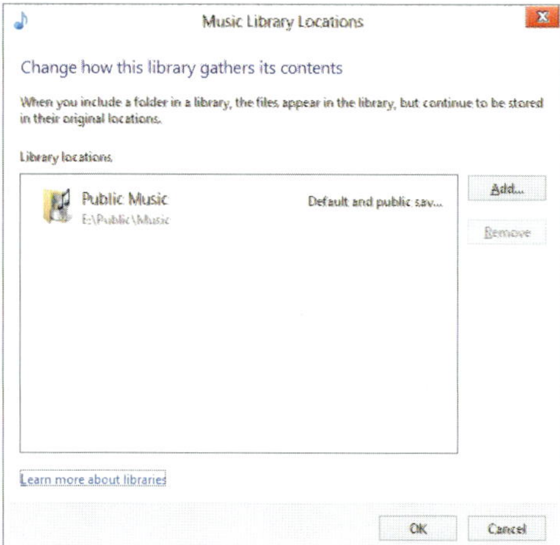

**D** The Music Library Locations folder



## To create a custom library:

- Right-click the Libraries icon **A** in the Navigation pane, select New, and then select Library.

- The first folder you add to a custom library is the default folder where content is saved.

## To create a Libraries tile on the tile-based Start screen:

Select the Pin To Start command from the Libraries context menu **A**.

## To add a folder to a library:

1. Open Windows Explorer, and click a library icon.

2. The ribbon changes to display a Library Tools section **C**.

3. Click the Library Tools label in the window title bar, then click the Manage tab.

4. Click the Manage Library icon at the left of the ribbon underneath the File tab **C**.

   A Library Locations folder appears **D**.

5. Click the Add button, and select a folder that you would like to add to the library. Close all open dialog boxes.

6. Click the Set Save Location button, and specify the folder you want to use.

7. If a library is mostly of a certain file type, then click the Optimize Library For icon, and select the file type from the drop-down menu.

   This allows the library to offer you the correct playback options and is helpful in indexing operations.

# Homegroups

The HomeGroup feature was introduced in Windows 7 as a means to allow people to share content and devices. A homegroup is a group of computers that can share resources. When you create a homegroup, you determine what resources you allow people to see (**READ**), and what resources you allow people to modify (**WRITE**). You can add picture, music, video, and document libraries, and you can share printers and other devices. Homegroups are password protected.

Use the HomeGroup control panel to change the libraries and devices you share, change streaming options, set passwords, and set advanced options. In the advanced options, you can enable network discovery, enable file and printer sharing, and allow Windows to manage homegroup connections. Other options allow you to set up public folder sharing, use encrypted file sharing connections, and turn password protection on or off. These options are found in the Network and Sharing Center control panel's Advanced settings.

Enabling these settings creates a homegroup that other systems (Windows 8 and Windows 7) can join. To modify more options, open the HomeGroup control panel.

## To create a homegroup:

1.  Press ⊞+C to open the Charms bar, click Setttings, and then click Change PC Settings.

2.  Click the HomeGroup section to view the HomeGroup page Ⓐ.

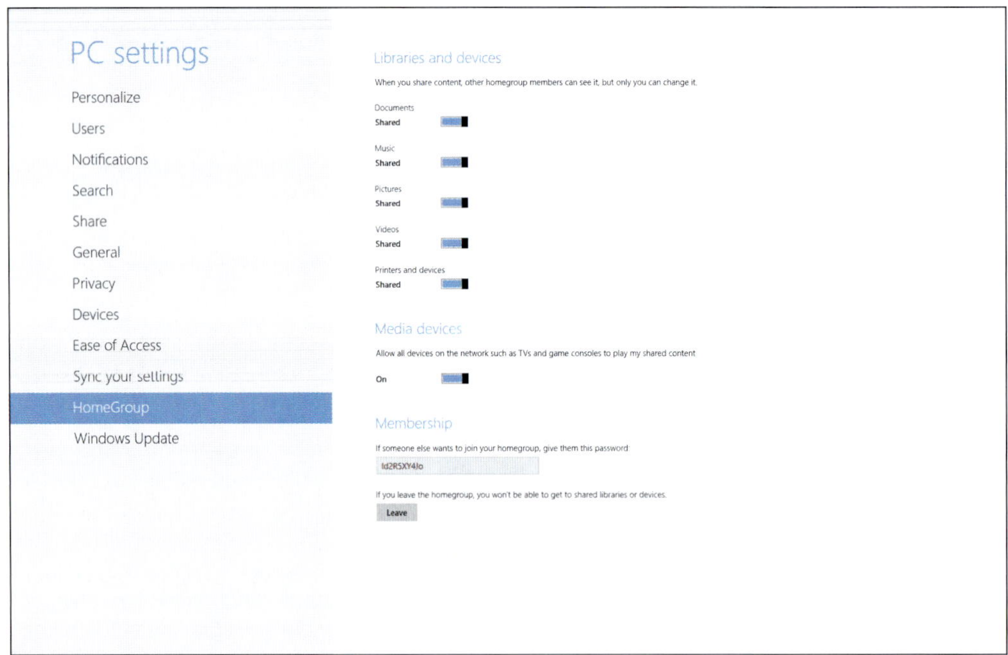


Ⓐ Create a homegroup by enabling the sliders for your libraries and devices on the HomeGroup page.

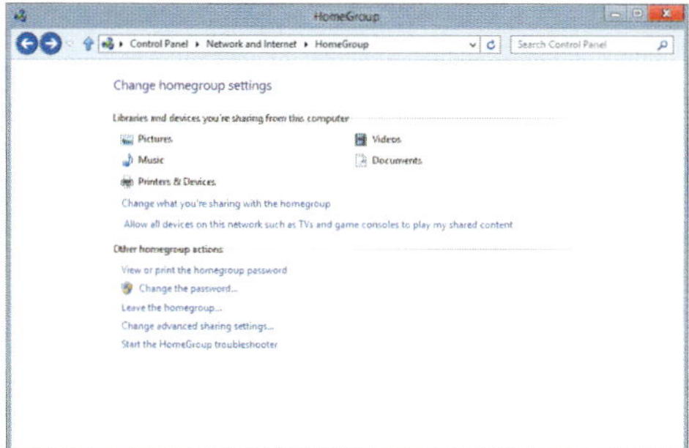

**B** The HomeGroup control panel allows you to enable more settings and modify your homegroup.

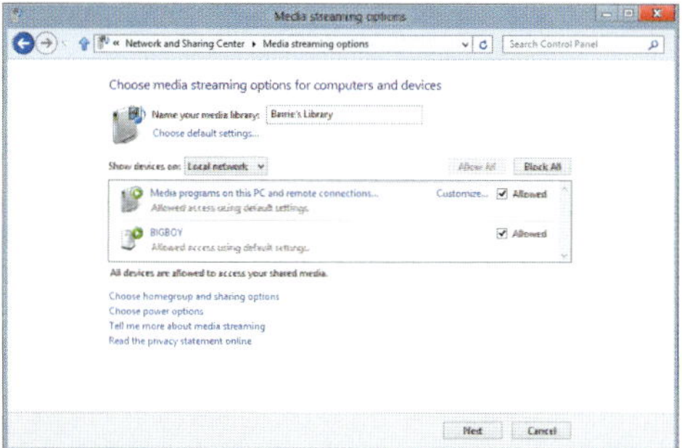

**C** Enable streaming to devices in the Media Streaming Options dialog box.

3. Move the sliders for each library that you wish to include in your homegroup.

By default, all of these sliders are disabled when you first install Windows 8.

4. Enable the Media Devices slider as well if you wish to share devices.

Note the Windows 8-generated password, because it provides access to the homegroup for you and for other connected computers. (This password is changed elsewhere.)

## To modify an existing homegroup:

1. Press ⊞+X or right-click the lower-left corner of the display to view the Computer Management menu, then select the Control Panel command.

2. In the Network and Internet section, tap or click the *Choose HomeGroup and sharing options* link to view the Home-Group control panel **B**.

3. Click the *Change what you're sharing with the homegroup* link to view and change the libraries that are part of your homegroup.

## To enable media streaming:

1. Click the *Allow all devices on this network such as TVs and game consoles to play my shared content* link.

2. In the Choose Media Streaming Options dialog box, tap or click the Turn On Media Streaming button, then tap or click OK.

3. In the Media Streaming Options dialog box **C**, name your library, and select which devices are allowed to stream content from your library; then click Next.

*continues on next page*

4. In the Share With Other Homegroup Members dialog box, select the permissions you wish to grant to other computers **D**. Click Next.

5. Note the password, and then click Finish.

## To join a homegroup:

1. Log in to Windows 8 or Windows 7 with a specific user account.

2. Open the HomeGroup control panel.

   The panel should have a section that shows that the homegroup was detected, as well as a Join Now button.

3. Click Join Now, enter the password, and click Next.

   Windows will post a message that you have successfully joined the homegroup.

   The homegroup that you joined appears in the Navigation panel of Windows Explorer. From there you can open the context menu **E** that you can use to modify your homegroup. Homegroups are a major upgrade from the older system of shared folders because they are containers that can provide access to multiple types of content and can provide permissions and streaming capabilities.

**TIP** Only one homegroup is allowed per network subnet.

**TIP** The Basic version of Windows 8 can join a homegroup but not create one.

**TIP** A Windows 8 member of a domain can join a homegroup but cannot share printers or folders.

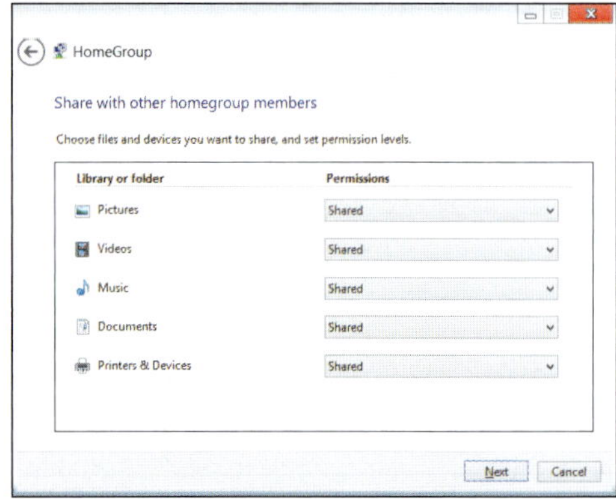

**D** Set streaming permissions in this dialog box.

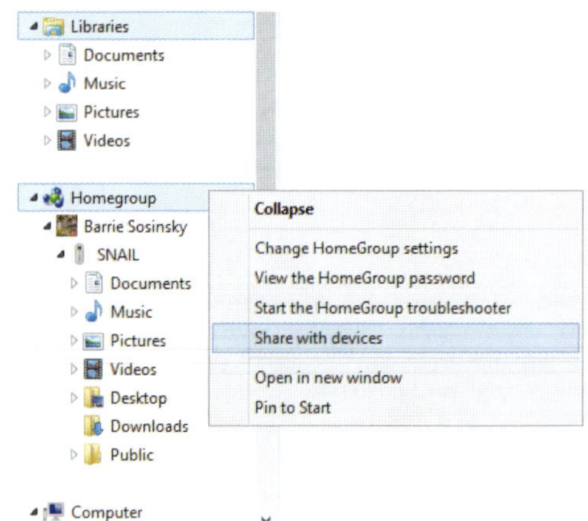

**E** You can modify a homegroup from within Windows Explorer using the Homegroup context menu.

Ⓐ The Search charm icon

# Search

Content is valuable only if you can find it, and with lots of content to manage, the Windows 8 search function is essential. In Chapter 10 you'll learn about how to use the Search box in Windows Explorer, as well as its advanced functions. But the tile-based interface comes with its own search function—the Search charm, which offers somewhat different methods for finding what you are looking for. In this section, we'll take a look at how to use the Search charm and learn about some principles that can make your searches more powerful.

## To go to Search:

On the Desktop or Start screen, press ⊞+C, and then click the Search charm Ⓐ; Search opens with Apps selected Ⓑ.

continues on next page

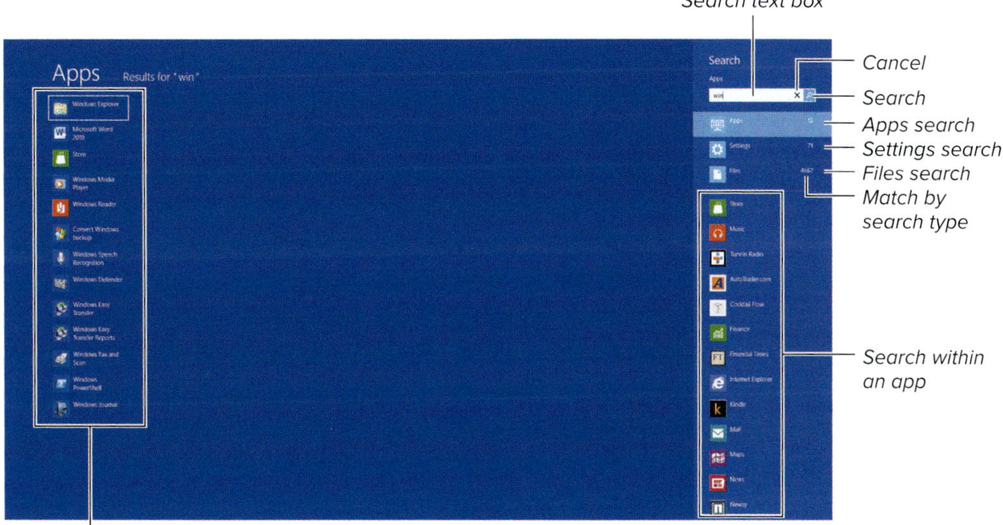


Ⓑ The tile-based Search app lets you search across app names, across settings (and Help topics), across filenames, and within individual tile-based apps.

- On the tile-based Start screen, start entering your search string, and Search opens with an Apps search.

- On the Desktop or in a tile-based app that supports the Search charm, press ⊞+Q. Search opens with an Apps search.

- On the Desktop, press ⊞+F. Search opens with a Files search.

- On the Desktop or in the tile-based interface, press ⊞+W. Search opens with a Settings search.

The "Search within an app" function is powerful and can save you a lot of time. If you search within Internet Explorer from here, the search is passed to your default search engine (which is Bing unless you change it). If you search within an app, then that app finds appropriate matches. People finds matching contacts; Music, Photos, and Videos find matching filenames; and the app Cocktail Flow shows you a matching drink. **C** shows matches to the search string "Win" in the Music app.

Notice that as you type a search string into the Search text box, Windows starts to display potential matches in the Search pane below the text box **D**. Those matches may get you where you want to go quickly.

**TIP** The tile-based interface Search supports wildcards and simple Booleans. Use ! to substitute for a single character, or * for multiple characters. Enclose a string with " " for an exact match of the string, and use "and" between search terms to search for matches to either string.

**TIP** Press Ctrl+Esc as an alternative to the ⊞ key. Many keyboards, especially older ones, don't come with a Windows key.

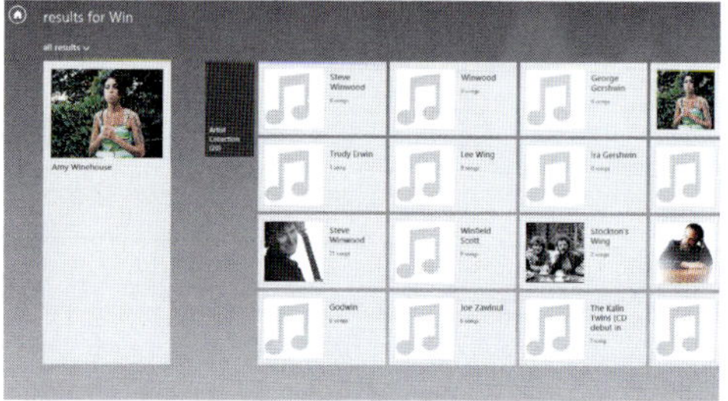

**C** The results of a search in the Music app

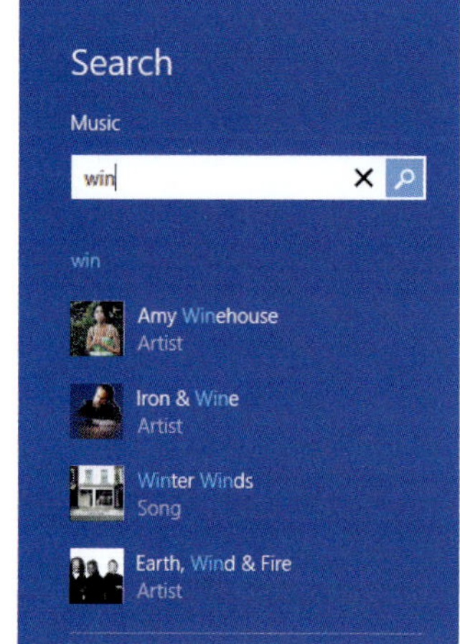

**D** Search gives you matches as you enter your search string.

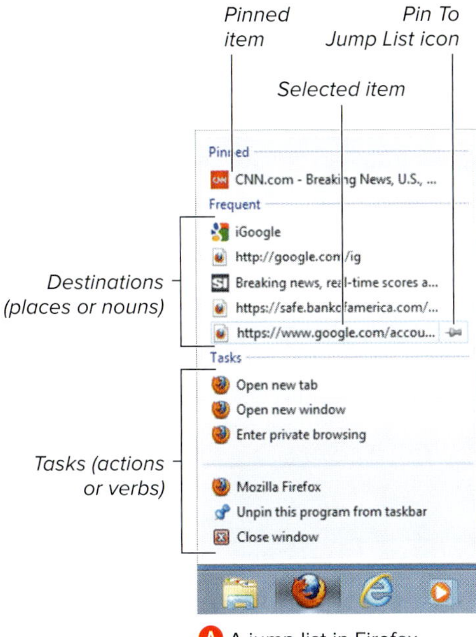



**A** A jump list in Firefox

# Jump Lists

A jump list **A** is a context menu for a Desktop taskbar icon. The list is organized into nouns and verbs and can contain useful actions. Nouns are categorized into pinned items, recent or frequent items, and custom categories. Tasks are usually separated into user tasks and taskbar tasks. What you see on a jump list is dependent on the application developer, but there are some development guidelines for jump lists—they are not just a list of the most recently used files that you see on most application's file menus.

## To use a jump list:

1. Right-click a taskbar icon on the Desktop.

   The icon displays a jump list **A**.

2. Select the command or object that you want to use.

   *or*

   Select an item so the Pin To Jump List icon becomes visible, and click that icon to have that destination always appear on the list.

   Only destinations can be pinned to the jump list.

**TIP** Items on a jump list can be dragged and dropped. For example, you can drag a document from a jump list to an email message.

**TIP** The jump lists for Start menu items are no more, because the Start menu is no more. However, jump lists were very popular and easy to use, and they served as the inspiration for the secondary tile feature in the tile-based interface in Windows 8.

# Sharing Content

The Clipboard allows you to share content between applications. You write selected content to volatile memory and then copy that content to another location using a Paste operation (Ctrl+V). You can choose to leave the content in the original location, which is a Copy operation (Ctrl+C), or delete the content you copy to the Clipboard, which is a Cut operation (Ctrl+X). The Clipboard supports the movement of rich data types, such as selected sets of files and folders, but it supports only one Copy operation at a time.

Third-party applications often extend the Clipboard to enable multiple stored operations, enable saving copied data, and other features. But wisely, Microsoft (and other operating system vendors) has opted to keep the Clipboard simple. Unlike previous versions of Windows, version 8 doesn't even come with a utility that lets you view the Clipboard. Applications such as Microsoft Office support an internal clipboard that is a stack and that allows you to perform multiple levels of undo and redo—but not Windows.

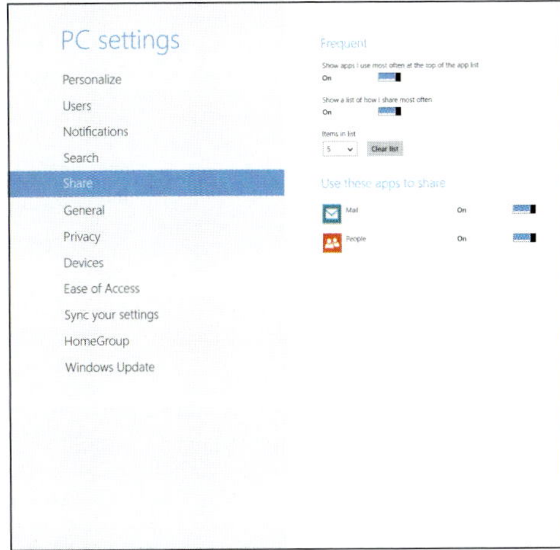



Ⓐ Enabling apps for sharing

Windows 8 introduces a new Sharing metaphor for tile-based applications that you access through the Share charm. Content can be shared between tile-based apps based on a "contract" between apps—a shared understanding about the nature of the relationship between the two apps. Thus, you can share pictures by using the Photos app with the Mail app.

What is shared and how an app uses the information is the app developer's decision. Sharing is a powerful new way for apps to interact.

## To enable sharing:

1. To open the Charms bar, press ⊞+C or swipe from the right edge. Click the Settings charm.

2. Tap or click the *Change PC Settings* link at the bottom of the bar, and then click the *Share* link in the left pane to view the Share settings Ⓐ.

3. Move the sliders to the right for the apps you wish to enable. As you add services such as Facebook, Twitter, and LinkedIn, they will appear on this page.

## To share a photo via email:

1. Open the tile-based Photos app, and select a photo.

2. Open the Charms bar, and tap or click the Share charm.

3. In the Share bar that appears on the right side of the screen, tap or click the Mail app 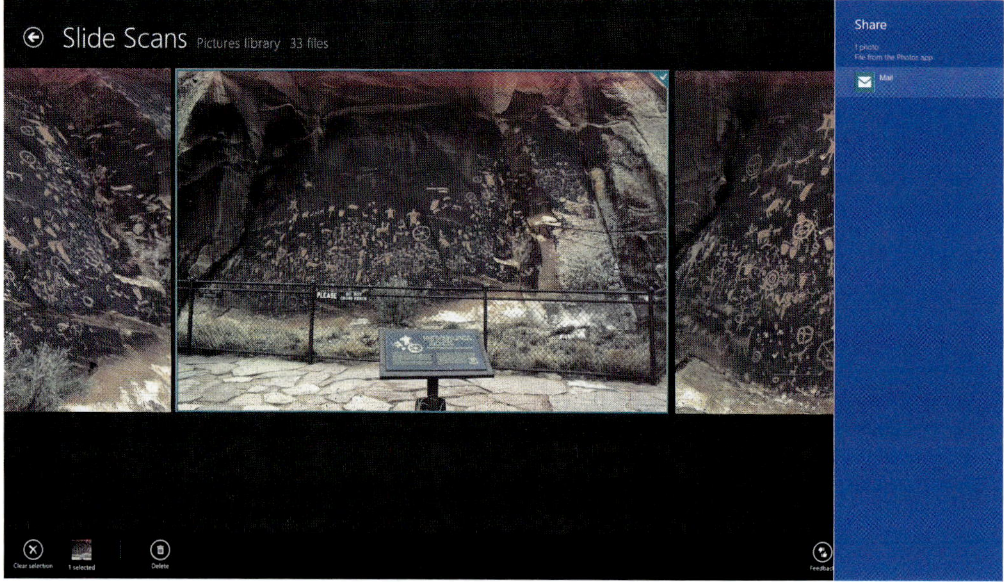.



**B** A photo is selected, and sharing with Mail is enabled.

4. Mail opens a message pane and attaches the photo to it. Enter an address, subject, and message, and then click the Send button to send the message on its way C.

**TIP** Although Internet Explorer isn't shown as a target app, it can serve as a source. If you see a webpage that you want to share, click the Share charm, select the Mail app from the list of target apps, and the page shows up referenced in the Mail app.

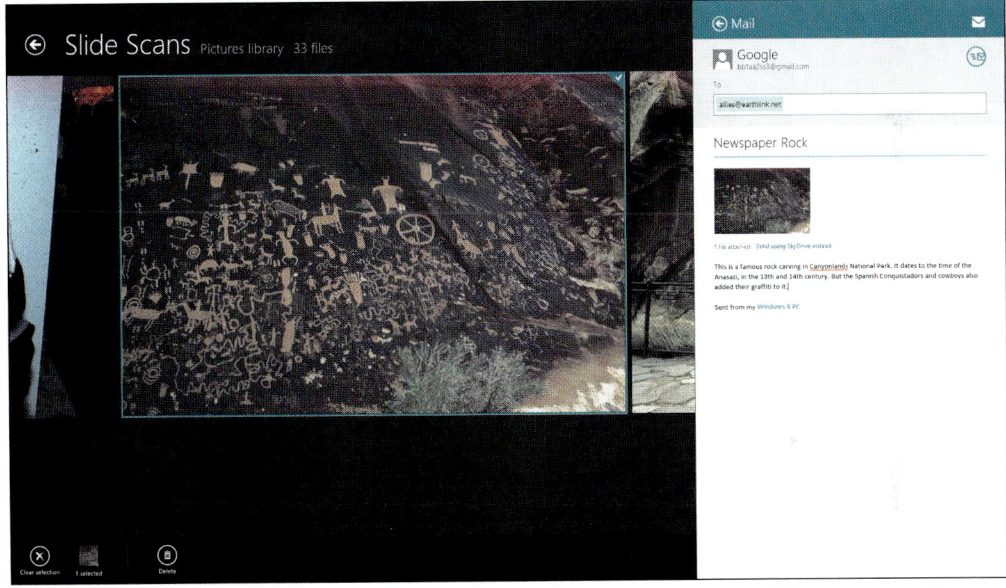


**C** Mail opens a message that allows you to send the photo directly through Mail.

# Putting It All Together

- A file is the building block of Windows, and files come in different file types.

- Learn to work with and use properties and metadata to organize your content and speed up your work.

- The Picker is a new touch-oriented utility for finding and selecting objects in the file system.

- A library is a special folder that can display folders from different locations together in a single place.

- Windows gives you four default libraries to work with: Documents, Music, Pictures, and Videos. But you can create your own custom libraries.

- Homegroups are network shares that allow you to make content available to other users logged into other systems.

- With the HomeGroup feature, you can share your libraries, stream video, share printers, and make content available to devices such as media-enabled televisions and Xbox 360 or PlayStation 3 consoles.

- The new tile-based Search function is powerful yet simple. You can search by apps, files, and settings or by using an individual app's content.

- A jump list is a context menu on a Desktop taskbar icon. A jump list can contain recent items accessed, favorite items, and tasks of various kinds. What's on a jump list is up to the developer.

- Use the Clipboard to cut, copy, and paste content from location to location. Although it is operationally simple, the Clipboard can support moving all sorts of rich data types.

- New to Windows 8 is an application sharing feature. Share allows one app to supply data or content to another app and provides the facilities to use that data immediately.

# Printers and Devices

If there is one area of technology that Windows leads in, it is device support. Since most desktop users are running Windows (and the operating system in second place isn't even close), manufacturers build printers, scanners, mice, displays, cameras, and other devices to work with Windows first and foremost. Microsoft has a long history of supporting device manufacturers, and it has developed a very rich device model.

Chances are that if you buy a mouse, keyboard, printer, display, or other device, it will work as soon as you plug it in—right out of the box. That's what Plug and Play (PnP) is supposed to do. Device support is built right into Windows, which is why the dialog boxes for mice, keyboards, displays, and printers all look roughly the same.

Windows recognizes simple devices such as keyboards or mice and applies a standard driver to them; that may be all that you need. However, any additional features added by the manufacturer—extra wheels or buttons on a mouse; programmable or non-standard keys on a keyboard; scan or fax features on a printer—will not be available from the default Windows drivers.

## In This Chapter

If you want those extra features to work, you will need to install the manufacturer's software and drivers.

Things do go wrong, and time changes all. Individual device support evolves over time, and not all device upgrades get pushed out over Windows Update, Microsoft's subscription upgrade system. So it's good to know how to upgrade and reinstall devices.

Windows 8 adds several new features to device support, primarily in the areas of touch-based app support, lightweight drivers, and better automated peripheral detection. Windows 8 can also automatically install a tile-based app from the Windows Store, provided that the manufacturer has made that app available.

In Windows 8, a new printer model was developed that can support a range of printers rather than just one specific printer. The intent is to have tile-based apps not rely on stored printer drivers, while supporting as many as 2500 of the most popular printers in use.

# Desktop Printer and Device Installation

In Windows, *printer* can refer to two separate entities: the physical printer and the printer software. The physical printer is the hardware device that creates output. The printer software is a virtual printer—a system containing a set of Input/Output routines and the configuration and management interface that translates program output into the mechanical actions that the hardware performs.

Physical printers are relatively low-speed devices, so printer software typically contains a buffer called a "print spooler" to store instructions until the physical printer can complete them. With a print spooler, you can continue working and specifying new print jobs while your old print jobs make their way from the queue to your printed output.

There are three basic ways to connect a printer to Windows 8:

- **Direct connections.** You plug a printer directly into your computer or tablet.

  About 75 percent of direct connections are made through USB ports, but Windows supports numerous other direct connections, including LPT, COM, and FireWire ports.

- **Wireless connections.** Most printers now come with a Wi-Fi transceiver, a Bluetooth transceiver, or both and can be detected by an access point or by a Bluetooth transceiver attached to your computer or device, often automatically.

  Thanks to the proliferation of tablets and smartphones, wireless printers (and other wireless devices) will become much more prevalent over time.

- **Network connections.** Most printers also now come with Ethernet connections and can be shared over a network. Windows can find network printers, access them, and print to them.

  The printer software that manages a network printer is called the *print server*, and through a print server, printers can be shared between computers.

  HomeGroup comes with capabilities for sharing a network printer in a workgroup.

Each of these methods of printer attachment requires its own driver type, but usually the printer installation software bundles them all in the same installation. To add a simple device or printer, just plug it in; if Windows recognizes and installs the printer, a dialog box will appear **A**. If your printer or device has additional features, use the manufacturer's installation software before you plug it in.

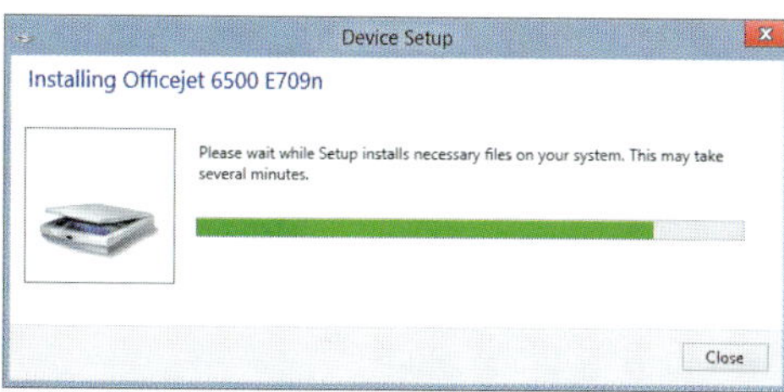



**A** When a device is automatically installed, you see a dialog box similar to this one.

## To install a local (directly connected or attached) printer from media:

1. Insert the CD or DVD that came with your printer into your device's optical drive.

2. Press ⊞+E, and open the optical disc's window.

3. Locate the Setup program and double-tap or double-click it to launch it.

4. Follow the installation wizard to completion.

5. You may be asked by User Account Control to allow the program to make changes. Click or tap Yes to continue.

   Steps in the wizard should ask you to name the printer, pick the printer port or specify a network printer, and perhaps share the printer (if it is a network printer), among other options.

6. Plug your printer into your personal computer or device when the software indicates that you should do so or after the software installation completes.

Note that the printer is attached at the end of the installation. If you attach the printer before performing the software installation, Windows may install a generic driver, which might not be the one you really want or the one that is the most up to date; in either case, you will not get all of the features that your printer is capable of.

If you do not have the installation disc, or if you want to install the latest version of the software, go to the manufacturer's website and download the software that contains the printer driver for your system. Then run that software directly.

If you want to simply install a print driver, use the Add Printer wizard.

**B** Open the Devices and Printers control panel from this link on the Control Panel home page.

## To install a printer driver using the Add Printer wizard:

1. Press ⊞+X or right-click the lower-left corner of the display to open the Computer Management menu; then select the Control Panel command.

2. On the Control Panel home page, click the *View devices and printers* link **B**.

3. In the Devices and Printers control panel, click the Add a Printer button **C**.

*continues on next page*

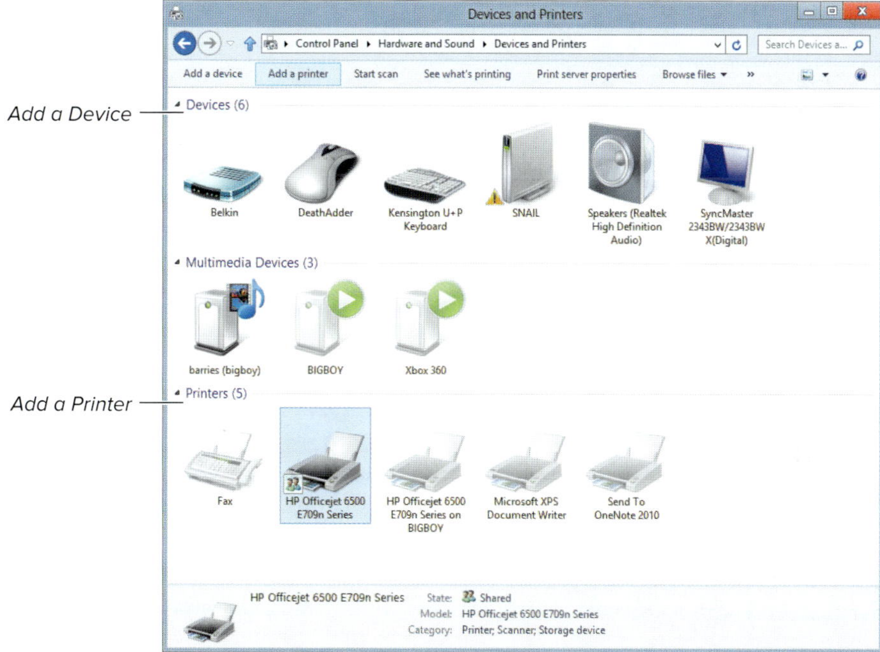

**C** Access the Add Printer wizard from the Devices and Printers control panel.

4. The Add Printer dialog box **D** appears, and Windows detects the available printers. Click the printer you wish to add, and click Next.

5. After adding the printer, the Add Printer wizard posts the dialog box shown in **E**. Enter the printer name, and click Next.

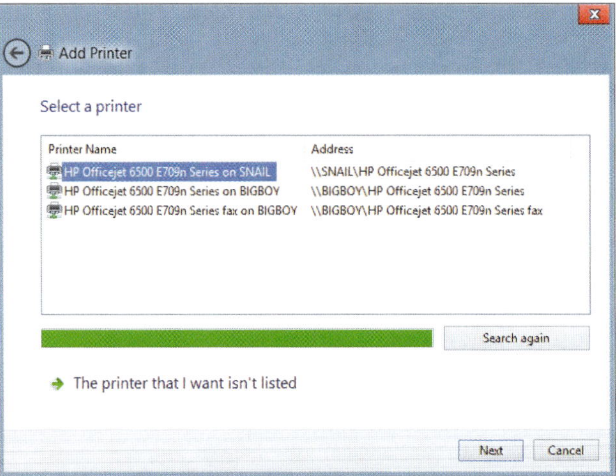


**D** Windows shows detected printers in the Add Printer dialog box.

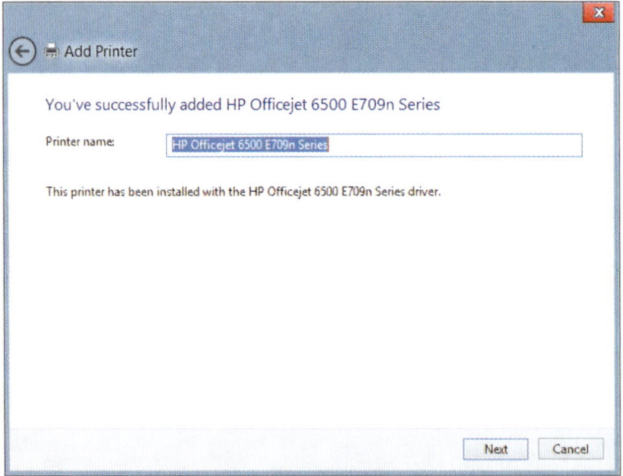


**E** This screen allows you to name your printer.

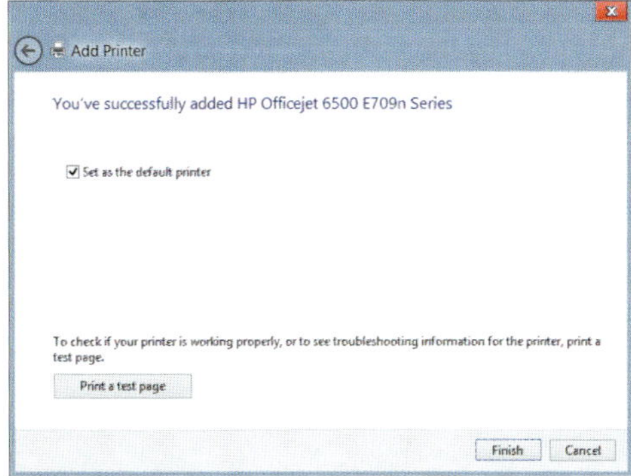



**F** The completion step of the Add Printer wizard

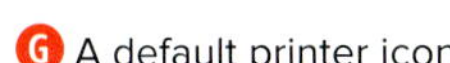

**G** A default printer icon

**6.** To set the new printer as the default, select the "Set as the default printer" check box **F**. Test the printer by tapping or clicking the Print a Test Page button. Click Finish.

When you designate a printer as the default printer, its icon displays a check mark **G**.

## To install a device using the Add Device wizard:

**1.** Press ⊞+X  or right-click the lower-left corner of the display to open the Computer Management menu; then select the Control Panel command.

**2.** On the Control Panel home page, click the *View Devices and Printers* link **B** in the Hardware and Sound section.

**3.** In the Devices and Printers control panel, click the Add a Device button.

**4.** The Add Device dialog box appears, and Windows detects the available devices. Click the device you wish to add, click Next, and finish the wizard.

**TIP** When you buy a new printer or device, don't assume that what came with the item is the latest software or even the correct software. Check the manufacturer's website to see if a better version of the software exists. This advice is particularly true when a new operating system is released. Although many devices come with software that performs automatic updating, many do not. It's a good idea to check the manufacturer's website to see if driver and software updates exist, and to install them if they do.

# Desktop Printing

Windows 8 printing from legacy (Desktop) applications is controlled by an application using operating system functions that are internal to Windows. That is, when you specify a print operation in an application, that application calls Windows system functions to send the output to the printer.

You can print from within an open file or directly from the Desktop—where you can print a single file, multiple files, or even multiple files from different applications.

If you are printing multiple documents or make a printing mistake, you will want to be able to manipulate the print queue. When you print to a device, Windows 8 places a Notification icon on the right side of the taskbar.

## To print a file from an application:

1. Open the file you want to print. Make sure that the Page Setup contains the options you want before printing.

2. Press Ctrl+P, or choose File > Print.

   A Print dialog box appears **A**. This dialog box will look similar in all applications. **A** shows the Print dialog box for Notepad, a simple text editor.

3. Tap or click the printer you wish to print to; the print options available to you may change when you do so.

4. Select any print options of interest to you, including the print range, the number of copies, collation, color options, and so forth. Tap or click Print.

   Windows 8 sends the print output to the print spooler for printing.

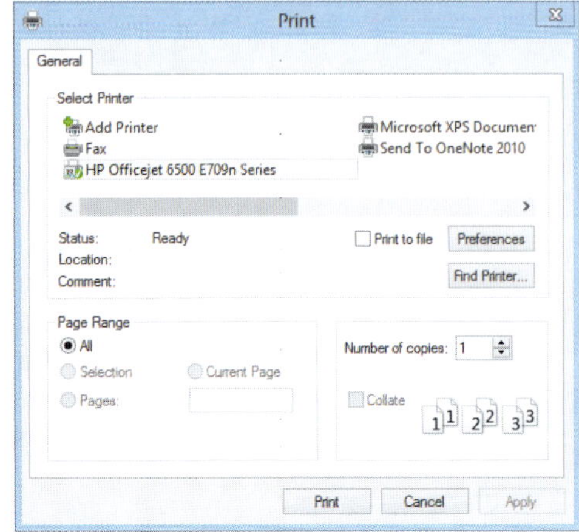

**A** A Print dialog box

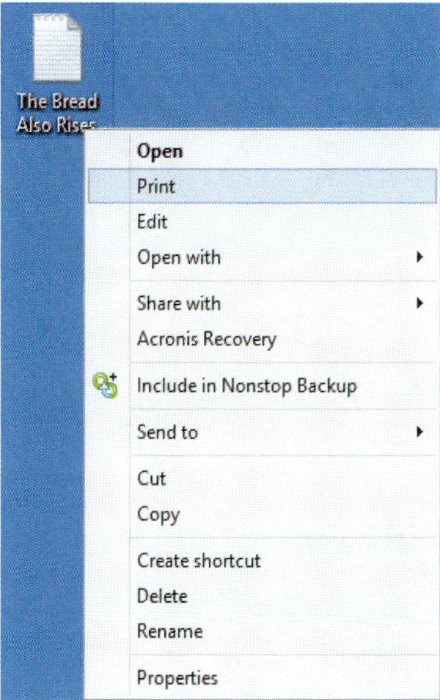

**B** The Print command on a file's context menu

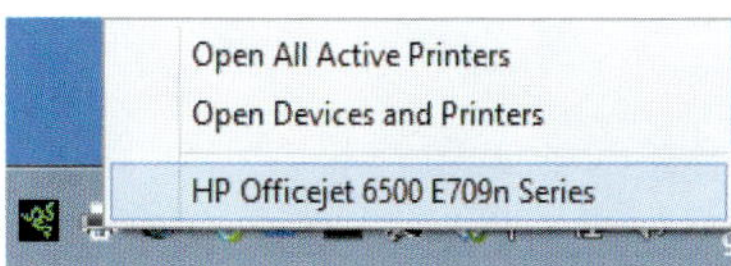

**C** The printer command opens this printer's print spooler.

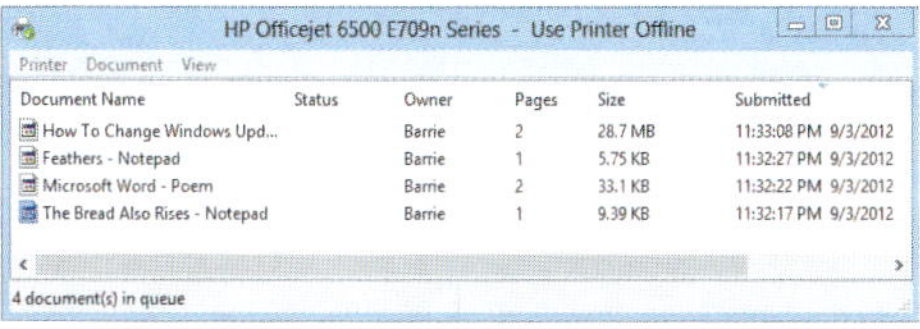

**D** A printer's print queue window

# To print files directly from the Desktop:

1. Select one or more files.

2. Right-click the selected file or files and select the Print command from the context menu **B**.

   *or*

   With the files selected, press Ctrl+P.

   Windows 8 will open the application responsible for the file, create the print job, send it to the spooler, and then close the application. If multiple file types are involved, Windows 8 opens the application for the second file type and prints those files. Any additional applications required for printing are opened and closed as needed.

# To view and modify a printer's print queue:

1. Tap and hold, or right-click, the printer's taskbar icon in the Notification area to view the Print Spooler menu **C**.

2. In the print queue window **D**, click the print job that you wish to modify.

3. From the Document menu, select Pause, Resume, Restart, or Cancel.

   From the Printer menu, you can connect to the printer, cancel all documents, pause printing, set the default printer, and perform other tasks.

**TIP** Use an application's Page Setup or Page Preview function to view your output before you print it. It will save time and expense.

# Start Screen Device Management

Devices and printers are managed differently in the tile-based UI than on the Desktop: Bringing a device or printer online is more automated, and there are fewer settings that you need to modfiy. That's to keep the settings you access from the Charms bar simple and accessible with your fingers. Devices are managed through the Devices section of the PC Settings screen. Let's take a look.

## To add a device to Windows 8 from the Start screen:

1. To view the Charms bar, swipe from the right side of your display or press ⊞+ C.

2. Tap or click the Settings charm **A**.

3. At the bottom of the Settings bar **B**, tap or click the *Change PC settings* link.

4. On the PC Settings page, tap or click the *Devices* link in the left-hand bar.

**A** The Settings charm

**B** The Settings bar

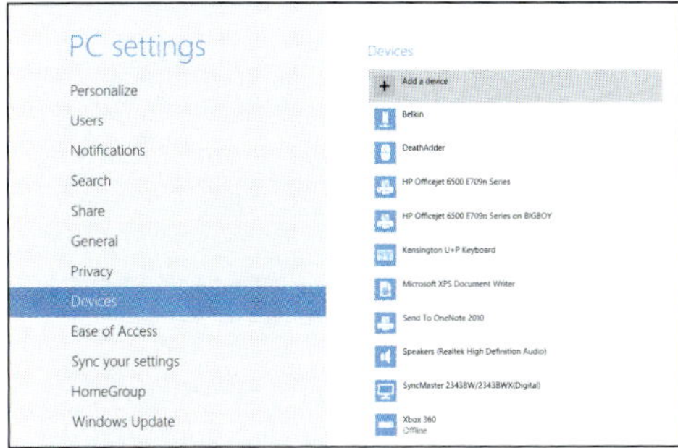



**C** The PC Settings Devices page

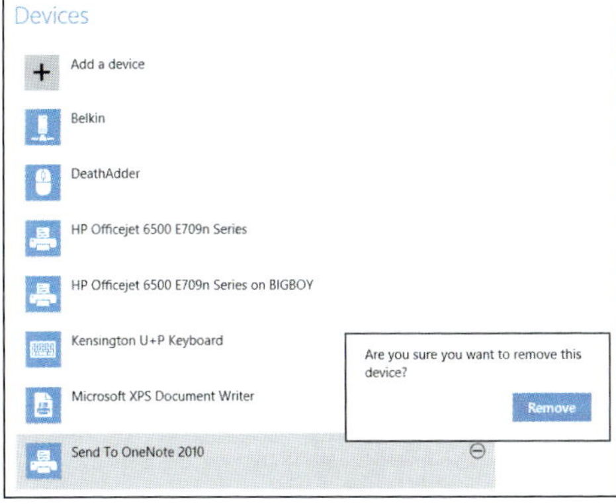



**D** The Device Removal dialog box

5. Tap or click the *Add a device* link in the main panel **C**.

6. Windows 8 opens a Searching for Devices dialog box that lists available devices. Tap or click the device you want to install on your system.

## To remove a device from your system:

1. On the PC Settings Devices page, tap or click the device that you want to remove.

2. Tap or click the Delete button that appears to the right of the device's button **D**.

3. In the "Are you sure you want to remove this device?" alert box, tap or click the Remove button.

That's pretty much all there is to device management in the new interface—it either works or it doesn't.

**TIP** You can print documents to files and use those files to print to devices later.

# Printing in Modern Apps

Printing in the tile-based UI is an app-specific function handled through the Devices interface. When you open the Devices charm, the devices you see are context sensitive. Whatever app or experience is currently open on your device, Windows 8 will populate the Devices pane with compatible devices. That is, each device is capable of printing the data that is output from the app.

### To print from a Modern app:

1. Press ⊞+K to open the Devices charm Ⓐ. If your printer is not on the list, add it by following the directions in the section "To install a printer driver using the Add Printer wizard."

2. Open the app that you want to print from.

3. Press Ctrl+P to open the Print bar Ⓑ.

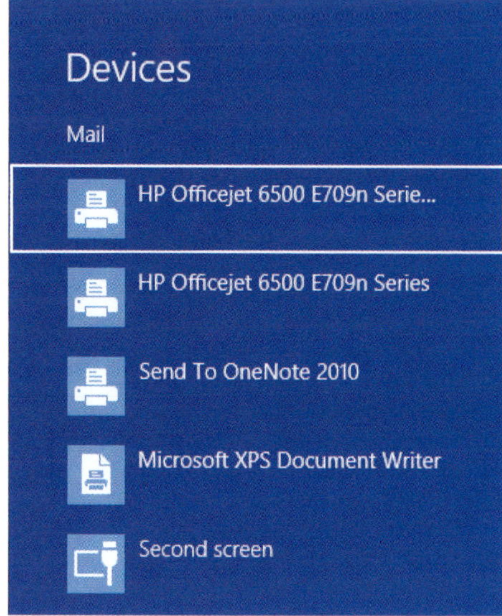

Ⓐ The Devices charm

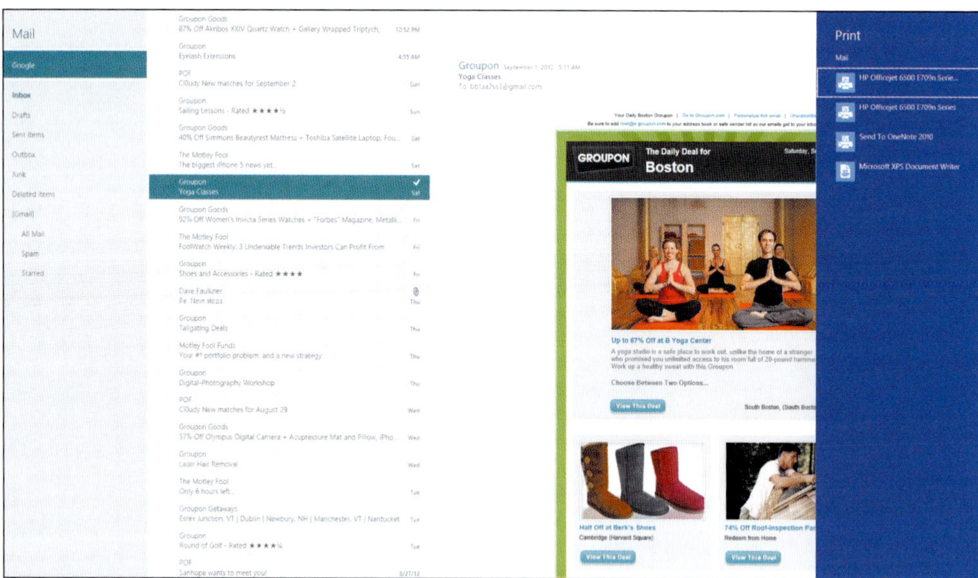

Ⓑ The Print bar

**C** The Print pane

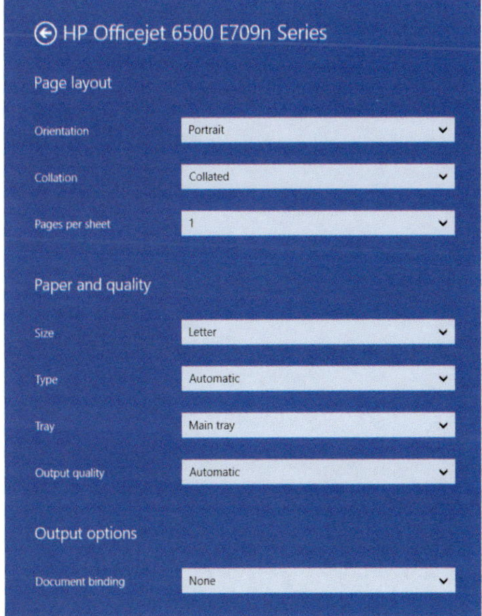


**D** The More Settings pane

4. Tap or click the printer you wish to use; the Print pane displays **C**.

5. Tap or click the print options you desire.

6. To explore additional settings, tap or click the *More settings* link **D**; return to the main Print panel using the Back button.

7. Tap or click the Print button to complete the operation.

**TIP** **Look for Print buttons in the interfaces of tile-based apps and in the Apps bar.**

# Device Manager

If you are using Windows RT on a Windows Phone 8 or tablet, then chances are that any device you need is already part of the package and has validated drivers. For PC users, though, adding new devices is part of the evolving experience you have with your system. At some point, you are going to upgrade your video card, add more memory, put in a sound card, or perform any of a hundred other changes. Or you might notice that a device doesn't work properly and wonder if it is functional. The one place you can go to check your system health down to an individual device level is the Device Manager.

Device Manager is a control panel applet that lets you view and control devices that are part of your system. That includes everything from chips on your motherboard to system components. When a device is malfunctioning, chances are that Device Manager will flag it for you and suggest some remediation. At least you'll be able to figure out what the offending component is.

In Device Manager you can do the following:

- Enable or disable a device

- Add a new driver for a device

- View device properties

## To view Device Manager:

- Press ⊞+X or right click the lower-left corner of the display to open the Computer Management menu, then select Device Manager.

- Press ⊞+W to search settings. Type **device manager**, and tap or click the Device Manager button.

- Press ⊞+R, enter **device manager** in the Run dialog box, and press Enter.

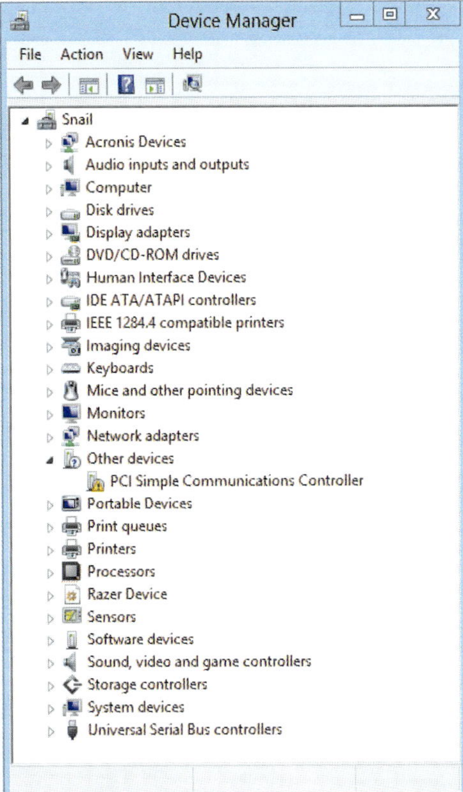



Ⓐ Device Manager

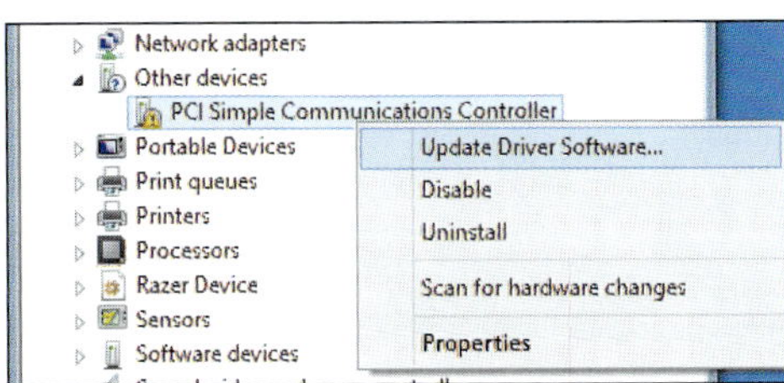



Ⓑ Update a driver using the Update Driver Software command on the context menu.

Whatever journey you took to get there, Device Manager appears Ⓐ.

A problematic device is shown open in its device type group. Here's what the status indicators mean:

- A gray downward arrow on the icon indicates that the device is disabled.

- A black exclamation point on a yellow triangle means that the device is not working properly.

- A yellow question mark indicates that the device isn't recognized.

- A blue I on a white field indicates that the device doesn't use the Use Automatic Settings feature.

Some standard error codes may appear next to the icon.

## To update a driver:

1. Right-click, or tap and hold, the device you wish to update to view the context menu Ⓑ.

2. Select the Update Driver Software command.

   Windows 8 will perform an automated search against its device driver database and attempt to perform the update.

**TIP** For a list of error codes and how to remediate them, go to support.microsoft.com/kb/310123. The Knowledge Base is Microsoft's internal service database, with detailed descriptions of problems and their solutions.

# Windows Update

Windows Update is Microsoft's push subscription service for system patches, device driver updates, device support, and security fixes. In these days of zero-day exploits, viruses, trojans, worms, and evolving hardware functionality, Windows Update is the front-line component for managing your device. (See Chapter 16 for more about these different security threats.)

Windows Update does the following things:

- Updates system software and components, including device drivers and hardware support

- Updates Microsoft software such as Internet Explorer, Microsoft Office, Windows Live applications, and some of Microsoft's developer tools

- Performs security updates (usually referred to as "patches") on the second Tuesday of each month, or as needed for more severe threats

You can choose to have Windows Update download updates and await your approval for installation, you can choose to have it automatically download and install updates, or you can disable it completely.

## To view Windows Update from the Start screen:

1. Press ⊞+W and enter **windows update** in the Settings text box.

2. Tap or click the Windows Update button.

   The Windows Update settings screen appears Ⓐ.

Windows Update is controlled more completely from inside its control panel app.

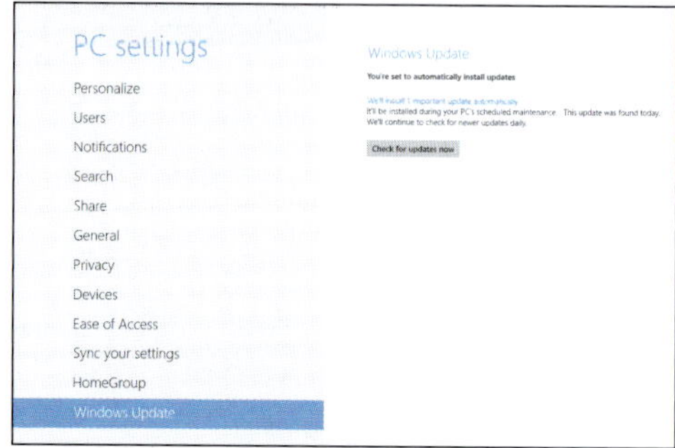


Ⓐ Windows Update settings screen

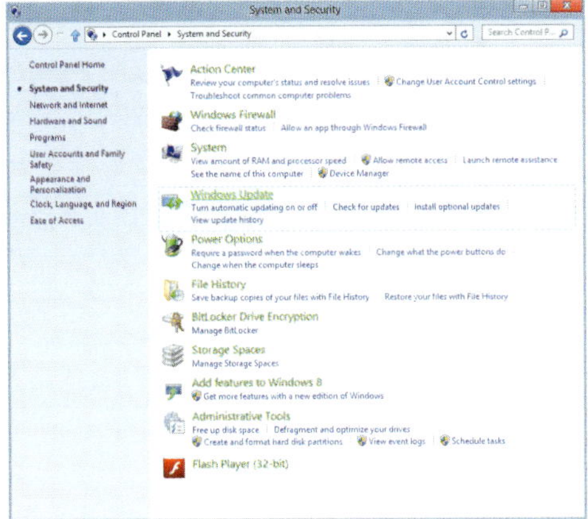

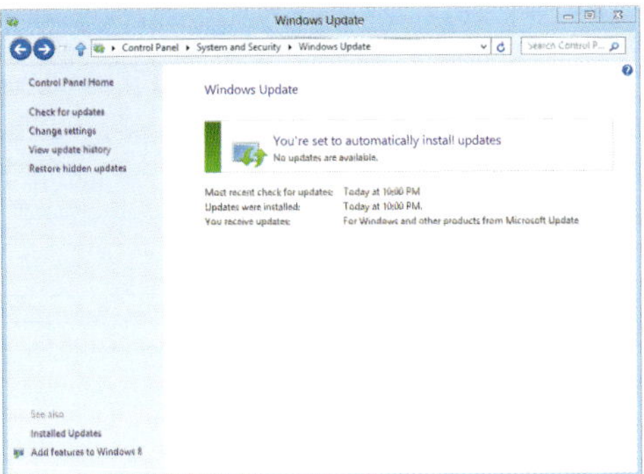

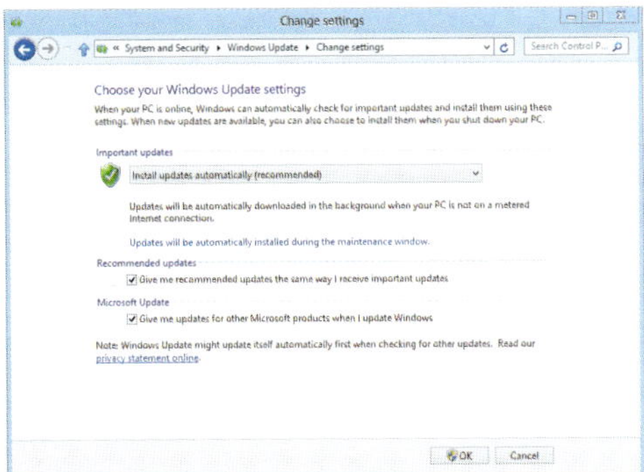

**B** The System and Security control panel

**C** The Windows Update control panel

**D** The Windows Update Change Settings control panel

## To change settings in the Windows Update control panel:

1. Press ⊞+X or right-click the lower-left corner of the display, and select the Control Panel command from the Computer Management menu.

2. Tap or click the *System and Security* link, then tap or click the *Windows Update* link **B**.

   The Windows Update control panel appears **C**.

3. Tap or click the *Change settings* link. View and change the current settings via the drop-down menu **D**.

4. Tap or click OK to enforce your new settings.

**TIP** Windows 8 lists updates that were applied by Windows Update in the Installed Updates control panel. Click the *Installed Updates* link in the Windows Update control panel to access this feature. You can remove a badly behaving update from that location, but the need to do that is rare indeed.

**TIP** It is recommended that you apply all updates to your system as soon as they are available. A Windows 8 installation is not considered complete until all updates are applied.

# Putting It All Together

- *Printer* refers to the hardware device used to print as well as to the software used to create and manage a print job.

- To connect a complex device or printer, use the manufacturer's software before you install the hardware.

- For simple devices, the generic drivers in Windows 8 may be all that you need, so just plug them in.

- Use the Devices and Printers control panel to see what is installed on your system and to access the Add Printer and Add Device wizards.

- Printing is controlled by applications, but the actual print system is a Windows system component.

- When you print, you create a print job, which is sent to a print queue (spooled) for the physical printer to print. You can manage the documents in the print queue.

- Windows 8 apps use a driverless print model, and printing is performed through the Settings and Devices charms.

- Use Device Manager to see what is attached to your personal computer and to troubleshoot problems.

- Windows Update is Microsoft's subscription push service for keeping your system current and secure. Apply all updates as soon as they are issued.

# 10

# Windows 8 Explorer

Windows Explorer is the central utility used to work with the Windows file system. It will play a major role in your everyday work: finding and selecting files and folders; searching for content; copying, pasting, moving, and deleting objects; and altering file and folder attributes—among many other things.

With the Windows 7 Start menu's powerful search function gone and the tile-based interface's search being incomplete, Explorer is where you can perform sophisticated searches in Windows. Get to know Explorer well and it will speed up your work.

Microsoft has enhanced Explorer from previous editions, adding a context-sensitive Microsoft Office-style ribbon. The Explorer interface now contains a better pane for previewing content, better tools for working with libraries, and improved property (metadata or tags) handling. Microsoft has also improved file operations such as copy and move, and although these differences are relatively minor, they are valuable.

## In This Chapter

# The Explorer Interface

Windows Explorer opens to display a file tree in the Navigation pane on the left, a Content pane in the middle, and a Display or Preview pane on the right. **A** shows Explorer with its ribbon open. That ribbon is context-sensitive and will open a different tab depending upon the current selection. You can modify what you see in the Explorer window by selecting options on the ribbon or from menus. The Layout group allows you to view the contents of a folder in many different ways: as icons, as tiles, by content, in a detailed spreadsheet-like style, and so forth. You can suppress the ribbon by toggling the Ribbon button on the right.

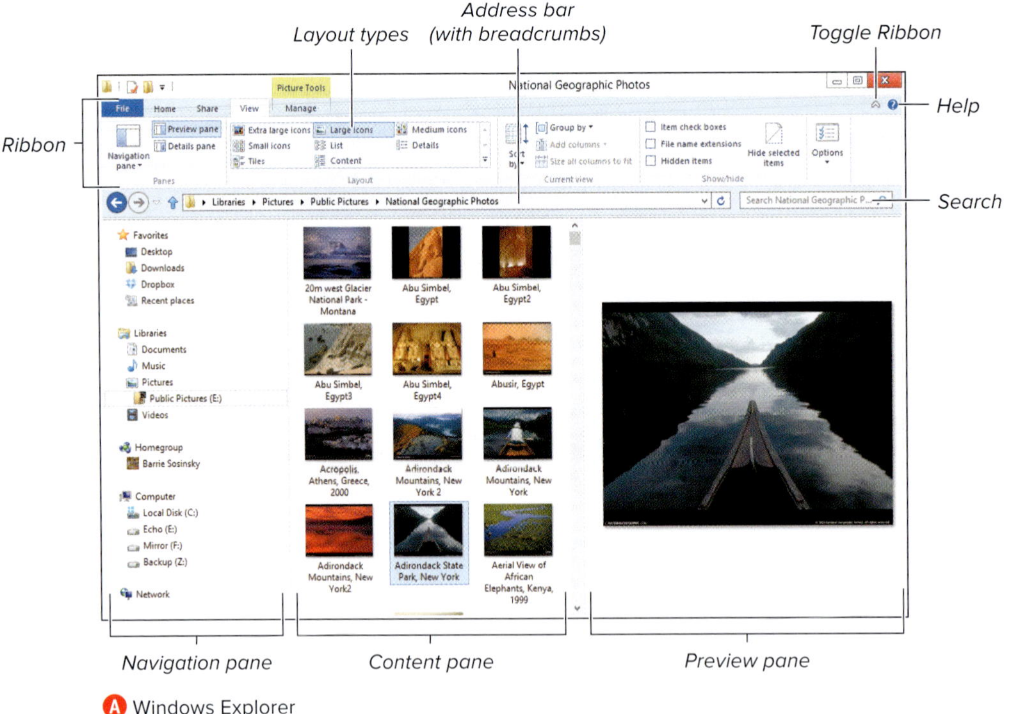


**A** Windows Explorer

Explorer uses the address bar to indicate your current position in the file system with a "breadcrumb." If you click in the address bar, the breadcrumb turns into a file path that you can copy and paste (for example, **E:\Public\Pictures\National Geographic Photos**). Click an element of the breadcrumb, and Explorer moves your view to that location.

When you click the Explorer tile in the tile-based interface, Explorer opens by default to the top of your libraries, which are virtual folders that can contain pointers to folders in many locations. The Refresh button updates the location in the address bar. The search functionality in Explorer is accessed by entering a search string into the Search box to the right of the address bar.

**TIP** You can move from tab to tab in Explorer by using the keystroke Alt+first letter. To move to the Home tab, for example, press Alt+H. When you do, you will notice that small boxes containing letters will appear on the ribbon. Enter the key shown to activate the feature you desire.

**TIP** If you click the Options button on the View tab of the ribbon, the Folder Options dialog box will open. This dialog box allows you to modify the way folders open in Explorer, the items you see in the Navigation pane, click behavior, what you can view, and how searching is performed. Windows hides system files and folders by default. As you become a more advanced user, you may need to access these items, and the Folder Options dialog box is where you do that.

# The File System

A disk drive can have one or more volumes, but volumes can have only one file system. The Windows file system is hierarchical and structured like a tree's canopy (A). Strangely, though, the top folder of the file system is called the "root," and each folder is a branch that can contain other folders or files. Folders represent positions in the file system; files are containers that hold data of various kinds and are classified by file type. Explorer gives you a flattened view of the file system.

There's one extra complexity you should be aware of: The file system can contain "virtual objects" (drives, folders, and files). In Unix or Linux these objects are called "pointers"; they point to a real object somewhere else. Windows calls these virtual objects *shortcuts*.

Several objects that you see, such as the Desktop and My Documents folders, are shortcuts to the same named folders in your user profile, found at *<Drive Letter>*/Users/*<User Name>*, but they are shown in artificial positions in the file system hierarchy that Explorer displays. Libraries are special virtual folders that can point to multiple locations on a local file system, as well as on other file systems. With this as background, let's run Explorer through its paces.



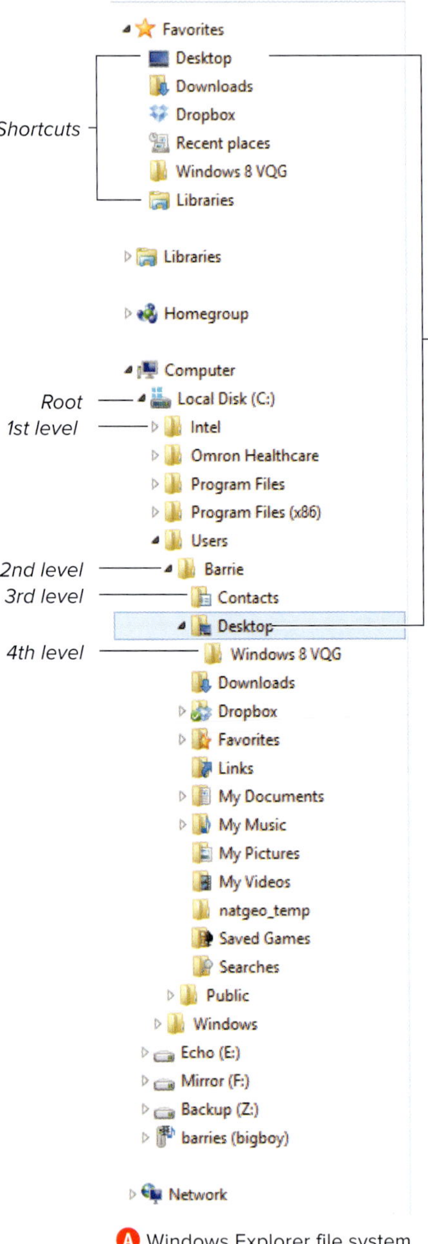 Windows Explorer file system

**B** Windows Explorer tile
in the metro interface

**C** Windows Explorer icon
in the desktop taskbar

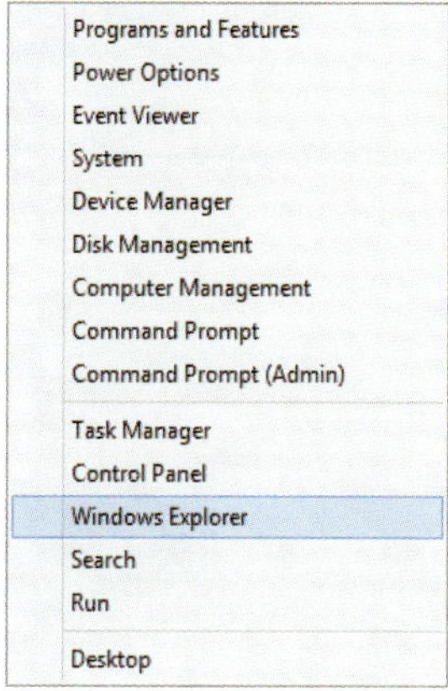

**D** Windows in
the Computer
Management menu

## To open Explorer:

- To show the Libraries folder, click the Explorer tile **B** in the tile-based interface, or the Explorer icon **C** in the Desktop taskbar.

- Right-click the lower-right corner of the Desktop, and select Windows Explorer from the Computer Management menu **D**. Explorer opens a system and devices view.

- To open Explorer to the Computer view **E**, with storage devices and a Computer ribbon, press ⊞+E.

**TIP** If there is a folder that you commonly use, you can add it to the Favorites section of the Navigation pane for easy access. Open the folder in the Content pane, right-click the Favorites icon, and select Add Current Location for Favorites from the context menu. The folder will now be listed whenever Explorer opens. You can also drag and drop folders to the Favorites list.

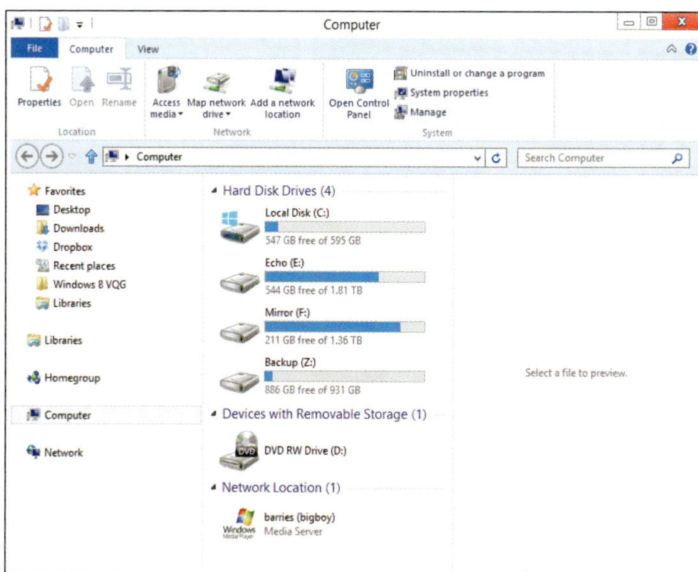

**E** Computer view

# Moving Around

Notice that in Ⓐ from the section "The File System," the word *Desktop* is selected, or highlighted in blue. Also notice that Ⓐ in "The Explorer Interface" has the words *Public Pictures* highlighted. Selections indicate your current position in the file system. To perform an action in Windows Explorer, you need to move to a position in the file system containing the object you want to examine or modify.

Let's consider how you can use Explorer to move around in the file system.

## To move directly to a place in the file system from anywhere:

Type the path directly into the address bar Ⓐ in Explorer, and then press Enter.

For example, type **C:** to go to the root directory of your C drive, or **C:\Users\<User Name>\My Documents** to go to your My Documents folder.

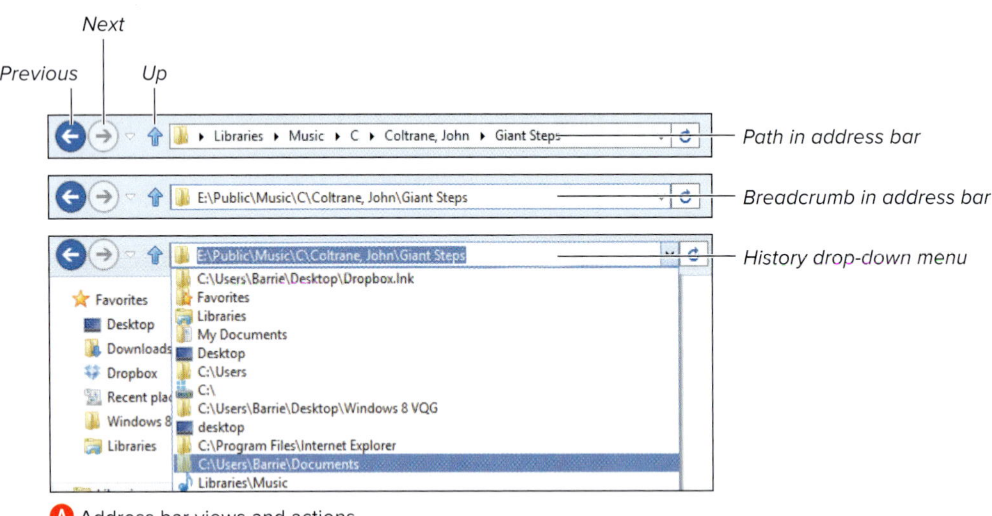


Ⓐ Address bar views and actions

## To move to a special virtual folder:

Enter the name of the folder (**Favorites**, **Desktop**, **Libraries**, and so on) into the address bar, then press Enter.

## To move to one of the folders in your current path:

Click any object in the breadcrumb to move to that folder.

## To move to a folder in Explorer:

Click the folder in the Navigation pane or Content pane.

## To move to your next or previous position:

Click the Previous or Next buttons. You can also press Alt+Left Arrow or Alt+Right Arrow, respectively, to perform the same task.

These buttons work just like they do in a browser.

## To move up a level:

Click the Up button or press Alt+Up Arrow.

## To move down a level:

Double-click a folder; or click once to select the folder, and then press Enter.

## To move to a place you've been before:

Click the arrow to the right of the address bar, and select the location from the History list.

**TIP** If you find that you need frequent access to a file or folder in a specific location, create a shortcut to it. To create a shortcut, right-click a blank portion of the Content pane and select **New > Shortcut** from the context menu. Then, in the Create Shortcut dialog box, click the Browse button, click **Next**, give the shortcut a name, and then click Finish.

# Working with Files

A file is an object in the file system that can store data. Files can be text, pictures, music, video, and so forth. Some file formats are universal; for example, TEXT (TXT), JPEG, RTF, and TIFF files can be interchanged (opened by) various programs. Other files are native (proprietary) to applications, such as DOCX to Microsft Word or PDF to Adobe Acrobat.

Windows does a good job indicating the file type by displaying an icon that is specific to that kind of file. A file also takes a three- or four-letter extension, such as .docx, that provides the file association with the program. However, Windows hides the file extension unless you set a hidden option to show them.

Explorer lets you work with files, open them, alter their properties, and perform a variety of tasks. Let's see how.

## To select a file:

Locate the file in the file system, and click once on the file to select it (which will highlight it).

## To select multiple files from the same folder:

- To select files located next to each other (a range), hold the Shift key and click the start and end of the range.

- To select files located next to each other (a range), drag a selection rectangle around your selection.

- To select files that are discontinuous, press Ctrl and click each item in your selection in turn.

## File Types

Some files store text characters in ASCII format. Letters, numbers, and symbols are all considered text—128 of them, along with another 128 symbols for old typewriter operations such as carriage return, ring the bell, and so forth. Word processor files contain additional formatting data and code; they are binary files. Picture files come in types such as JPEG, TIFF, PNG, and WMF. Files that are based on industry standards are meant to be opened by many different programs and are called *interchange formats*. Most picture files are compressed to save space.

Some files are meant to be opened only by the program that created them. Those are called *native formats*, and they are proprietary. For example, Microsoft Excel saves spreadsheets in the XLSX format, which is native, along with CVS and other formats that are standards. Non-native, or interchange, file formats require translators be written to read or write to a format.

**TIP** If you start to type the name of a file, Explorer will move to the first matching file name and select it.

**TIP** You can select two or more items only from the same folder; you can't select items from different folders.

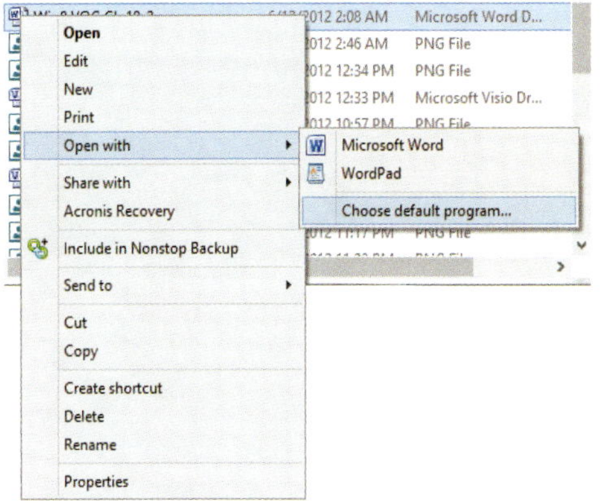

**A** A context menu for a selected file

## To select all items in a folder:

Click the Select All button in the Select group of the Home tab of the ribbon, or press Ctrl+A.

## To deselect all items in a folder:

Click the Select None button in the Select group of the Home tab of the ribbon, or click anywhere on a blank area of the folder.

## To invert your selection:

Click the Invert Selection button in the Select group of the Home tab of the ribbon. This option is valuable when you have a complex set of items selected and want to delete the items that are *not* selected.

Once a file or files are selected, you can move, copy, delete, or rename them, examine or alter properties, and more.

## To open a file or files:

- Double-click a file to open it in its default program.

- With a file or files selected, press Enter. All selected files open in the programs that they are associated with.

- To open a file with its default program, right-click the file name and select Open **A** from the context menu.

- Enter a path into the address bar with the file name at the end of the path, and press Enter.

## To change the default program that opens a file:

1. Tap and hold, or right-click, and select Open With **Ⓐ** from the context menu.

2. Select Choose Default Program from the submenu.

3. Select the program from the How Do You Want To Open This File? dialog box **Ⓑ**.

   *or*

   Click the *More Options* link, then scroll the list.

   If the program isn't on the list, use the *Look for an app in the Store* link or the *Look for another app on this PC* link to view other options.

4. Select the Use This App For All Files check box to make this program the default program for opening this file type.

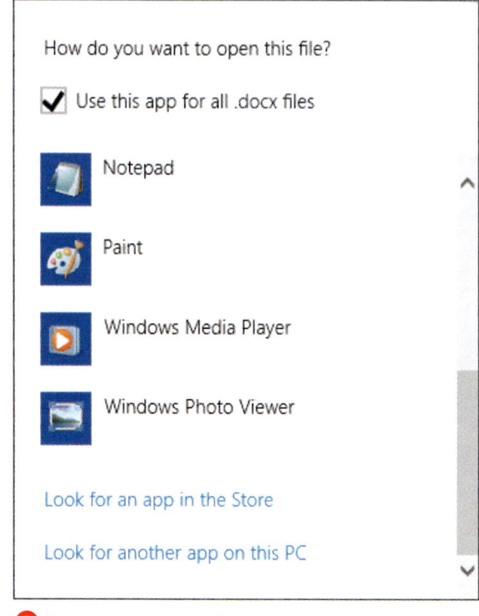


**Ⓑ** Program selection list

## To work with the Clipboard:

With a file selected, the Home tab of the ribbon is shown **Ⓒ**. This tab has buttons that allow you to perform file operatons.

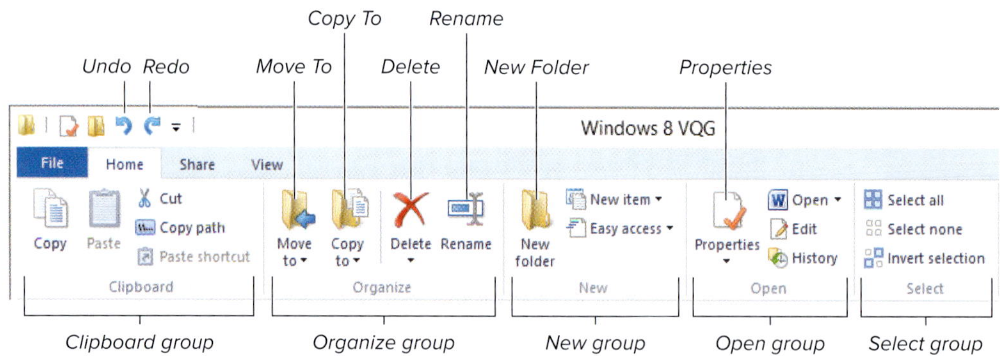


**Ⓒ** The Home tab of the ribbon

- Use the Cut, Copy, and Paste buttons
  Ⓒ in the Clipboard section of the
  ribbon to move a selection to the
  Clipboard, to copy a selection to
  the Clipboard, or to place what is
  on the Clipboard at your current location, respectively. Or press Ctrl+X,
  Ctrl+C, or Ctrl+V, respectively.

- Use the Copy To or Move To buttons in
  the Organize section of the ribbon to
  place your selection in another location.

**TIP** If you want to restore or undo your deletion, click the Undo button on the Quick Access toolbar or press Ctrl+Z. If you change your mind again, the Redo button or Ctrl+Y redoes an undo.

## To delete a file or folder

With the file or folder selected, click the Delete icon, or press Delete.

## To change a file or folder name:

- Click Rename. Explorer places the
  name of the file into an edit text box for
  you to alter.

- Click New Folder to create new folders
  and files.

- Use the buttons in the Open section to
  open files or to alter the file's properties.

## To pause a copy or move operation:

When you copy or move a file or folder, Windows displays a file transfer dialog box 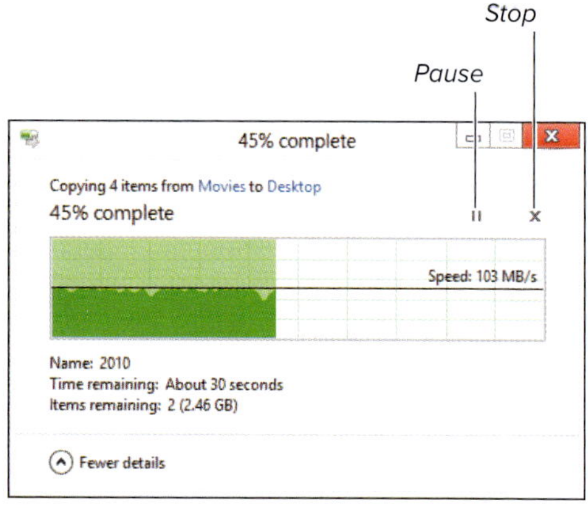 that shows the progress of the transfer or move. This new feature allows you to pause an operation that is taking too long or to delay the operation until a more convenient time. Yeah!

Click the Pause button ( ‖ ).

## To end a copy or move operation:

Click the Stop button ( X ).

This new dialog box shows transfer rates graphically and numerically and gives a much more accurate indication of the time remaining than previous versions did.

**TIP** The ribbon can be navigated completely with your keyboard. Hold the Alt key and press a tab name's first letter. When you release that keystroke, a set of boxes with letters will appear. Press a letter to activate that ribbon feature.



**D** File transfer dialog box

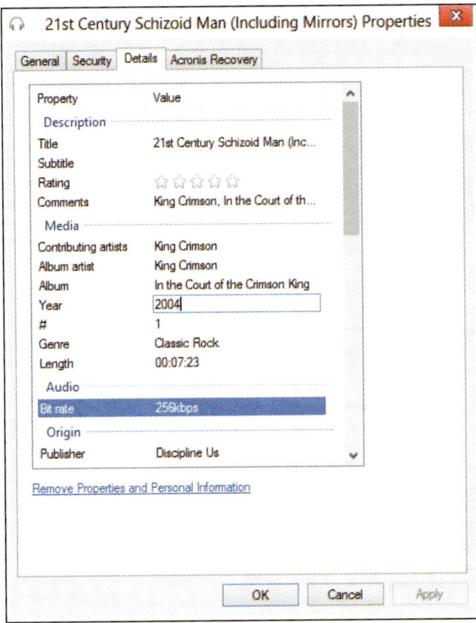



**A** File properties

# Properties

Files have descriptive data written into them that tells a viewer more information about the file's contents. Data about data is called *metadata*, but the Windows operating system calls this data *properties*. Properties are also called *tags* or *attributes* **A**.

Properties are important because they control what you see in Explorer and how you see it. Properties allow you to organize your content, search for and find items, back up and protect your files, and much more.

## To view and modify an object's properties in the file system:

- Select the object, right-click it, and select the Properties command.

- With the object selected, click the Properties button on the Home tab of the ribbon.

## To view properties in the Details view of a folder:

Not all properties can be edited from within a Properties dialog box; it depends on the file type. Music files and photos are two categories of objects for which a large number or properties may be edited. An example of an MP3 music file's Properties dialog box is shown in **B**.

To get some idea of how this affects your view in Explorer, lets take a look at the Details view of this music album **B**.

1.  Open the folder of interest.

2.  Click the View tab, then click the Details button to change to that view.

3.  Right-click the column header to view the properties that are displayed as columns in that view.

4.  Click a property to enable its view (add the check mark) in the listing; or click to disable the view of a property (remove the check mark).

**TIP** Notice that the folder is sorted by the Name property. You can sort on any property by clicking the Sort arrow to the right of the column (property) name. Just as you can in a spreadsheet, you can drag a column header border to resize the column, and you can drag the header itself to move the column from left to right.

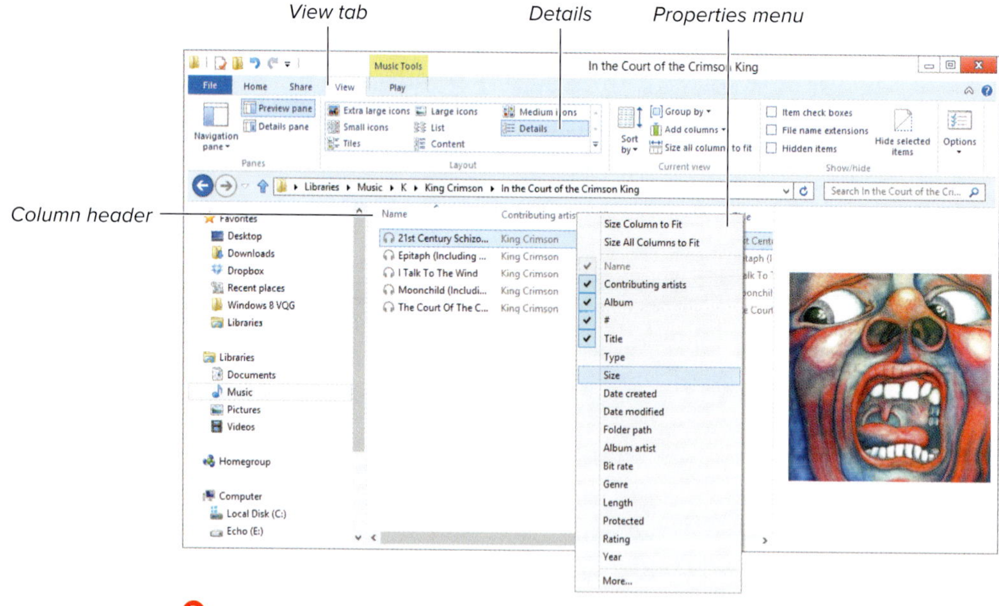



**B** MP3 file properties

# Searches

One of the more important functions that Windows Explorer provides in Windows 8 is an advanced search capability. There's nowhere else in Windows that offers this capability (although there are third-party tools that do so).

When you click in the Search box to the right of the address bar, Explorer displays a Search tab that provides a number of search options 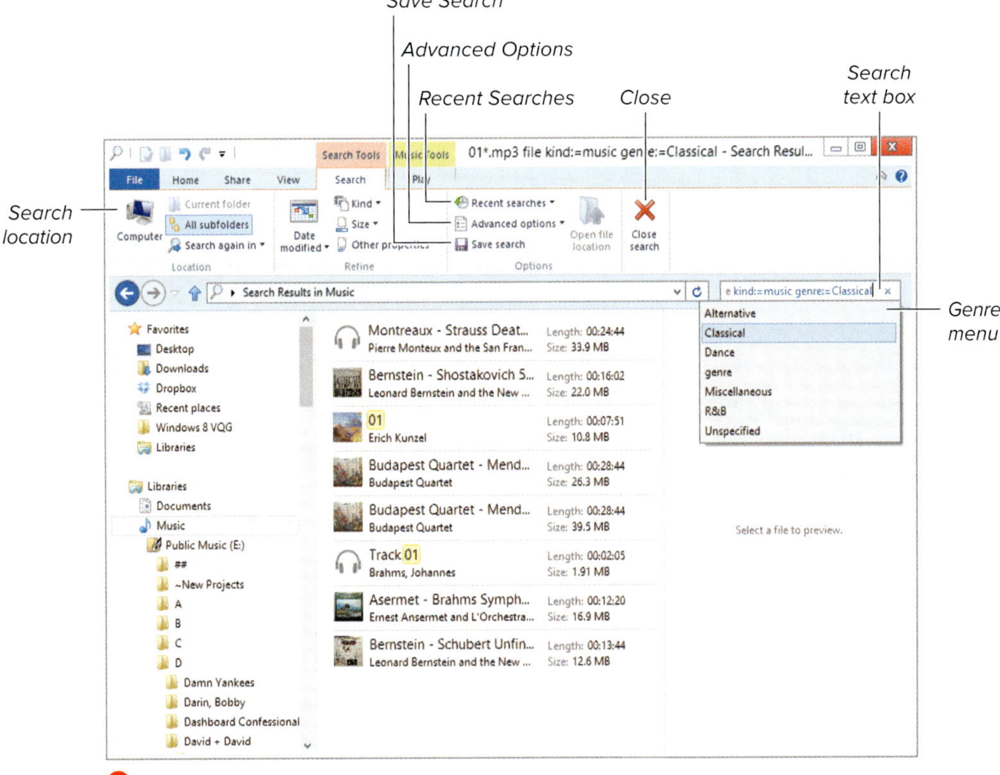



**A** The Search Tools tab of the ribbon

## To perform a simple search:

- Enter a search string in the Search text box, and then press Enter.

- Use the wildcard * for any string of characters, and ? for a single character.

- Use " " (quotation marks) around text to perform an exact search for the content in the string.

## To perform an advanced search:

- To sort by location, click the buttons in the Location group of the ribbon and select a search drive or folder.

  The default is to search all subfolders, but you can use Search in your Home group, your libraries, or on the Internet.

- Sort by Date Modified, Kind, Size, or Other properties by clicking the buttons in the Refine group. You might search by date to find work you did yesterday or last week.

When you select these filters from the Refine group on the Search ribbon, Explorer enters the filter into the Search box to accompany the string you search for. In the example Ⓐ, the filter for Genre was selected from Other Properties and the drop-down menu appeared in the Search box, letting you select Classical from the choices.

## To perform a search you have recently done:

Click the Recent Searches button in the ribbon, and select the search from the drop-down menu.

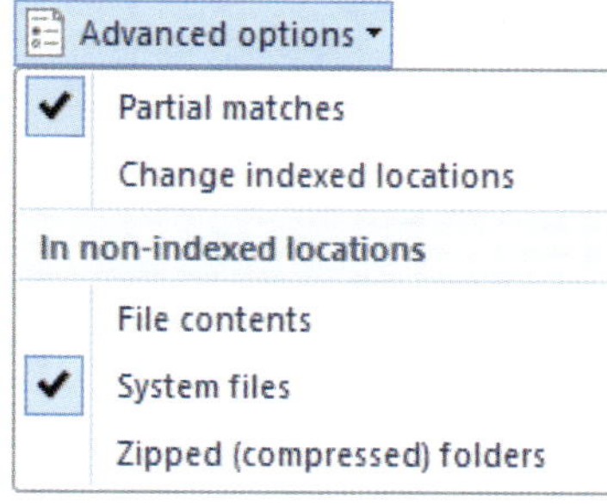

**B** Advanced Options menu. You can select multiple options on the Advanced Options menu.

## To use advanced options:

- Select the Change Indexed Locations command from the Advanced Options drop-down menu **B** to move searches to different indexed locations.

- Select Partial Matches to search for partial matches to your string at your current location.

- Select the File Contents command to search within a file's content.

- Select the Change Indexed Locations command, and then select that location in the Indexing Options dialog box that the appears to move searches to different indexed locations.

- Select the Zipped (compressed folders) command in the Advanced Options menu to search within zipped or compressed files.

## To save a search for later use:

1. Perform your search.
2. Click the Save Search button.
3. Give the search a name you can remember.

## To close a search:

Click the Close button (X) to the right of the Search ribbon; or click another folder, object, or location.

**TIP** Searching indexed locations is much faster than searching non-indexed locations. If you find a location that you intend to search regularly, index it.

**TIP** A library can organize an information type across multiple locations—music or photos, for example. Library searches are therefore very powerful.

# Putting It All Together

- Windows Explorer is a desktop application that lets you view the contents of your file systems.

- You can open Explorer from its tile, from a taskbar icon, from the Desktop Start (management) menu, or by simply typing **explorer** when you are on the Start screen.

- Explorer shows you content in several panes: a Navigation pane, a Content pane, and a Preview pane.

- What you see on the ribbon is context sensitive and changes depending upon what is currently selected.

- The file system is a hierarchical tree structure, and Explorer shows you a flattened view of it.

- Some special virtual folders act as shortcuts, or pointers, to various locations important to the user. Some of these special folders (such as the Libraries folder) can show you the contents of several locations at once.

- You can use the Navigation pane, ribbon, and other Explorer tools to move around the file system.

- You can edit the properties for files, folders, and other objects within Explorer.

- Files have file types that define how the content is handled by Windows applications.

- Explorer offers the means to access object properties, and those properties affect what you see inside Explorer.

- Explorer is the most advanced location in which you can perform searches to find and organize content.

# Diagnosis and Recovery

There are many ways in which Windows 8 can misbehave. Hardware can be defective, third-party software can be poorly written, or a combination of circumstances that hasn't been fully tested can crash the system. The upside of Windows is that it supports more programs and devices than any other operating system.

This chapter describes two ways you can use to figure out what has gone wrong on your system: Windows Task Manager and Windows Recovery Environment. Task Manager displays what is running on your system. It also offers the ability to end applications and processes. Windows 8 borrowed from Microsoft's server technologies to give Task Manager a very significant upgrade.

Sometimes problems are easier to fix than they are to figure out; other times your system fails and you need to restart from a known good state. The Windows 8 team reconceptualized what to do with a malfunctioning computer and came up with the equivalent of a reset button: the Windows Recovery Environment. It allows you to refresh your system or even restore it to a factory new condition.

# Task Manager

Task Manager is Windows 8's premier diagnostic tool for examining the applications, processes, services, and performance characteristics of your system. A version of Task Manager has shipped with every version of Windows desktop and server since Windows 3.1. The version in Windows 8 contains a number of improvements that desktop users haven't seen before, many of which carry over from Microsoft's server operating system.

Task Manager replaces a bookload of arcane Linux/Unix command-line commands with an elegant, easy-to-use form that any Windows user can appreciate. (Windows also has those commands as part of its Command Prompt arsenal.)

With Task Manager, you can do the following:

- Find out which applications are running on your system.

- Switch between applications or shut down an application.

- Determine which processes are running on your system, determine the resources each process is utilizing, and if necessary, kill a process.

- Monitor your CPU, memory, and network usage in the Resource Monitor.

- Shut down or restart your system.

When you first open Task Manager, it will appear in the Compact view 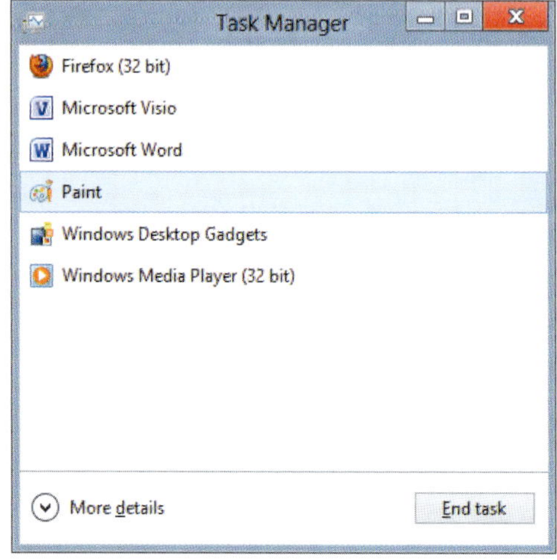 and display your running applications in a window. If an application is not responsive, you will see a note indicating this condition.

When you kill an application, Task Manager doesn't ask you first if you are sure, it simply closes the application. If you have unsaved work in the application, Task



**A** Task Manager in Compact view

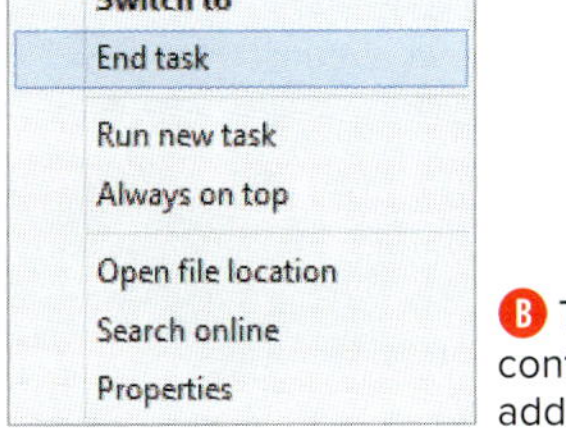

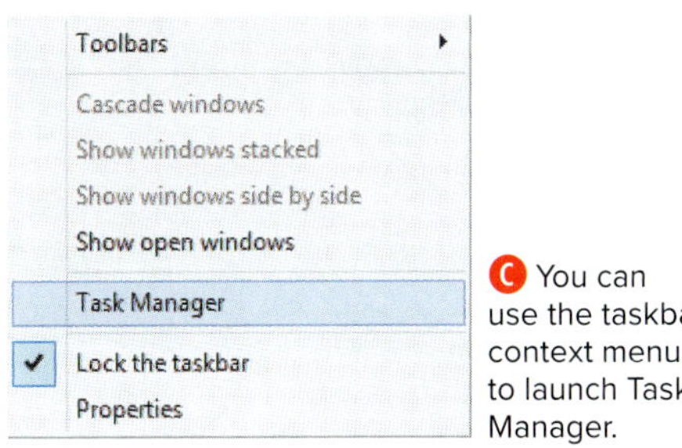



**B** The Task Manager context menu provides additional functionality.



**C** You can use the taskbar context menu to launch Task Manager.

Manager will end the application without asking you to save your work first.

This simplified version of Task Manager has a few more tricks up its sleeve: If you right-click (or tap and hold) a running program, a context menu opens **B**.

## To launch Task Manager:

- Press Ctrl+Shift+Esc.

- Right-click the Desktop taskbar, and select Task Manager from the context menu **C**.

- Press ⊞+R, enter **taskmgr**, and press Enter.

- Press Ctrl+Alt+Del to view the Task screen, and click the Task Manager button.

- Press ⊞+Q, enter **Task Manager** in the Apps search box, and click the Task Manager button.

- On the tile-based Start screen, type **Task Manager** in search until you see its button appear.

## To kill an application:

- Tap or click the application in Task Manager, and then tap or click the End Task button.

- Select the End Task command from an app's context menu.

## To switch to another application:

- Switch to the selected app by selecting the Switch To command or by pressing Alt+Tab or ⊞+Tab. Switching applications can be useful when an application is unresponsive.

- Double-tap or double-click the app you want to switch to.

## To learn more about an application:

- Select Open File Location from the Task Manager context menu B to view the folder that contains the program's executable file.

- Select the Search Online command from the Task Manager context menu B to use your browser's search engine to search for information about the program file.

- Select the Properties command from the Task Manager context menu B to view the executable file's Properties dialog box.

## To create a new task:

1. Select Run New Task from the Task Manager context menu B.

2. In the Create New Task dialog box D, enter the program, folder, document, or Internet resource into the Open text box; then click OK.

   The Create New Task dialog box is similar to the Run dialog box.

**TIP** If you have multiple application windows open when you use the End Task function, all windows are terminated and you will lose any unsaved work.

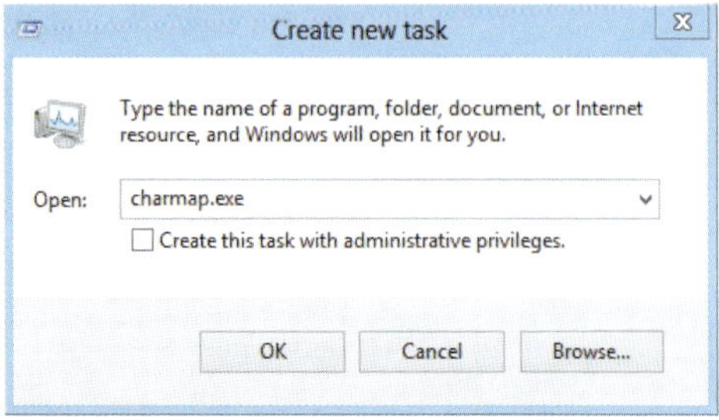

D Use the Create New Task dialog box to run new programs, open folders and documents, open web pages, and more.

# The Processes Tab

In the Compact view, Task Manager doesn't display much detail—it doesn't even show you tile-based programs that are in use. But Task Manager is a very rich diagnostic tool. Among its best uses are determining which programs are resource hogs, figuring out what's running on your system, and learning about how well your components are being used. You can do all these things through the Processes tab in Task Manager's Detailed view.

The standout feature of the Processes tab is the "heat map." Task Manager color-codes applications and processes to represent low to high usage rates. The colors make it very easy to spot which applications or processes are making your system sluggish. Task Manager uses a set of small programs, called "counters," that count various aspects of system performance. This data is collected and reported in the Processes tab.

While it is generally safe to terminate a program, terminating background processes and some services can cause your computer to malfunction. That's why Windows 8 includes tools to view properties and search for a name using your browser. These tools can help you determine whether it is safe to end a process.

Microsoft has put a lot of effort into changing the arcane programmer-type names in Task Manager into friendly names. So you now see "Print driver host for applications," whereas in Windows 7 you would have seen `splwow64.exe`.

## To open Task Manager's Detailed view:

Open Task Manager, and click the More Details button at the bottom of the window 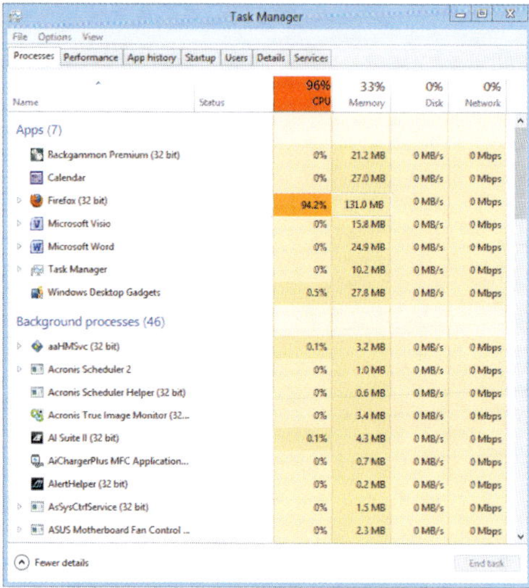.

The Detailed view groups windows under their application **B**. And where you once saw "Synchost" in multiple listings, now Task Manager groups the Service Host processes into logical groupings and lists the services by their friendly names **C**.

**TIP** In the Processes, App History, Startup, Users, Details, and Services tabs, you can click the column headers to sort the display by that item.

**A** Task Manager's Processes tab displays a "heat map" that shows which applications are using the most resources.

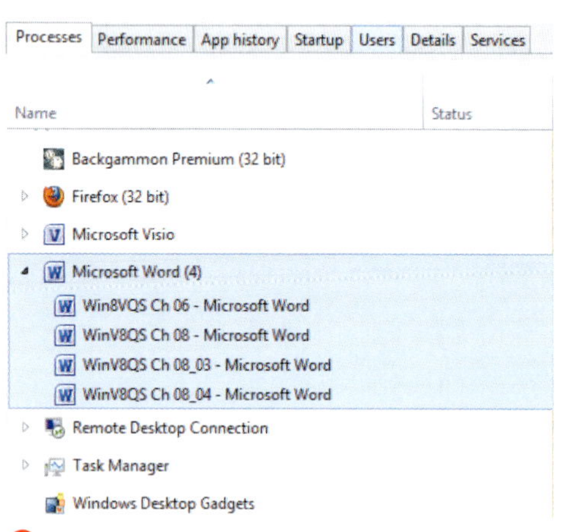

**B** Task Manager groups application windows.

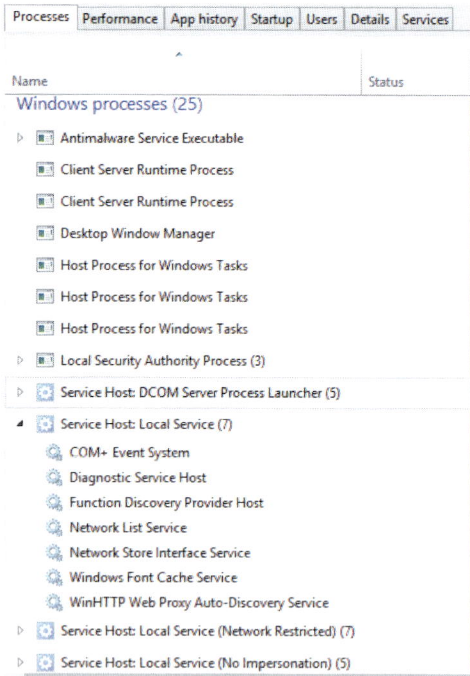

**C** The enigmatic "Synchost" is finally revealed using friendly names, a commonsense new feature of the Windows 8 Task Manager.

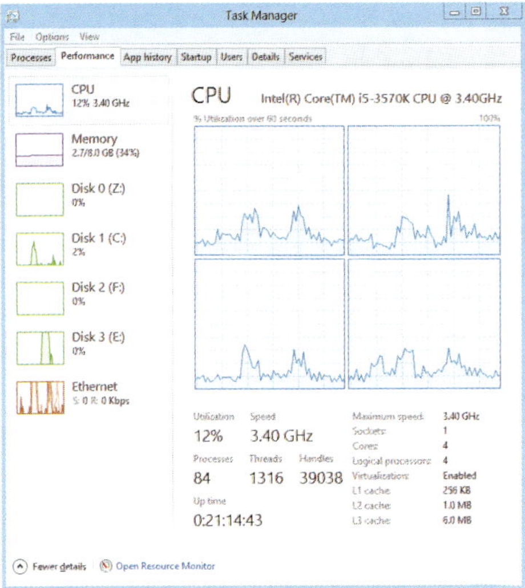



**A** The utilization rates of each core in a four-core CPU

# The Performance and App History Tabs

Most people spend about 80 percent of their time (based on Microsoft's telemetry-based research) using the Processes tab of the Task Manager. But there's much more to be learned about your system on the remaining tabs. The two next most important tabs are Performance and App History. Performance shows you a real-time graph of your system's four main resource components: CPU (processor), memory, disk, and network **A**.

If you look closely at **A**, you will see that all four cores are loaded at about the same levels, but that all of the curves are unique. This illustrates one of the important "under the hood" features of Windows 8. Microsoft rewrote the operating system so that it fully utilizes all cores during run times. That's one of the reasons that Windows 8 starts up more quickly than Windows 7, and why its systems are more responsive. It's an important advance.

Notice also that there is a link to the
Resource Manager on the Performance
tab. Basically, Resource Manager **B** is a
fancier version of the Performance display;
it lets you isolate individual factors one at
at time or by group.

Although the Performance tab provides
immediate feedback, the information you
see on the App History tab **C** is endlessly
fascinating. In its heat map display, you can
learn which apps have been running since
statistics were measured. The display lists
tile-based apps and websites.

**TIP** **The context menus of objects on the
Performance tab let you hide information
and switch to a summary display, as well as
copy what you see so you can store a record
elsewhere.**

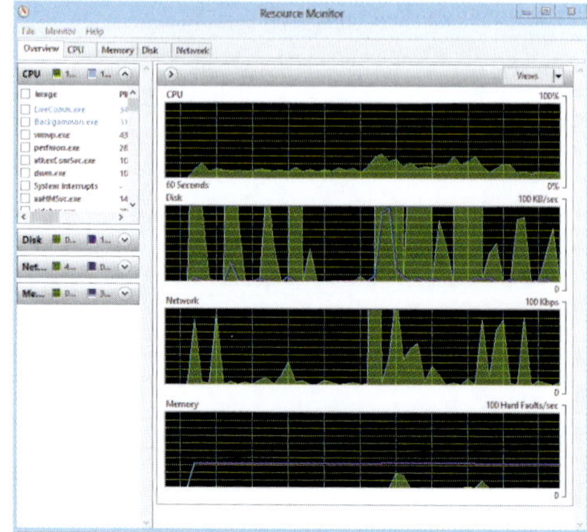

**B** Resource Manager is a more advanced
performance diagnostic tool than Task Manager.

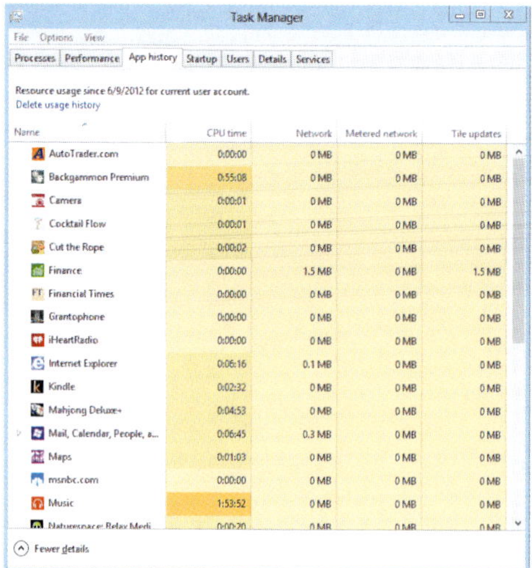

**C** App History shows how long tile-based apps
and websites have been open.

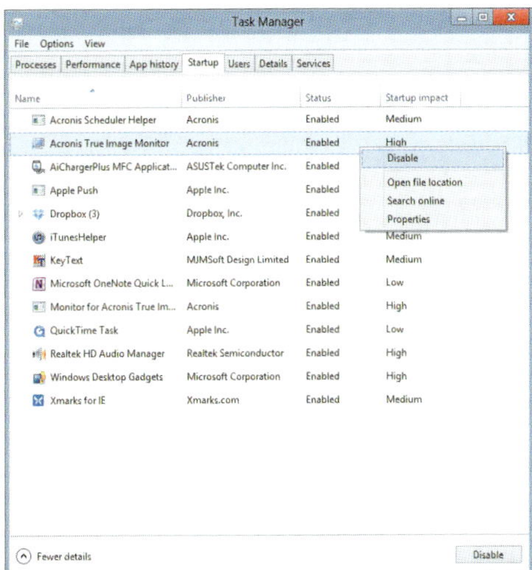

**A** Startup lists the applications that automatically launch. It allows you to disable an app, which can be useful for diagnostic purposes when your system exhibits unstable or unusual behaviors.

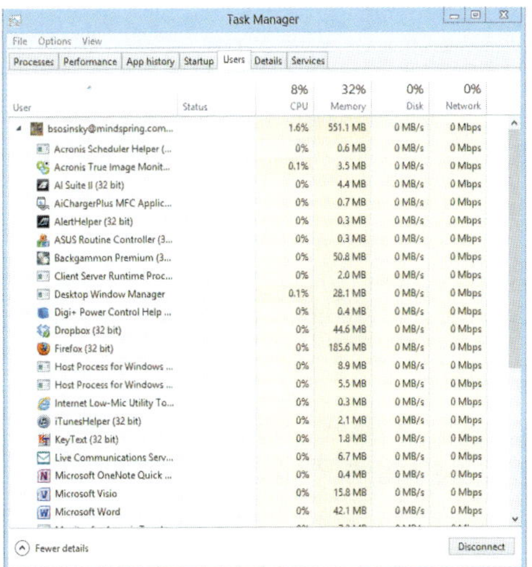

**B** Users is an alphabetical listing of running applications and processes broken out by connected user accounts. You can use it to end a user's session and terminate apps or services.

# The Startup, Users, Details, and Services Tabs

The remaining tabs of the Task Manager are less used, but you might find them useful from time to time.

The Startup tab maintains a list of the applications that automatically launch when you start your system **A**. Note that applications you launch after your system starts up are not included in this list. The list shows the amount of resources that the app consumes.

You can use this list to enable or disable an application's startup behavior.

The Users tab **B** is a variation of the Processes tab, but it lists apps and services alphabetically by user—again in heat map format. You can use this diagnostic feature to stop startup programs if they are consuming too many resources or contributing to a very slow startup.

The Details tab **C** is an alphabetical listing of apps and services running on your system. It can be useful when you want to quickly find something without having to search categories first.

Notice that tile-based apps show a state of "Suspended" **C** when you work on the Desktop. When you switch away from a tile-based app, the program's state is saved to disk and is no longer running. That's why tile-based apps require so little time to start back up, and why you aren't required to close them when you aren't using it. The Backgammon app highlighted in **C** is a tile-based app.

The Services tab **D** is worthy of some attention. Services are processes that run in the background and are used whenever required. Some processes are loaded into memory and perform periodic functions; other processes are suspended and their state is stored until they are called for; other processes run continually.

Click the *Open Services* link at the bottom of the window to open the Services control panel and alter a service's behavior. Be careful, though, because some services are essential to keep Windows running, and many services have dependencies that require other specific services be running for them to work. You can garner information on the dependencies from descriptions found in the Services control panel.

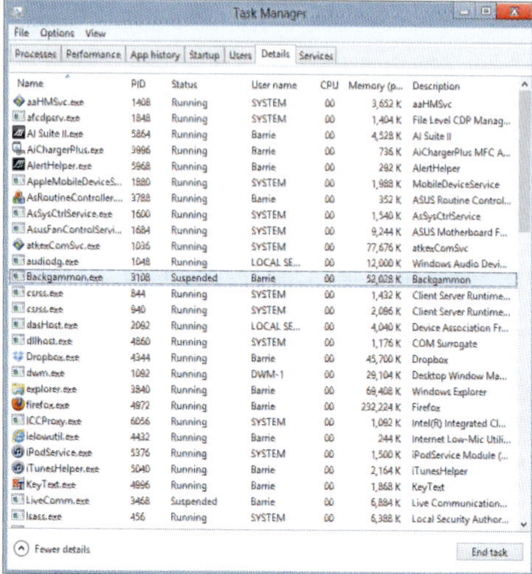

**C** The Details tab is an alphabetical listing of apps and processes running on your system.

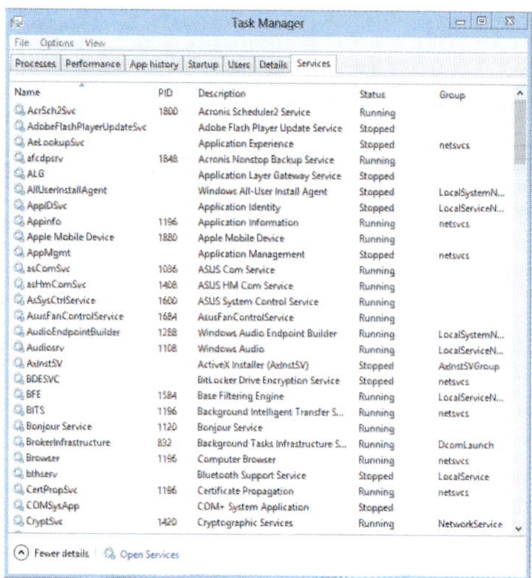

**D** The Services tab

### To enable or disable a startup app:

1. Tap and hold, or right-click, an application to view its context menu.

2. Select the Disable command to pause a running application.

   *or*

   Select the Enable command to run a paused app again.

### To disconnect a user:

1. Tap or click the user account to select it.

2. Tap or click the Disconnect button to end that user's session.

### To terminate an app or process:

1. Tap or click an app or process to select it.

2. Tap or click the Disconnect button to terminate that app or process.

**TIP** Many services are optional but are installed anyway. Hardcore gamers often turn off services to optimize their systems; you can get advice on this from www.blackviper.com. The average user probably shouldn't bother.

**TIP** There are better tools than Task Manager for managing startup activities. One competent application is the System Configuration utility, which ships with Windows 8. Go to the Run dialog box, type `msconfig`, and press Enter to view this utility.

# Refresh and Reset

Consumers have gotten used to the idea that when their phone or tablet misbehaves, all they have to do is unfold a paper clip, stick it in a tiny hole, and wait four seconds, and their device will reset to a factory state. Microsoft decided it was time to reimagine for software the concept of the hardware reset button—to emulate the return to a factory state and provide an easier way to roll back or revert to past "known good" configurations. Windows has had the "last known good configuration" feature for a while—if you had an installation DVD handy, you could restore a Windows sytem without losing your data by replacing key system files. Windows 8 makes this process easier.

With Windows 8, you can do the following:

- **Reset your PC.** When you reset your device, Windows deletes your data, apps, and settings and gives you a clean install. You reset your computer when you want to nuke it before you give it to someone else.

- **Refresh your PC.** When you refresh your device, Windows keeps all your data, tile-based apps, and settings and reinstalls Windows. You refresh your system when your system is misbehaving or crashing because you installed an evil device driver on it.

Refresh preserves your wireless connections and broadband settings, Bitlocker settings, drive letters, and personalization settings. Refresh alters file type associations, display settings, and Windows firewall settings. You may need to manually restore these altered settings (and some Desktop applications) when the refresh is complete.

*Advanced Startup menu*          *Reset your PC*

Ⓐ The General section of the PC Settings screen contains the Reset, Refresh, and Advanced Startup options.

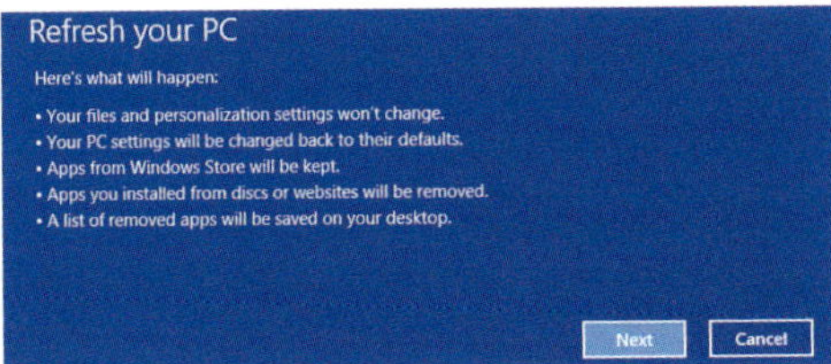


Ⓑ Use the Refresh Your PC repair operation when your system is experiencing problems.

# To reset or refresh your system:

1. To view the Charms bar, swipe from the right edge, move your cursor to the upper-right corner of your display, or press ⊞+C. Tap or click the Settings charm.

2. Tap or click the *Change PC Settings* link at the bottom of the Settings bar.

3. Tap or click the *General* link Ⓐ.

4. To completely replace your Windows installation, skip to step 6.

   To refresh your system when it is not performing correctly, tap or click the Get Started button in the Refresh Your PC Without Affecting Your Files section.

   Windows posts an alert box Ⓑ explaining that Refresh will repair your system.

5. Click Next, and you will be asked to supply the Windows installation media (DVD).

   Your system restarts, and Windows replaces system files and rolls your system back to the last known good configuration. When you log in to your system, you may find that a recent application or device installation has been reversed, but all of your data and system settings will be intact. Skip the rest of these steps.

*continues on next page*

6. To completely replace your Windows installation, tap or click the Get Started button in the Remove Everything And Reinstall Windows section.

   Windows posts an alert box 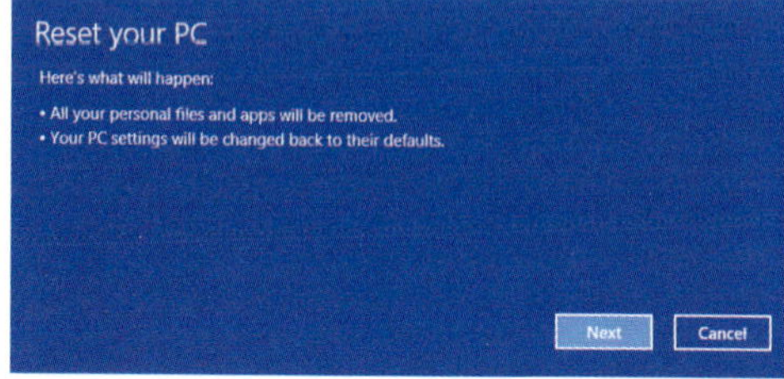 that describes the action.

7. Tap or click Next. You are prompted to supply the installation media (DVD) before proceeding.

   Windows overwrites your data and files, reinstalling a fresh copy of Windows.

8. In the How Do You Want To Remove Your Personal Files dialog box, there are two options: tap or click the Thoroughly button to reformat your disk; tap or click the Quickly button to simply remove and replace the files and file system but leave your old data on the disk.

Refresh and Reset are great options when you can boot your computer. But if you can't boot into Windows, the system will post the Troubleshoot dialog box 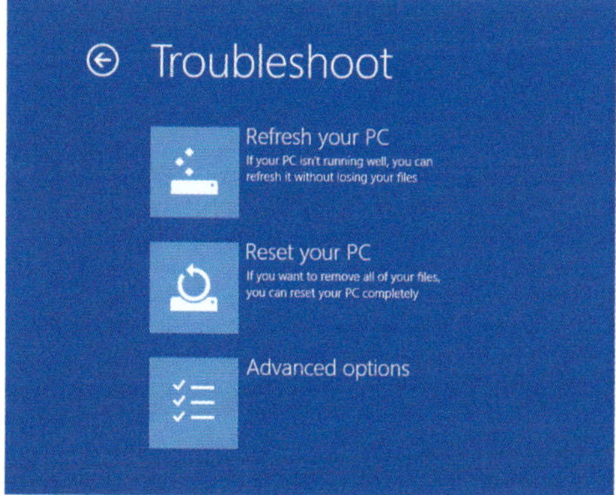. This is your entry back into the Refresh and Reset options. The third option, Advanced Options, is described in the next section.

**TIP** Windows 8 has new option that allows you to create a bootable USB flash drive. If your system can't boot, you can use this flash drive installation to fix or repair a problem. Some manufacturers supply a recovery partition, which is yet another way to get back up and running.



**C** WARNING: This option removes all settings and applications, creating a fresh installation of Windows. Use this when you give away or sell your PC.



**D** Troubleshoot appears when your system can't boot. From here, you can refresh or reset your system.

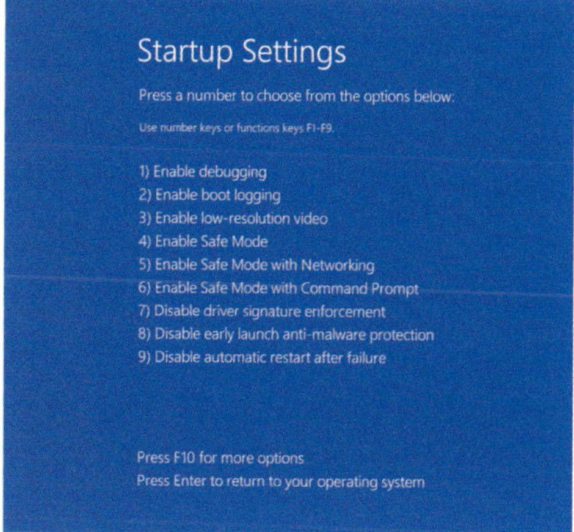


**A** Startup Settings describes some of the options that the Advanced Boot menu offers.



**B** The Startup Settings screen will restart your system and put you into a debugging, logging, low-resolution video, safe mode, or recovery environment.

# Windows Recovery Environment

Refresh will solve most of your computer's woes automatically. But you may run into situations where Refresh doesn't work and you don't want to start over or revert to a system image. Windows comes with a number of troubleshooting options that you can use to save the day:

- **System Restore** restarts your system, has you log in, and then allows you to take your system back to a stored state.

- **System Image Recovery** uses an image to revert your system back to a stored state.

- **Automatic repair** runs a diagnostic program that attempts to find problems and restore your system to a working state.

- **Command Prompt** opens an administrator Command Prompt into which you can enter commands that will fix or modify your system.

- **Startup Settings** opens the Advanced Boot menu option **A**.

If you select the Startup Settings button, you see the Startup Settings screen **B**, which allows you to choose one of several options to help you fix your system.

Space precludes a complete discussion of these startup options, but here's a brief description of each:

- **Repair Your Computer.** This option will appear if your system has a System Reserved partition that you can repair from.

- **Enable Safe Mode (with Networking or Command Prompt).** Safe Mode loads a minimal set of drivers and services so you can boot successfully to Windows and fix what's broken. This works well with damaged device drivers and hardware issues.

- **Enable boot logging.** This method will write the **ntbtlog.txt** file, which contains the installed drivers that you can use for troubleshooting.

- **Enable low-resolution video.** For display problems, you can use this option to boot into 640 x 480 pixel resolution and install new display drivers.

- **Enable debugging.** This mode allows a trained professional to diagnose your system by loading it step by step.

- **Disable driver signature enforcement.** This option allows your system to load drivers that aren't properly signed or certified.

- **Disable early launch anti-malware driver.** ELAM drivers load first and can interfere with software that they deem malware.

- **Start Windows Normally.** This will ignore all options and boot to Windows.

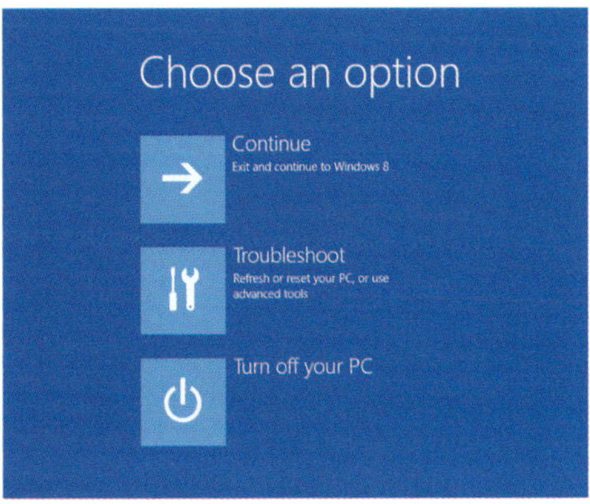



**C** The Choose An Option screen

## To boot to the Advanced Options menu:

1. Open the General page of the PC Settings screen (**A** in the previous section).

2. In the Advanced Startup section, click the Restart Now button.

   When your computer restarts, you will see the Choose An Option screen **C**.

3. Click Troubleshoot.

4. On the Troubleshoot screen, click the Advanced Options button to view the Advanced Options screen **D**.

**TIP** The Recovery control panel has options to create a recovery drive, open the system restore feature, and create a system restore point.

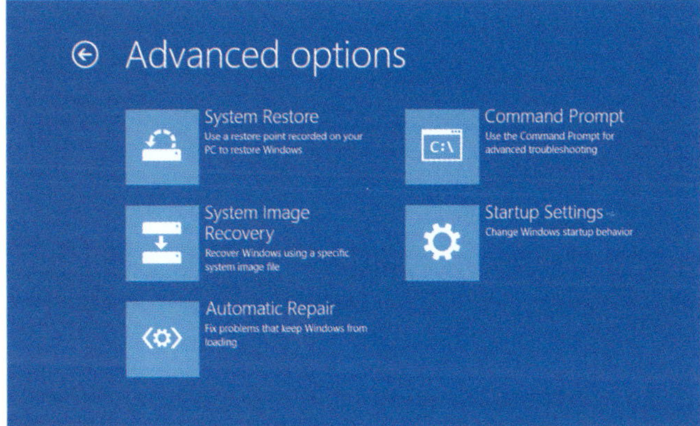



**D** The Advanced Options menu

# System Images

When your system is in a condition or state that you want to preserve, you should create a system image. A system image is a snapshot of your system and contains a bit-for-bit copy of your system in a single container file. Inside that file are all of your system's files in an unencrypted state.

Normally, the container file is an ISO image file. An ISO file is archive file—you can write an ISO file to disk and restore your system from it. Windows comes with a built-in command-line utility—recimg.exe— for creating a system image.

When you create a recovery image and store it to disk, Windows 8 uses it to perform a refresh operation and restore your system. That is, you are creating a custom recovery image that will be used in place of the one that Windows wrote when it last wrote this archive to disk. If you store several images, you can use the **/setcurrent** and **/deregister** switches to determine which image Windows uses. The **/showcurrent** switch will indicate which image is the current one.

System images are an excellent method for backing up a computer, but only when you use them on a regular basis. With Windows Backup gone from Windows 8, you are forced to consider other methods to back up your system, and imaging is the way to go.

What you really want is to take snapshots periodically and restore from the last snapshot. The first snapshot is a full backup, but additional snapshots are differential files that store only the changes.

As with many Windows utilities, Microsoft gives you a solid baseline tool, but it's not the tool you'd want to use in your everyday work. I use Acronis True Image Home on my systems because I can set it up to automatically image my disks. If it's automatic, it will get done—if it's not, it won't.

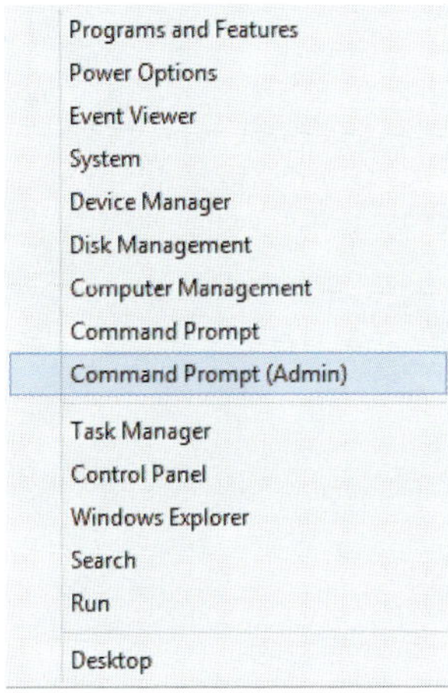



Ⓐ The Computer Management menu

## To create a system image:

1. Press ⊞+X or right-click the lower-left corner of the display to view the Computer Management menu Ⓐ. Choose the Command Prompt (Admin) command.

2. The User Account Control posts a dialog box asking you if you agree to elevate privileges. Tap or click Yes.

   The Administrator: Command Prompt dialog box appears, with **C:\Windows\system32** as the current directory Ⓑ.

3. Enter the command **recimg –createimage c:\RecoveryImage** into the Command Prompt window, and press Enter.

   This command tells Windows to run the **recimg** command, create an image, and put that image into the **C:\RecoveryImage** directory. It takes a while to write the image to disk. It's a good idea to create a fresh system image from time to time.

**TIP** You can use **recimg /?** (the help switch) to get an explanation of the **recimg** command.

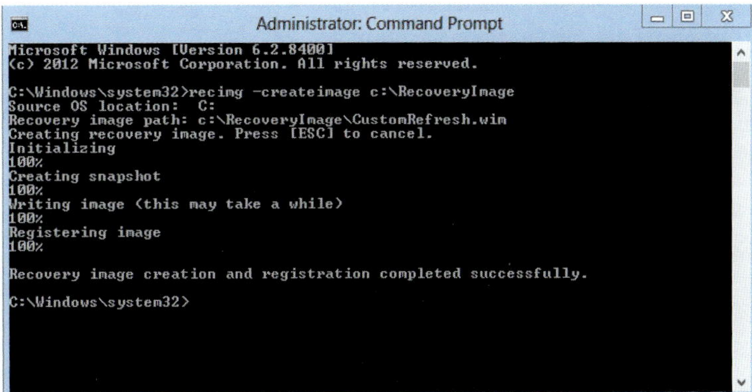



Ⓑ The Command Prompt window after the **recimg** program has written a system image to disk

# Putting It All Together

- Use Task Manager to find out what applications, processes, and services are running on your system.

- Task Manager can help you isolate an application or process that is ruining your system's performance, and shows you consumption in the form of a heat map.

- When your system freezes, you can use Task Manager to terminate a program or switch to another program.

- Refresh is a process that brings your system back to a known good state and retains all of your applications and settings.

- Reset is a process that completely wipes out Windows 8 and creates a new installation. You can choose to do a thorough reset and overwrite all previous data, or a quick reset and just rewrite system files.

- The Advanced Options menu has additional methods for restoring a damaged Windows installation, including Safe Mode, Enable Low-Resolution Video, and more.

- System images are the preferred method for backing up Windows 8. They take a complete snapshot of your system.

# Disks and Storage Devices

Modern computers manage and store vast quantities of information. These days, when you can hold the digital equivalent of all the books in a library in your hand, storage is truly a technological marvel. Windows 8 supports the widest variety of storage devices of any operating system in the industry, and it can connect to, configure, and manage those devices. In this chapter, you will learn how.

The bulk of this chapter discusses how to use hard drives, because they are the most commonly used storage devices. Hard drives can be used individually or in groups, and this chapter tells you how to format and configure drives and provides details about what storage configurations are possible. This is a large subject—and this is a small book—so you really only learn the highlights of what is possible.

This chapter also gives you some basic information on solid-state drives (SSDs), optical discs, and USB thumbdrives—just a few of the other storage devices that you are likely to use in your daily work.

## In This Chapter

# Simple Volumes

When you attach a "raw" disk to Windows 8, the operating system recognizes the disk, launches a wizard, and asks you to prepare the disk so that you can use it. A disk can be a hard drive, a USB thumbdrive, a solid-state drive, or many other storage devices. When you prepare a storage device for use, you create a partition (literally a part of a drive) and then place a volume in that partition. More correctly, you create a *logical volume*. If you use the entire drive for your partition and have one volume within it, the terms *volume* and *partition* are synonymous. These terms are often interchanged, but they are not identical. Most manufacturers ship storage devices to you with one partition on it—that is, if they bother to partition and format the drive for you at all.

You can create multiple partitions on a storage device. When you do, each partition acts as if it were its own storage device. You can subdivide partitions into more than one volume. On one physical drive, Windows allows you to create up to four primary partitions: three with a single volume each, and one extended partition that can contain multiple volumes.

When you format a volume, Windows marks the drive into areas that have addresses and writes a file system that keeps track of what data is stored at which addresses in the first addressable sections, which contain the master boot record. Newer systems use a scheme called a globally unique identifier partition table, which is supported by the new Unified Extensible Firmware Interface (UEFI) BIOS now coming into common use. A BIOS, or Basic Input Output System, is the instructions used by your computer's chipset to boot and to communicate with memory, peripherals, and other devices.

For a hard drive with optical platters, the operation writes concentric rings and creates slices by writing magnetic diameter lines. The arc-shaped slices are called *sectors*, and individual areas within the sectors are called *clusters*. Windows 8 installs the NTFS (New Technology File System) onto hard drives. Older and smaller systems like thumbdrives use different file systems, such as FAT32 (file access table). DVDs and CDs use a file system called CDFS and have different methods for addressing storage.

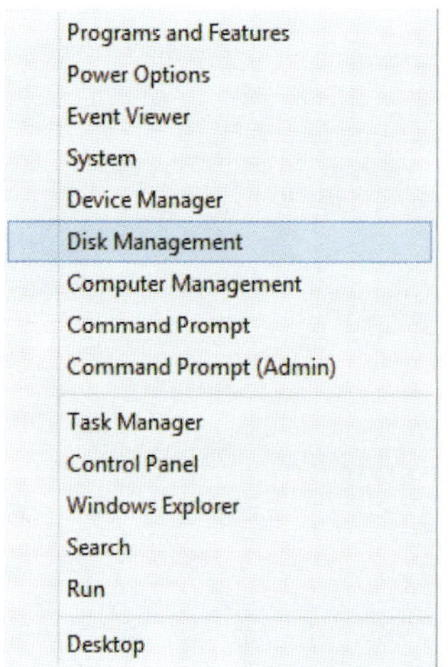



# To create and format a new partition or volume:

1. Press ⊞+X or right-click the lower-left corner of the display, and select Management > Disk Management **A**.

   If your account is not an Administrator account, you will be prompted to elevate your privileges. Windows 8 connects to the virtual disk service, displays all of your disks, and finds their states **B**.

continues on next page

**A** Select Disk Management to create partitions and volumes and to format disks.

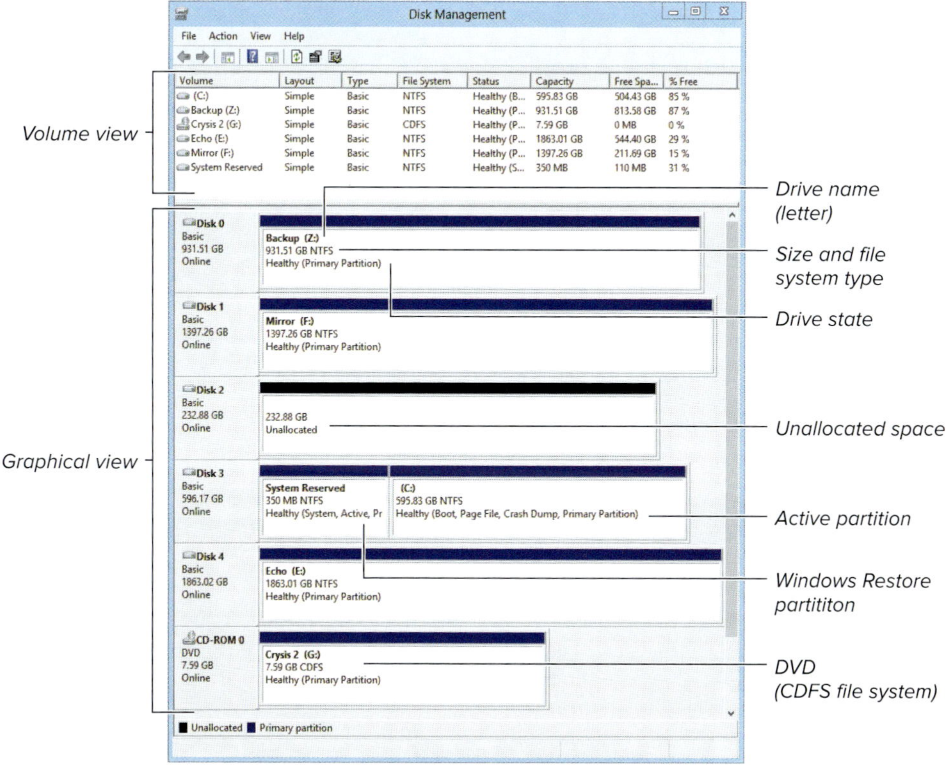


The Disk Management window shows the following volume-view table:

| Volume | Layout | Type | File System | Status | Capacity | Free Spa... | % Free |
|---|---|---|---|---|---|---|---|
| (C:) | Simple | Basic | NTFS | Healthy (B... | 595.83 GB | 504.43 GB | 85 % |
| Backup (Z:) | Simple | Basic | NTFS | Healthy (P... | 931.51 GB | 813.58 GB | 87 % |
| Crysis 2 (G:) | Simple | Basic | CDFS | Healthy (P... | 7.59 GB | 0 MB | 0 % |
| Echo (E:) | Simple | Basic | NTFS | Healthy (P... | 1863.01 GB | 544.40 GB | 29 % |
| Mirror (F:) | Simple | Basic | NTFS | Healthy (P... | 1397.26 GB | 211.69 GB | 15 % |
| System Reserved | Simple | Basic | NTFS | Healthy (S... | 350 MB | 110 MB | 31 % |

Graphical view:

- Disk 0 — Basic, 931.51 GB, Online — Backup (Z:), 931.51 GB NTFS, Healthy (Primary Partition)
- Disk 1 — Basic, 1397.26 GB, Online — Mirror (F:), 1397.26 GB NTFS, Healthy (Primary Partition)
- Disk 2 — Basic, 232.88 GB, Online — 232.88 GB, Unallocated
- Disk 3 — Basic, 596.17 GB, Online — System Reserved, 350 MB NTFS, Healthy (System, Active, Pr | (C:), 595.83 GB NTFS, Healthy (Boot, Page File, Crash Dump, Primary Partition)
- Disk 4 — Basic, 1863.02 GB, Online — Echo (E:), 1863.01 GB NTFS, Healthy (Primary Partition)
- CD-ROM 0 — DVD, 7.59 GB, Online — Crysis 2 (G:), 7.59 GB CDFS, Healthy (Primary Partition)

■ Unallocated  ■ Primary partition

**B** Notice that the size (length) of the disks in the graphical view is not to scale with their rated capacities. Disk Management is a Microsoft Management Console snap-in, and Computer Management is an application container called a framework (described in Chapter 5).

2. Tap and hold, or right-click, an unallocated space, and select New Simple Volume from the context menu 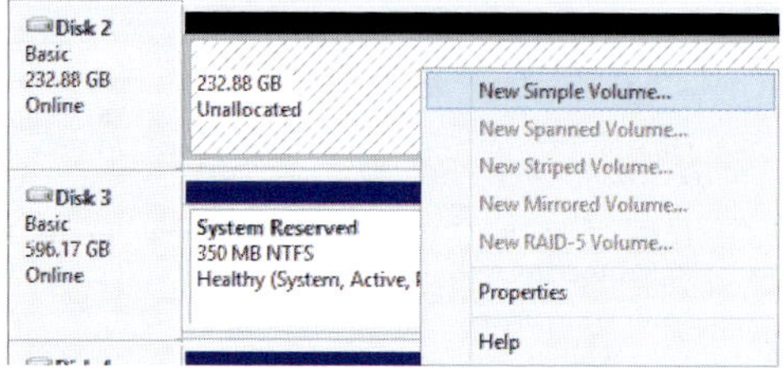 **C**.

   The New Simple Volume Wizard appears **D**

3. Click Next.

4. In the Specify Volume Size screen **E**, enter the size of the volume you want to create, or accept the disk's maximum size. Tap or click Next.

5. In the Assign Drive Letter Or Path screen **F**, give the volume a letter label or have the volume contents displayed within a shortcut folder at the path you specify.

   You can also choose not to assign a drive letter or path; you can do so later, in the Disk Management utility. Drive letters must be unique, and it is typical (though not required) to use C: for your boot or system drive and D: for your DVD or optical drive. Once upon a time, A: and B: drives were often used for floppy disks.

**C** Select the New Simple Volume command to create a new volume and format it. If a drive has never been used, its state will show as Raw; if the volume has been deleted and the area of the disk is formatted but has no file system, its state will show as Unallocated.

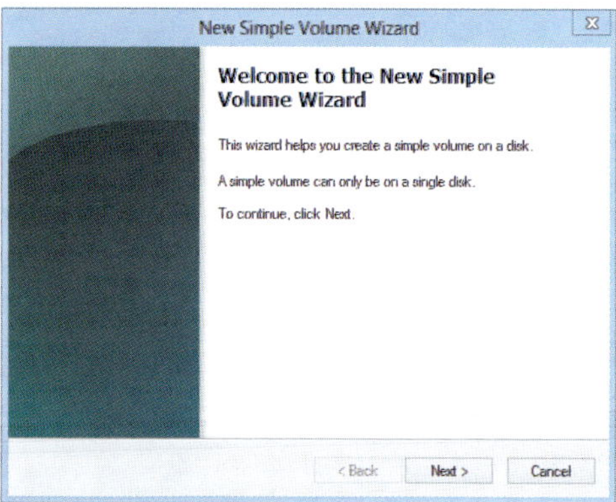

**D** The New Simple Volume Wizard

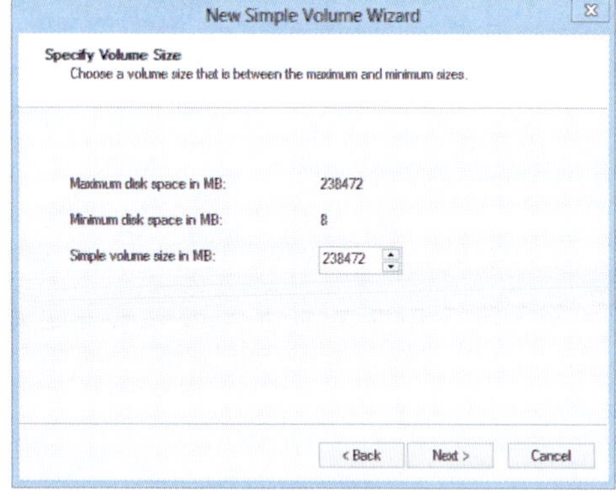

**E** You can enter a value for the new volume size up to the maximum size of the unallocated space; any space you don't use remains unallocated.

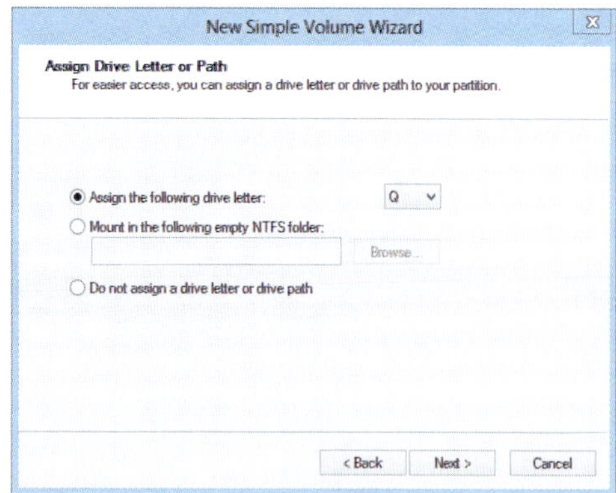

**F** Assigning a drive letter or mount point (path)

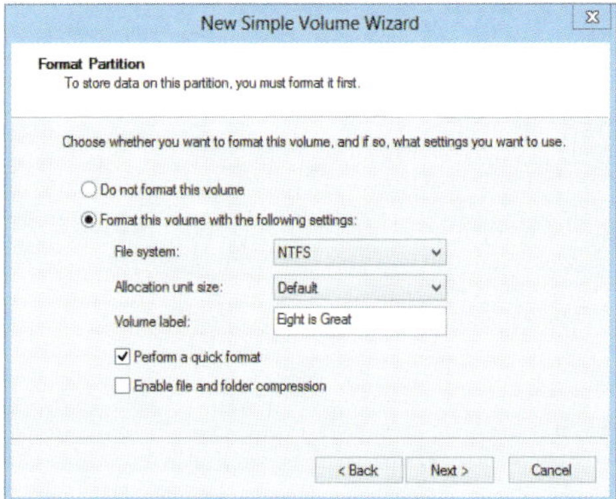

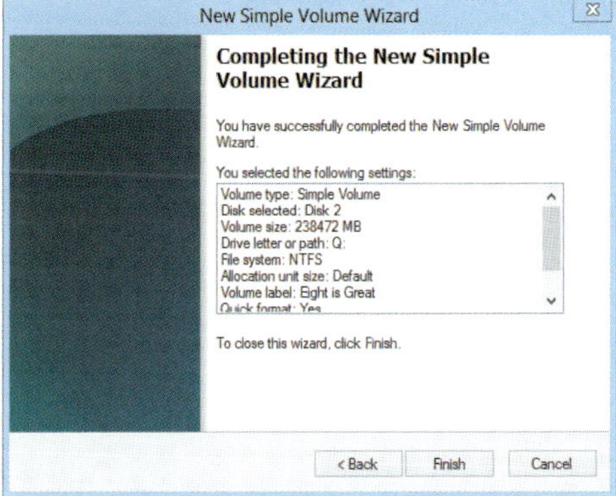

**G** Set the format types and properties using the Format Partition screen of the wizard.

**H** The final screen of the wizard lets you review your selections before creating the volume.

6. In the Format Partition screen **G**, select the file system, the type, and the volume properties, or select Do Not Format This Volume. Tap or click Next to proceed to the review screen.

   Usually, you will want to keep the default NTFS system and default allocation size. The Volume Label field controls what you see displayed as a title for the volume in Internet Explorer. Selecting the Perform A Quick Format check box writes a file system but does not reformat your volume. Enabling file and folder compression will give you some additional storage at the cost of reduced performance.

   If you chose the quick format option, then formatting your drive will take a few seconds to a minute. If you chose to perform a full format (by deselecting the Perform A Quick Format check box), then it will take from minutes to hours to create the volume, depending on your drive size and the power of your CPU.

7. Review your selections on the Completing The New Simple Volume Wizard screen **H**; then click Finish to create the volume.

## To format an existing partition or volume:

1. In the Disk Management utility, right-click (or tap and hold) the volume you wish to reformat, and then select Format from the context menu. The Format dialog appears 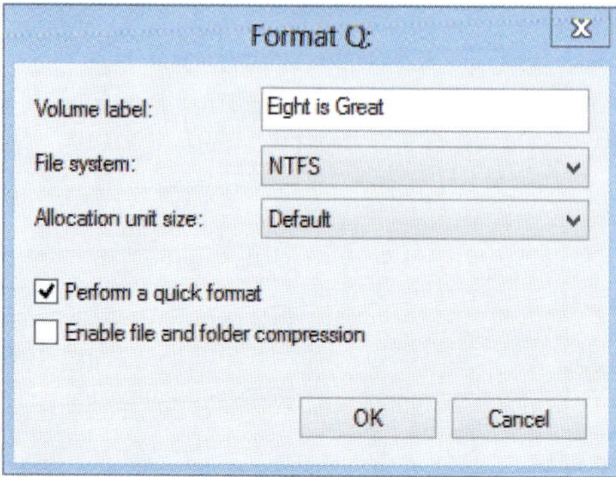.

2. Windows displays an alert box 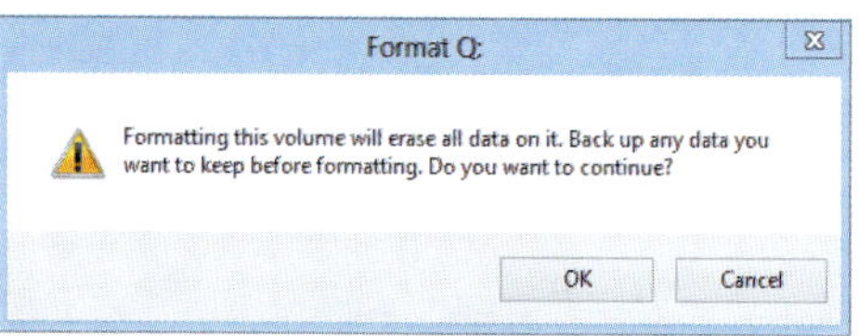. Tap or click OK to proceed. Windows then formats your partition or volume.

   To protect users against accidental errors, Windows 8 does not allow you to reformat the system or the boot (active) partition unless you start your system from another partition.

## To extend a volume:

1. Right-click, or tap and hold, the volume in the Disk Management utility, and select Extend Volume from the context menu to launch the Extend Volume wizard.

2. Click Next to view the Select Disks screen 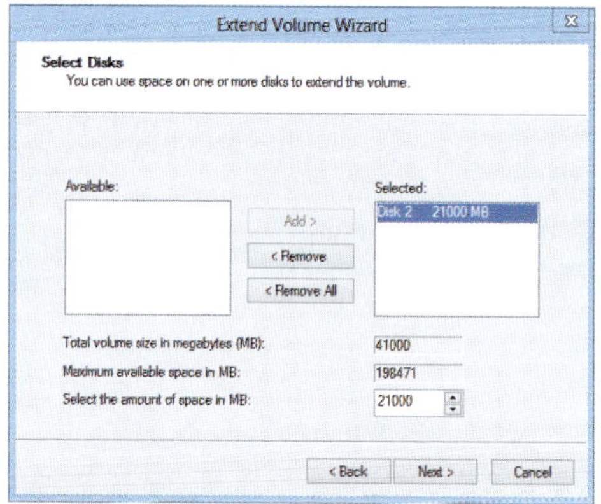.

3. Add additional available disks (optional), and then enter the amount of additional space you desire in the Select The Amount Of Space In MB field.

4. Tap or click Next, and complete the wizard. Windows 8 adds additional space to your volume.

**I** The Format dialog box offers the same options you saw in **G**.

**J** The Format alert box; ignore it at your peril.

**K** In the Extend Volume Wizard, specify the amount of additional space you wish to add to your volume.

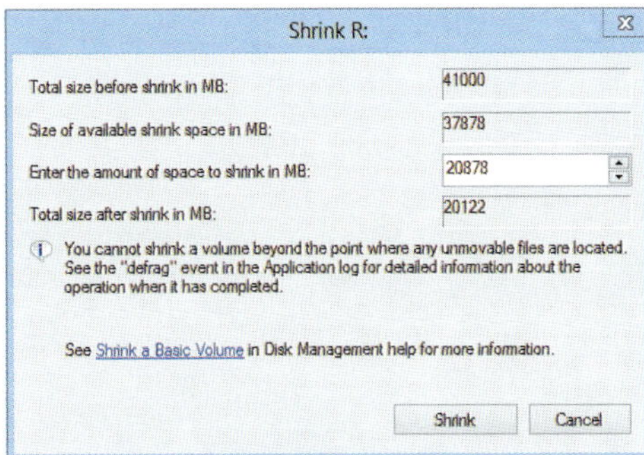



**L** In the Shrink dialog box, enter the amount of space you wish to remove from your volume.

## To shrink a volume:

1. Right-click, or tap and hold, the volume in the Disk Management utility, and select Shrink Volume from the context menu to launch the Shrink Volume wizard.

2. Click Next to view the Shrink dialog box, and then enter the amount you wish to remove from your volume **L**.

3. Click the Shrink button, and you are returned to the Disk Management utility, where your disk is shown at its smaller size.

   Shrink can remove only space that doesn't have files on it, so you may need to defrag the volume before shrinking it.

**TIP** A quick format overwrites the file table but doesn't overwrite data that is on disk. A regular format will take much longer but zeros out all data, making it much harder for others to recover the information. A regular format is always the better option from a security standpoint.

**TIP** Although Windows 8 lets you use either a master boot record (MBR) or a globally unique identifier partition table (GPT) for systems that come with the UEFI BIOS, MBR is preferred for any disk that is less than 2 TB.

# Dynamic Disks

A basic disk is one that contains primary partitions and logical volumes, with each having its own file system. In **A**, you see a disk subdivided into the maximum four partitions: three primary partitions and one extended partition that contains multiple volumes. For most Windows users, basic disks and simple volumes are all they will ever need.

You can do the following with basic disks using the disk's context menu and the Disk Management menu commands:

- Create and delete both primary and extended partitions

- Create and delete logical volumes (drives) inside an extended partition

- Format a specific partition and mark it active so that Windows 8 can boot from it

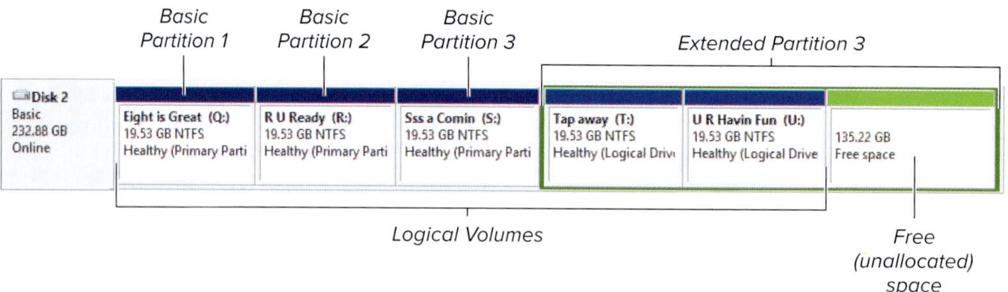


**A** A drive with the maximum number of allowable partitions, one of which is an extended partition

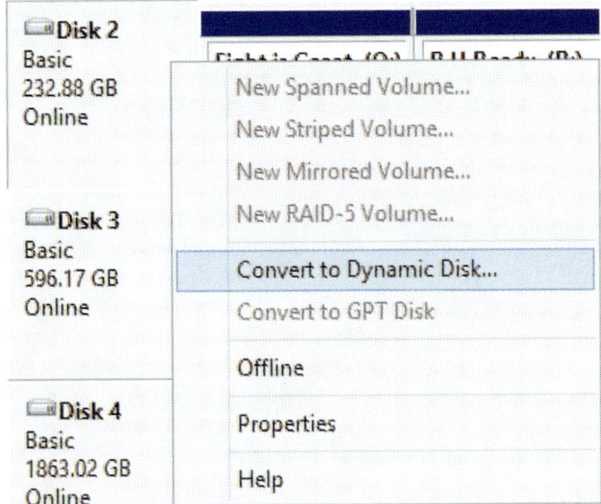



**B** The Convert to Dynamic Disk command in the Disk Management utility

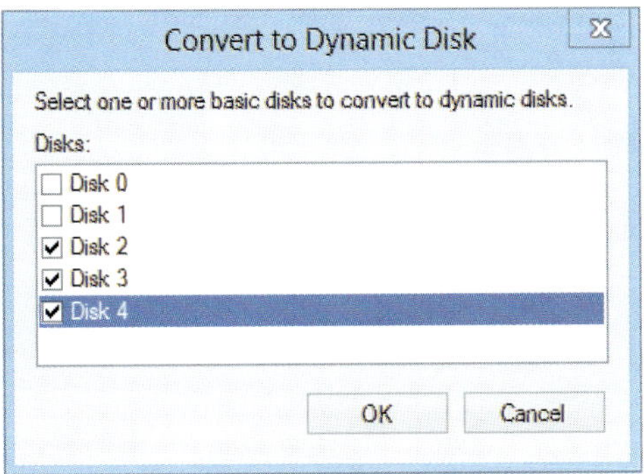



**C** The Convert To Dynamic Disk dialog box

In Windows 8, you can create what are called dynamic disks, which contain dynamic volumes. With dynamic disks, you can have volumes that do the following:

- **Span** across two or more locations on the disk and across two or more disks.

- **Stripe** (RAID 0) your data across multiple disks, which allows for faster performance because more disk heads are in operation at the same time.

- **Mirror** (RAID 1) data from one disk to a second so that you can survive a disk failure by using the working disk.

- Create a **RAID** (redundant array of independent disks) so that you can survive a disk failure.

One popular RAID level is RAID-5, which stripes data across three or more disks and writes redundant data across all three disks. It improves performance and allows you to survive a disk failure. When a disk fails, you replace it and rebuild the array from the redundant data.

## To create a dynamic disk:

1. Tap and hold, or right-click, the Disk label in the Disk Management utility to view the context menu **B**.

2. Select Convert To Dynamic Disk.

3. Windows displays the Convert To Dynamic Disk dialog box **C**. Select the disks you want to convert, and then tap or click OK.

4. The Disks To Convert dialog box appears, confirming your selections. Tap or click Convert to proceed.

*continues on next page*

**5.** Windows 8 displays an alert box **D**
Informing you of the consequences of
your actions. Tap or click Yes to perform
the operation.

When the dynamic disk is complete, the
disk label will show the word *Dynamic*
under its name in the graphical bar that
represents the disk in the Disk Manager.

Once you create dynamic disks, the commands to create volume sets are enabled.
Each command you see on the menu **B**
(all of which will now be enabled) launches
a wizard to guide you through the process.

## To change a dynamic disk to a basic disk:

Delete all dynamic volumes on the disk.

## To create spanned, striped, mirrored, or RAID volumes:

**1.** Create two or more dynamic disks on
your system.

**2.** Tap or right-click a drive label to view
the context menu.

**3.** Select New Spanned Volume, New
Striped Volume, New Mirrored Volume,
or New RAID-5 Volume from the context
menu **B**.

**4.** Each command launches a wizard
that guides you through the process
of creating that particular storage
configuration.

**TIP** The different dynamic disk configurations
(spanning, striping, mirroring, and RAID) are
valuable ways to get additional performance
from a bunch of disks. With solid-state drives,
the performance benefits are less likely to be
important to you, but the data protection features are valuable. Wikipedia's article on RAID
(http://en.wikipedia.org/wiki/RAID) can provide
you with more information on this topic.

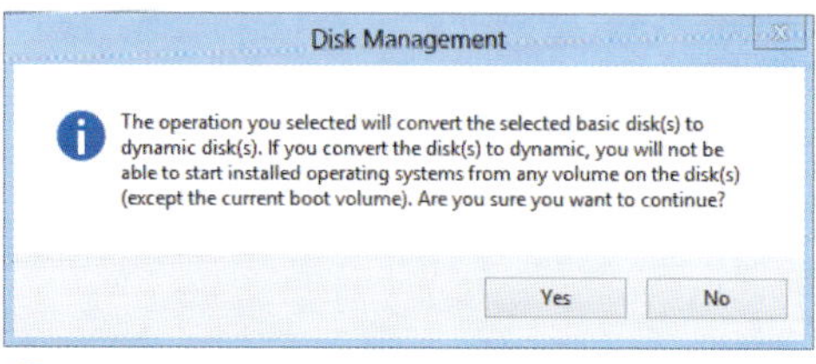

**D** Windows 8 will let you know the consequences
of your actions.

# Drive Properties and Tools

Windows stores a lot of information about your disk drives, along with some useful tools for disk maintenance, in their Properties dialog boxes. You can determine what type of disk you are using, specify how you want to share the disk, set up security, and more.

You can view properties for any device you see in Windows Explorer: hard disk, optical drive, SSD drive, USB thumbdrive, and so on. You'll find the following tabs in the Properties dialog box:

- **General.** Here you can view disk statistics, run Disk Cleanup, and set up compression and indexing.

- **Tools.** This tab lets you do a disk check (error checking) and run a defragmentation routine.

- **Hardware.** Lists all of your physical disks.

- **Sharing.** Here you can allow your disk contents to be shared by others and set their privileges.

- **Security.** This tab allows you to control which user accounts can access your disk and what rights they have (**READ** or **WRITE**).

- **Quota.** On this tab you can limit the amount of space each user account is allowed.

- **Acronis Recovery.** This is a custom tab installed by Acronis True Image software and is not part of standard Windows 8.

In Ⓐ, you see the General tab of the Properties dialog box for a system boot drive. This is the tab you will visit the most. The General tab allows you to do the following:

- Change the disk name
- View the file system
- View disk utilization statistics
- Open the Disk Cleanup utility
- Compress files on the disk
- Index files for faster searches

## To view the Properties dialog box:

1. Press ⊞+E to view Windows Explorer.

2. Tap and hold, or right-click, the disk of interest, then select Properties from the context menu.

**TIP** You might wonder why the General tab shows two different sizes next to the Used Space legend. The larger number to the left is the size used on disk, whereas the number on the right is the actual amount of disk space the files themselves consume. The size of the files on disk includes the amount of disk space that is currently assigned and cannot be used. Since files are placed into units in sectors and don't always fill up a sector, the additional unused but unassignable space is what makes the size on disk larger than the size.

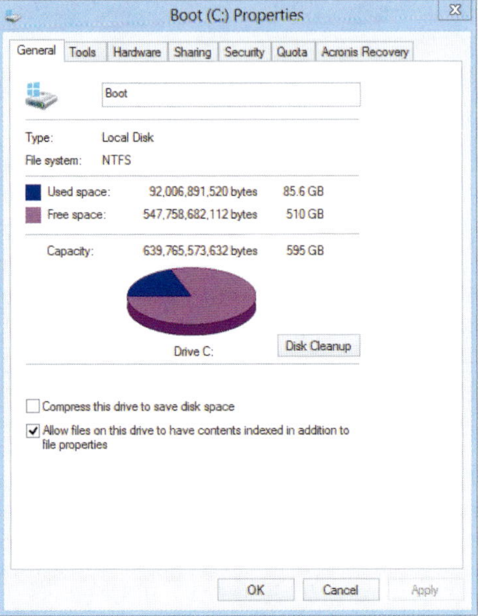

Ⓐ The General tab of a hard disk's Properties dialog box

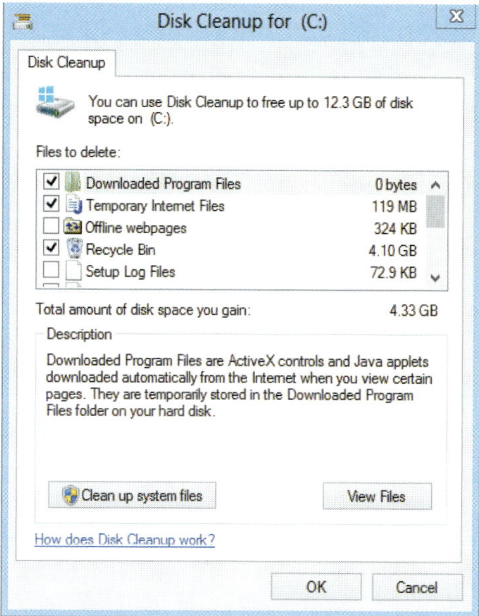

**A** Use Disk Cleanup to free up additional space on your drive.

# Disk Cleanup and Check Disk

Disk Cleanup is used to delete files and objects from your disk to clear additional free space when your disk gets full. It will also make your drive perform a little faster.

All disks suffer errors and corruptions over the course of their lifetimes. Indeed, optical disks are so large and their written areas so small that they can be damaged by all sorts of things: the magnetic head coming too close to the surface of the optical platter, a speck of dust, the stray cosmic ray, you name it. Disk drives are designed to find and mark off damaged areas and to find and fix soft errors. (SSDs are memory chips and don't suffer from this defect.)

The primary tool in Windows 8 that performs this magic is called Check Disk (**chkdsk.exe**), and in Windows 8 this utility's operational mode has changed so that it is running in the background fixing errors as it detects them. This will greatly reduce the time you need to spend fixing your disks. When Check Disk detects an error, it will post a "Scan drive for errors" message in the Action center. You can run Check Disk on all attached drives while your system runs, but to run it on the system disk you have to reboot your system and wait for the process to complete.

## To run Disk Cleanup:

1.  Click the Disk Cleanup button on the General tab of a disk drive's Properties dialog box (**A** in the previous section).

2.  When the Disk Cleanup dialog box appears **A**, select the files you want to remove and click OK.

3.  Confirm your action in the alert box.

## To run Check Disk:

1. Click the Tools tab in the disk drive's Properties dialog box 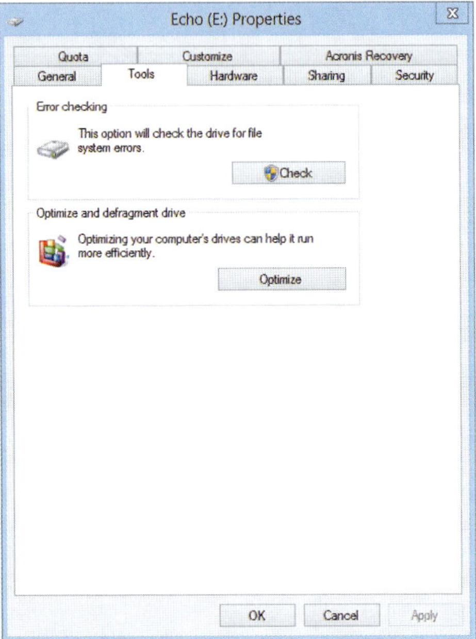, then tap or click the Check button in the Error Checking section.

2. The Error Checking dialog box appears **C**. Select Scan And Repair Drive.

   If this is the boot drive (system disk), you will be asked to reboot your system and the Check Disk utility will run prior to startup.

**TIP** Hard disk errors can be transient and sometimes aren't detected immediately by Windows 8's background scanning. If your computer freezes or reboots and you can't track down a software bug, try running Check Disk on your drive.

**B** The Tools tab of a disk drive's Properties dialog box

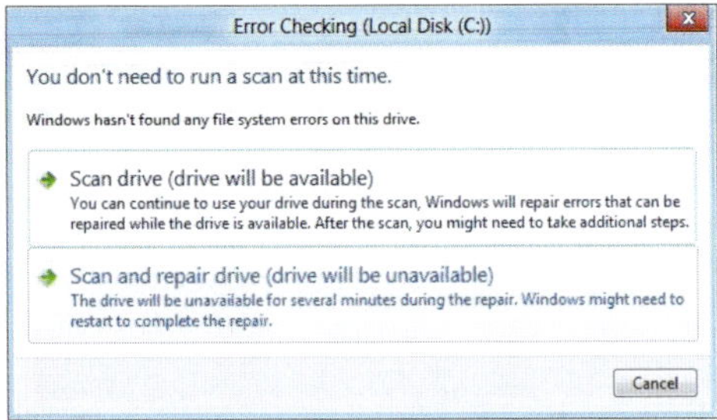

**C** The Error Checking dialog box

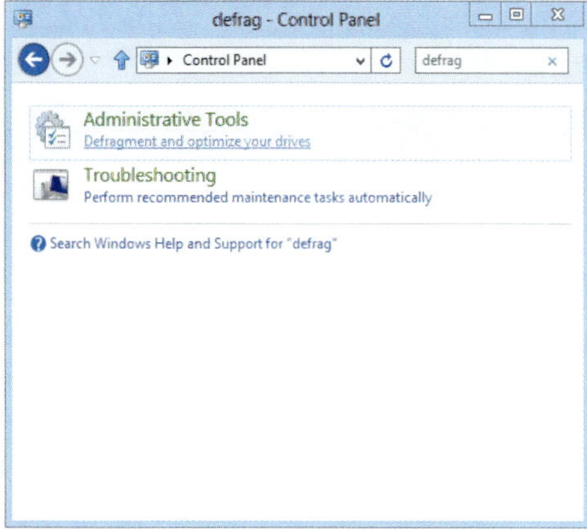



A Search for the Defrag control panel to open this tool.

# Defragment and Optimize Drives

As you operate a hard drive, Windows 8 deletes files in some places and writes files in other places using available free space on disk. Your system uses the free space available, and when the available free space in one contiguous area on disk isn't large enough to fit a file, Windows will write part of the file to one location and another part of the file to another location. That is called file or disk fragmentation, because the file is split up into fragments.

Fragmentation extracts a performance penalty on your system because a disk head is forced to move locations to read data (called a "seek") as it performs a READ operation. For magneto-optical hard drives, the performance penalty can be on the order of 10 to 20 percent, which is not insignificant but not a major penalty. Still, there are programs called "defraggers" that you can use to move files around so that they are contiguous, as well as to place commonly used files like system files together on disk in optimal locations. It's good to perform defrags on your disks every two to four weeks. Windows 8 ships with a utility called Optimize Drives that allows you to perform this operation.

## To perform a defrag on a hard drive:

1. Press ⊞+I and tap or click the *Control Panel* link that appears in the Settings bar.

2. In the Defrag control panel, enter defrag into the Search field and press Enter or tap the Find icon A.

*continues on next page*

3. Click the *Defragment and optimize your drive* link to open the Optimize Drives dialog box **B**.

   Defragmentation can take from several minutes to several hours, depending on the size of the disk, the number of files, and the degree of fragmentation that must be optimized.

4. To analyze a disk's fragmentation, select the drive and tap or click the Analyze button.

5. To optimize a disk, select the drive and tap or click the Optimize button.

6. Tap or click Close when the operation is finished.

## To schedule defragmentation:

1. Tap or click the Change Settings button in the Schedule Optimization section of the Optimize Drives dialog box .

2. Select a frequency from the Frequency drop-down menu **C**.

3. Click the Choose button and select the drives you wish to optimize. Tap or click the OK button.

4. Tap or click the OK button on the Optimization Schedule screen.

**TIP** You can optimize all attached hard drives, as well as certain solid-state devices. Solid-state drives also suffer from defragmentation, but they use an alternate form of defragmentation routine, called TRIM, which is built into their firmware. TRIM is a command name, not an acronym.

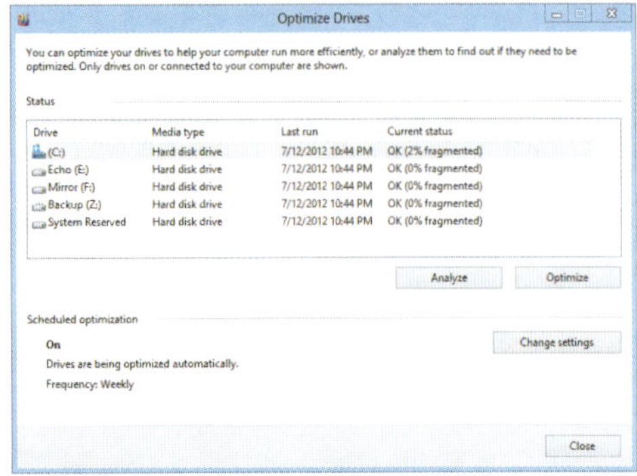

**B** The Optimize Drives dialog box

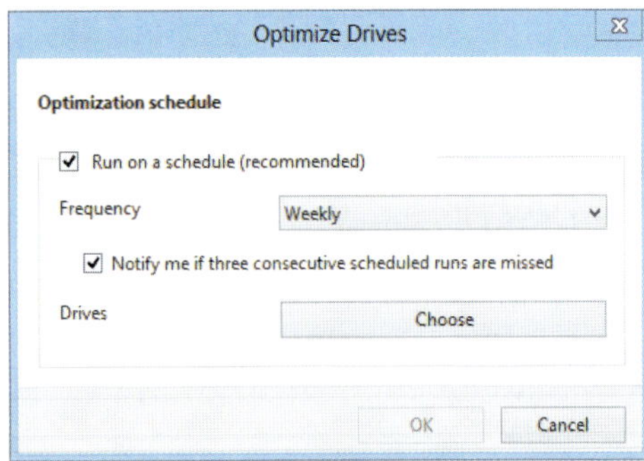

**C** The Optimization Schedule screen

# Solid-State Drives

Solid-state drives (SSDs) are a technological wonder. Adding an SSD drive vastly improves system performance by making access to stored data an order of magnitude faster. Since SSDs are memory chips, there are no moving parts, so they also greatly reduce power consumption. Soon, the majority of laptops and desktop PCs will use SSDs as their system disk. For tablets and phones, SSDs are already standard.

An SSD drive is a set of memory chips inside an enclosure, which has a built-in drive bus interface controller card. Typically, SSD drives are sold with the SATA III interface, just like hard drives and optical drives. Older drives, now deprecated, use SATA II. Some high-performance SSDs are sold as PCI cards, but they are expensive and uncommon. When you connect a SATA II or III SSD card, you may be required to switch to AHCI from SATA mode in your system's BIOS/UEFI.

A modern PC with Windows 8 on an SSD can boot in under 10 seconds. Compare that to Windows 7 on a hard drive, which can take from 45 to 60 seconds. Now we're getting somewhere.

Over time, SSD devices fragment, just like all storage devices. You can defragment an SSD just like you do any other drive—by using the Optimize Drives utility that was discussed in the previous section. When you run the optimization, you will notice that the Current Status field indicates the percentage of the device that has been "trimmed." **TRIM** is the command used to rewrite an SSD so that it is optimized.

## To install Windows on an SSD drive:

1. Disconnect all drives on your system, except the SSD drive and the drive containing your Windows 8 installation files (your DVD drive perhaps).

2. Boot up using your Windows 8 installation disk, and start the **SETUP** program that is located on your installation media.

3. Windows should recognize your SSD device. Continue with the installation, allowing Windows to format the disk and install Windows on the SSD.

   Installing Windows 8 on an SSD works best as a fresh install.

**TIP** Western Digital sells a line of hybrid hard drives with large SSD caches in them. These devices offer the benefits of SSDs, along with high disk capacities, at a much lower price.

**TIP** Intel's Smart Response Technology (SRT) allows an **SSD** to be first-level storage (cache) in front of hard drives that serve as second-level storage. The system places system files and commonly used files on the **SSD**, while moving less commonly used files to the hard disk. You will find **SRT** on modern motherboards, and the feature is supported by drivers for Windows 8. It can speed up a system by 40 percent over a hard drive Windows 8 installation.

# Storage Spaces

With the appearance of Windows 8, Microsoft has decided to end its development of Windows Home Server. Since Windows 8 can serve as a media server, the unique disk pooling solution of Home Server has been moved into Windows 8, where it's called Storage Spaces.

Storage Spaces are logical containers that combine a group of physical disks into a resource pool to which a drive letter is assigned. The resource pool can be any size, and the disks it contains can be any size or type—both SATA and USB drives can be used. If the drive manager can recognize the storage device, it can be added to a pool. This ad hoc addition of storage is known as *thin provisioning*.

Since a Storage Space is an abstract container, it can be "larger" than the available disk space. As you run out of real available space, Windows 8 will ask you to add more disks. So, for example, you could create a 2 TB space called Document Space and a 6 TB space called Media Space even though your Storage Space pool contains a set of disks that add up to only 3 TB Ⓐ.

A space protects the data it contains by either mirroring it (RAID 1) or using disk parity (RAID 3). Mirrors and parity require that data be stored on multiple physical drives. If a mirror or parity disk fails, an alert box informs you of the problem. If you have enough free disk space in the right place, Storage Spaces rebuilds the lost redundant element. Otherwise, you need to install another disk. It's kind of like a credit default swap, but for your data.

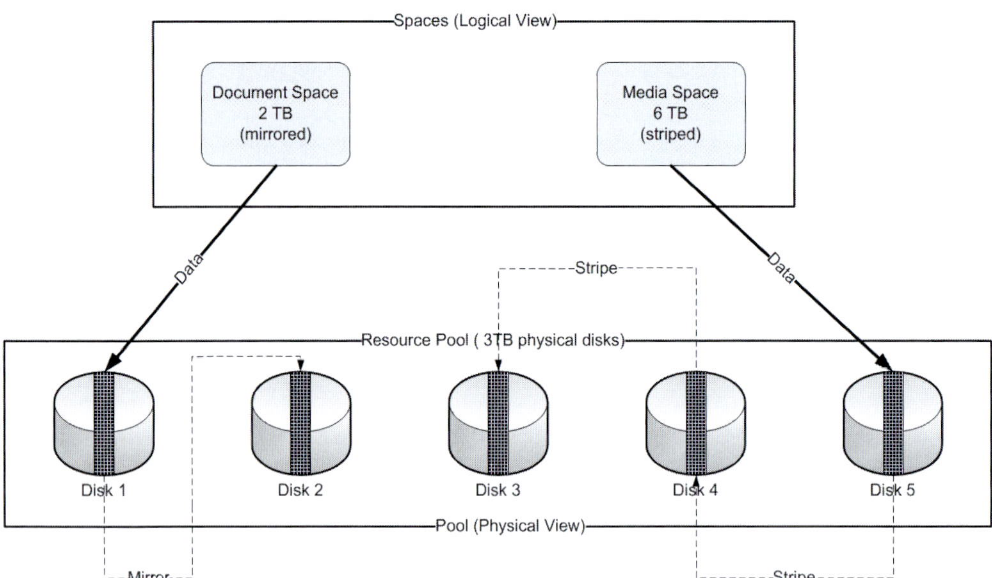


Ⓐ Storage Spaces lets you create and manage protected pools of storage.

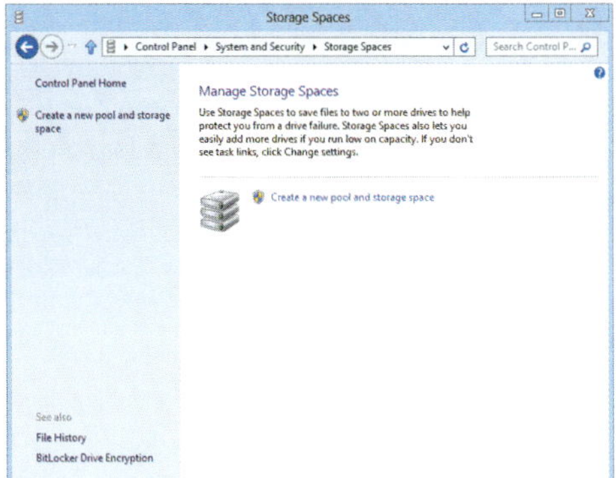

**B** The Storage Spaces control panel

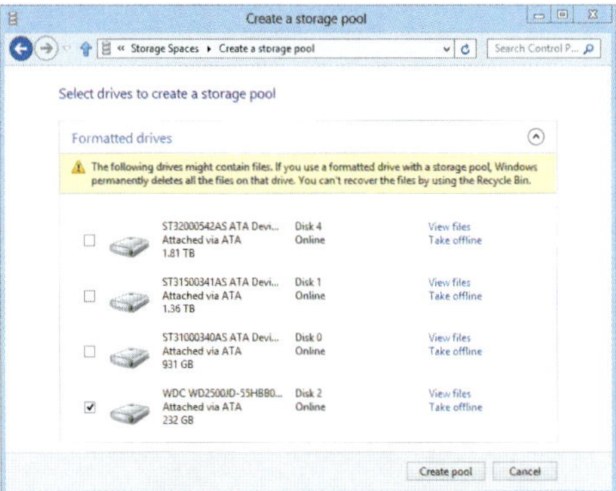

**C** Select the drives you wish to include in your storage pool.

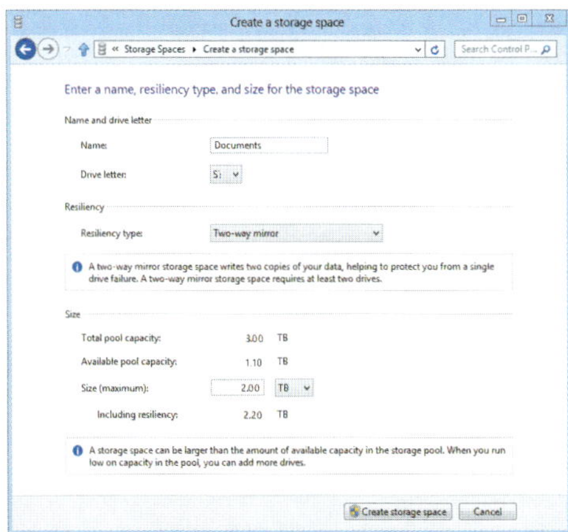

**D** The Create A Storage Space screen allows you to define the name, type of resiliency, and size of the Storage Space.

## To create a Storage Space:

1. Press ⊞+X or right-click the lower-left corner of your display to open the Management menu.

2. Select the Control Panel command to open the Control Panel dialog box. Click System And Security, and then click Storage Spaces. The Storage Spaces control panel appears **B**.

3. Click the *Create a new pool and storage space* link. You will be asked to elevate your privileges to administrator. Tap or click Yes.

4. In the Create A Storage Pool dialog box **C**, select the drives you want to use and click OK.

5. Give the storage space a name **D**; choose a setting from the Resiliency Type menu; and give the storage space a size. Tap or click the Create Storage Space button.

   After you create a Storage Space, you can modify its size. Click the *Manage Storage Space* link to open a dialog box that lets you add and remove disks from the resource pool.

**TIP** A Storage Space is only useful if it protects your data, so always mirror or stripe your Storage Spaces. Striping gives higher performance but uses more disk space than a 2-way mirror.

# Optical Discs

Hard drives are devices with platters that can be read and written to using magnetic fields generated at the tips of moving drive heads. They are great for applications where data is meant to be written and rewritten many times at a single location. For applications where you intend to write the data less frequently or perhaps permanently, optical discs are used. CDs and DVDs are made of photosensitive materials embedded in plastic, and they can be modified by focused light, usually in the form of a laser beam. Laptops, desktop computers, and some tablets come with an optical drive.

A CD-ROM disc can contain up to about 800 MB of information. For this reason, CDs are most commonly used for audio and picture files, often bundled into albums. DVDs can support from 4.7 GB for a single layer to up to 8.5 GB for double-layer discs, making them useful for applications, games, and movies. Blu-ray discs can contain about 40 GB of information and are used for high-definition movies.

The suffix ROM (read-only memory) is used for a disc that is permanently written and can only be read; R is used when the disc is read-only once you have written to it once; and RW is used when you can read and write to the disc. A plus (+) or minus (-) sign indicates the technology that is used to work with that kind of disc; for example, DVD+RW and DVD-RW are two different formats. Modern optical drives can read and write to a variety of, but not all, formats, so you need to make sure that a particular format will work in your drive.

The Mastered format is a write-once format. When you add files and master the disc, you "burn" the files and the disc becomes read-only. With the Live File System, you can continue to write to the disc over time. If the disc is an R disc, then the files are added until you fill up the disc. For RW, you can overwrite deleted files and use the disk again.

The latest and highest-capacity optical drives are Blu-ray discs. They are often used for very high-quality movie playback, and less frequently to back up data on. A single-layer Blu-ray disc can hold 25 GB; a double-layer disc can hold 50 GB. The name Blu-ray comes from the use of a blue-violet laser in place of the red lasers used in the DVD format. Advanced PCs may come with this type of optical drive. Blu-ray technology requires its own set of drivers, but it is managed similarly to other optical disc types.

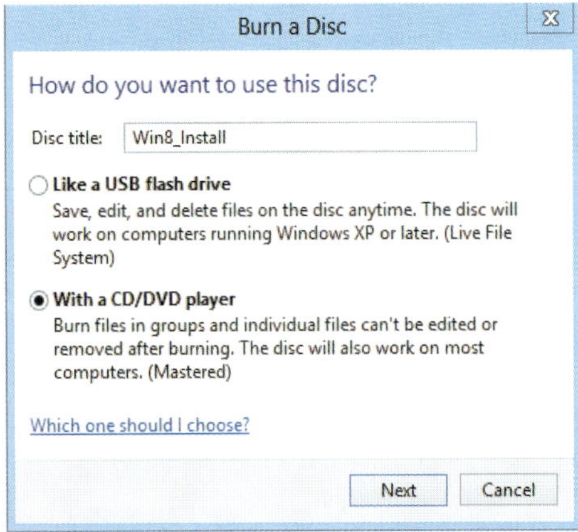


**A** When you insert a writable optical disc,
Windows 8 offers you two formatting options.

## To format a CD or DVD:

1. Insert the blank disc into your drive.

2. The Burn A Disc dialog box opens **A**.
   Enter a title for the disc.

3. Select either the Like A USB Flash Drive
   radio button or the With A CD/DVD
   Player radio button, and tap or click
   Next.

4. When the format operation is complete, open the disc window and drag
   and drop the files you want to copy to
   the disc.

## To play a file on an optical disc:

Double-click the file. Windows will launch
the software player that is associated with
that file type.

Windows 8 has an AutoPlay feature that
will detect the files on an optical disc and
play them automatically when you insert
them. Audio and video files require the use
of a conversion program called a codec.
Although a variety of audio and video
codecs are included in Windows 8, Microsoft for some reason has decided to once
again omit the movie playback codec. You
will need to either purchase or download
a movie playback program. When you purchase a DVD drive, this software is often
included in the package. You can download the Media Player Codec Pack from
CNET's Download.com site.

**TIP** You can find a more complete listing of disc types at http://windows.
microsoft.com/en-US/windows-vista/
Which-CD-or-DVD-format-should-I-use.

# USB Flash Drives

A flash drive, or thumbdrive, is a set of memory chips packaged into a container with a bus controller. Nearly all thumbdrives are USB drives, and over time the capacity of these drives has grown substantially while the price has plummeted. Small USB drives are given away as prizes in cereal boxes.

Modern flash drives have very long duty cycles, in keeping with their solid-state construction. Most USB drives are preformatted. The smaller drives come with the FAT file system, which is universally supported. Larger USB drives are formatted with FAT32. You can use and run disk diagnostic utilities on thumbdrives, and you can partition them.

## To format a flash drive:

1. Press ⊞+E. Tap and hold, or right-click, the flash drive icon in Windows Explorer, and select Format from the context menu Ⓐ.

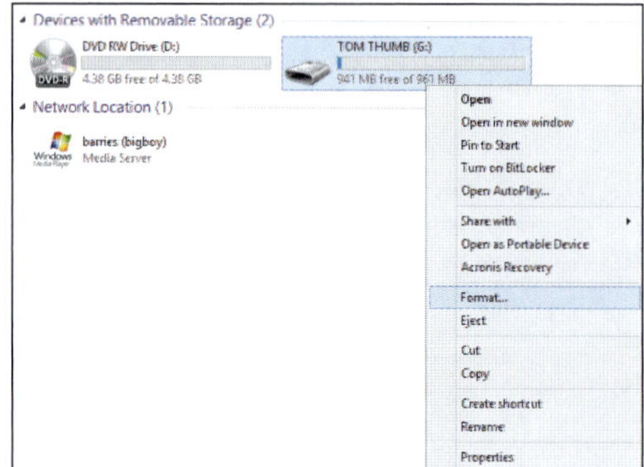


Ⓐ The Format command for a USB drive

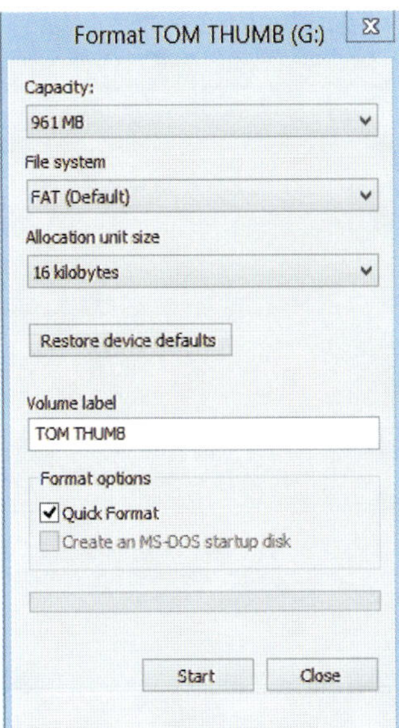



**B** The Format dialog box for a USB drive has options for different file systems.

2. In the Format dialog box **B**, select the file system you want (FAT, FAT32, NTFS, or exFAT), enter a name for the drive, and click the Start button.

Most of the options you see in the Format dialog box are identical to the options you see for hard drives. The formatting process writes the addressing scheme differently, but it is functionally equivalent.

Here are some uses for flash drives:

- Create a Windows to Go installation, which is a portable version of Windows on a USB drive (see Chapter 15). Windows To Go is only available with Windows 8 Enterprise edition.

- Install a lightweight bootable operating system, along with disk utilities, antivirus programs, and portable apps.

- Encrypt the drive to secure your files on it.

- Turn the flash drive into a device key by using Predator software (you can get this from Download.com).

- Use the flash drive with Windows ReadyBoost.

**TIP** ReadyBoost is a Windows-specific feature that allows you to use a USB flash drive as a cache for your system memory. In laptops, for example, you can speed up your system by extending the system memory in this manner. Enable ReadyBoost in the ReadyBoost tab of the Properties dialog box for the USB flash drive.

# Putting It All Together

- Disk drives can be divided into partitions, and partitions into volumes, which must be formatted for use.

- Each volume contains a file system and appears as an independent disk in the file system.

- Simple volumes occupy space on a single basic disk.

- Dynamic disks can participate in more advanced types of volumes, including ones that span disks, are striped across disks, and are written with redundant information called parity.

- Windows 8 supports different RAID levels, such as 0 (striping), 1 (mirroring), and 5 (striping with parity).

- Windows 8 comes with utilities that can remove unnecessary files, check a disk for errors, or defragment a disk.

- Solid-state drives (SSDs) are best used as boot, or startup, drives.

- Storage Spaces lets you create a pool of disks that are mirrored or striped for protection and lets you assign portions of that pool to different uses.

- You can format and use a variety of optical media in Windows 8.

- To play movies in Windows 8, you will need to install a movie codec.

- Flash drives are portable solid-state drives that can be used for a variety of purposes.

# Networking

The design goal for Windows 8 networking was to make mobile connectivity ubiquitous and easy to use. Microsoft has kept the networking part of the tile-based interface simple, with only a handful of features exposed. The focus is on getting users connected automatically and keeping them connected even as they move from place to place. In networking, as in all things Windows 8, the word is mobile.

Windows 8 has made it much easier to connect devices to mobile broadband services such as 3G and 4G networks. New drivers are pushed automatically to your device using the Windows Update service. Devices that conform to the new Mobile Broadband Interface Model specification are now supported in Windows 8.

The wide range of network device and protocol support in previous versions of Windows has been retained within a variety of control panels. Central to accessing Windows' powerful networking support is a control panel called Network and Sharing Center.

## In This Chapter

# Network and Sharing Center

Windows 8 tries to make things simple for users. When you plug a network adapter into your system, Windows 8 will recognize it and in most instances install a driver for it. A driver is a low-level program that communicates with the I/O (input/output) functions of your system's chipset. Automatic installation is part of what is called Universal Plug and Play (UPnP). UPnP works for networks, printers, USB, Bluetooth, and many other types of buses and devices. Plug and Play (PnP) by contrast is when devices connected directly to your system are recognized automatically.

When a network interface is installed, numerous protocols attempt to automatically configure the adapter so that it can connect to available networks. For network adapters, Windows 8 dynamically assigns a network address and a name resolution server using two network services: DHCP (Dynamic Host Configuration Protocol) and DNS (Domain Name Service). These services configure your system so that your network connectivity is established without your manual intervention.

Wireless or other radio-based networks will also auto-negotiate from a variety of connection protocols to find the best type of connection to send and receive on. For example, a Wi-Fi adapter that conforms to the IEEE 802.11g standard will negotiate with an access point running the newer, multi-band 802.11n protocol so that the connection drops down to the lower g-standard speed.

Network settings in the Charms bar offer very simple options:

- Switch networks
- Turn sharing on and off
- Turn airplane mode on or off

  Airplane mode turns off all signals that could potentially interfere with a plane's communications; it is required by airline authorities.

This is all well and good when everything works, but when it doesn't you will need to pay a visit to the Network and Sharing Center panel, where all the advanced networking options in Windows 8 are found.

One common task is to manually set up your network adapter. This is an essential skill, so we'll take a look at how the task is performed.

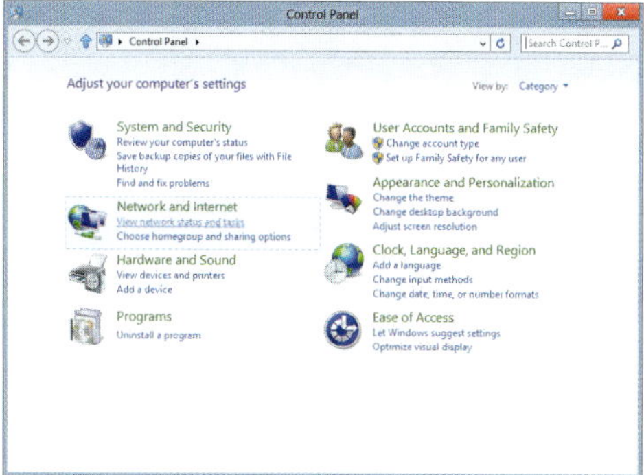

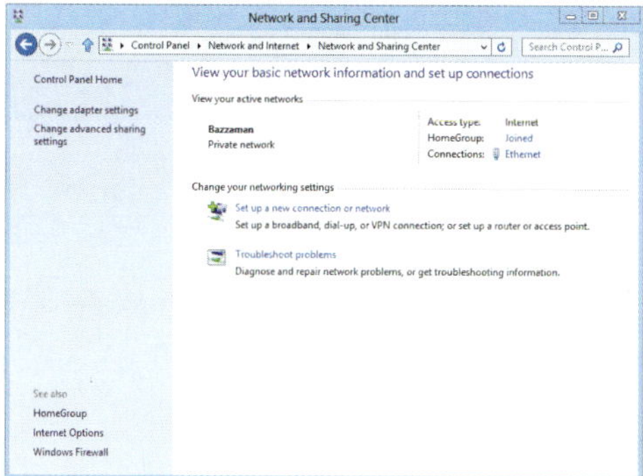

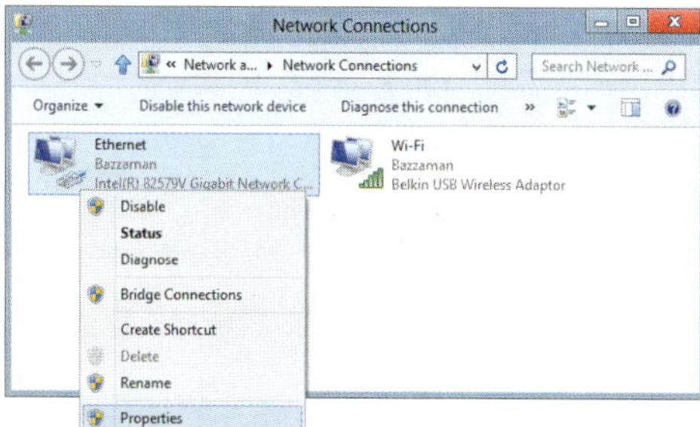

**A** You can access the Network and Sharing Center panel from the Control Panel home page.

**B** The Network and Sharing Center panel provides access to advanced network configuration options.

**C** Open a network adapter's Properties dialog box to view its network settings.

## To open the Network and Sharing Center panel from the Computer Management menu:

1. On the Desktop, press ⊞+X, or right-click, the lower-right corner of the display, and select Computer Management > Control Panel.

2. In the Network and Internet section, click the *View network status and tasks* link **A**.

## To open the Network and Sharing Center panel from the taskbar:

1. Right-click the Network icon in the Notification area of the taskbar.

2. Select Open Network And Sharing Center from the pop-up menu.

   The Network and Sharing Center panel appears **B**.

## To change a network adapter's settings:

1. Click the *Change adapter settings* link in the left pane of the Network and Sharing Center panel **B**.

2. In the Network Connections dialog box, right-click the network adapter of interest and select the Properties command from the context menu **C**.

*continues on next page*

3. In the Ethernet Properties dialog box, scroll down and select Internet Protocol Version 4 **D**. Click the Properties button.

   For a dynamically assigned address, both the Obtain An IP Address Automatically and Obtain DNS Server Address Automatically options are selected.

4. To assign a static (fixed) IP address and your own DNS server and gateway, click Use The Following IP Address **E** and fill in the address, subnet mask, and default gateway in the appropriate text boxes.

5. Continue by filling in at least one (but preferably two) DNS server in the Use The Following DNS Server Addresses text box, and click OK. Click OK again to close the second dialog box and return to the Network and Sharing Center panel.

The Internet Protocol Version 4 dialog box allows you to set a fixed IP address, which can be useful when you want your device to always appear with a known address; for example, when you want to configure a PC as a media server. For most laptops, tablets, or phones that are mobile devices, you will want your device to have a dynamic address, but it's still useful to know where these settings can be accessed so you know that your dynamic settings are configurable.

**TIP** You can use more than one network adapter at the same time, and one or more adapter types. This can speed up network performance and ensures that you have a backup should one adapter go down. You can also use one adapter to connect to one type of network and the other to connect to another type or to a different network at the same time.

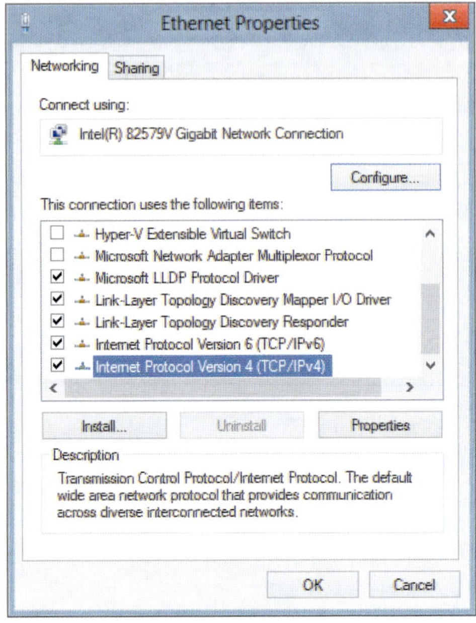

**D** The Ethernet Properties dialog box

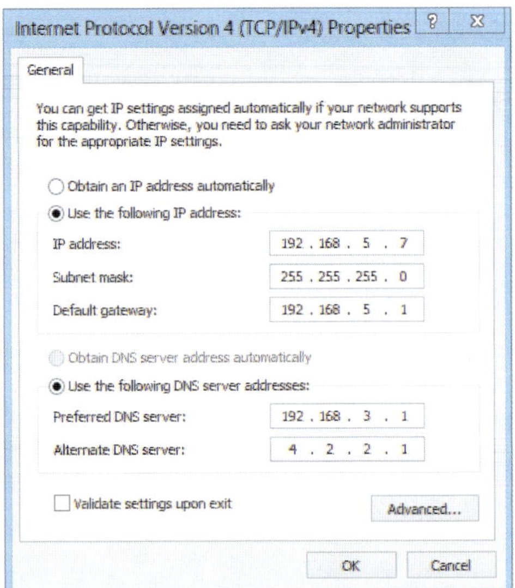

**E** The Internet Protocol Version 4 Properties dialog box

# Network Connections

When you set up your computer, you give it a name. This friendly name, or hostname, is what you see when you browse a network. However, a hostname isn't what a network uses to send traffic back and forth between systems. Networks use network addresses—they are the recognized endpoints where traffic is sent or received.

One computer can have multiple network connections, each connected through a single piece of hardware called a network adapter (or network interface card). A network adapter contains a transceiver that is given a unique machine address. Ethernet cards and Wi-Fi adapters all have unique MAC (media access control) addresses assigned to them by the hardware manufacturer. We assign networking addresses to individual MAC addresses as part of our network setup, either automatically or manually.

For TCP/IP networking, which is the dominant networking protocol in use today, an IP address and subnet type is given to each network interface. To configure a network connection, you also have to assign an address for the system that is the "gateway" to outside networks. Since we use friendly names, DNS maps the friendly names to IP addresses, and vice versa, so that systems can be located. So you also have to specify which DNS servers perform name resolution for your network interface so that your connection can find and be recognized by other endpoints on a network.

Network services have been developed to automatically supply this information so that network connections can be automatically configured as dynamic assignments.

On local Microsoft networks, other services provide name resolution; they are built into Windows 8 and do not need to be configured.

## To view your current network connection:

- On the Desktop, move your mouse cursor over the Network icon in the Notification area 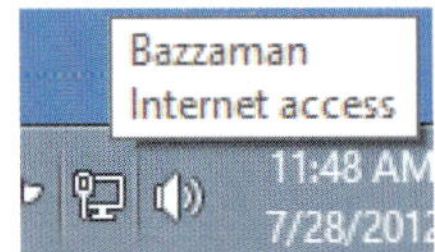.

- Tap or click the Network icon **A** to open the Networks bar **B**.

- Press Ctrl+C or swipe from the right edge to open the Charms bar. Tap or click the Settings charm, and then tap or click the Network icon in the Settings bar **C** to view the Networks bar **B**.

The Networks bar shows the available wired or wireless networks for a computer. When you right-click the connection and select the Turn Sharing On Or Off command from the pop-up menu, the Sharing dialog box opens, which allows you to view and be viewed by other network devices.

**TIP** You can check your network devices using Command Prompt. To open Command Prompt, open the Run dialog box, type `cmd`, and press Enter. If you enter `ipconfig`, Windows 8 will list all of your network adapters and their properties. Type `ipconfig /release` to release dynamically assigned addresses and `ipconfig /renew` to get a new address. Type `ipconfig /?` for help with this command. Note that the spaces in `ipconfig /release` and `ipconfig /renew` and `ipconfig /?` are intentional.

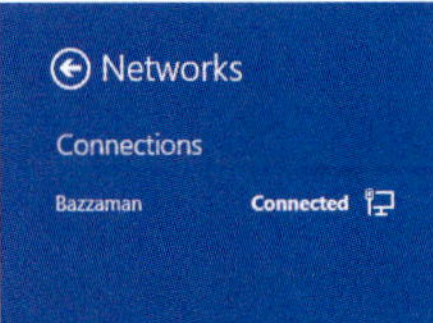

**A** The Network icon in the Notification area shows the currently connected network in its tooltip.

*Wireless Network Adapter connection*  *Ethernet Network Adapter connection*

**B** The Networks bar when you connect with a wireless (Wi-Fi) adapter (left) and with an Ethernet adapter (right)

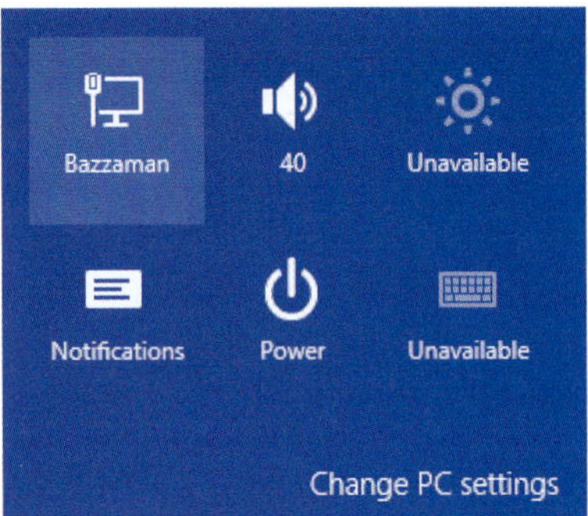

**C** The Network icon in the Settings bar

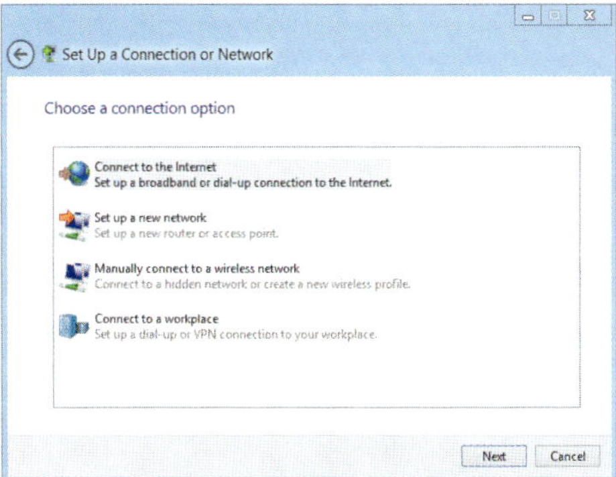

**A** The Set Up a Connection or Network wizard

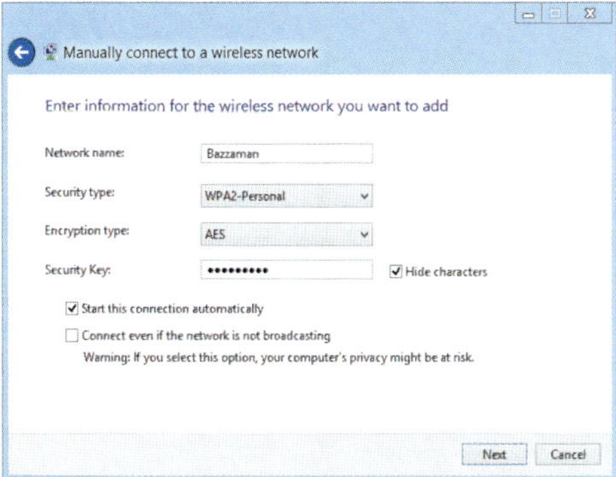

**B** The Manually Connect to a Wireless Network dialog box

# Set Up a Connection or Network

You can use the Set Up a Connection or Network wizard in any of the following scenarios:

- To connect to the Internet via broadband or dialup (modem)

- To set up a new network connection through a router or access point

- To manually connect to a hidden wireless network or create a new wireless profile

- To connect to a business network using either a dial-up or virtual private network (VPN) connection

You will usually only have to do this once, when you connect to a network or configure your router or access point the first time. The *Set up a new network* link **A** polls your network to find available routers, modems, and access points that you can connect to.

## To set up a network:

1. Open the Network and Sharing Center panel, as described earlier.

2. In the Change Your Network Settings section of the Network and Sharing Center panel, click the *Set up a new connection or network* link.

   The Set Up a Connection or Network wizard appears **A**.

3. Tap or click the *Manually connect to a wireless network* link **B**.

*continues on next page*

4. Enter the information required for your wireless network, then tap or click Next.

   If you have difficulty getting the password right, deselect the Hide Characters check box to see what you are typing.

5. Windows 8 posts a success dialog box; click Close to complete the process.

The *Connect to a workplace* link lets you connect either by using a secure VPN connection or by dialing directly with a modem 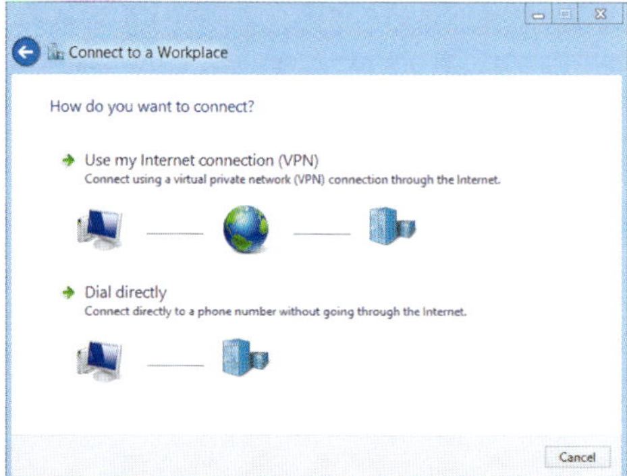.

## To connect to the Internet through a broadband modem:

1. Open the Set Up a Connection or Network wizard.

2. Click the *Connect to the Internet* link in the Set Up a Connection or Network screen Ⓐ to open the dialog box shown in Ⓓ.

   (PPPoE stands for point-to-point protocol over Ethernet, which is a protocol for DSL services.)

3. Fill in the Broadband Connection configuration screen Ⓔ.

4. Click the Connect button.

**TIP** As a general rule, Ethernet broadband connections are faster than Wi-Fi, which in turn is faster than 3G or 4G networks.

**TIP** A feature called DirectAccess is available in Windows 8 to users accessing a network with a Windows server. This type of remote access connection lets users securely access enterprise shares, websites, and applications without connecting through a VPN. To use this feature, an administrator must run RRAS on the server and your device must be an authenticated client.

Ⓒ The Connect to a Workplace dialog box lets you connect to another network via VPN or dial-up.

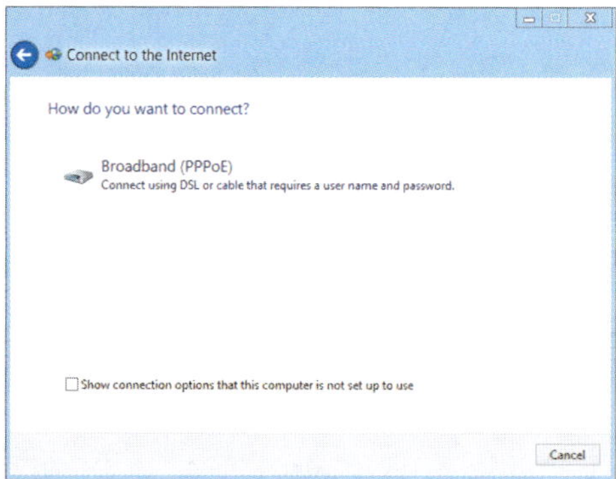

Ⓓ The Connect to the Internet dialog box lets you connect to the Internet through a broadband connection.

Ⓔ You enter your broadband connection's configuration details in this dialog box.

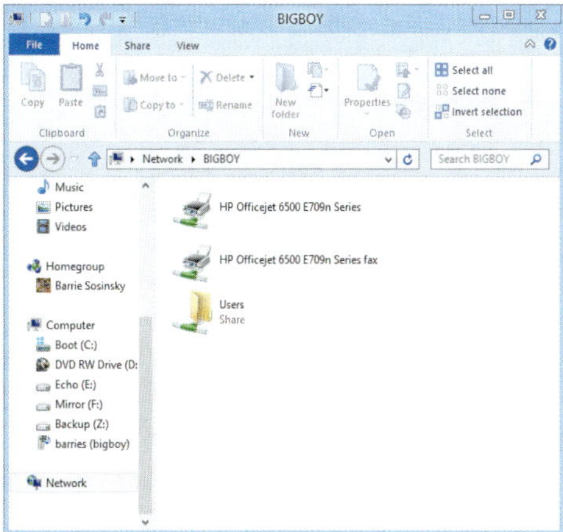

**A** Network shares within a connected host

# The Network Folder

The Network folder is one of those special folders that you can place on your Desktop or view from within Internet Explorer. It shows you what devices are viewable on your network and provides buttons for adding network devices and printers, establishing a remote connection, and more.

In the Network folder, you can highlight a computer and double-click it or press the Open button on the Network tab of the ribbon to drill down into the contents of the host. In this manner, you can expose whatever shared content or devices exist on that system. For example, when the host BIGBOY is opened **A**, you see that there are two network printer shares available, as well as a network share called Users. You can tell that they are network resources because the icons display network cables. Whether you can actually access these shares depends on whether the owner gave you the rights to do so.

Notice that the address in the address bar is >Network>BIGBOY, which is in the "breadcrumbs" format. As you learned in Chapter 10, you can click elements of a breadcrumb to move around. If you click inside the address bar, it changes to **\\BIGBOY**, which is the actual address in UNC (Uniform Naming Convention) notation. The Users folder would have the path **\\BIGBOY\Users**. If you enter this string into the address bar or into the Run dialog box, Windows Explorer will show the contents of the Users folder.

## To view your network and currently connected devices from Windows Explorer:

1. Press ⊞+E to open Windows Explorer.

2. In the left pane, scroll to the bottom and tap or click Network.

## To view your network and currently connected devices from the tile-based Start screen:

1. On the tile-based Start screen, start typing **network**.

2. Select the Network app when it appears.

   The Network folder opens **B**.

**TIP** I like to show the Computer, User's Files, Network, Recycle Bin, and Control Panel folders on my Desktop. To do this, open the Desktop Icon Settings control panel and enable those check boxes.

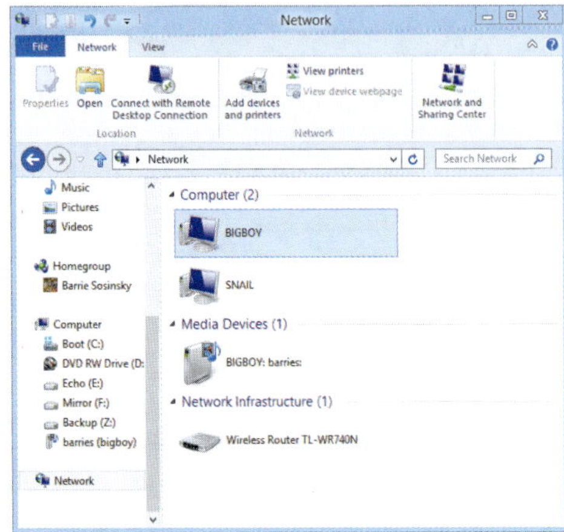

**B** The Network folder

# Wireless Connections

Wireless connections use radio signals to send and receive transmissions. The two dominant forms of wireless connection are Wi-Fi, which is based on the IEEE 802.11 standards, and broadband connections that use cellular phone networks such as 3G and 4G.

Microsoft has put a lot of development effort into making wireless networking seamless and easy to use. If your wireless adapter is enabled, chances are that it will be automatically configured for you and will detect available networks. You just need to know how to select a wireless network and authenticate your device.

You can set all of your wireless and network settings in the Wireless section of the PC Settings page, which is accessed from the Settings charm. Windows learns your network preferences over time and prioritizes one wireless or mobile broadband network over others. Since Wi-Fi is cheaper, has lower latencies (greater transfer rates), and allows for higher data caps, when Wi-Fi is available mobile broadband connections are not used. On a mobile device, this also has the effect of lengthening battery life. When Wi-Fi isn't available, your device switches back to your broadband connection.

Microsoft has put a lot of effort into making mobile broadband easy to use. When you insert a SIM card or a USB transceiver into your PC, Windows 8 automatically recognizes which vendor's device it is, installs the correct drivers, and connects you to the

service's network. That's pretty slick. If the device is unlocked and can access multiple service providers, Windows 8 allows you to choose from the different possibilities within the Networks bar. You can also choose another network provider and even be directed to subscribe to a service.

One new feature you might not notice is that when you reconnect a PC to a Wi-Fi network, it connects in about a second—even faster than your display is available. Windows 7, by comparison, took about 12 seconds to establish a network connection.

If you have a limited bandwidth connection, you may want to show the estimated data usage and set it as a metered connection.

The metered connection option is useful if you are on a 3G or 4G network and have a limited data bucket. When this option is enabled, device software and app updates will not download over your broadband connection. Those data transfers are performed when another network connection, such as a home Wi-Fi network, is enabled.

Windows 8 introduces a feature called "airplane mode," which turns on and off all wireless communications with a single switch. In airplane mode, Wi-Fi, Bluetooth, and any other wireless connections are taken offline. Airplane mode is not available when your device is connected to an Ethernet network. When Windows 8 is offline, a variety of system functions, such as Live Tiles and automatic updates, do not function. You access airplane mode from the Networks bar in the Settings charm.

## To switch wireless networks:

1. Open the Networks bar , and click or tap the network you want to connect to.

2. If you want to connect automatically to this network, leave the Connect Automatically check box (the default) selected and then tap or click Connect.

3. Enter the network security key **B**, then tap or click Next.

4. For public networks, tap or click the No, Don't Turn On Sharing Or Connect To Devices button.

   *or*

   For private networks, tap or click the Yes, Turn On Sharing And Connect To Devices button **C**.

   You are joined to the new wireless network. Each wireless adapter has a unique address and can be connected to one wireless network at a time.

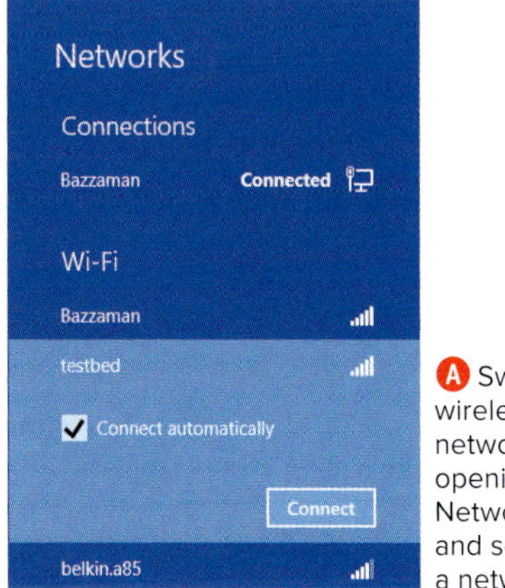

**A** Switch wireless networks by opening the Networks bar and selecting a network.

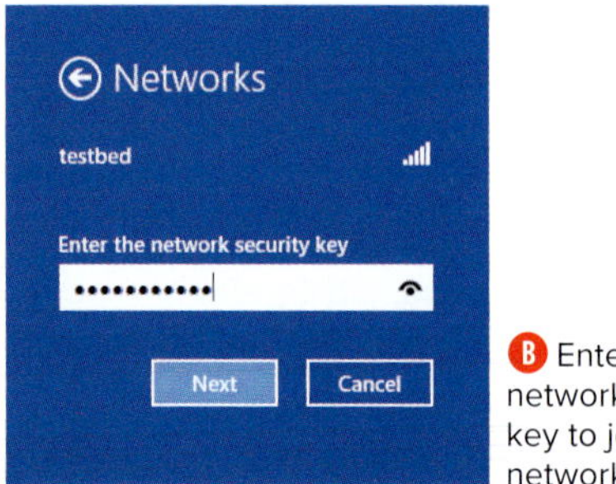

**B** Enter the network security key to join the network.

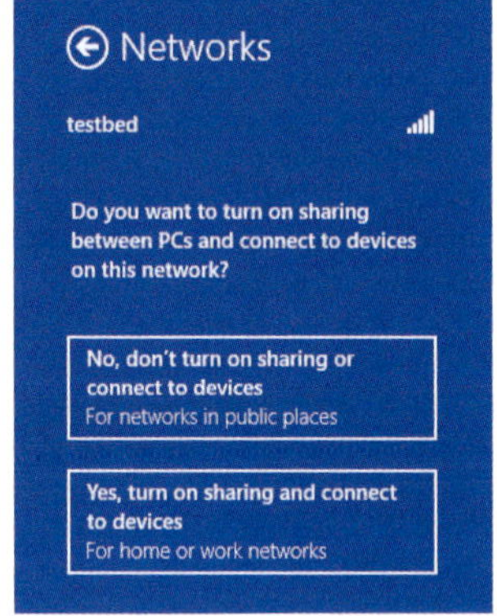

**C** Turn network discovery and device sharing on or off here.

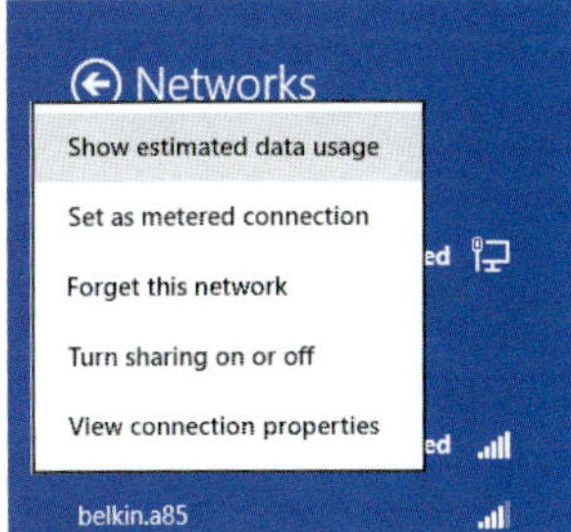



**D** The Show Estimated Data Usage command

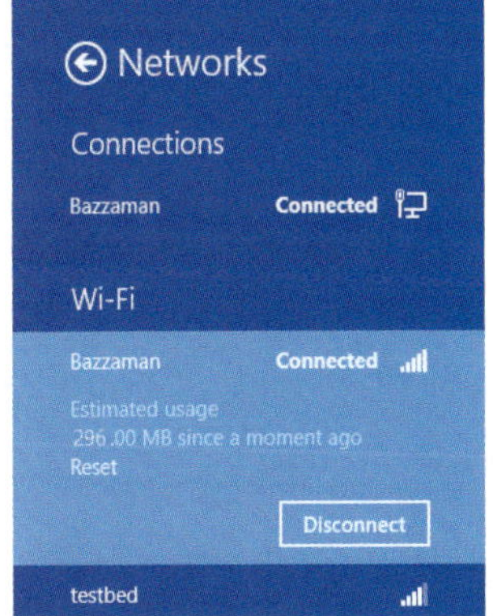



**E** The estimated data transferred since you last reset the counter is shown in MB.

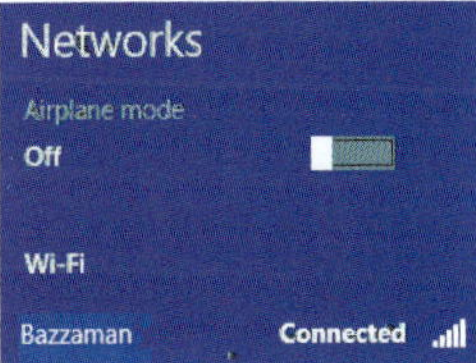



**F** Airplane mode is available only when you are wirelessly connected.

## To show your wireless network's estimated data usage:

1. Open the Networks bar **A**. Tap and hold, or right-click, the wireless network to which you are connected.

   The pop-up menu **D** appears.

2. Select the Show Estimated Data Usage command; Windows 8 displays the usage statistics **E**.

   This same setting may be found in the Devices section of the PC Settings page (which you can access from the Settings charm).

## To turn airplane mode on or off:

Open the Networks bar and move the Airplane Mode slider **F** to On or Off, as desired.

**TIP** The Windows 8 Task Manager contains detailed information on the history of your wireless apps. In this application, you can check your broadband connection to determine how much data has been used, see connection times, and check whether an application is metered or not. This information is found on the App History tab.

# Sharing Settings

Windows 8 comes with different network settings so you can control who has access to what network resources on your devices.

Three types of networks are defined:

- **Private.** Your private network would be a home network on which you are the only user or on which other members of the network are trusted.

- **Guest or Public.** Guest or public network sharing is restricted to reduce the possibility of access to sensitive resources.

- **All Networks.** This profile controls access to public folders, media streaming options, file sharing, and password protection.

Among the sharing settings you can control are network discovery, file and printer sharing, HomeGroup connectivity, media streaming, and password protection. Network discovery allows your computer to be seen on the network by others and allows your computer to find other devices. Turning off network discovery provides some measure of protection. These settings also allow you to share files on the network, encrypt file transfers, and make sure that people authenticate themselves with a user ID and password to gain access to your files.

Folders, printers, and even entire drives can be shared over a network. You share these objects by opening their Properties dialog box and creating the share on the Sharing tab.

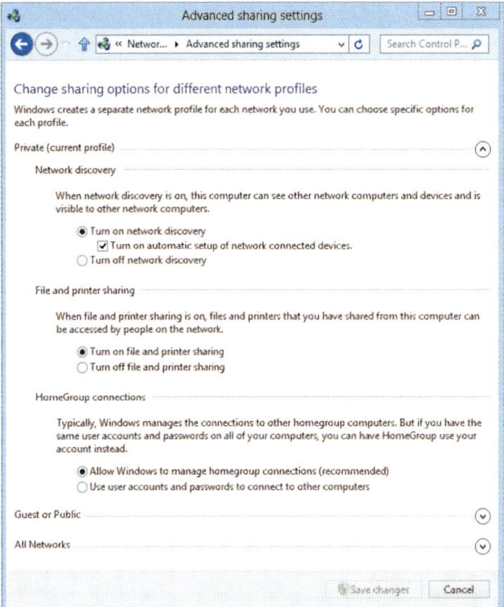

**A** The Private sharing profile settings in the Advanced Sharing Settings dialog box

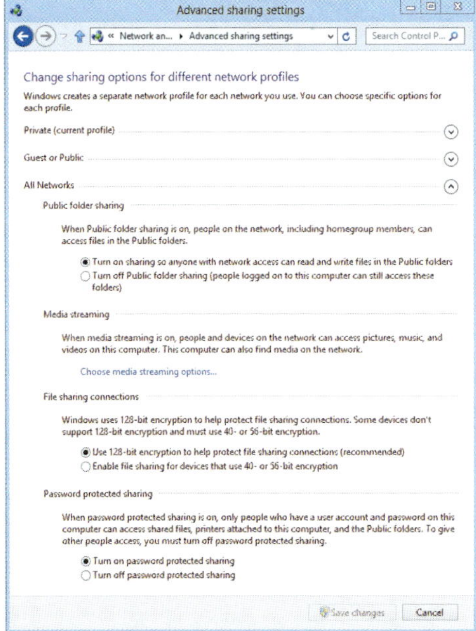

**B** The All Networks sharing profile contains options for access to network shares, media streaming, and password protection.

## To access sharing settings:

1. Open the Network and Sharing Center panel, and tap or click the *Change advanced sharing settings* link in the left pane.

2. Select the profile you wish to alter **A**.

3. Select the options you wish to turn on or off, then click the Save Changes button.

The Guest or Public sharing profile is the most restrictive—you have control over only network discovery and file and printer sharing. **B** shows the settings available for All Networks.

## To create a folder share:

1. On the Desktop, tap and hold (or right-click) a folder, select Properties, and then click the Sharing tab.

   Disks and printers also have a Sharing tab.

*continues on next page*

2. On the Sharing tab **C**, click the Share button.

3. In the File Sharing dialog box **D**, click the drop-down menu or the Add button to allow specific users access to the folder.

4. Click the Permission Level column and select the level of access you wish to allow for the share; then click the Share button.

The File Sharing confirmation dialog box appears **E**. From here, you can email people about the share or copy and paste the link to the share.

**TIP** One nice solution for sharing files and folders across multiple machines is Dropbox. When you install Dropbox, it looks like a local drive on your system, but your files are stored in the cloud. Microsoft's SkyDrive that you will learn about in Chapter 17 provides a similar and equally useful function.

**TIP** The Advanced Sharing button **C** lets you limit the number of simultaneously connected users, set access permissions, and allow users to cache content on their system when they are offline and aren't connected to your system. If you set the option for password protection, users must supply a password before they can connect to your share.

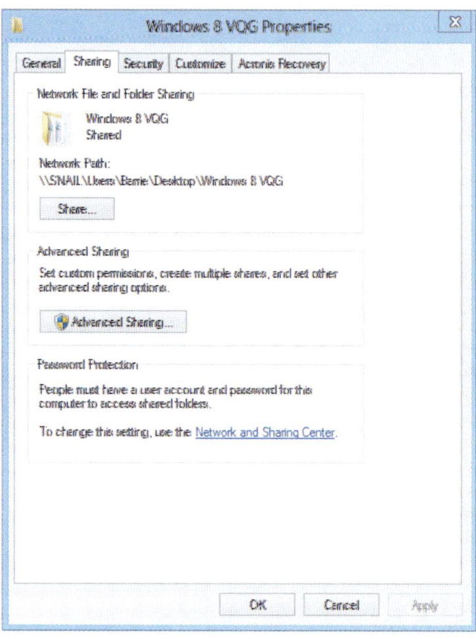

**C** The Sharing tab in the Properties dialog box

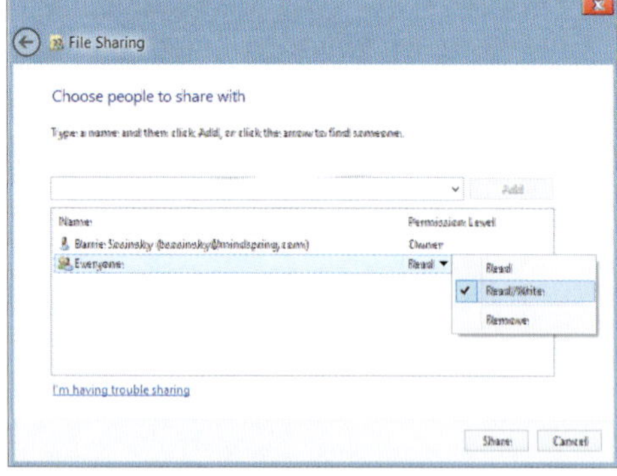

**D** The File Sharing dialog box lets you share folders (or other objects) with other users.

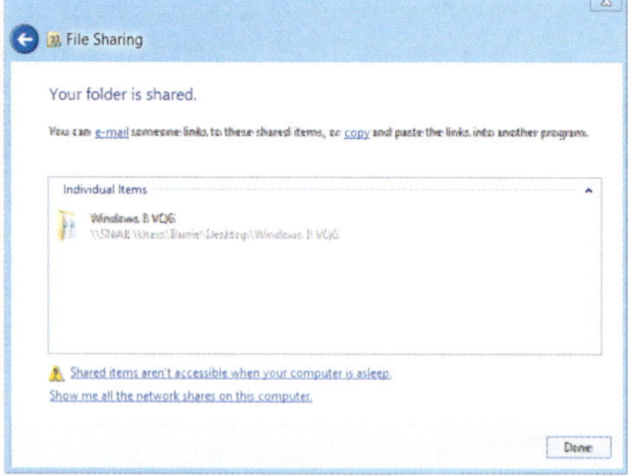

**E** The File Sharing confirmation dialog box gives you the path to the newly created network share.

# Bluetooth

Although we don't tend to think of Bluetooth as a networking service, it is. Bluetooth is a wireless technology with a 25-foot range that allows you to connect all manner of peripherals to your device, including mice, keyboards, printers, and so on. You can form Bluetooth connections between two such enabled Windows 8 phones or tablets to transfer information. Bluetooth isn't a high-speed connection, but it is sufficient for these purposes.

Nearly all mobile devices come with Bluetooth built in. For PCs, you may have to add a Bluetooth transceiver to your system; they are most commonly added by plugging in a small USB key. Normally, Bluetooth network adapters are automatically recognized and configured by a PC, with no intervention needed.

When you bring a Bluetooth device within range of another Bluetooth device, they detect each other and automatically negotiate to see if they can communicate.

Devices come with their own "profiles," which are sets of properties that they support. If the two devices have the same profile, Windows will ask if you would like to join the remote Bluetooth device to your system. The master Bluetooth device (your USB transceiver or phone) can add up to seven slave devices, and masters and slaves can switch places. The network uses a round-robin polling method to transfer data between devices.

There's little to configure with Bluetooth in Windows 8; devices are either compatible or they are not. For the most part, when a device claims to be Windows compatible, it almost always is—even if the compatibility was for an earlier version of Windows.

**TIP** Keep in mind Bluetooth's 25-foot limit when using devices. Unlike Wi-Fi, Bluetooth can't penetrate walls. Its low speed also makes it primarily a peripheral-only network.

# Putting It All Together

- Windows 8 does a great job of automatically configuring your network interfaces and connecting to available networks, even without your intervention.

- For advanced network configuration, open the Network and Sharing Center panel and investigate the options you find there.

- You can share printers, folders, disks, and other network resources attached to your system or the network.

- A network connection uses your network adapter as its interface and assigns a network address to it.

- The Network and Sharing Center panel has a number of options for connecting to networks, which include connections to a broadband or cable modem, VPN, and router or wireless access points.

- Once you connect to a network, you can use the Network folder from within Windows Explorer to browse your network and find resources.

- Wireless, or Wi-Fi, connections are detected by Windows 8 automatically. You can use the Networks section of the Settings bar to switch networks.

- New wireless network features allow you to configure a wireless connection for metered usage, as well as use airplane mode for turning off all radio networks while on a plane.

- You can enforce a number of settings that control access to shared resources, including who can write to a folder, whether passwords are needed, and streaming options.

- Bluetooth works seamlessly with Windows 8 and is great for connecting peripheral devices, but it can be used only over a short distance.

# Internet Explorer 10

No application better exemplifies Windows 8 than the brand new version of its browser, Internet Explorer 10 (IE10). Internet Explorer is one of the few native applications that have both a tile-based interface and a Desktop, or legacy, interface.

When you open the tile-based version of Internet Explorer, the browser opens full screen to give you an immersive experience. Since you are navigating primarily with touch, actions such as scrolling, page turns, settings, and so forth are kept operationally simple. The tile-based IE was clearly meant to satisfy tablet and smartphone users.

IE10 comes with the new Trident rendering engine, which is HTML5 compliant, as well as the Microsoft Chakra JavaScript engine, which first appeared in Internet Explorer 9. Adobe Flash is built into the tile-based IE browser, which enables you to view video on websites without extra effort.

Legacy sites that require plugins work with Desktop IE10. This version of the browser won't seem too different from Internet Explorer 9, but there are many new features in Desktop IE that you will find quite practical.

## In This Chapter

# Tile-based IE10

The tile-based version of Internet Explorer is meant to be an immersive experience. A website should be displayed with little or no browser interface shown onscreen, thus maximizing the content's size. What you see in Ⓐ is the *New York Times* website in full-screen mode. Notice that not one interface element shows on the page.

When you need to alter the content of the browser, a gesture will either allow you to perform an action or open an area of the screen in which you can use touch commands.

You can perform edge swipes to open an address box and enter text with the virtual keyboard; open the Charms bar to change settings; or open a panel containing tabs, recent pages, or favorites all displayed as tiles. Tile-based IE10 has corresponding mouse and keyboard equivalents, but the interface was designed with touch in mind. Menu systems are gone in the tile-based interface: When you need to make selections, a small dialog box with a limited number of choices appears.

There are a number of features built into the tile-based IE10 that make the browsing experience faster and more natural. It's easy to take them for granted. For example, Microsoft has built in a prefetch feature that looks for the link to the next page; when you are reading a story online, tile-based IE10 takes you to the next page with a

Ⓐ Metro Internet Explorer 10 full-screen mode

right-to-left swipe without you having to locate that next link and click it. When you enter text from the virtual keyboard, the browser predicts what your next entry might be and displays sites you have been to, displays sites that are popular, and offers word recognition and auto-correct. The goal is to get you where you want to be as quickly as possible.

Since tile-based IE and Desktop IE are not separate programs, when you create a favorite site it appears in both versions of the interface. You can pin your favorite sites or pages to the Start screen and launch the browser to that page with a single tap or click. If you log into Windows Live, your favorites, your history, and other settings are synchronized across several devices.

## To scroll:

- Swipe up to scroll down a page.

- Swipe down to scroll up a page.

- Use your mouse's scroll wheel to scroll up or down a page.

- Use the page's scroll bars to scroll up or down a page.

**TIP** **You may like the responsiveness of the tile-based interface but need the tools that you find in the Desktop version. If you are using a multi-monitor display, put the tile-based version on one monitor and Desktop on another.**

# Working with Content

The page in tile-based IE10 is dynamic, and you can interact with it. It reacts to touches, swipes, and dynamic gestures such as pinch and expand. You can perform several actions to get to the content you want to see in a web page in a form that you want to see it in.

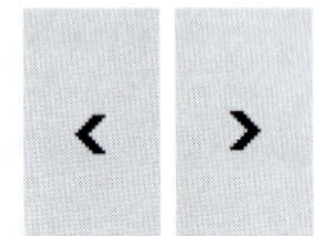

Ⓐ Previous and Next arrows

## To move to the next page of a story:

One of the nice new features in the tile-based IE is that it picks up the *Next* link in a story and moves you there when you ask it for the next page.

- Swipe from the right or left to move forward or back, respectively.

- Move your mouse to the right or left edge until a faint arrow appears Ⓐ, then click.

## To zoom in or out:

- To zoom in for a closer view, touch the display with two fingers and move them out from one another.

- To zoom out and see more of the screen, pinch two fingers together.

- To alter the screen zoom with your mouse or by touch, open the Settings charm, select Internet Options, and move the Zoom slider.

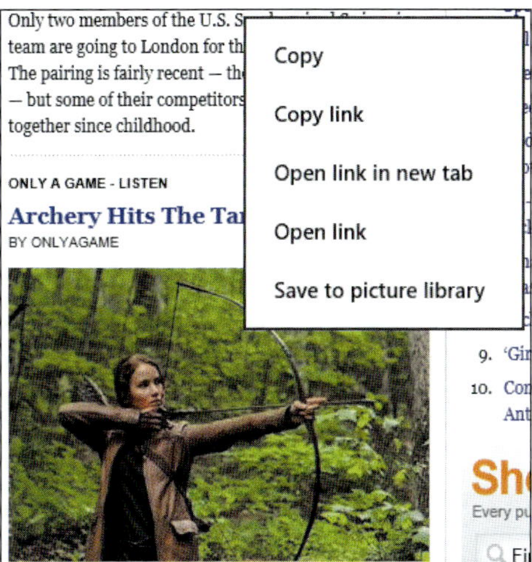


**B** Context menu for active content

## To activate content:

- Tap or click a link to open that page.

- Tap or click a Flash video to play that video.

- Tap and hold an item, or right-click it, and select an option from the context menu **B**.

## To copy to the Clipboard:

1. Tap and drag, or click and drag, to select the desired text.

2. Hold your finger on the selection or right-click to view the Copy menu.

3. Select Copy to place the text on the Clipboard.

   *or*

   Press Ctrl+C.

**TIP** If you see a Flash video on a page, double-click it to play it full screen. Double-click again to restore it to its previous style.

# Working with Tabs

The tile-based IE shows a single browser window on your display, without an address bar or tabs opened. You can display the interface elements using a set of simple gestures.

If you have selected another browser as your default, Windows 8 disables the tile-based IE10 and displays the Internet Explorer tile **A**. When you tap the tile, the Desktop version of Internet Explorer 10 launches instead of the tile-based version.

### To open the tile-based IE10:

Open the Start screen, and tap or click the Internet Explorer tile **B**.

### To view the tile-based tab thumbnails and address bar:

- With the tile-based browser open, swipe down from the top edge of the screen.

- Right-click the open browser.

- Press ⊞+Z.

The tabs and address bar display **C**.

### To view a tab:

Tap or click a tab in the tab group.

**A** Desktop Internet Explorer tile

**B** The tile-based Internet Explorer tile

## To open a new tab to a page:

1. Tap or click the New Tab button (+) at the top of the window, or press Ctrl+T.

2. Tap or click the address bar.

3. Enter the address into the address bar using either the virtual keyboard or a real one.

   Notice that as you enter characters, tile-based IE offers suggestions of known websites, places you have visited, and favorites to speed your selection. Once the page opens, the web page's favicon (website-specific icon) appears in the address bar to the left of the URL.

4. Tap or click the Forward button or press Enter.

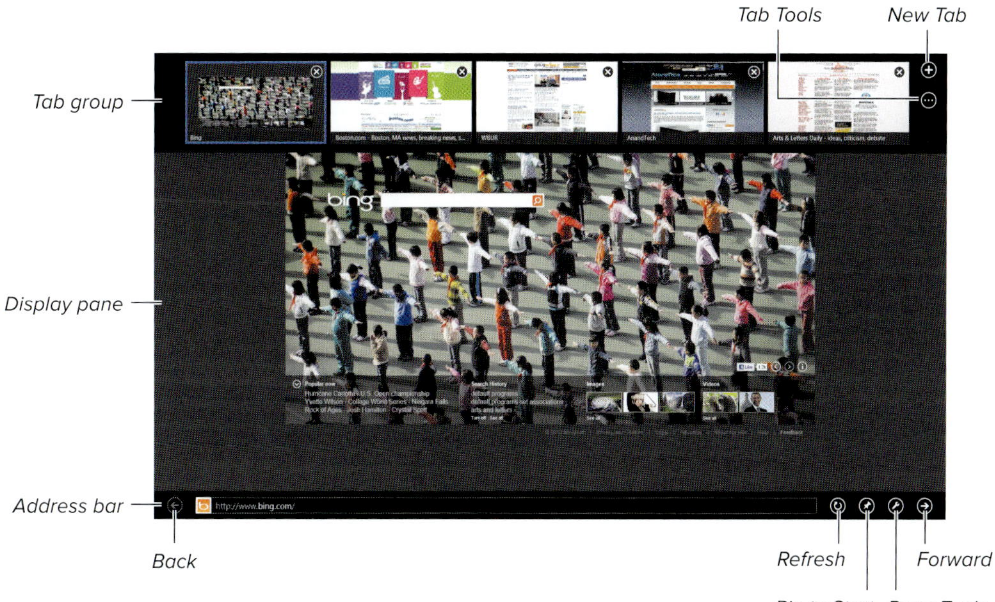


C The tile-based IE10 with tab group and address bar

## To close a tab:

Tap or click the Close button (X) on the upper-right corner of the tab's thumbnail.

Up to ten tabs are displayed at a time. As you open more than ten tabs, the tile-based IE10 closes your old tabs to make room for the new ones.

## To close all tabs:

1. Tap or click the Tab Tools button to open the Tab Tools menu.

2. Tap or click Close Tabs **D**.

## To open a private tab:

1. Tap or click the Tab Tools button.

2. Tap or click New InPrivate Tab.

When you select the New InPrivate Tab option **D**, the tile-based IE10 opens a browsing session that does not save cookies and does not permit personal information to be sent to websites. Microsoft calls this feature Do Not Track (DNT), and it is new to Windows 8. DNT is also available in Desktop IE10.

**TIP** You can always tell if a tab is InPrivate. It displays a blue InPrivate box on the thumbnail name of the tab as well as on the left of the address bar.

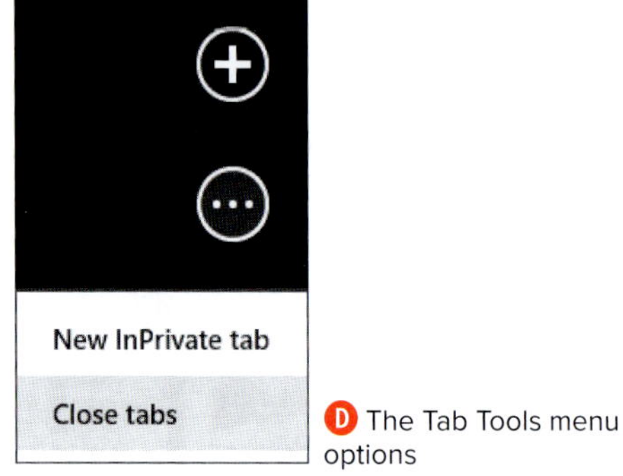

**D** The Tab Tools menu options

**A** When the address bar is selected (gets the focus), it shows you tiles.

**B** Entering an address into the address bar

**C** The address bar during a page load

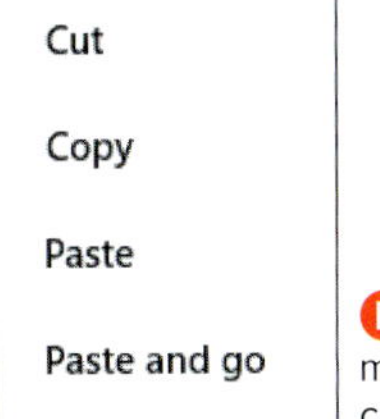

**D** The address bar Clipboard menu features a new command called Paste And Go.

# The Address Bar

The address bar in the tile-based interface allows you to enter an address or URL (Uniform Resource Locator) using touch. It works using your mouse as well. When you touch or click the address bar, it changes to look like it does in **A**.

When you start to enter text into the address bar, it changes to look like it does in **B**. As you enter text, Windows 8 suggests sites you might want to go to based on your history, well-known sites, and auto-entry. This is an option you can disable, but it's useful here because you can click one of the choices if it's what you want. On a touch-sensitive display, the keyboard will open to allow you to enter text into the address bar.

Once you've entered the address, click the Forward button or press Enter to go to the address. As the site loads, the address bar changes to **C**: You see a dot animation, and the Refresh button changes to an X. Tap or click X to stop the page load; the X changes back to the Refresh button.

The address bar supports Clipboard operations: Copy and Paste, as well as a new command called Paste And Go.

### To view Clipboard commands:

- Tap and hold the address bar.
- Right-click the address bar **D**.

**TIP** Paste And Go is equivalent to pasting content into the address bar and then tapping the Forward button or pressing Enter.

# Tiles and Pinning

If there is a site or web page that you will return to, you can choose to pin this page to your Start screen. When you pin a page, it becomes a tile that you can tap or click to return to that page instantly.

## To create a Start screen tile:

1. Go to the page you wish to save as a pinned site.

2. Tap or click the Pin To Start button (the pushpin) **A**.

3. Enter a name for the tile, or edit the current label.

4. Tap or click the Pin To Start button.

Once you pin a web page to the Start screen, it appears as a tile at the right of your other tile groups. In the tile-based interface, the tile takes the predominant color of the web page and displays the website's favicon or a badge.

It is convenient to have a section of your favorite sites; they make navigation very convenient, and they appear in the Favorites section above the address bar whenever you enter a new page. In **B**, you can see a section of tiles for some of the websites that I visit often.

Web page tiles are like other tiles on the Start screen—they are live. If the website developer supports it, the tile can display live information, changing background and information as time goes by.

## To go to a recent or favorite (pinned) page:

Tap or click a tile in the Frequent or Pinned sections above the address bar. You can swipe right or left, or scroll, to see additional choices.

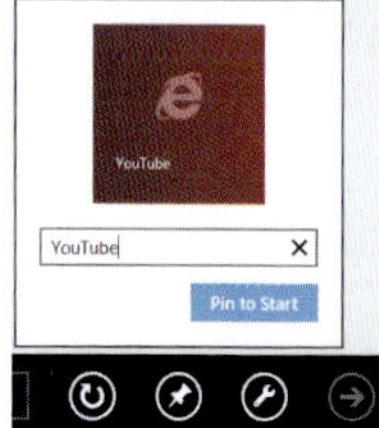

**A** Create a custom Start screen tile using the push pin button.

**B** A section of tiles shown as a labeled group

**TIP** If the tile for Internet Explorer gets unpinned from the Start screen and is missing, you can easily restore it. Open the Search charm, click Apps, and enter Internet Explorer into the Search field. Right-click the Internet Explorer result, and select Pin To Start from the Apps bar at the bottom of the screen.

**A** The Page Tools menu



**B** The Find On Page tools on the address bar

# Page Tools

The tile-based IE10 offers you a few Page Tools options **A**, as well as application-specific charms. The choices offered to you by these tools are both limited and important.

The Page Tools menu lets you:

- Get an app for this site

- Find items on a page

- Switch to the Desktop interface

Notice that the Page Tools button (**C** in "Working with Tabs") has a + (plus sign) on it. This indicates that the website offers some special content, usually an application that you can download from the Windows Store. Without this option, the Get App For This Site option is disabled and you don't see the plus sign on the tool icon.

## To search on the current page:

1. Click the Page Tools button.

2. Select the Find On Page command **A**.

3. Enter the search string into the Find field that appears to the right of the address bar **B**.

4. Tap or click the Next button to find the next match beyond your current position on the page.

   *or*

   Tap or click the Previous button to search back before your current position.

As you enter a search string, the tile-based IE displays the number of matches it finds and highlights them in yellow on the page. The current position is indicated by a blue highlight.

## To switch from the tile-based IE10 to Desktop IE10:

1. Click the Page Tools button.

2. Select the View On The Desktop command A.

   The same page you are viewing appears in Desktop IE.

## To show the tile-based IE as a sidebar of the Desktop:

1. Drag the browser to the side of the screen, as shown in C.

2. Use the slider to enlarge the browser to two-thirds of the display, close it, or make it full screen.

**TIP** Press Ctrl+. (period) to move the tile-based IE10 sidebar to the other side of the display.

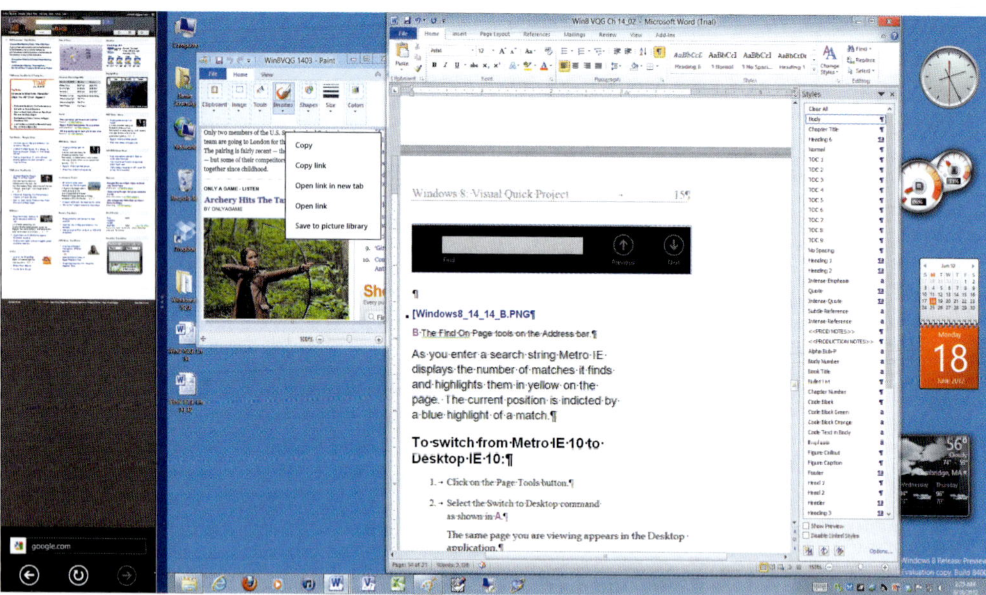

C The tile-based IE appears here as the left sidebar, with the Desktop to the right.

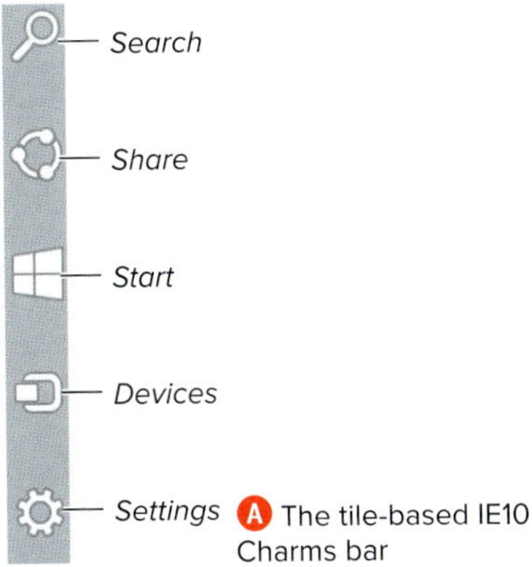



**A** The tile-based IE10 Charms bar

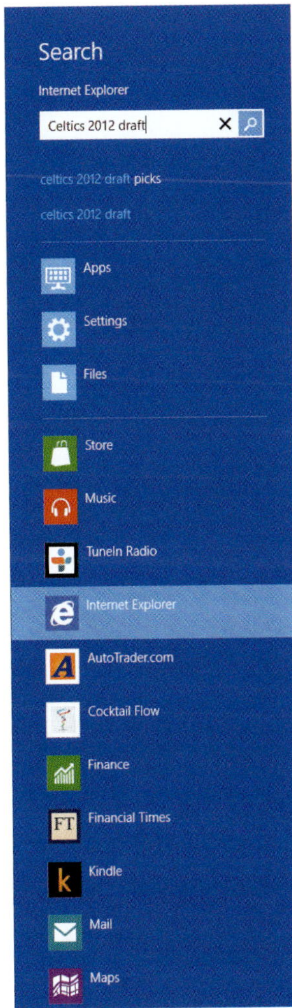



**B** The Search bar

# Settings

The tile-based IE10 offers a very limited number of settings that you can alter, but the important ones are illustrated here. Desktop IE10 has many more tools for changing browsing behavior, as you will see in a moment.

The tile-based IE10's Charms bar **A** allows you to open settings pages related to Internet Explorer.

### To display the tile-based IE10's Charms bar:

- Swipe to the right side of a display.

- Place the cursor in the lower-right corner of the screen and hold it for a second.

### To search for an item:

1. Click the Search charm in the Charms bar **A**.

2. Enter a search string into the Search field **B**.

3. Click the Find button (magnifying glass) to the right of the Search field.

   Notice that Internet Explorer is automatically selected for you. When you first open this Search bar, the name of your default search engine appears in the Search field. The charms and this same search function are available within the Desktop version of IE10 as well.

### To share pages or links:

Click the Share charm, and select either the Mail or People application to send that content to your intended audience.

The Start charm sends you to the Start screen and is a system-wide function. You can perform the same action by pressing the Windows ⊞ key on your keyboard. Devices is also a system function, sending your page or selection to a printer or to a program like One Note.

## To display Internet options:

1. Click the Settings charm in the Charms bar **A**.

2. Select Internet Options from the Settings bar **C**.

   The Internet Explorer Settings bar appears **D**.

## To delete your browsing history:

Click the Delete button in the Internet Explorer Settings bar **D** to delete your cookies, history list, temp files, and stored passwords.

## To remove geolocation permission:

Use the Ask For Location slider to turn off the ability of a website to locate you—even sites you previously allowed.

## To zoom in or out:

Use the Zoom slider.

## To turn off the Flip Ahead function:

Use the Turn On Flip Ahead slider to enable or disable this feature. It's hard to foresee a situation when you would want to turn this useful feature off.

## To enable page encoding:

1. Move the Select Encoding Automatically slider to On.

2. Select the encoding type from the drop-down list.

3. Select whether the document is encoded left-to-right or right-to-left.

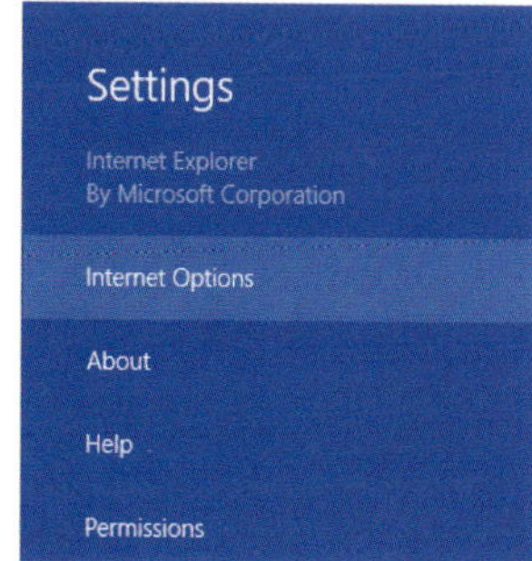

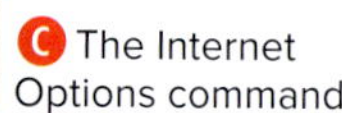

**C** The Internet Options command

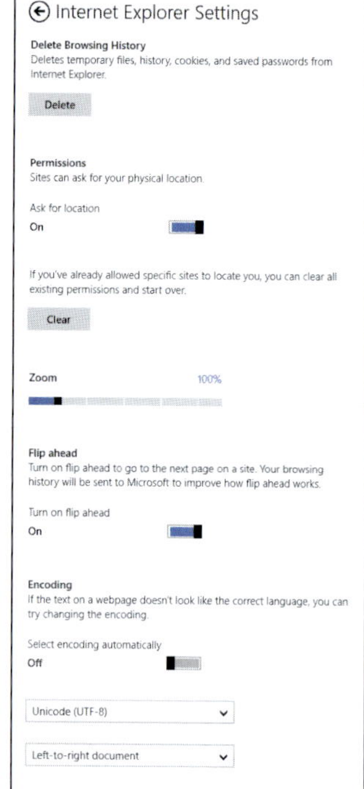

**D** The Internet Explorer Settings bar

**TIP** To go directly to the Internet Explorer Settings bar, press ⊞+I.

**TIP** Hold the cursor in the upper-right corner of the display to show charms related to Windows 8.

**TIP** Use encoding only when the web page is in another language.

# Desktop IE10

If you have used Internet Explorer in previous versions of Windows, then the Desktop IE in Windows 8 will seem familiar to you. The remainder of this chapter is devoted to the important features of the Desktop IE that are not found in the tile-based IE.

## To open Desktop IE10:

- Click the Internet Explorer icon in the taskbar **A**.

- Click a tile on the Start screen that opens a website that contains legacy content, and the Desktop version of IE will launch.

- Select the View On The Desktop command from the Page Tools menu in the tile-based IE (**A** in "Page Tools").

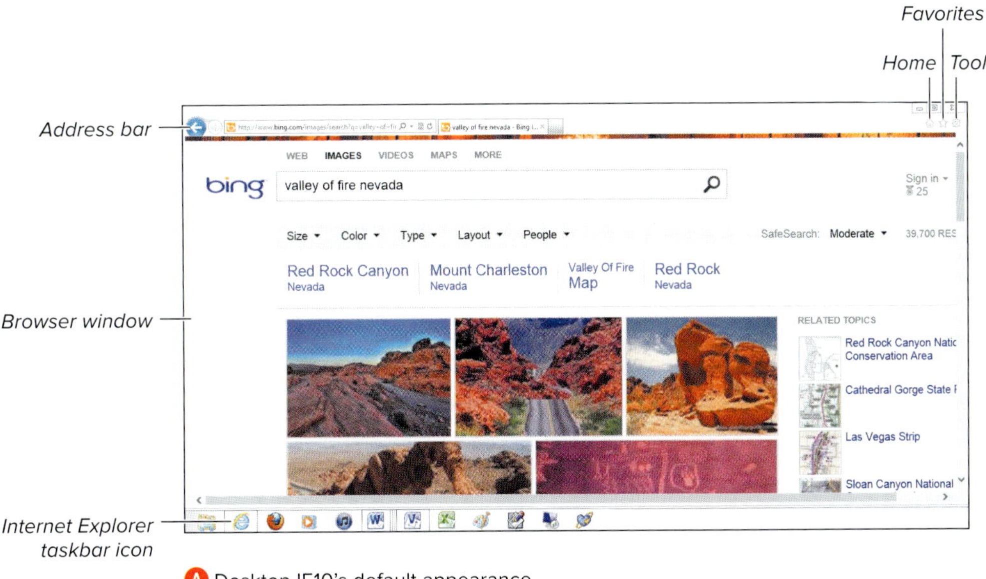


**A** Desktop IE10's default appearance

The first time you open Desktop IE, all the interface tools—menus, favorites, and so forth—are turned off 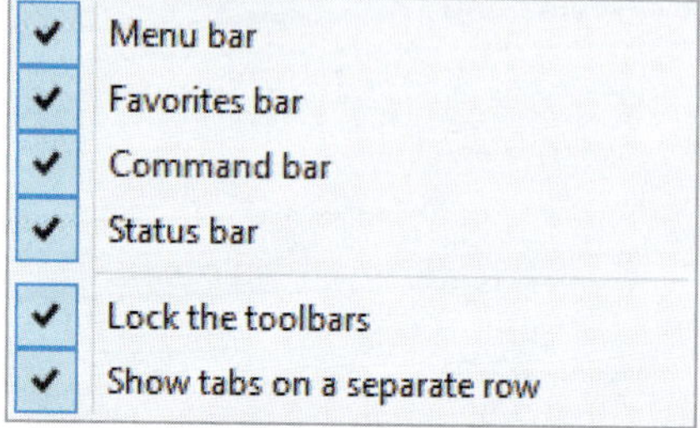. Both the Favorites button and the Tools button display a drop-down menu with choices, but if you are on a large monitor, you might want to see traditional menus and toolbars.

## To display toolbars and menus:

1. Right-click the address bar to show the Tools menu **B**.

2. Select the menus and taskbars you wish to see.

3. Desktop IE changes its display **C**.

**TIP** **Press Alt+Home to go to your home page. The Home and End keys take you to the top and bottom of the page, respectively. Page Up and Page Down take you up and down one full screen.**

**B** The Tools menu in Desktop IE

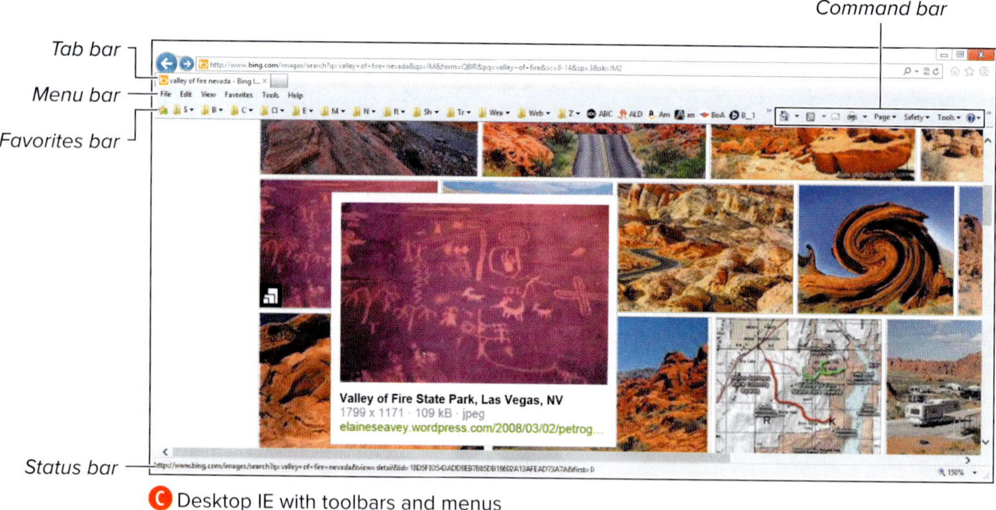


**C** Desktop IE with toolbars and menus

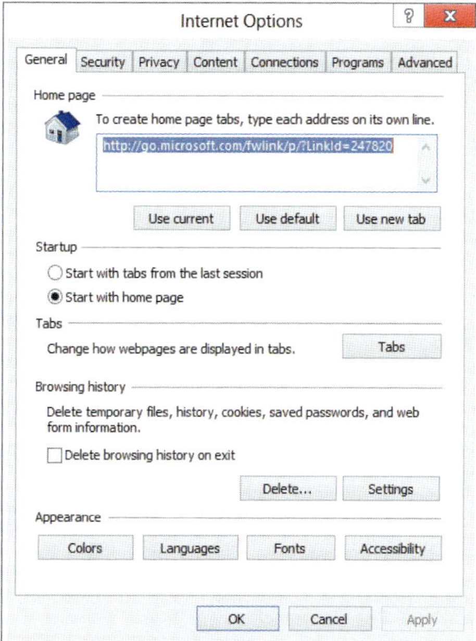

A The General tab of the Internet Options dialog box

# Options and Tools

Desktop IE gives you access to a number of important settings. This section highlights some of the more important ones. To begin with, you probably want to explore the Internet Options dialog box, because it sets the home page, connection types, default behaviors, and a number of advanced features.

## To open the Internet Options dialog box:

Click the Tools menu and select the Internet Options command from the bottom of the menu. The General tab appears **A**.

## To set your home page:

1. Enter the page address into the Home Page text box.

   *or*

   Click the Use Current button to set the current page as your home page.

2. Click Apply to set the page and continue making changes, or click OK to set the page and close the dialog box.

## Internet Options dialog box tabs:

- Click the **General** tab to change IE10's appearance, how it starts up, and how tabs are displayed, and to delete all personal information from a session upon exit.

- Click the **Security** tab to set limits on what sites you can connect to.

- Click the **Privacy** tab to limit actions that are allowed by connected sites. For example, you can turn off geolocation, suppress pop-ups, and turn off tool-bars and extensions when in InPrivate browsing mode.

- Click the **Content** tab to set family safety and content display options, control the use of site certificates, turn AutoComplete on or off, and turn on or off feeds and web slices (a web slice is a subscription technology that pushes content to your browser).

- Click the **Connections** tab to control your Internet connection, including set-ting the address of a proxy server, set-ting up a VPN, and connecting to your local area network (LAN).

- Click the **Programs** tab 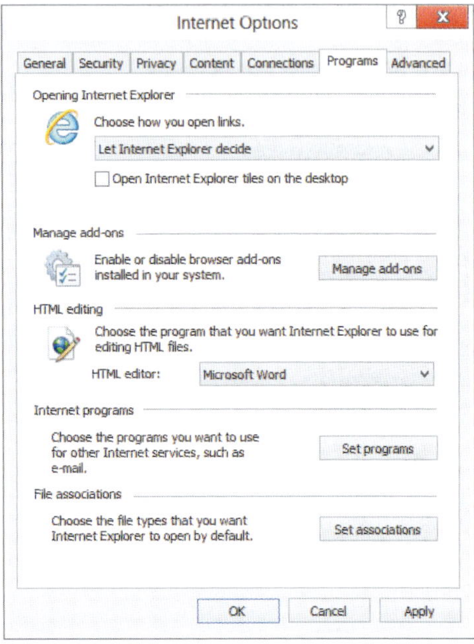 to deter-mine which version of Internet Explorer opens by default and how content is handled. You can also use the Set Programs button to change your default browser.

- The **Advanced** tab has many options that modify rendering, accessibility, multimedia, and security behaviors. Most of these settings are rarely changed in everyday use.

The Command bar moves many of the more popular Internet Options commands onto a menu, where they are easier to view. Here are a few of the most important commands.

**B** The Programs tab of the Internet Options dialog box. Settings you modify here affect both the tile-based and Desktop IE, since they are one and the same program.

## To set Page menu options:

- Use the **Compatibility View** command if a website doesn't load correctly.

- Use the **Zoom** command to zoom in or out.

- Use the **Text Size** command to change the font size on your screen.

- Use the **View Source** command to see the code from which your page was rendered.

## To set Safety menu options:

- Use the **Delete Browsing History** command to remove all stored session information.

- Use the **InPrivate Browsing** command to delete session information for a tab.

- Use the **Tracking Protection** command to disable geolocation by websites.

## To set Tools menu options:

- Use the **Popup Blocker** menu to suppress pop-ups or allow them on a per site basis.

- Use the **View Downloads** command to view the Download dialog box and access downloads.

- Use the **Full Screen** command to remove the Desktop IE interface and view only site content.

**TIP** Press Ctrl++(plus) and Ctrl+– (minus) to zoom in and out.

**TIP** Press Ctrl+J to show your downloads.

**TIP** Press F11 to toggle between a full-screen display and your previous display.

**TIP** Press F1 to access help.

# Putting It All Together

- Internet Explorer is one program, but it comes with two different interfaces: tile-based and Desktop. Changes you make in one interface also show up in the other.

- The tile-based IE10 is immersive and has been optimized for touch and gestures.

- Features such as AutoComplete make filling out forms in the tile-based IE easier than you might imagine.

- Desktop IE has many more options than its tile-based brother and is better navigated using a keyboard and mouse.

- Spend some time experimenting with tile-based IE by using touches, swipes, touch and holds, edge swipes, pinches, and other gestures to see how you can interact with content on a page.

- It is quite useful to pin favorite websites and pages as tiles on the Start screen.

- New security options, such as InPrivate Browsing and Do Not Track, make IE10 more secure out of the box.

- Use the Internet Options dialog box of Desktop IE to alter many default behaviors and customize your browsing sessions.

- Use the Desktop version of IE to open sites that require plugins or sites that have legacy features. You can install plugins and turn on a compatibility view to enable successful page viewing there.

# Mobile Computing

Mobile computing is what Windows 8 is all about. Windows 7 is a great operating system, but it wasn't built for small screens, ubiquitous networking, on-the-fly social media, and cloud computing. In Windows 7, those were add-ons; in Windows 8 they are basic plumbing.

Windows 8's killer feature is that it implements the core operating system across PCs, laptops, tablets, and phones. A developer creating a game on one platform has a simple port to another. The same DirectX graphics that power *Angry Birds* on your PC will have them flying across your Windows Phone 8 as well.

This chapter focuses on some of the main features that aid mobile users. Although most of this book was written with PCs and laptops in mind, this chapter starts off with a section on Windows Phone 8. Windows Phone 8 is a generational leap forward from its predecessor, supporting high-resolution screens, multi-core processors, NFC (near-field communication) tap-and-buy and tap-and-send transactions, and more.

Windows Mobility Center, a supporting utility for mobile devices, ships with
Windows 8 (it first appeared in Vista); it is
basically a hardware control panel for your
laptop or tablet. It's just a keystroke away.
Windows 8 users will also benefit from
Sync Center, a way of keeping your data
and settings synchronized between your
mobile devices. Microsoft's dream is that
you run around with a Microsoft tablet or
laptop, call from a Microsoft phone, and
work on a Microsoft PC at your home or
office—all connected through Microsoft's
Windows Live cloud platform and with
Windows Azure apps (covered in Chapter 17). The Windows 8 operating system
is Microsoft's attempt to turn the dream
into a reality.

Since there are networks everywhere,
you expect your Windows 8 device to be
able to keep you constantly connected
by switching networks as you move from
place to place during the day. For the most
part, Windows 8 does this without much
intervention on your part. However, it is
good to know how Windows 8 is connecting and to be able to control networking
to use your preferred provider. A section
in this chapter rounds out the networking
discussion started in Chapter 13 and tells
you how to manage multiple networks with
your mobile device.

In the final section of this chapter you will
learn how to gauge power consumption
and how to create and manage power
plans. Windows 8 introduces a new connected standby mode for the tile-based
apps to conserve resources.

# Windows Phone 8 Features

Microsoft's plan is to have Windows 8 running on mobile laptops, tablets, and phones. Laptops and certain tablets are based on the Intel IA x86 processors, and are feature for feature the same as Windows 8 on a desktop PC. You will be able to upgrade these devices from Windows 7 with few concessions.

Other tablets run the ARM processor and a stripped-down version of the operating system called Windows RT.

When you buy a Windows Phone 8, chances are that it will also run RT. Windows RT is new and contains features that aren't immediately compatible with the Windows Phone 7, which ran the Windows CE core. So an upgrade of a Windows Phone 7 will include a Start screen **A** as an interim version of the Windows 8 operating system and may be given the version number 7.8.

The Windows Phone 8 moves to something that Microsoft is calling the "common core." In the common core that is shared by these new Windows 8 phones and tablets are the operating system kernel, file system, networking, and common graphics and multimedia functions, including DirectX. Most importantly, the Windows Phone 8 contains the same driver model, meaning that devices that work on one hardware platform will work on another. Developers just love this stuff because it means that hardware is easily portable and their apps will run across platforms with few modifications.

**A** On Windows Phone 8, the Start screen has three sizes of Live Tiles that can be scrolled.

Windows Phone 7 was limited to single core CPUs and a display resolution of 800 x 480 pixels. Windows Phone 8 supports dual- and quad-core processors and 720p (1280 x 720) and WXGA (1280 x 768) hi-def screen resolutions. The next generation of phones will also have microSD card slots for memory expansion. This means that Windows Phone 8 will be competitive with the most powerful Androids and iPhones on the market today.

The Windows Phone 8 also supports the new Internet Explorer 10 browser with HTML5 and JavaScript, as well as a new rendering engine that will improve gaming. Many security features found on the desktop platform—such as the disk encryption BitLocker feature, secure boot, device and software security signing, SmartScreen, and Microsoft's anti-phishing features—are on the phone browser. With the inclusion of a touch-oriented version of Microsoft Office and SharePoint integration into these phones, Windows Phone 8 may become a corporate favorite.

NFC technology allows Windows Phone 8 to participate in secure payment systems that use tap-to-pay. NFC technology also allows in-proximity data transfers. That is, you can put two NFC-enabled phones near each other and press a software button to transfer data wirelessly in a peer-to-peer connection. NFC is incorporated into devices through an NFC transceiver, and you transfer data through a tap-to-send action. In one example of a tap-to-send application, you can put your phone next to a kiosk with an NFC transceiver to initiate a data transfer.

Wallet, the most prominent software addition, uses NFC . It uses Secure SIM cards that are portable between phones. It can be used with credit cards, coupon programs, and purchase transactions inside phone apps. In Wallet, you can select a credit card, enter an amount and a password, and then tap to send your purchase to a payment station that looks a little like a bar code scanner.

Microsoft's partnership with Nokia adds that company's global mapping technology, NAVTEQ, to Windows mobile devices. NAVTEQ support GPS-style turn-by-turn directions and can even provide map support for phones that are disconnected from a network. A feature called Nokia City Lens lets you sweep a phone's camera to create a picture of what you see, and then this feature overlays data on the picture that highlights local businesses.

**TIP** **Windows Phone 8 will download apps and games from the Windows Store. Companies can also create their own Windows Phone 8 Hub with custom apps and business information.**



**B** Microsoft Wallet uses NFC to tap-to-pay and tap-to-send data between mobile devices in proximity.

# Windows Mobility Center

Windows Mobility Center is a handy little utility that puts all the commonly used mobile device settings in one place.

With Windows Mobility Center you can:

- Adjust screen brightness.
- Adjust sound volume.
- Display battery status.
- Change your screen orientation from portrait to landscape and vice versa.
- Change monitor output either by adjusting display settings or by projecting your screen on an external monitor. For example, when you make a presentation, Windows 8 turns off system notifications.
- Monitor Sync Center to change settings and check your synchronization status.

Mobile device manufacturers can modify Mobility Center, adding additional tiles and functionality to it. Note that Mobility Center is available only on laptops and tablets; it is not available on PCs or mobile phones.

## To open Windows Mobility Center:

- Press ⊞+X. (This keystroke works on mobile devices only. On a PC, it will open the Computer Management menu.)
- Tap or click the Mobility Center tile on the Start screen that came with your device.
- Open the Control Panel, change the view to small icons, and click the Windows Mobility Center icon.

Whichever method you use to get there, Windows Mobility Center appears on your screen Ⓐ.

**TIP** All the icons in the Windows Mobility Center are shortcuts to control panel features. For example, you can click the Brightness icon to modify the screen's display in the power plan.

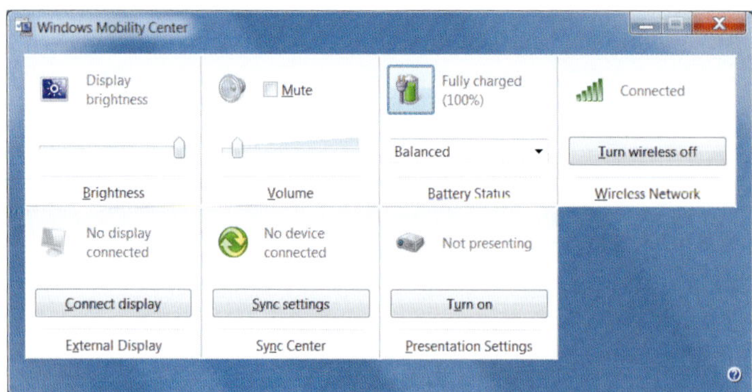


Ⓐ Use Windows Mobility Center to quickly adjust your laptop or tablet's hardware settings.

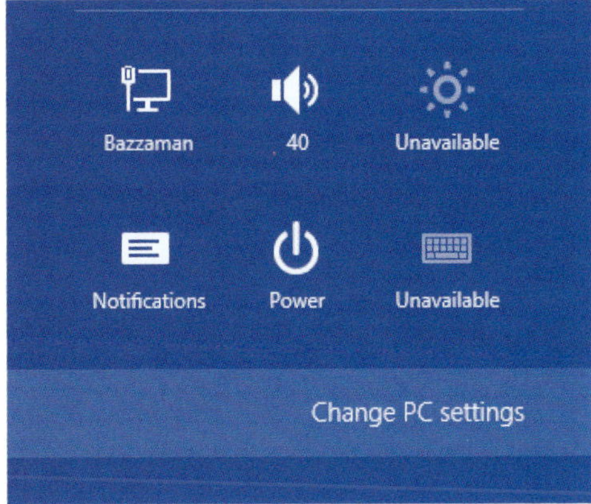

**A** The Settings charm

**B** The *Change PC settings* link

# Data Synchronization

Windows 8 allows you to run the same apps on PCs, tablets, and phones. Chances are that you will want to use the same data and settings as you move from device to device. The best way to do that is to synchronize your data. If you use a local account on a PC, you will have to use a third-party solution to perform data synchronization. But if you log in to your computer with a Windows Live account, you can synchronize some of your app settings and passwords, your personalization settings, and settings for devices such as your mouse and keyboard.

## To set up data synchronization:

1. Press ⊞+C to open the Charms bar, and then tap or click the Settings charm **A**.

2. Click the *Change PC settings* link at the bottom of the Settings bar **B**.

*continues on next page*

3. Click the *Users* link in the left navigation bar, and then log in to your Microsoft account **C**.

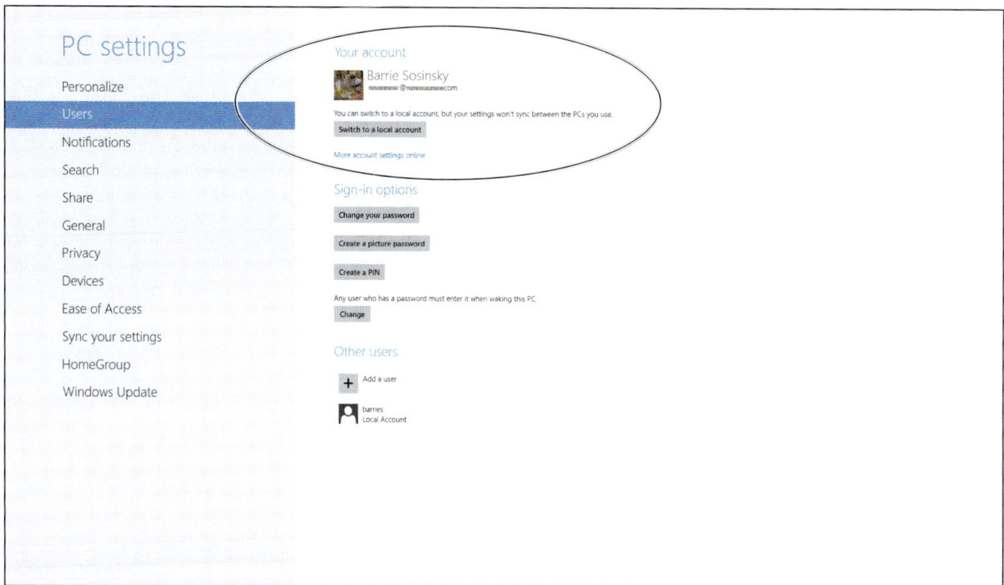

**C** Log in to your Microsoft account on the Users page.

**4.** Click the *Sync your settings* link in the PC Settings bar, and then drag the sliders to synchronize data elements **D**.

**TIP** **You might want to consider turning off the setting that allows synchronizing when your device is on a metered connection, because that could add to your data charges. You also may want to turn off the setting that allows synchronizing while you are roaming, which will add to data charges and may drain your battery faster than you might like.**

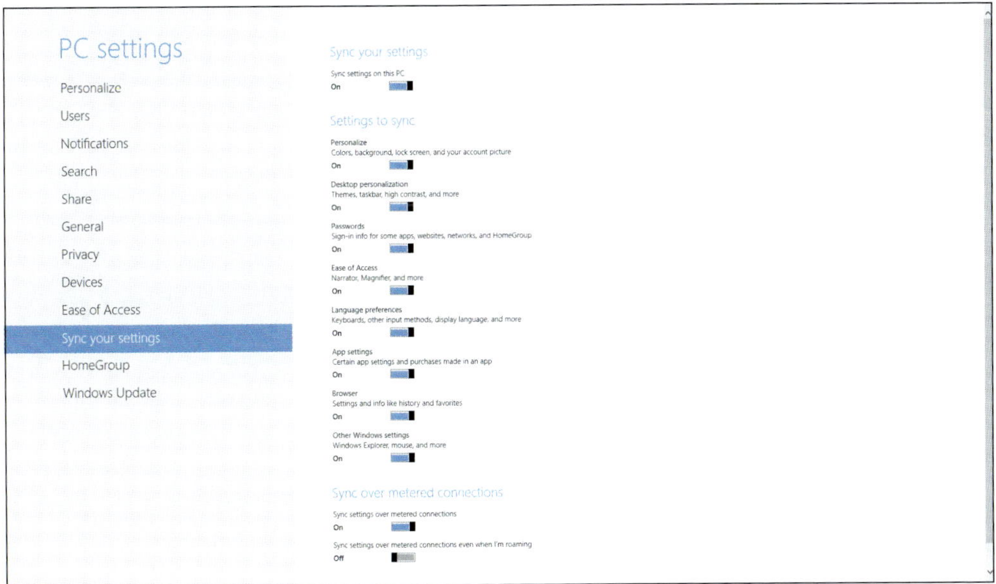


**D** Turn on the Sync Your Settings features on this page, and your data synchronizes through Windows Live.

# Smart Network Switching

Although the Start screen may be Windows 8's most visible feature, pervasive networking has seen the greatest improvements in this new operating system. Mobility means that users expect to be connected from anywhere and to anything. Microsoft's solution for Windows 8 adds new forms of Wi-Fi and broadband connectivity, metered connections, and network switching and prioritization.

This is bits and bytes that only übergeeks appreciate, but the effect on your everyday laptop, tablet, or phone is that Microsoft offers customers industry-leading connectivity in a simple-to-use interface that won't take you long to learn. In Chapter 13, you learned how to configure mobile network connections; in this section, let's consider how you manage those connections.

Windows has the following connection priority order:

1. Ethernet is connected first since it is hard-wired to a router or network hub and is assumed to be faster and cheaper than wireless connections.

2. Wi-Fi networks are connected next.

3. Mobile broadband is connected last.

The reason for this order lies in the assumption that Ethernet is your fastest and cheapest connection, Wi-Fi is slower and may cost more, and mobile broadband connections such as 3G and 4G are expensive and may be metered.

Windows 8 handles Wi-Fi in this manner:

- It lists all Wi-Fi networks that are currently within range in order of their signal strength.

- When you connect to a Wi-Fi network, Windows 8 stays connected to that Wi-Fi network whenever it is in range.

- Should you connect to a second Wi-Fi network, Windows 8 connects to that network first whenever it is in range.

Connections to mobile broadband networks are handled a little strangely, although it makes perfect sense if you think about it.

With mobile broadband:

- When you manually connect to a mobile broadband network and there are Wi-Fi networks in range, you stay connected to the mobile broadband network for as long as the session (connection) lasts.

- When you are disconnected from mobile broadband, you are reconnected to a Wi-Fi network.

Again, it is assumed that your mobile broadband connection is both expensive and metered.

**TIP** When you are connected to a Wi-Fi network and you prefer to force Windows 8 to connect to mobile broadband, open the Wi-Fi Networks list and click the Disconnect button. Windows won't connect to that Wi-Fi network again automatically. You can also hide a network by selecting the Forget This Network command in the network's context menu.

**TIP** Windows 8 comes with a feature that turns off all radio devices: airplane mode. It is covered in Chapter 13.

## The `netshell` Command

You can handle most simple network connection tasks within the Windows 8 network interface or from the Network and Internet control panel (see Chapter 13).

Some wireless network connection operations aren't in either of those two places and require a more powerful method: the **netshell** command. You enter **netshell** commands at the Command Prompt, which as you may recall is opened by pressing ⊞+R, entering **cmd** into the Run dialog box, and tapping or pressing Enter. You can also select the Run command from the Computer Management menu.

Here are some **netshell** commands you can use. Substitute *ProfileName* with the actual name of the profile:

- **netsh wlan show profiles** lists all wireless connections.

- **netsh wlan delete profile  name=*ProfileName*** deletes the named connection.

- **netsh wlan set profileparameter  name=*ProfileName* connectionmode=manual** stops connecting to a network that is currently out of range.

- **netsh wlan show profile  name=*ProfileName*** deletes a network connection that is out of range.

# Managing Power Consumption

With Windows 8's increasing focus on mobile devices, a lot of development work has gone into ensuring that:

- The system boots faster and more efficiently

- Applications use less power when they run

- Applications run in the background only when they are performing a task you started before you switched away

- Apps consume as few resources as possible when they aren't displayed and active

This last improvement is particularly true of the tile-based apps and makes it unnecessary (as a general rule) to close these apps when you aren't using them. That will take some getting used to for many of us.

Most of these improvements aren't in the user's control because they are built into Windows 8's internals. But you certainly will recognize the changes, because your laptop, tablet, and phone will be more responsive and have longer battery life.

On solid-state devices, you will find that after the screen dims and turns off, the system falls into a type of sleep called "connected standby," where Desktop apps are suspended but tile-based apps continue to run in a low-power mode. For PCs, all apps are suspended when the system goes to sleep **Ⓐ**.

Some processes have to stay active in the background:

- Music players

- File downloads

- Refreshing Live Tiles on the Start screen

- Background printing

- Receiving an IM (instant message), a VOIP (Voice over IP) call, or an email

- Sharing content, such as uploading photos to Facebook

- Synchronizing content with a tethered device (tethered devices are connected by a short-distance connection like Bluetooth)

Windows 8's new touch interface has few controls that let you manage power settings; it is expected that equipment manufacturers of cell phones and Windows RT tablets will optimize those settings for you. However, if you are working with Windows 8 on a system with the Desktop, you have a number of power consumption settings available to you through the Power Options and System Settings control panels.

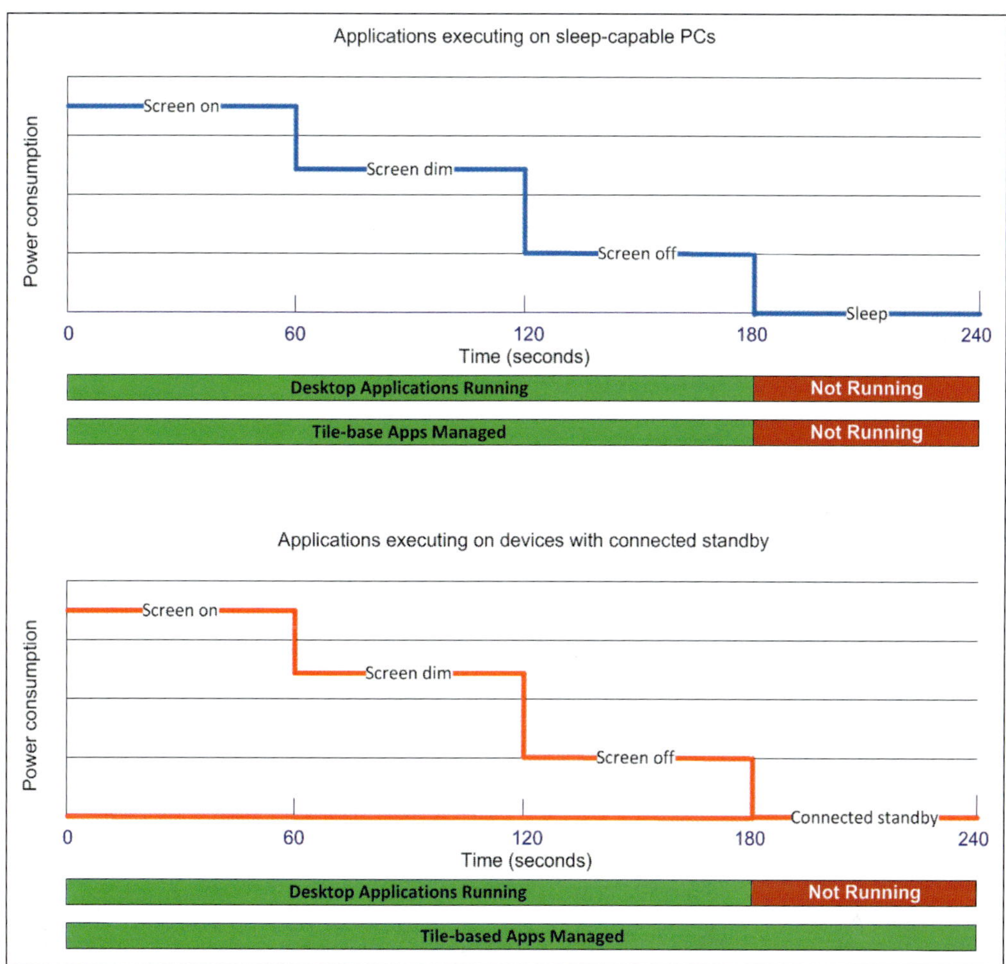


**A** Depending on the device hardware, Windows 8 will power down and suspend all apps or power down and leave the tile-based apps in a quiescent state.

## To change the power plan on a battery-powered device:

Click the battery icon in the Notification area, and select either the Balanced or High Performance plan **B**.

Desktop PCs don't have a battery icon, so to choose a plan on a PC you will have to open the Power Options control panel. You can get there from the *More power options* link **B** or by following the procedure in the next section.

## To change the power plan on a PC:

1. Press **⊞**+X, or right-click, the lower-left corner of your display, and select the Control Panel command.

2. On the Control Panel home page, click the *System and Security* link and then the *Power Options* link to view the Power Options control panel **C**.

3. Select one of the three plans: Balanced, Power Saver, or High Performance.

   *or*

   Click the *Create a power plan* link to open a wizard that sets the amount of time before your screen dims and turns off and your system goes to sleep.

   You can apply settings to each of the plans.

You may notice that Windows 8 PCs have a Power menu containing Sleep, Shut Down, and Restart commands. Gone from the menu is the hibernation feature, where memory contents are written to disk before shutting down and are read when starting up. You can change what the Power button does and restore the Hibernate command to its menu in the Power Options control panel.

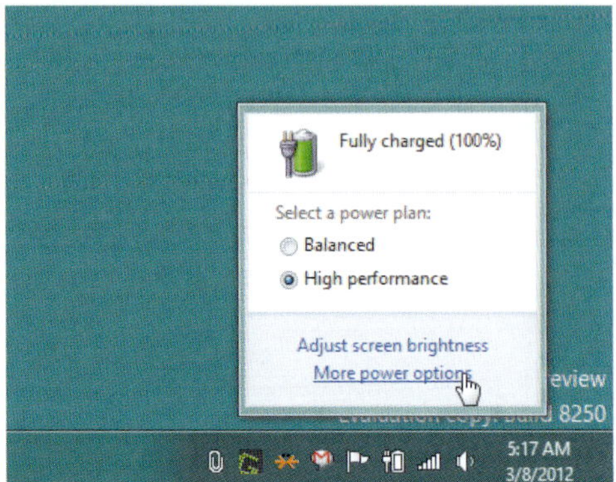



**B** Changing the power consumption plan

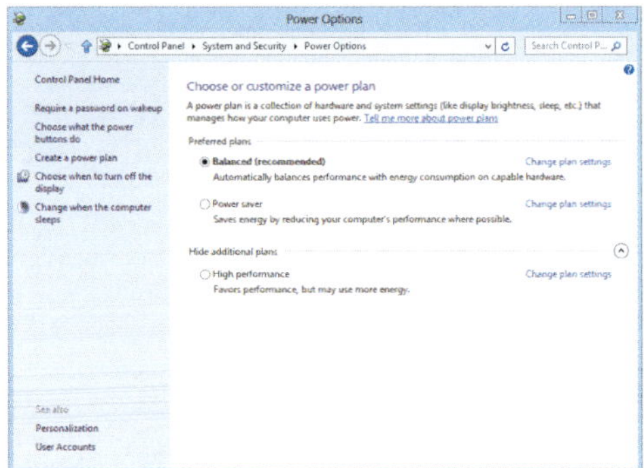

**C** The Power Options control panel is where you select a power plan or create a custom one.

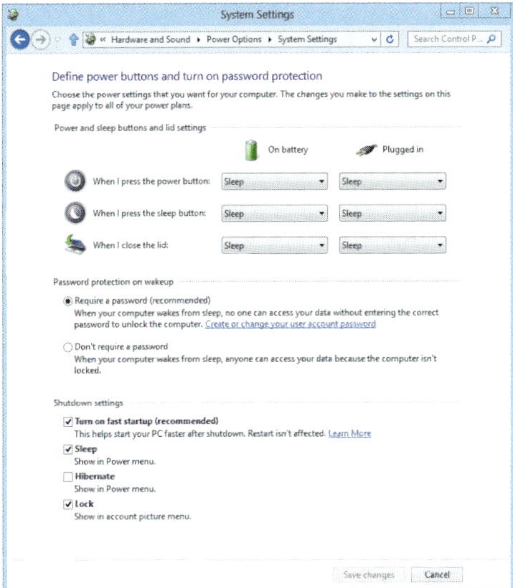

**D** Use the System Settings control panel to control what the Power and Sleep buttons do.

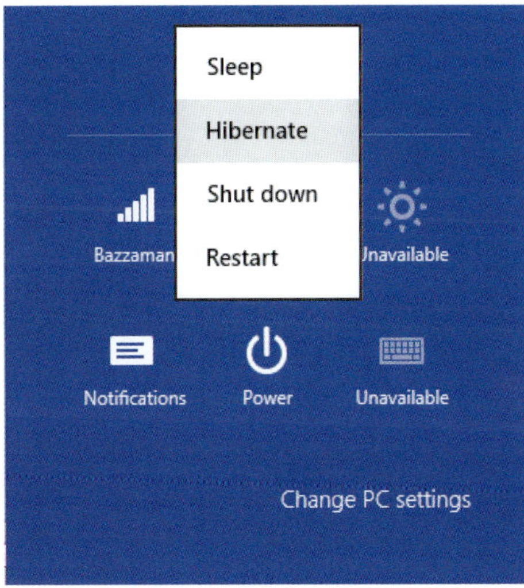


**E** The Power menu showing the Hibernate command

## To change the Power button's action:

1. Click the *Choose what the power buttons do* link in the Power Options control panel **C** to view the System Settings control panel **D**.

2. Select a function for the Power button and the Sleep button from the two drop-down lists.

   For a mobile device, you will want to keep the time it takes to dim the screen or put the device to sleep relatively short, and to use the Power Saver plan. For a laptop, you will see options for what happens when you close the lid **D**.

## To restore the Hibernate option to the Power menu:

Select the Hibernate check box in the System Settings panel **D**.

The Power menu will now include the Hibernate command **E**.

**TIP** New mobile devices that come with hard drives benefit from the fastest sleep times you can live with. On a solid-state device, the component that draws the most power is the display—minimize its dimming time to get the most battery life.

# Putting It All Together

- Windows Phone 8 supports powerful hardware using a Windows 8 common core.

- Windows Mobility Center is a control panel utility that allows you to conveniently modify your mobile device's hardware settings.

- The data synchronization feature allows you to synchronize your data and settings across your Windows 8 devices wherever you go.

- Windows has a preferred order in which it connects to networks: Ethernet, then Wi-Fi, and then mobile broadband.

- Mobile broadband connections are assumed to be expensive and metered, and Windows 8 adds a means to monitor your data usage when connected to them (or to Wi-Fi).

- Microsoft has completely reworked the Windows 8 hardware usage model to make mobile devices more power efficient, boot faster, and use fewer resources.

- When a tile-based app is not on the screen, it is generally inactive—unless you had started a task that you would expect to process in the background (such as printing).

- Some apps do stay active in the background, particularly those associated with media and telephony, printing, content sharing, and synchronization.

- You can assign power plans that control how your device is powered down when inactive.

# 16

# Security

Security is a very high priority for Microsoft and has been for a long time. Each successive version of Windows continues to improve security in some way. *Windows security* is no longer an oxymoron.

Windows 8 has the same security model as Windows 7, although there are some minor improvements, particularly in the area of browser security. So in this chapter, you will learn about the important security features that you need to know to secure a PC, laptop, or tablet running Windows 8. I'll also highlight the new features you'll want to learn.

Windows 8 security functions are manifold and competent. Windows Firewall, Windows Defender, encryption, and browser settings are all that you need to secure your system against almost all attacks or exploits. Security is built into the fabric of Windows. This chapter introduces you to safe computing practices and explains how to use these security functions to safely go about your business.

## In This Chapter

# Safe Computing

Windows 8 is a very complex operating system that was designed to allow developers to do just about anything you can think of. Microsoft has certain rules of the road that developers and the programs they create must follow to keep users safe. For the most part, users aren't expected to have to think about safety; Microsoft tried to engineer automated security into Windows 8. However, vulnerabilities can be exploited. You can eliminate 95 percent of the serious problems you might encounter by obeying the following ten commandments.

**Commandment 1.** *Thou shalt update your Windows 8 computer immediately and completely.*

Windows Update is Microsoft's push subscription service for delivering Windows operating system and Microsoft Office upgrades and patches. Since the bad guys watch for patches and vulnerabilities and attack them as soon as they can, you need to use Windows Update **A** to immediately install updates.

**Commandment 2.** *A user shalt thou be.*

Always log in as a user, not as an administrator. You can view and change your account privileges in the User Accounts control panel to give you the access you need on a daily basis. When you run as an administrator **B**, your privileges are too broad and can be used to compromise your system. Elevate your privileges only when you are installing software or performing a task that requires it. Also, you should never give away your account login information.

**A** The Windows Update icon

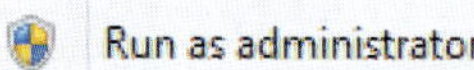

**B** The Run As Administrator command

**C** The Windows Firewall icon

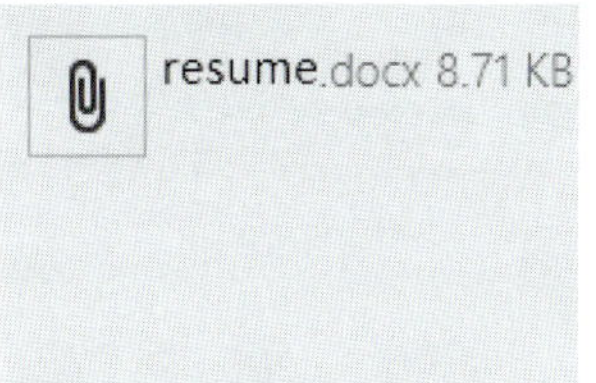


**D** The Windows Defender icon

**E** Beware of attachments.



**F** Beware of links—especially deals that are too good to be true.



**G** Know whence thy download comes.

**Commandment 3.** *Thou shalt hide behind the firewall.*

When you place your computer behind a router or firewall, it becomes much harder for evildoers to find your system and attack it. You should turn on Windows Firewall **C** and allow only the types of incoming traffic you approve. (See the "Windows Firewall" section that follows.)

**Commandment 4.** *Thou shalt run an antivirus program.*

Windows Defender **D**, described later in this chapter, is a very competent program and is turned on by default. If you don't have an antivirus program running, Windows 8 will complain.

**Commandment 5.** *Thou shalt not open email attachments from unknown sources.*

When you open an email attachment **E**, you run the risk of running a program that can modify your system. Attachments that are programs are no longer labeled as such, so make sure that you are certain of the source of the attachment and its purpose before opening it.

**Commandment 6.** *Thou shalt not tap or click links in emails from unknown sources.*

A link **F** may take you to a web page that contains programs that compromise your system.

**Commandment 7.** *Thou shalt not download files from untrusted sources.*

Evil knows no limits. Avoid the ten plagues contained in unknown files by downloading **G** only from known sources.

**Commandment 8.** *Thou shalt not expose thyself to others.*

The dark forces want to know who you are; indeed, they want to know everything about you. With just your name and social security or credit card number, almost anything is possible. Be especially careful when entering personal information into a computer. Make sure that a site's URL matches what you expect to see, and that you are using an HTTPS connection. Impersonation, or *phishing*, is a common technique used to compromise your system.

**Commandment 9.** *Thou shalt use strong passwords (but not strong language).*

A strong password **H** has the following attributes: It is not a word; it is not a name; it does not appear in a dictionary or encyclopedia; it cannot be looked up on a search engine; it contains both upper- and lowercase letters; it contains at least one number or symbol. The longer the password, the better.

UseStrongPasswords!

**H** Use numbers, symbols, and a mix of upper- and lowercase letters.

**Commandment 10.** *Thou shalt back up not once, not twice, but thrice.*

Avert Armageddon: Store three copies of every file—one on two different types of media, and one copy stored at a separate location. This is called 3-2-1 backup **❶**, a philosophy outlined by Peter Krogh in his book *The DAM Book: Digital Access Management for Photographers.*

Hosanna to Leo Laporte at TWiT.tv for proselytizing for safe computing on his many podcasts. These commandments are based in part on his advice.

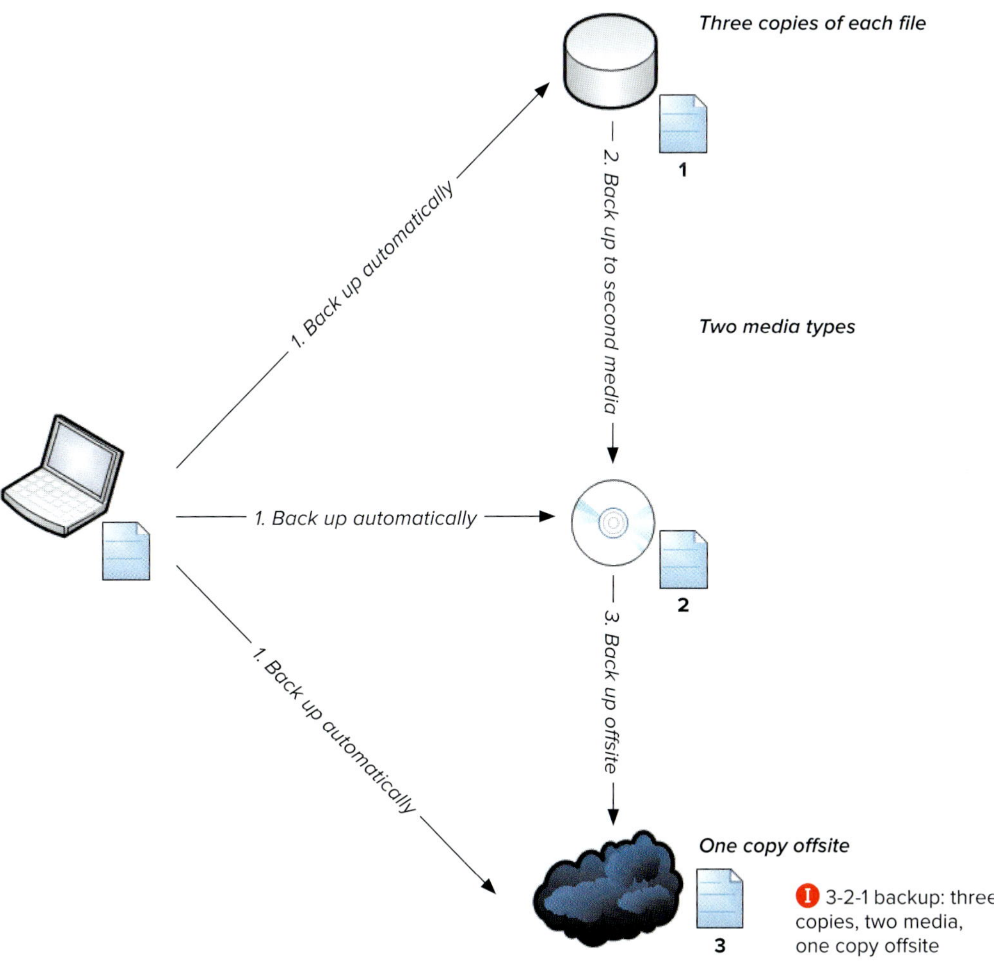

Advice on good security practices could fill a book; this chapter can provide only some of the basic information. Microsoft maintains an extensive security site called the Microsoft Safety & Security Center **J** (www.microsoft.com/security/), which provides background information, tips, updates, and fixes.

**TIP** **Never rely on manual systems for protection. Set up your backups to run automatically so that you are always protected.**

**J** The Windows Safety & Security Center is a good place to learn about safe computing on Windows 8.

# Windows Firewall

A firewall is hardware or software that examines network traffic and either allows the traffic to pass through it or blocks it, based on the contents of the traffic—the address it was sent to, the protocol used for the message, and the network port used to receive the message, among other things. Firewalls provide protection against worms and hackers probing your system. You also need the protection against viruses, malware, and spyware that programs like Windows Defender provide.

Your system should always be behind a hardware router. A hardware router provides network isolation by hiding your computer's network address on a different subnet. Routers can also be firewalls. And Microsoft provides a software program called Microsoft Firewall, which you should always have turned on.

Firewalls should be turned on:

- For all types of networks (public, private, and domains)

- For all network connections (Ethernet, Wi-Fi, and mobile broadband)

- For all inbound traffic types—except traffic that you wish to allow

    Among the ports you may want to allow are HTTP, HTTPS, FTP, and POP.

## To open the Windows Firewall control panel:

- Press ⊞+W and type **firewall**. Tap or click the Windows Firewall button that appears in your search.

- Press ⊞+X, select the Control Panel command from the Computer Management menu, click the *System and Security* link on the Control Panel home page, and click the *Windows Firewalls* link.

Windows Firewall Ⓐ has links that allow you to turn the firewall on or off, change notifications, and allow an app or feature through the firewall.

## To turn Windows Firewall on or off:

1. Tap or click the *Turn Windows Firewall on or off* link in the left pane of the Windows Firewall control panel.

   The Customize Settings control panel appears Ⓑ.

2. Tap or click the Turn on Windows Firewall option.

   *or*

   Tap or click the Turn off Windows Firewall (not recommended) option.

The only time you should turn off Windows Firewall is when you are installing a third-party firewall in its place.

## To change firewall notifications:

Tap or click the *Change notification settings* link in the Windows Firewall control panel to view the Customize Settings control panel Ⓑ.

Select the Block All Incoming Connections check box to block all attempts by outside sources to connect to your PC and provide

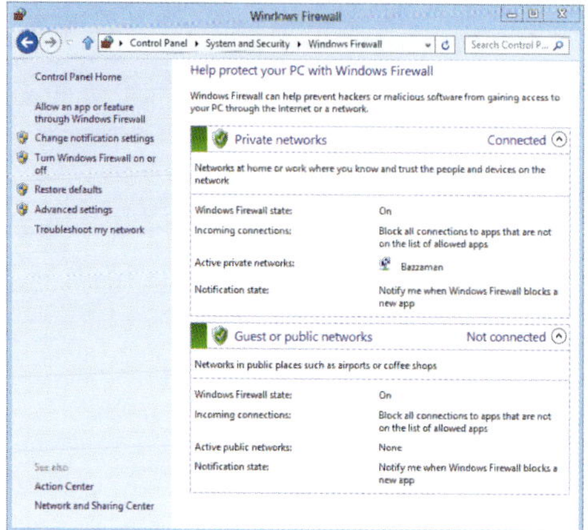

Ⓐ The Windows Firewall control panel

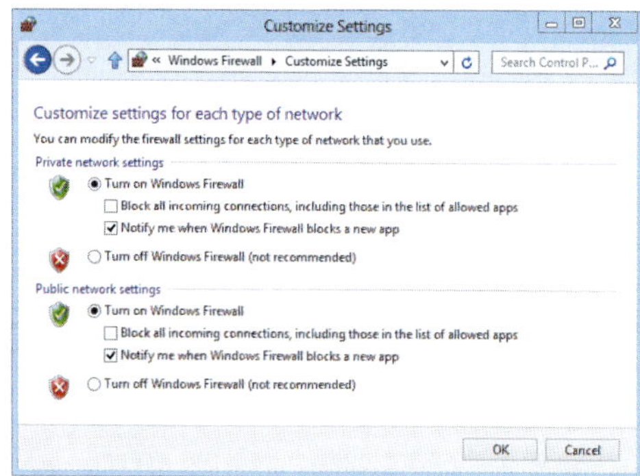

Ⓑ The Customize Settings control panel

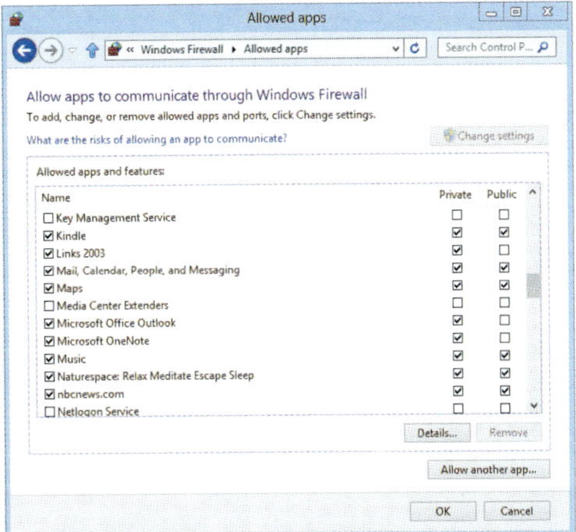

C The Allowed Apps control panel

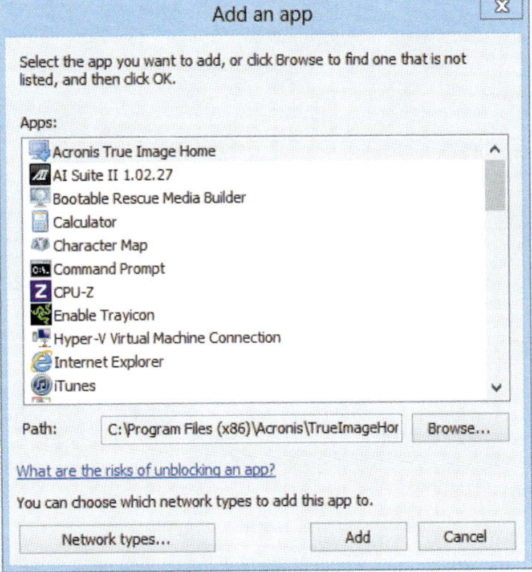

D The Add an App dialog box

maximum protection for public networks; you can achieve the same result by turning off sharing or connections in the Network and Sharing Center. Select the Notify Me When Windows Firewall Blocks a New App check box to see an alert when an application tries to connect to your system; the alert also allows you to unblock the port for that particular app. Note that you can block domains through Group Policy settings.

## To allow an application through Windows Firewall:

1. Tap or click the *Allow an app or feature through Windows Firewall* link in the left pane of the Windows Firewall control panel.

   The Allowed Apps control panel appears C.

2. Tap or click the check box for the app you want to allow or deny access to; then click the Public or Private check box to enable that access.

3. To add more programs to this list, tap or click the Allow Another App button to open the Add an App dialog box D. Highlight the app, and then click Add.

4. Tap or click OK to enforce your changes.

**TIP** There are many third-party firewall solutions that you can install, but you only need to have one firewall active at a time. Windows Firewall is adequate for most users' purposes.

**TIP** It's a good idea to examine the Allowed Apps list and remove programs that you aren't using or that are unfamiliar to you. Before you remove an app, a file, or anything else, check that what you are removing isn't required by your system to operate correctly. Search online to research the function before committing to an action.

# Windows Defender

Finally. Windows 8 is the first version of this operating system to ship with an antivirus/malware system installed by default. Although "Genuine Windows" users could download and install Windows Security Essentials with Defender technology for Windows 7, an upgraded version of this program is now part of the base install. Windows Defender protects from viruses, trojans, worms, rootkits, spyware, malware, and other bad guys right from the start. You can argue that there are more effective packages you might want to install, but simply keeping Windows Defender on and updated will keep your computer from turning into a zombie or grinding to a halt.

### To open Windows Defender:

Press ⊞+W to open the Search bar for settings, enter **defender** in the search box, and click the Windows Defender button to launch the program Ⓐ.

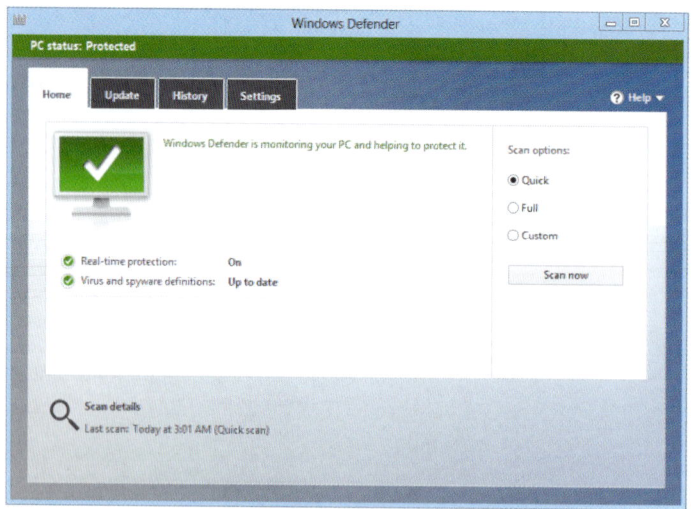

Ⓐ Here comes Windows Defender to save the day.

Windows Defender is on by default, and the only time you would want to turn it off is when you install another antivirus program. It's not a good idea to have two antivirus programs running at the same time because they tend to step on each other's toes. You can turn off Defender by deselecting the Turn On Real-time Protection check box found on the Settings tab of the Windows Defender screen.

By default, Windows Defender runs a quick scan for known viruses, spyware, and unwanted software. Every so often you will want to run a full scan, which scans all the files on your attached drives.

I recommend that you run a full system scan of all of your connected drives about once a month, or whenever your system acts strangely or is sluggish.

## To run a full system scan:

Tap or click the Full option in the Scan Options section; then click the Scan Now button.

**TIP** For systems that are seriously compromised, consider creating a Windows Defender Offline installation on a CD, DVD, or USB flash drive. Instructions can be found at windows.microsoft.com/en-US/windows/what-is-windows-defender-offline. When you boot from this drive and run the Offline version, it may bring your system back to life.

**TIP** The Malicious Software Removal tool detects viruses, spyware, and other malware. It is used internally by Windows every so often; for example, when you apply a large system patch or point upgrade. You can download the current version of the tool from www.microsoft.com/security/pc-security/malware-removal.aspx.

**TIP** The site www.safety.live.com redirects you to the Microsoft Safety Scanner. This is a downloadable tool that you can use to check your PC for viruses, spyware, and malware. The tool is free but expires after ten days; you have to download it again to run it a second time.

# Action Center

Windows 8 Action Center is a control panel that monitors your system's configuration, notifies you when it detects a security or configuration problem, and can help you take action to remedy problems it finds. In most cases, Action Center sits in the background and doesn't require intervention.

But when there is a problem, Action Center makes itself known by posting a warning and turning the notification icon on the taskbar red or yellow 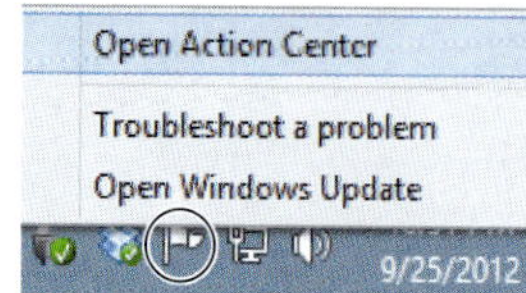. A red item indicates that the problem is significant and needs to be addressed immediately; a yellow item is a recommendation. The notification icon gives you quick access to Action Center 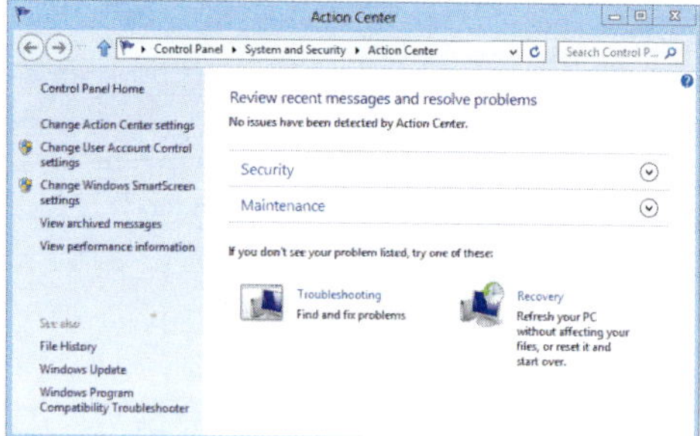. Using the Security button, you can access the state of Action Center, its Security section 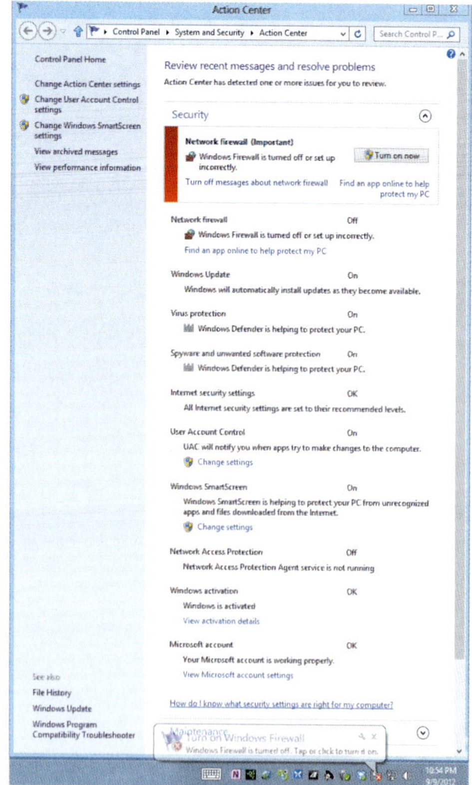, and the notification icon when Windows Firewall is turned off. Action Center also provides a button to remediate the problem.



Ⓐ The Action Center notification icon and its pop-up menu are a quick path to the Action Center control panel.

Ⓑ Action Center

Ⓒ A critical system problem indicated in Action Center

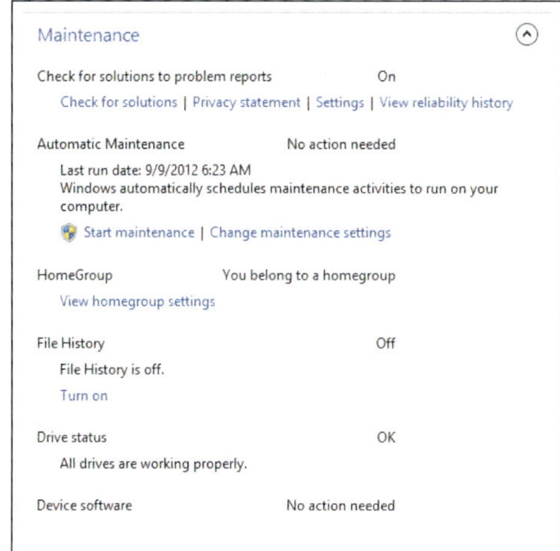



**D** The Maintenance section lets you run checks on your system status, check your HomeGroup, and turn File History on or off.

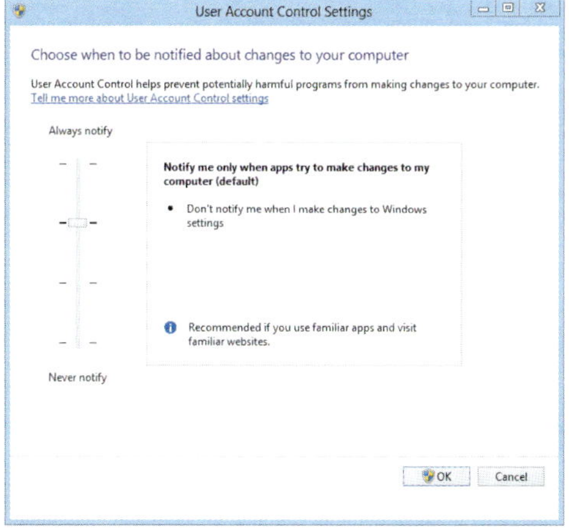



**E** The User Account Control Settings dialog box

Using the Maintenance button in Action Center **B**, you can access the Maintenance section **D**, check the status of your drives and devices, do a maintenance check, and turn on File History. File History backs up files on your primary drive and in your libraries, files on your desktop, your contacts, and your favorites to a secondary drive. It's always a good idea to have an extra way to recover files in case of an emergency.

You can access two other important Windows 8 security features from Action Center: User Account Control and Windows SmartScreen settings. Links to these are in the left pane of the Action Center control panel **B**.

When you tap or click the *Change User Account Control settings* link, the User Account Control Settings dialog box opens **E**. User Account Control notifies you when a change requires administrator privileges and allows you to elevate your privileges to perform the operation. The choices are:

- **Always notify me.** For all changes that require administrator privileges, the screen dims and a dialog box appears. This is the most secure setting.

- **Notify me only when apps try to make changes to my computer.** This is the default setting. Your changes to Windows settings are allowed, but apps' changes to your PC require rights elevation.

- **Notify me only when apps try to make changes to my computer (don't dim my desktop).** This choice is the same as the one above but doesn't dim the screen.

- **Never notify me.** If a change requires administrator privileges and you are signed in as an administrator, the change is allowed. If you are signed in as a user, the change is denied.

Windows SmartScreen is technology that can block apps from the Internet from running on your system unless you elevate your privileges to administrator level. The *Change Windows SmartSceen settings* link opens the dialog box shown in 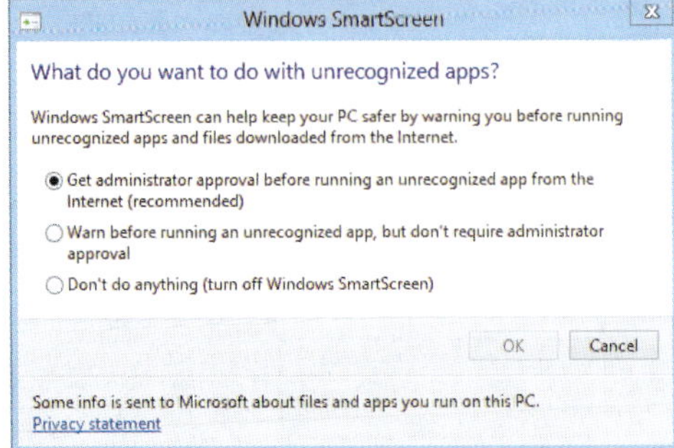. I can think of no good reason to alter this setting.

## To open Action Center:

1. Tap and hold, or right-click, the Action Center icon in the Notification area on the taskbar.

2. Select the Action Center command from the pop-up menu.

   Action Center appears B.



F The Windows SmartScreen dialog box

# BitLocker Drive Encryption

BitLocker Drive Encryption is a feature that encrypts a logical volume so the data on disk can't be read by outside parties. If your laptop is lost or stolen, BitLocker protects your data from being accessed by others. As you might recall from Chapter 12, a logical volume is a disk partition or set of partitions and can be part of a disk or can even be combinations of partitions that span one or more disks. With BitLocker, the boot partition remains unencrypted.

BitLocker appeared in Microsoft Vista and has been carried over with some improvements into Windows 8 Pro and Windows 8 Enterprise; it is not available on Windows 8 and Windows 8 RT. The notable improvements are:

- **User password and PIN selection.** Users can now set their passwords and PINs without having administrative privileges.

- **Used disk space encryption.** The latest version of BitLocker encrypts the whole volume.

- **Pre-provisioning.** You can encrypt a hard drive and install Windows 8 on it.

  You should use pre-provisioning only on a new, fully encrypted hard drive. If you pre-provision an already used drive, only the used parts of the drive will be encrypted. Any unused parts of any volume will contain unencrypted data that can be read. That is, any files you may have created (and perhaps even deleted) will still be on your drive in an unencrypted form and can be read by others.

*continues on next page*

- **Hardware hard drive encryption.**
  BitLocker can recognize whether a
  hard drive is encrypted and will use the
  drive's hardware instead of the CPU to
  read and write data.

Files you add to your encrypted drive will
be encrypted. If you copy those files to
an unencrypted drive, they will be unencrypted on that drive.

Encrypted File System (EFS) allows you to
encrypt sensitive files on your computer
without using BitLocker to encrypt the
drive. EFS is described in the next section.

## To use BitLocker to encrypt a volume:

1. Press ⊞+W and type **bitlocker**. Tap
   or click the BitLocker button to display
   the BitLocker Drive Encryption control
   panel 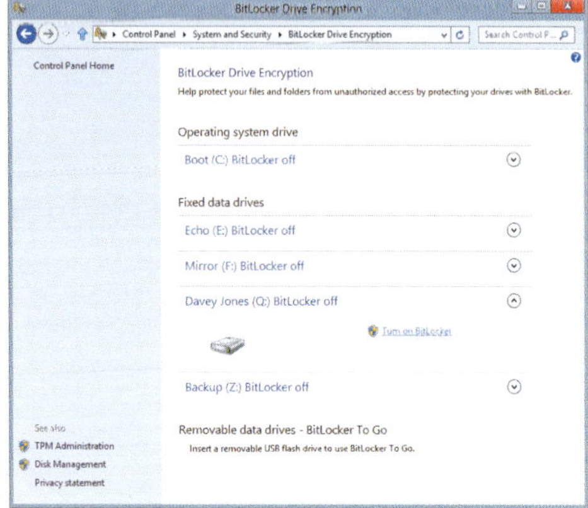.

   You can also open BitLocker from the
   System and Security section of the
   Control Panel.

2. Click the *Turn on BitLocker* link for the
   volume you wish to encrypt to launch
   the BitLocker wizard.

3. In the Choose How You Want to Unlock
   This Drive screen 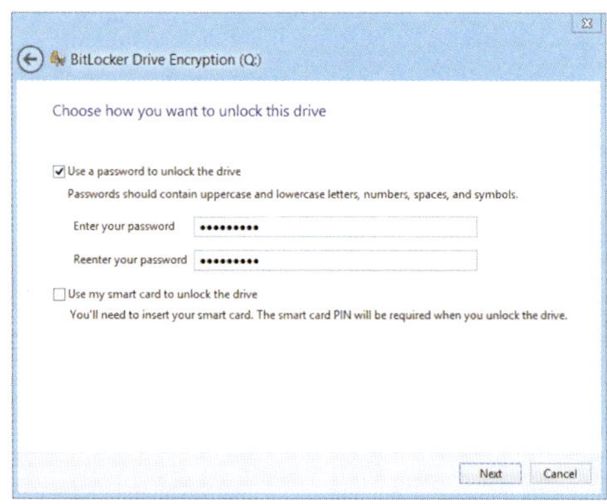, enable either the
   password or smart card option to cre-
   ate the access key; type the password
   twice, and press Enter.

Ⓐ The BitLocker control panel

Ⓑ Step 1 of the BitLocker wizard

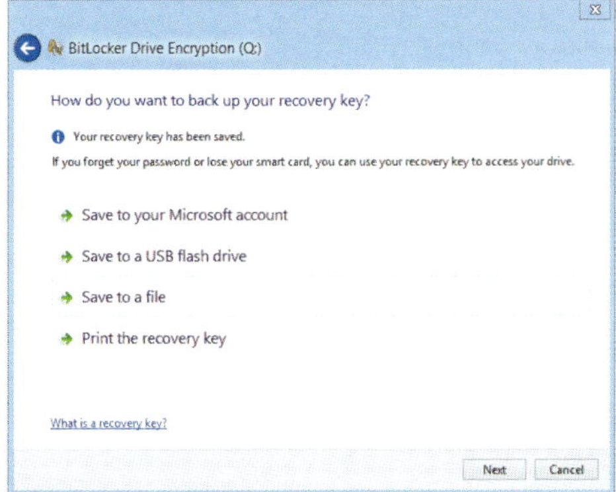

**C** Step 2 of the BitLocker wizard

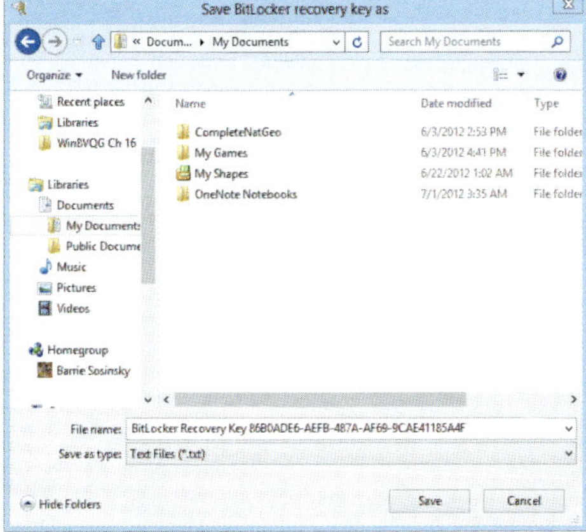

**D** Pick a location to save the recovery key file to. If you save the key to your USB drive or SkyDrive, you can access it should you lose the local copy.

**E** This alert box tells you to save the recovery key to another PC or device.

4. In the How Do You Want To Back Up Your Recovery Key screen (step 2 of the wizard) **C**, click a location.

You can choose more than one location, which is a good idea. The backup key is required in case you can't access your drive. Placing the key on the same drive that is encrypted means that you may lose access to that copy of the key. That's why a backup somewhere else is essential. The Save To Your Microsoft Account option saves the backup key to the cloud. If you click Save To A File, you will be prompted to pick a location to save the recovery key file to **D**; if you choose a local drive, you will see an alert box **E** that informs you that it is more secure to save the file to another PC or device.

*continues on next page*

5. In the "Choose how much of your drive to encrypt" screen (step 3 of the wizard) **F**, choose to encrypt either the used disk space or the entire drive. Click Next.

6. In the final step of the wizard **G**, click the Start Encrypting button.

   Windows 8 displays a notice indicating that the drive is being encrypted **H**.

**TIP** Use the BitLocker to Go feature to protect data files stored on removable devices such as external hard drives or USB flash drives. This feature is available only on Windows 8 Enterprise.

**TIP** If you tap or click the *Manage BitLocker* link in the System and Security section of the Control Panel, you can back up the recovery key, change or remove your password, add a smart card, turn on auto-unlock, or turn Bit-Locker off for your encrypted drive.

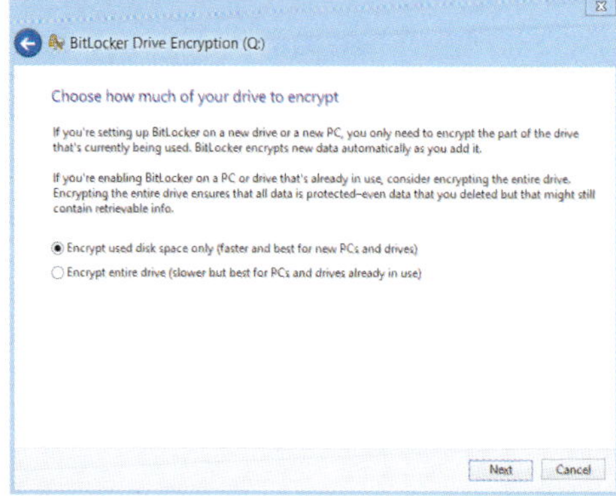

**F** Encrypt either the used disk space or the entire volume.

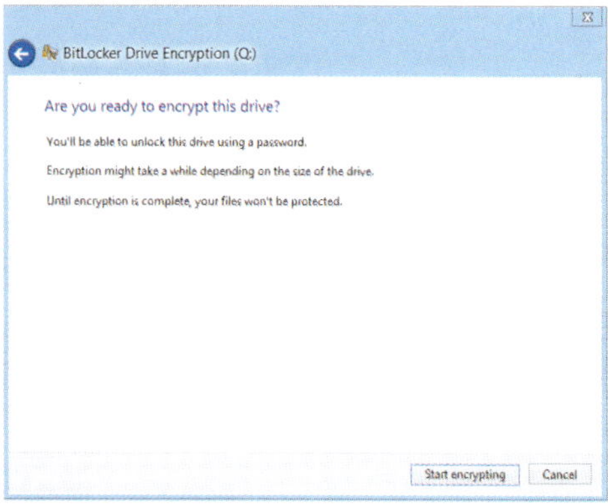

**G** The final step of the wizard

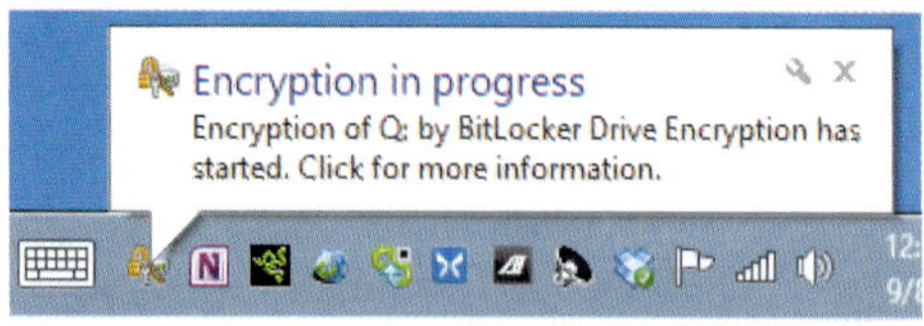


**H** Drive encryption is in progress.

# Encrypting File System

Encrypting File System (EFS) allows you to encrypt data that is stored on drives on a file-by-file and folder-by-folder basis. Data in an encrypted file cannot be read without supplying the correct encryption key.

When you encrypt a file, Windows 8 automatically creates the private key that users need to access the encrypted file and associates it with your Windows password. If you use a strong password and don't allow people physical access to your computer, then your encrypted file is safe. When you look at an encrypted file or folder, the only way you can tell that it is encrypted is to examine its properties. If you created the file, you can access the folder or file transparently and work with it as you normally would because Windows automatically decrypts it for you.

When you encrypt a folder, all items in that folder are encrypted. When you add items to the folder, they are also encrypted. When you move an encrypted file in the file system, it remains encrypted, but if you move an item to a different drive, the file or folder is decrypted. Should you lose the user's private key when you reinstall the operating system or create a new user, you can use the EFS recovery agent to decrypt your files. Administrators on corporate networks can create a Group Policy that imports the recovery certificate into the Active Directory and allows them to decrypt files should the key be lost or should the user leave the company.

## To encrypt a file or folder with EFS:

1. Right-click the file or folder icon that you want to encrypt. Select the Properties command from the context menu.

2. On the General tab of the Properties dialog box **A**, click the Advanced button to open the Advanced Attributes dialog box **B**.

3. Select the Encrypt Contents To Secure Data check box. Tap or click OK.

   The file or folder is encrypted to disk.

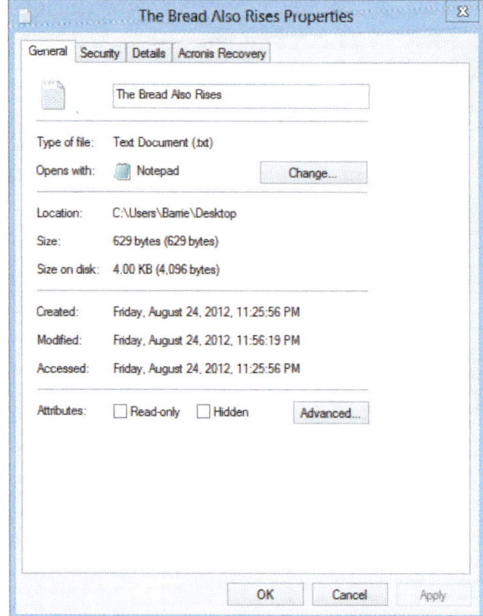

**A** The General tab of a folder's Properties dialog box

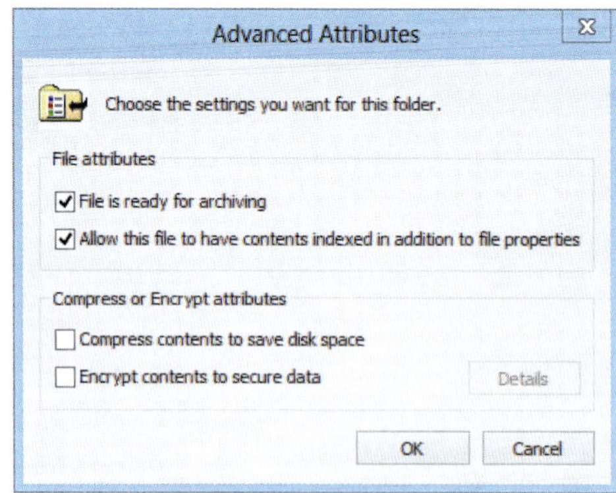

**B** The Advanced Attributes dialog box

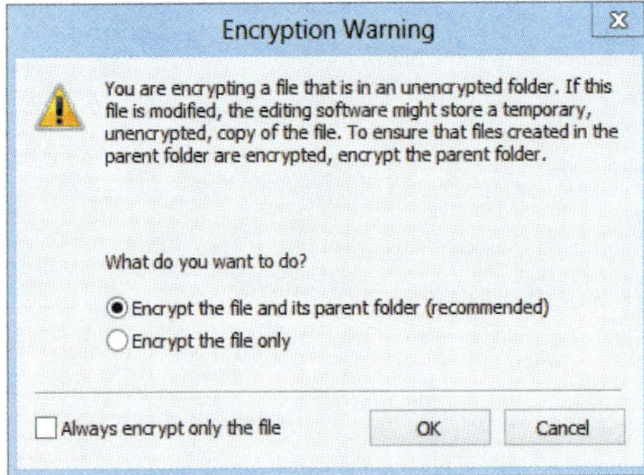


**C** The Encryption Warning dialog box

4. If you encrypt a file in an unencrypted folder, you will see a warning **C** indicating that using the file can make temporary copies of the file available in an unencrypted form. Encrypt either the file or the folder and then tap or click OK.

**TIP** Folder encryption offers more protection than file encryption and should be preferred when possible. Also, since the secret to encryption is the strength of your login password, be sure to use a strong password and protect it from others.

# Securing Internet Explorer

Browsers are particularly troublesome programs from a security perspective because, if you let them, they allow people on the outside to run programs inside your computer. All the things that make browsers so much fun—like playing Missile Command on www.atari.com/arcade, which uses Java, or running movies on a streaming media player—can be a backdoor into Windows 8.

All browsers have security settings built into them. Although there are arguments as to which browser is the most secure, all are actively updated against threats. Internet Explorer 10 is used as the example here because that's the browser that ships with Windows 8. IE10's Safety menu is your access to managing its security features 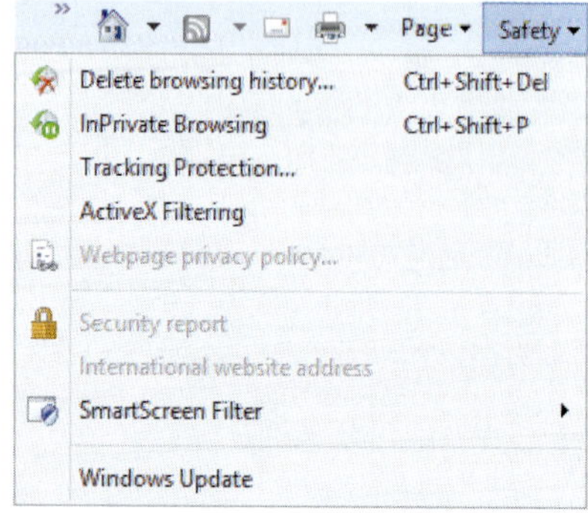.



**A** Internet Explorer 10's Safety menu

The Delete Browsing History command deletes downloaded content, cookies, temporary files, browsing history, download history, form data, passwords, ActiveX filtering, and tracking protection data; this can be a good reset, making it harder for outsiders to compromise your system. With InPrivate Browsing (new in Windows 8) turned on, all stored data in a browsing session is deleted when you close your browser. ActiveX Filtering prevents ActiveX programs from executing on a site. All of these features can make your session safer, but they limit what IE10 is capable of.

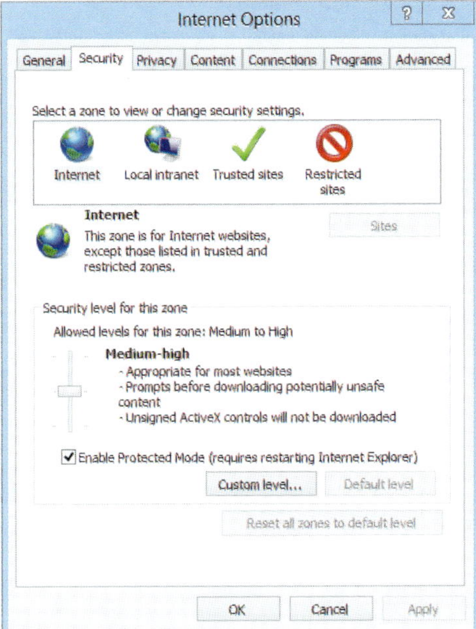



**B** The Security tab of the Internet Options dialog box

Most of the settings for security and privacy in Internet Explorer 10 are contained in the Internet Options dialog box **B**, particularly on the Security and Privacy tabs. The default settings on those tabs are adequate for most purposes, but you can customize them for special purposes.

### To view Internet Explorer 10's Safety menu:

Tap or click the Safety menu found on the IE10 command bar **A**.

### To open Internet Explorer 10's Security settings:

1. Tap or click the Tools menu on the IE10 command bar, and select the Internet Options command.

2. Tap or click the Security tab to view the security settings **B**.

**TIP** When entering sensitive information into a browser, always look to see that the protocol is HTTPS and that the address bar has a lock icon on the left.

# Putting It All Together

- Follow the ten commandments of safe computing.

- Use Windows Update, and always apply all patches and upgrades as soon as possible.

- Turn on and use Windows Firewall and Windows Defender.

- Do not click links, open attachments, or download content from unknown sources.

- Always log in as a user, and use administrator privileges only when you need to accomplish a task that requires them.

- Use 3-2-1 backup to protect your data from loss.

- Windows Firewall prevents access to your computer on a program-by-program basis.

- Windows Defender scans your system for viruses, trojans, malware, and spyware.

- Monitor your system status and correct security problems in Action Center.

- Use the BitLocker feature to encrypt drives so they can't be read by others.

- Use Encrypting File System to encrypt files or folders.

- Internet Explorer 10 ships with several new security features that can remove session data, block sites and apps from running, and more.

- Visit the Windows Safety & Security Center to learn more about current security issues, find tools, and get advice.

- Allow firewall access only to programs that you are familiar with.

- Run full Windows Defender scans every month or so.

# Cloud Connections

Microsoft has a vision that you will go to work, turn on your Windows 8 PC, and be a happy, productive worker. Then you will leave for home, whipping out your Windows 8 tablet to answer mail, read, or play games during your commute. At home, you will pick up a Windows 8 laptop to conduct your personal business and to socialize through Microsoft social media. Throughout the day, you will answer calls on your Windows Phone 8.

When you add a contact on one device, it appears on all of your devices. Your calendar and address book are similarly synchronized. How does it all work? It works because you are always connected to the cloud, where your apps and data reside as well as on your local device. Gone are computer stores with shrink-wrapped software; only Windows Store remains.

## In This Chapter

Microsoft sees the cloud as just another platform. To Microsoft, the cloud is a version of the Windows operating system itself—one that is omnipresent, distributed, and enabling. With Windows 8, you log in to your Microsoft account and gain access to all of Microsoft's web services. Many of the apps and services you see in Windows 8 were once part of the Windows Live service; now those services are front-ended by many of the new, tile-based apps.

For developers, Microsoft's vision means that the applications they create can run on all versions of Windows, either locally or in the cloud. With minimal development effort, the same application can run exactly the same way on a desktop, on a server, or remotely in the Microsoft Azure cloud. *Microsoft Azure* is the name of the cloud services that Microsoft offers to developers.

Microsoft's vision is a powerful one, and Microsoft is a major force in the cloud-computing world. They are a leading "Platform as a Service" provider through the Microsoft Azure service. In this chapter, you will learn about cloud computing and how Windows 8 uses what Microsoft has built.

# Windows Store

Windows Store is Microsoft's new marketplace for digital content distribution. On Windows Store, you will find both free and paid applications, trial offers, and content of various kinds. There's no web address for Windows Store; you access it from the Store app on the Start screen.

You can think of Windows Store as the Microsoft equivalent of Apple's App Store or of the Google Play store for Android tablets and phones. Windows Store distributes tile-based apps and pushes updates for the apps you purchase when they become available.

Windows Store requires that apps go through a certification process before becoming available. This certification process checks that the app meets certain guidelines, including those for robustness, legality, lack of moral turpitude, and other factors. Microsoft takes a 30 percent cut of the retail sales from developers, which drops to 20 percent when sales reach $25,000. Developers wishing to sell apps in this marketplace should visit the Windows Store Dashboard (msdn.microsoft.com/en-us/windows/apps/br216180).

Windows Store lists apps in the following categories:

- Spotlight
- Games
- Social
- Entertainment
- Photo
- Music & Video
- Sports
- Books & References
- News & Weather
- Health & Fitness
- Food & Dining
- Lifestyle
- Shopping
- Travel
- Finance
- Productivity
- Tools
- Security
- Business
- Education
- Government

Each of these areas typically has tiles for All Stars, Top Free, and New Releases; some have tiles for Top Paid and Popular Now groups.

When you purchase an app, Windows Store associates it with your Microsoft account and allows you to install the app on up to five devices. To install an app you've purchased on a different device, simply open Windows Store on that device and install the app.

## To open Windows Store:

Tap or click the Store tile Ⓐ.

The Windows Store app appears Ⓑ.

Ⓐ The Windows Store tile

Ⓑ Windows Store

## To review and purchase an app from Windows Store:

1. Tap or click the app tile that you are interested in to view the app's Overview screen Ⓒ.

2. Tap or click Details to view release notes, recommended hardware, supported processors, language versions, and app permissions.

3. Tap or click the *Reviews* link to see reviews submitted by users and the app's rating.

4. Tap or click the Install button to purchase the app.

5. If the app is free, it will automatically be installed; if not, complete your purchase.

   The newly installed app appears as a tile on the Start screen.

As upgrades appear for any of your downloaded apps (free or purchased), they will be listed in Windows Store's Live Tile Ⓐ, and an upgrade link will appear in the Windows Store app Ⓑ. From the standpoint of Windows Store, any app you download is considered to be "purchased," even if it was free.

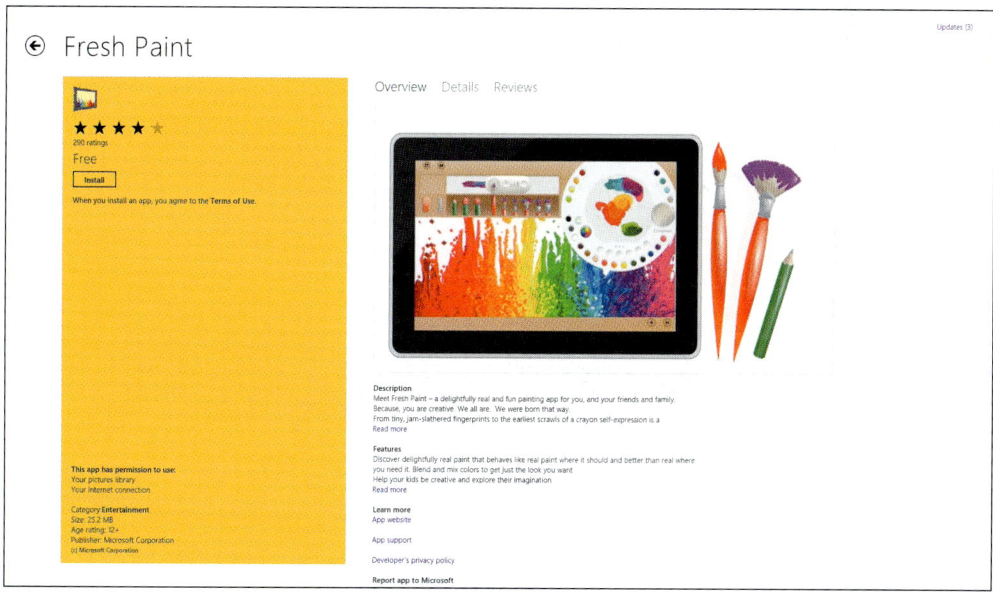


Ⓒ Click the Install button to install an app from Windows Store.

## To search Windows Store:

1. While in Windows Store, swipe from the right edge of the display.

   *or*

   Drag down from the upper-right corner of the display, and click the Search charm.

   The Search bar appears, with the Windows Store app selected **D**.

2. Enter any part of an app's name to view potential matches.

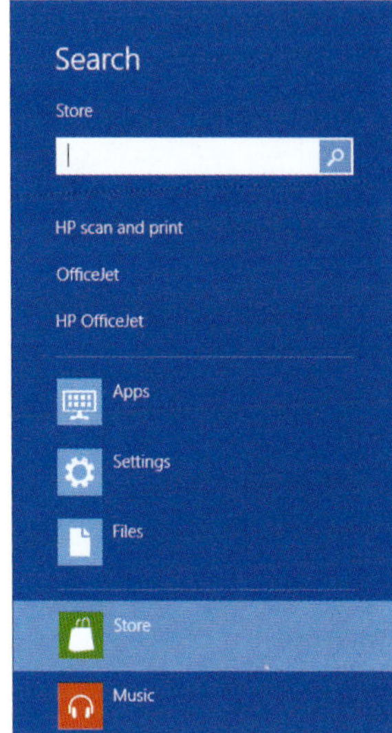



**D** The Search bar for Windows Store

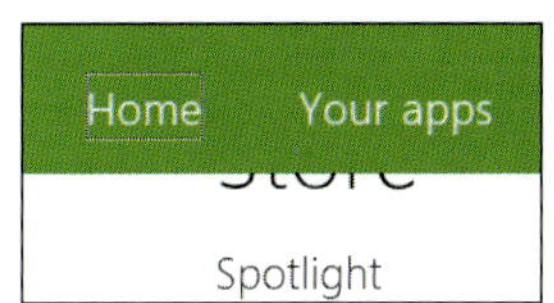


**E** Click the Your Apps button to view all of your installed Windows Store apps.

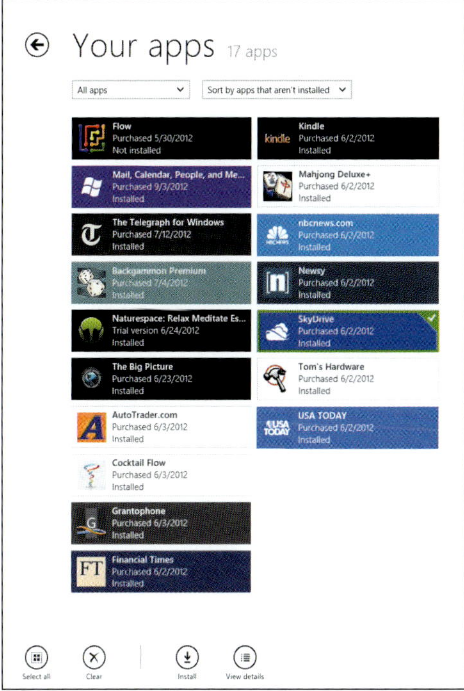


**F** The Your Apps screen

## To install Windows Store apps:

1. Swipe from the top edge or right-click the Windows Store background to view the Apps bar.

2. Tap or click the Your Apps button **E**.

   The Your Apps screen appears **F**.

3. Tap or click the All Apps pop-up menu to view apps not installed on your device.

4. Tap or click the Install button.

**TIP** Use the Apps Group button in the lower-right corner of the display to view a smaller version of the Windows Store app groups.

**TIP** If you are not able to find an installed app's tile by searching, simply go to Windows Store and reinstall the app.

# Microsoft Account

When you installed Windows 8, one of the steps had you create a Microsoft account, if you didn't have one already. This was covered in the "Installing Windows 8" section of Chapter 1. You can create a new Microsoft account at login.live.com.

Microsoft account is a single sign-on validation service that allows you to log on once and gain access to many websites and services. Microsoft account has been known as Wallet, Passport, .NET Passport, Passport Network, and, most recently, Windows Live ID. Microsoft account consolidates accounts from Windows Live ID, Hotmail, Zune, and Xbox Live.

The service ties a user name to an email account and a password and is backed up by a system of Microsoft account authorization servers. You can use your personal email address or a Hotmail or Live.com address. Once you log in to this service over a secure SSL (HTTPS) connection, your credentials are passed to any of the Microsoft digital properties you might visit; a "digital property" can be a website, a domain, or a service. Your Microsoft account stores your credentials, settings, and data in the cloud so that the information is available to any device that is signed in to your Microsoft account and connected to the Internet.

You can have your login stored on your device. Once your login is authenticated, a time-limited cookie is stored on your system and an encrypted ID tag is created that you can use as your ticket to other websites. The authentication server validates you to the site or service you are trying to gain access to.

The following information is stored with your Microsoft account:

- User information, like your name and address
- User preferences, such as your language and email settings
- Billing and transactions

You can log in to Windows 8 using a local account, a domain account, or your Microsoft account. When you use your Microsoft account, you are cloud-connected to services such as backup and synchronization. When you log in to your device with a local account, you lose access to all the cloud-connected apps and their data. However, you can convert your local account to a Microsoft account.

When you log in to a Windows 8 device with a Microsoft account, your settings are pushed to your current device from the cloud. You can sync settings for personalization, passwords, Ease of Access, certain apps, browsers, Windows Explorer, your mouse, and more.

## To convert a local account to a Microsoft account:

1. Sign in to Windows, press ⊞+C to open the Charms bar, and then tap or click the *Change PC settings* link.

2. Tap or click the *Users* link.

3. Tap or click the Switch to a Microsoft account button **A**.

4. Confirm your local account password **B**. Tap or click Next.

5. Provide your Microsoft account email address **C**. Tap or click Next.

*continues on next page*

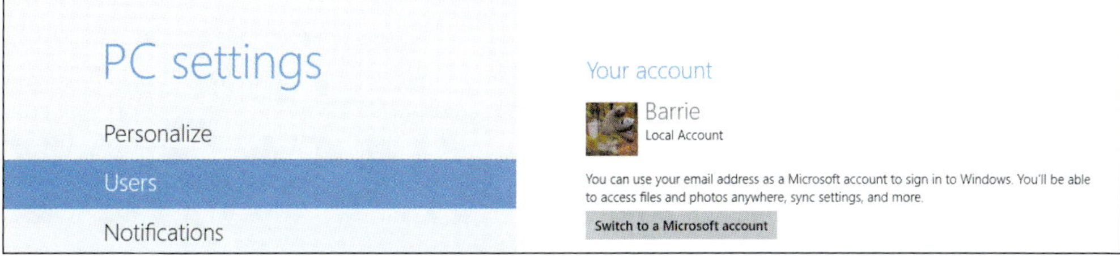

**A** The current account login

**B** Provide your local account password.

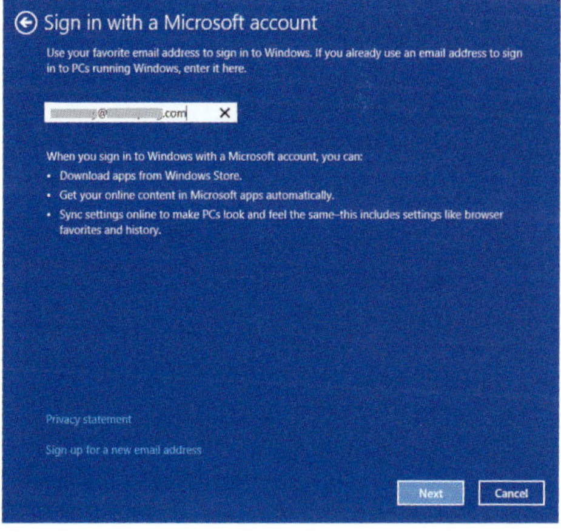

**C** Provide your Microsoft account email address.

6. Enter your Microsoft account email address and password **D**. Tap or click Next.

7. The Add Security Info screen **E** appears. Enter your country code and phone number, and tap or click Next.

   The final Sign In screen appears **F**.

8. Tap or click Finish to link the local account to your Microsoft account.

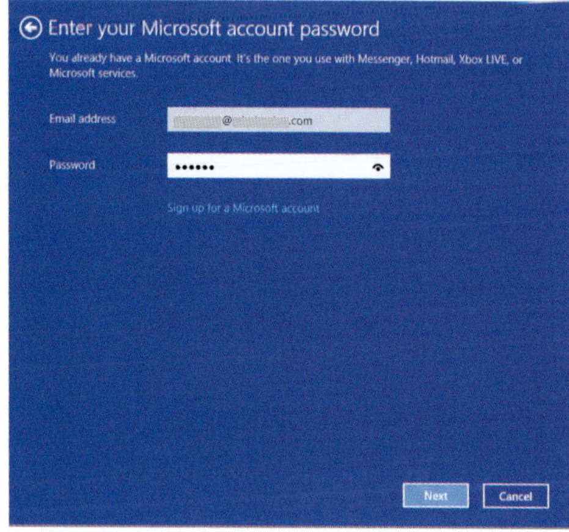
**D** Enter the Microsoft account email address and password here.

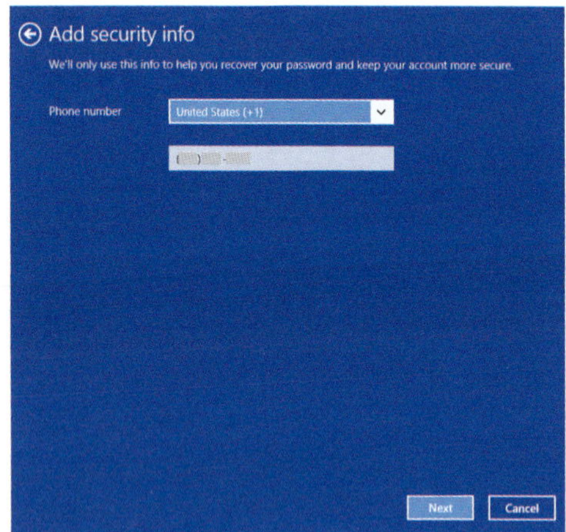
**E** Enter your country code and phone number.

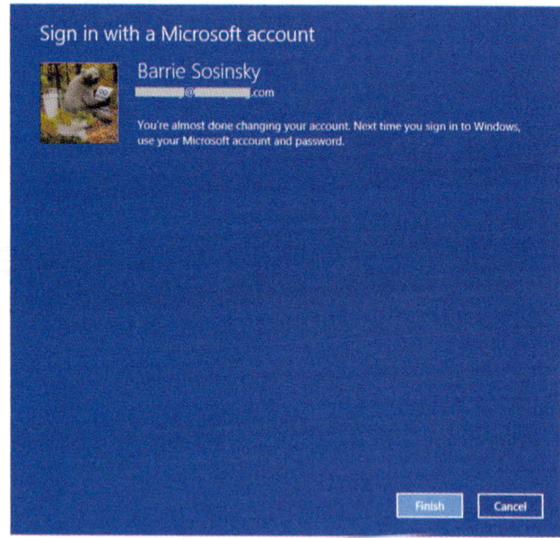
**F** The final screen linking your Microsoft account to your local account

When you link your local and Microsoft accounts, they share the same settings.

When you log in again, use your Microsoft account **G**.

Notice the *More account settings online* link **G**. That link opens Internet Explorer and displays (and allows you to change) your Microsoft account settings **H**; the first time you visit this site, you may be asked to supply a verification code that is sent to your phone. **I** shows the billing and payments screen for a Microsoft account. Other screens let you change personal information and perform other tasks.

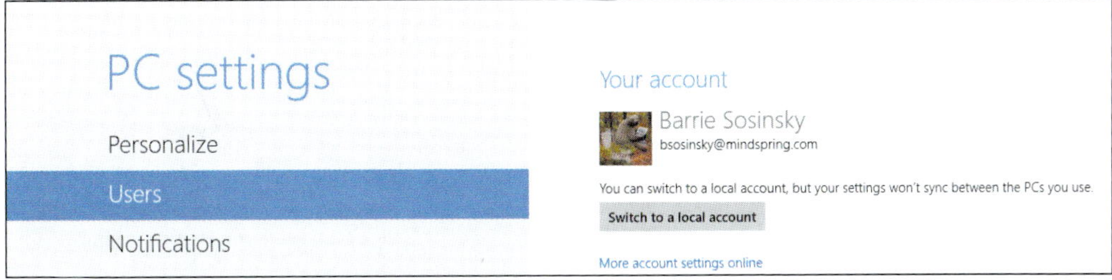

**G** Your user settings now show that you are logged in to a Microsoft account.

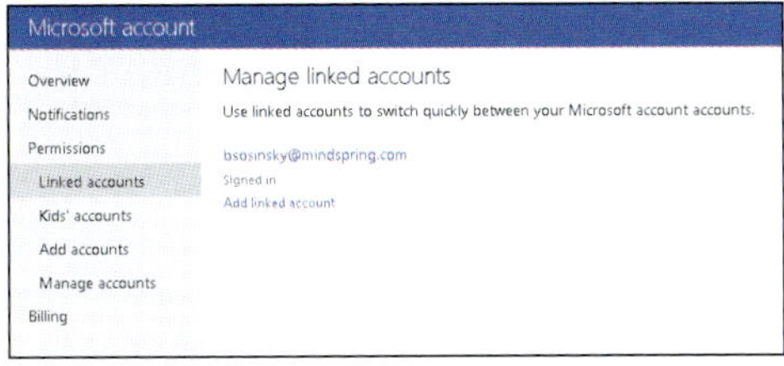

**H** The Managed Linked Accounts screen

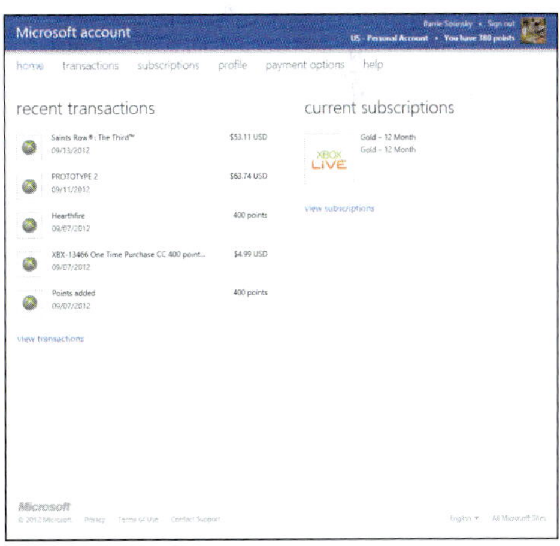

**I** The billing and payments screen for your Microsoft account lets you view your online purchases and transactions.

## To enable a roaming profile:

1. Press ⊞+I, and tap or click the *Change PC settings* link.

2. Tap or click the *Sync your settings* link in the PC Settings bar 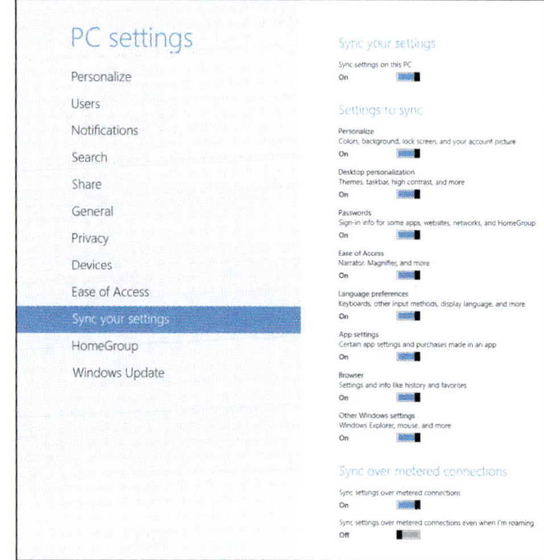.

3. Drag the sliders to turn on the sync settings you want.

**TIP** You can connect your Microsoft account to your domain account using the same general procedure. In the Users pane, tap or click the *Connect your Microsoft Account* link and then enter your Microsoft account email address. A domain account is used in corporate settings and usually isn't linked to a Microsoft account.

**J** The Sync Your Settings sliders allow your device to pick up elements of your profile when you are roaming.

# Windows Live

Windows Live (Live.com) is Microsoft's branded set of web applications and web services. It is the seventh most heavily trafficked website in the world. Live services include:

- Windows Essentials applications (covered in the next section)
- Web services
- Mobile services

Microsoft estimates that nearly 500 million people use Windows Live services every month: Hotmail is the world's leading free email service; Messenger is the world's leading instant messaging service, with between 300 and 350 million active users; Microsoft's SkyDrive online storage service has 130 million users; and Windows Live Mail is second only to Outlook as a mail client.

The name Windows Live is being phased out, but the services will remain. The apps you see on the Start screen—People, Calendar, Mail, Photos, Messages, SkyDrive, and so forth—are the front-end apps that make Live services a seamless part of the Windows operating system. SkyDrive is the service that makes Windows 8's built-in data and settings synchronization work. Similarly, other services formerly branded as "Live," such as Xbox Live and Office Live, are losing Live in their names.

There was always the feeling that Windows Live apps were not part of the Windows *experience*. Not any more—in Windows 8 they are a natural expression of the web services they represent. Even the Family Safety service is now built right into Windows 8. **Ⓐ** shows the relationship between Windows Live services and Windows 8.

| Service | Windows 8 Desktop | Windows Phone 8 | Web (Live.com) | API Used | Previous Versions |
|---|---|---|---|---|---|
| Account | Microsoft account | Microsoft account | Account.live.com | OAUTH | Windows Live ID, Passport |
| Storage/ Docs | SkyDrive app, SkyDrive Desktop | SkyDrive app, Office app | SkyDrive.com | REST, JSON | FolderShare, Live Mesh, Windows Live Mesh |
| Email | Mail app | Mail app | Hotmail.com | EAS | Windows Live Mail, Outlook Express |
| Calendar | Calendar app | Calendar app | Calendar.live.com | EAS, REST | Windows Live Mail, Windows Calendar |
| Contacts | People app | People app | People.live.com | EAS, REST | Windows Contacts |
| Messaging | Messaging app | Messaging app | Integrated in Hotmail and SkyDrive | XMPP | MSN Messenger |
| Photos/ Videos | Photos app, Photo Gallery, Movie Maker | Photos app, Camera Roll | Photos.live.com | REST, JSON (via SkyDrive) | Windows Live Photo Gallery, Windows Live Movie Maker |

Reference: http://blogs.msdn.com/b/b8/archive/2012/05/02/cloud-services-for-windows-8-and-windows-phone-windows-live-reimagined.aspx.

**Ⓐ** Windows Live services and apps as deployed across platforms

Live.com now redirects you to the Hotmail login screen **B**. Hotmail is being rebranded as Outlook.com, so when users switch from the Hotmail user interface to the Outlook.com user interface, they will log in directly to their Inbox instead of to Windows Live Home. The Live Home page will be deprecated and will disappear over time.

**TIP** If you have a Hotmail account, when you go to Outlook.com your account will automatically be transferred to the new interface. The process is painless, and the interface is a great upgrade.

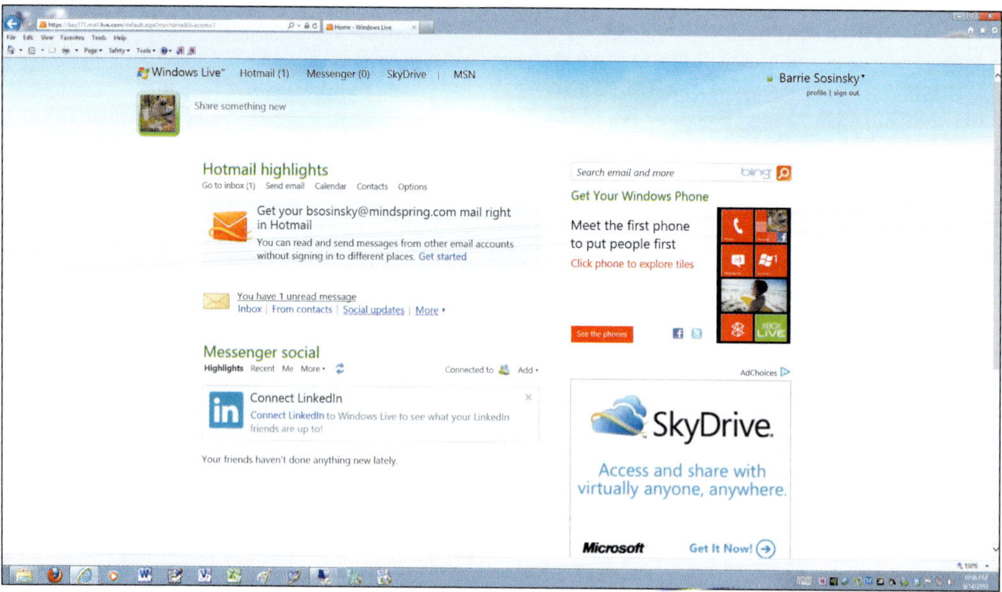

**B** Live.com redirects to the Hotmail login page.

# Windows Essentials

Windows Essentials, formerly known as Windows Live Essentials, is a set of free applications that Microsoft offers for download via an installer **A**.

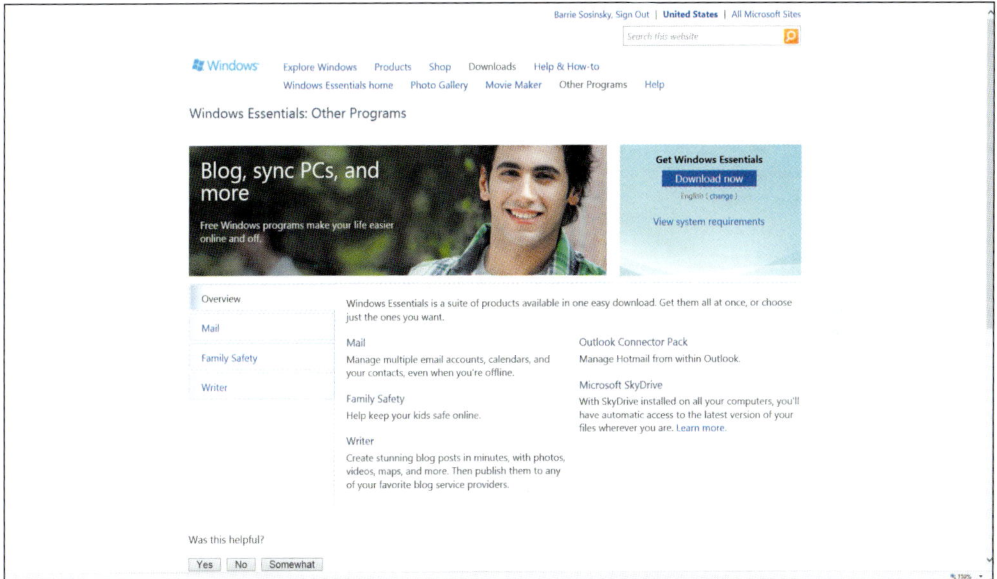


**A** The Windows Essentials home page allows you to download a set of useful tools.

Windows Essentials includes the following downloadable applications:

- **Mail.** The Mail app contains functionality that you will find in the Mail, Calendar, and People apps.

- **Messenger.** Unlike the tile-based Messenger app, the Desktop version offered in Essentials is windowed and allows you to move back and forth between work and chat sessions. That's something you will appreciate.

- **Movie Maker.** Movie Maker is a video editor **B**. Its tools for editing audio and video, as well as the video stabilization feature, allow you to create nearly professional-quality movies. You can also add free background music to your movies. Movie Maker may be the best part of the Windows Essentials package.

- **Photo Gallery.** This application has much better photo acquisition features and photo editing capabilities than the tile-based Photos app.

- **SkyDrive.** SkyDrive is Windows' cloud-based storage service. With SkyDrive, you get an Internet Explorer interface to your remote files, and you can access your files from any connected PC.

- **Writer.** Writer is a blog writer. It's a small, efficient, easy-to-use tool that also handles media, such as photos.

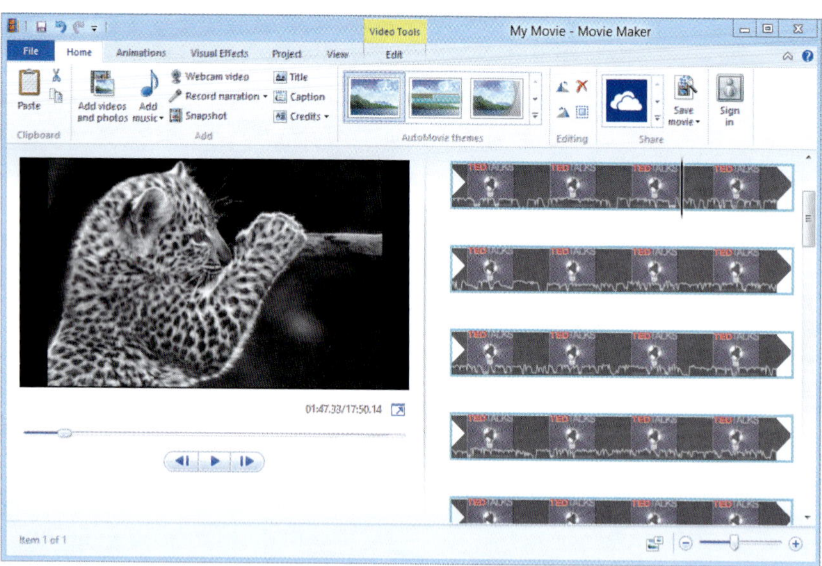

**B** Movie Maker

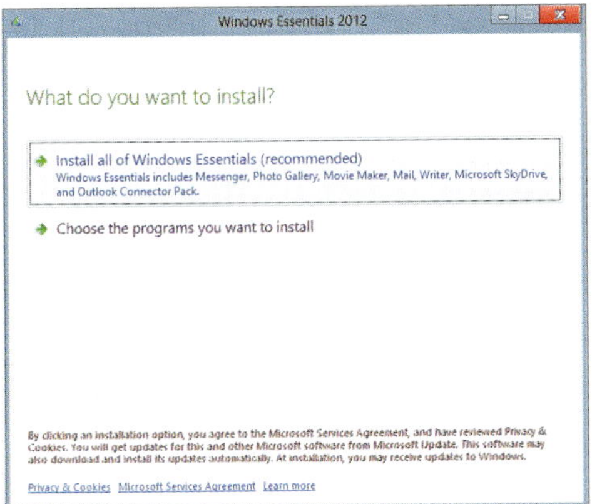

C Install all or some of the Windows Essentials applications.

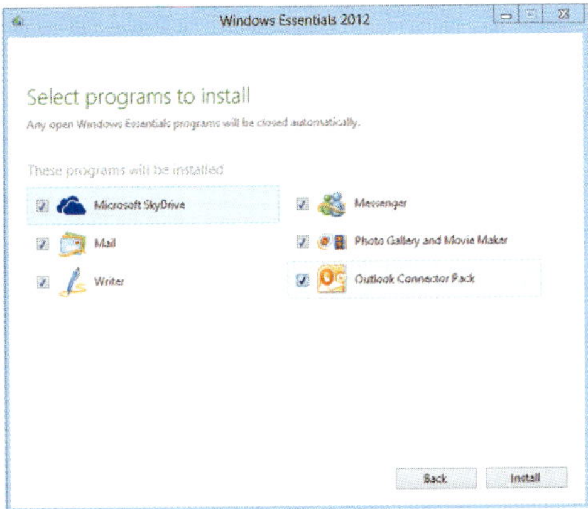

D The Custom Installation page

The Photos, Messenger, and Mail apps that appear on the tile-based interface aren't as full-featured as the applications that are found in the Essentials package. Movie Maker and Writer are applications that you will find useful, but they do not have a tile-based app counterpart.

Family Safety is gone from the Essentials package; it is now part of Windows 8 settings. Family Safety allows you to control who can be connected to the Internet during what times, and to place content and site restrictions on your family's user accounts. Also missing from this version of Essentials are the Bing Bar, Outlook Connector (Outlook 2013), and Windows Live Mesh.

## To install Windows Essentials:

1. Open your browser, go to windows. microsoft.com/en-US/windows-live/ essentials-home, and tap or click the Download Now button A.

   A dialog box asks if you want to save or run the program.

2. Save the setup file (wlsetup-web.exe) to a known location, and download the file.

3. Launch the wlsetup-web.exe file by double-clicking or double-tapping it. If necessary, elevate your privileges by tapping or clicking the OK button in the User Account Control dialog box.

4. In the Windows Essentials dialog box C tap or click either the Install All or the Choose The Programs button to proceed.

   If you select Install All, skip to step 6.

5. Select the programs you want, and then tap or click the Install button D.

*continues on next page*

6. When the Done dialog box appears, tap or click Close.

7. When the Windows Essentials End User License Agreement appears, tap or click the Accept button.

8. In the Welcome Back dialog box 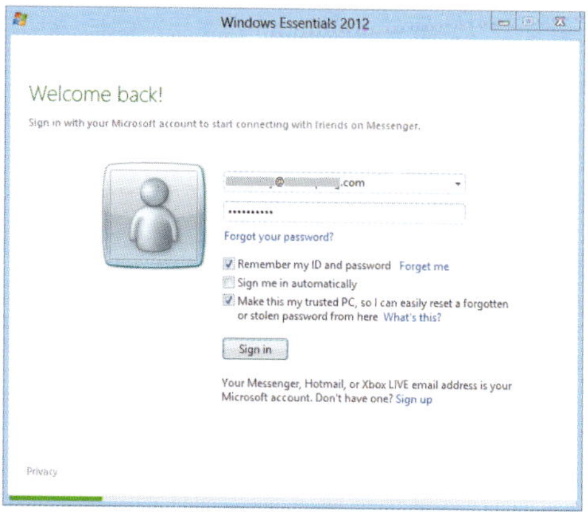, enter your Microsoft account information and tap or click Sign In.

9. In the Connect Your Favorite Services dialog box, you can connect Windows Essentials to Facebook or LinkedIn, or you can click the Close button to continue without connecting to those sites.

   The Desktop version of Messenger appears **F**.

After you install Windows Essentials, you will see a new application group at the right of your Start screen, with a tile for each installed application **G**. You will also notice that SkyDrive is integrated into Windows Explorer for you to use immediately.

**TIP** You may also want to download Microsoft Security Essentials (windows.microsoft.com/mse) and Windows Essentials Codec Pack (www.mediacodec.org).

**E** The Microsoft account login screen for Windows Essentials

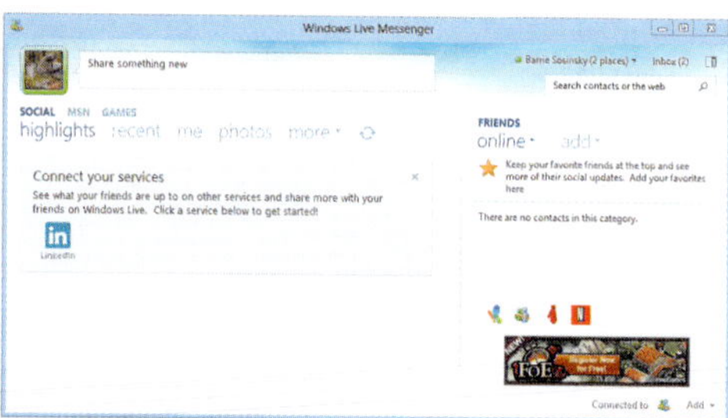

**F** The Desktop version of Messenger

**G** The Windows Essentials tile group

# SkyDrive

Microsoft SkyDrive, previously known as Windows Live SkyDrive and then as Windows Live Folders, is a cloud-based file hosting service. You get 7 GB of storage with your Microsoft account and can purchase additional storage as needed. You can upload files of up to 300 MB to SkyDrive.

SkyDrive files can be made available to any device that is logged in to your Microsoft account, including notebooks, tablets, phones, and Macs.

SkyDrive is accessible in three different locations:

- The tile-based SkyDrive app
- Internet Explorer
- SkyDrive.live.com

Since SkyDrive is based on HTML5 technology, you can drag-and-drop files and folders to and from your browser, as well as access SkyDrive from Internet Explorer. The tile-based SkyDrive app is part of the Windows 8 standard installation. The Desktop SkyDrive app is part of the Windows Essentials package; the tile that the Windows Essentials installer creates is a shortcut to the SkyDrive folder in Windows Explorer.

When you add a file to SkyDrive, the file type is retained and the appropriate icon is displayed. SkyDrive has application viewers that let you open and use documents right in the drive. You can search within SkyDrive, but the search works only for Microsoft Office formats.

There's also some additional functionality in SkyDrive that might not be clear to you at first glance. SkyDrive can:

- Save documents from Hotmail/Outlook and share them with other connected devices.
- Allow you to edit Microsoft Office documents in a browser (using Office Web Apps).
- Integrate with save and share features, as exemplified by the integration with Bing, Microsoft's search engine.
- Enable you to share files from social media sites such as Facebook, Twitter, and LinkedIn.
- Run a photo slideshow.
- Store folders as a ZIP file (compressed archive).

  The limit for a ZIP file is 4 GB or 65,000 files.

From a Windows 8 perspective, the most important thing SkyDrive does is serve as the mechanism by which settings and files are stored and synchronized.

Almost anything you can do in Windows Explorer, you can do in SkyDrive.

SkyDrive is built into Windows Explorer, and you don't have to do anything special to work with it there. It is fully drag-and-drop enabled.

When you open SkyDrive in Windows Explorer for the first time, a wizard appears that asks if you want to change the default location of your local SkyDrive folder (**C:\Users*<username>*\SkyDrive**). You will also see an option that allows you to share files in that folder with other connected devices. Content in that folder is synchronized with your cloud storage.

## To add a file to the tile-based SkyDrive app:

1. Tap or click the SkyDrive tile **Ⓐ**. SkyDrive opens.

2. Swipe from the bottom or right-click SkyDrive to view the Apps bar **Ⓑ**.

3. Click the Add button **Ⓑ** to open the SkyDrive tile-based picker.

**Ⓐ** The SkyDrive tile

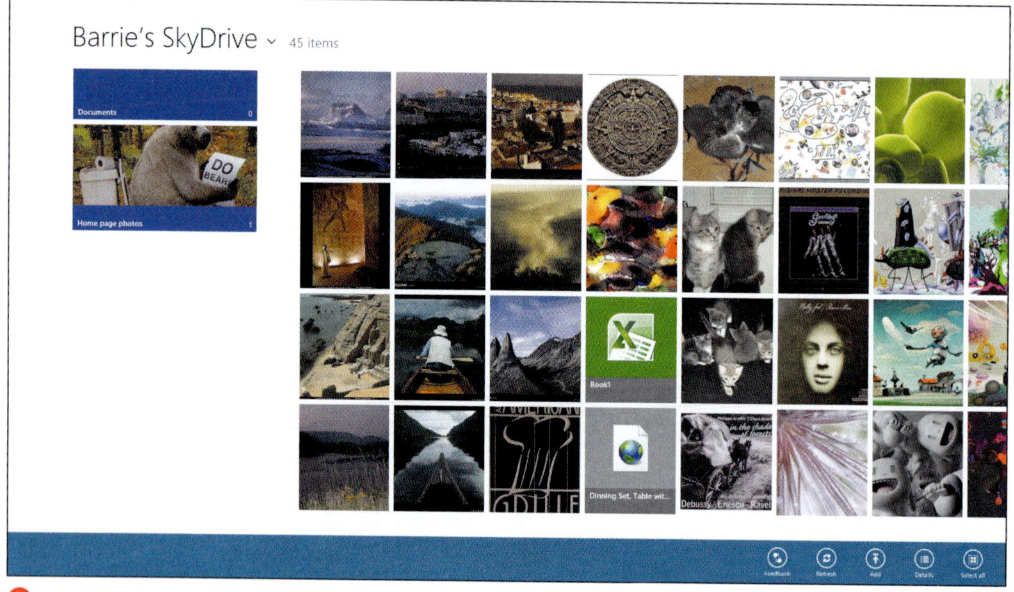


**Ⓑ** SkyDrive with the Apps bar showing. The Add button is the center button in the bar.

4. Select the file you wish to add **C**.

5. Tap or click the drop-down menu **D** to move to another folder within SkyDrive.

**C** SkyDrive's file picker allows you to navigate the file system and select files to add.

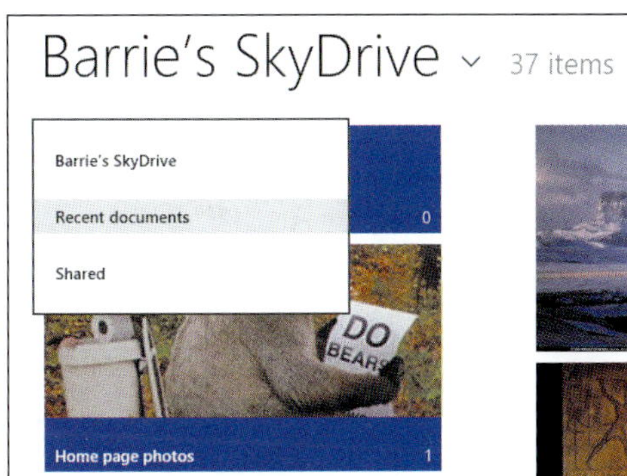

**D** Use the drop-down menu to move between SkyDrive's built-in folders.

# To open SkyDrive inside Windows Explorer:

1. Press ⊞+E.

2. Tap or click the SkyDrive icon in the Navigation pane **E**.

Notice that in **B** and **E**, pictures appear as pictures, folders as folders, and many of the documents appear with their document icons. SkyDrive knows about these files, so just double-tap or double-click on objects to open them. Files open in tile-based apps unless the file is a legacy (Desktop) file type.

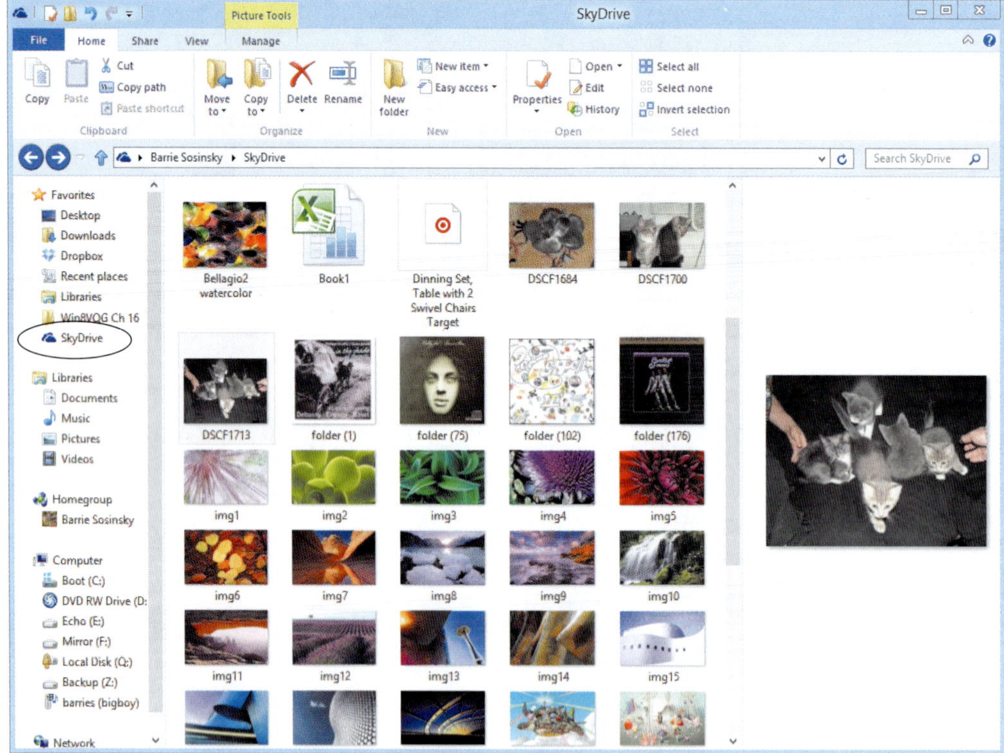

**E** SkyDrive shows up as a folder in Internet Explorer. This folder is a local folder synchronized to the cloud.

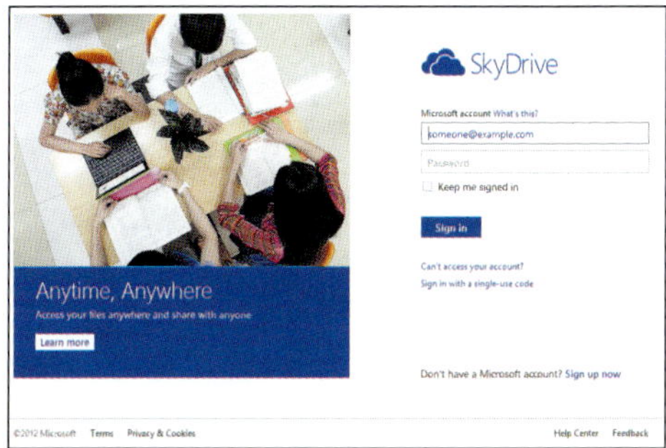



**F** The SkyDrive login screen is where you enter your Microsoft account information.

## To access SkyDrive from a browser:

1. Enter **skydrive.com** into your browser's address bar, and press Enter.

   The SkyDrive login page opens **F**.

2. Enter your Microsoft account credentials and then tap or press the Sign In button.

   SkyDrive.live.com appears **G**.

**TIP** In the browser version of SkyDrive, there is a *Get SkyDrive apps* link. From that page, you can download apps for a variety of mobile devices, including the Windows Phone, the iPhone and iPad, and Android phones.

**TIP** What's unfortunately missing from SkyDrive is automated backup. For now, you should invest in third-party products such as Acronis True Image to perform this function.

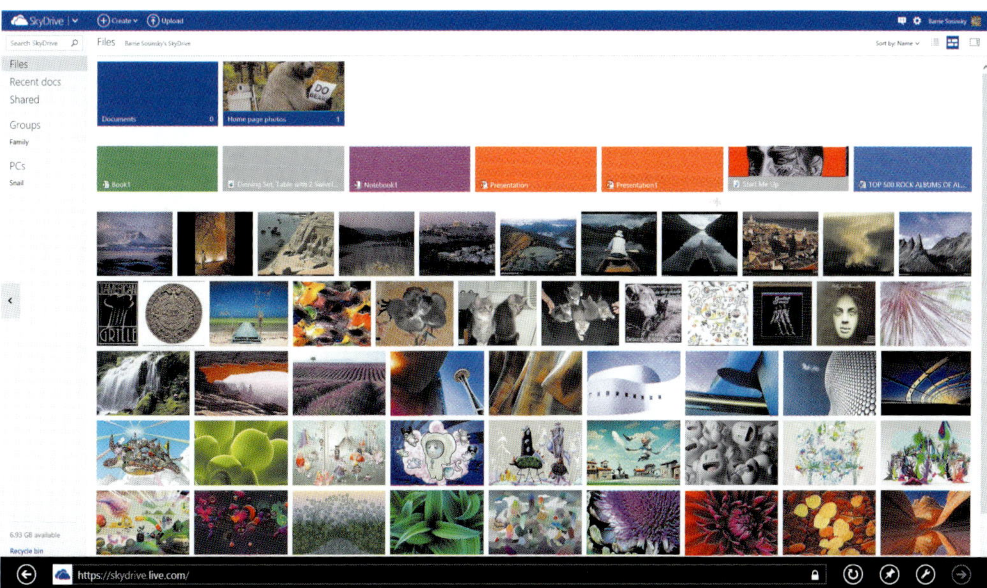



**G** SkyDrive.live.com shown in the tile-based Internet Explorer 10 app

# Office 2013

For many people, Microsoft Office is the reason they buy Windows in the first place. Corporations have standardized on Office, and it's a product suite with a long tradition. Over time, Microsoft intends to move Office online and have users pay for it as a service.

To this end, Office 365 (www.microsoft.com/office365) was launched. The online versions of Word, Excel, and PowerPoint aren't nearly as feature-complete as the shrink-wrapped Office 10 applications, but they can read and write files and perform basic content modification. You can purchase a subscription plan for Office 365, and depending upon the plan you get a subscription to Office 2010 Desktop applications as well as access to Exchange Server, SharePoint Server, and Lync Server. This is a corporate play to compete with both OpenOffice (which is free) and, more importantly, Google Docs. Plans for enterprises, small business, and education exist for this product.

The next version of Microsoft Office is Microsoft Office 2013. This is the successor to Office 2010, and it is in early beta. The early technical release shows a tile-based interface, with a ribbon and a Windows 8 look and feel. You can get a look at the preview home page 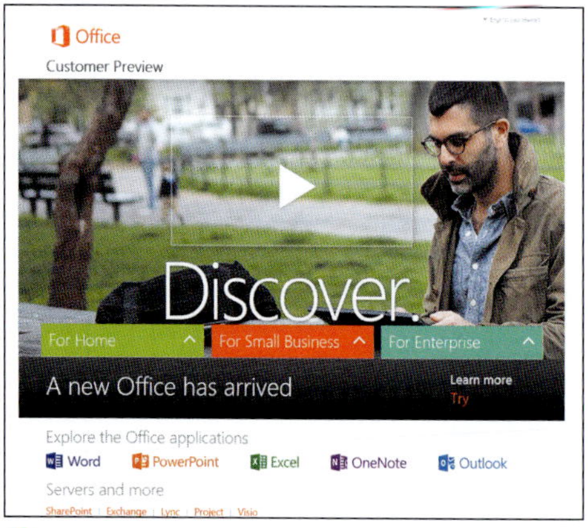 by visiting www.microsoft.com/office/preview.

Office 2013 is an important development because it is the first large Desktop legacy application suite to be converted into the tile-based interface; this will affect the conversion of all of the other major Desktop applications on the Windows platform. Microsoft views Office 2013 as a cloud-connected service, and it will use a model similar to the one you are now seeing in the tile-based apps.

**A** The Office 2013 preview page. These apps will set the standard for the conversion of Windows legacy applications to the new, tile-based apps.

**TIP** You can preview Office 2013 by downloading it from www.microsoft.com/office/preview/en/try-office-preview.

# Putting It All Together

- The cloud is the glue that makes the data and services you use on your Windows 8 device available on your other connected devices, and vice versa.

- Windows Store is the distribution method for all tile-based apps, with some apps available for free and others paid for through your Microsoft account.

- Windows Store keeps track of what you purchase, lets you download upgrades, and restores missing or corrupted apps.

- Windows Store comes with a powerful search function.

- Your Microsoft account is the key to accessing Microsoft's cloud-based services.

- Microsoft account consolidates accounts from Windows Live, Hotmail, Zune, and Xbox.

- You can convert a local account or a domain account to a Microsoft account, as well as link them.

- You can enable a roaming profile by syncing your settings through the tile-based interface's Sync Your Settings panel.

- Windows Live is a set of online applications, web services, and mobile services that is being merged into the Windows 8 platform.

- Windows Essentials is a package of apps that can replace or supplement apps that are currently installed in Windows.

- Several of the Windows Essentials apps are more powerful than the default apps; a few offer unique functionality that you should take advantage of.

- SkyDrive is Microsoft's cloud-based storage app. It is available through a tile-based app, in Windows Explorer, and at skydrive.com.

- SkyDrive synchronizes content between cloud storage and local folders, and can be accessed from any Windows connected device via your Microsoft account.

- The development work being done to convert Office to the new, tile-based interface will affect the conversion of all of the other major Desktop applications on the Windows platform.

# Index

# K

keyboard, closing apps from, 111

Keyboard icon, 84

keyboard shortcuts

    Charms bar, 22, 47

    Close command, 75

    Computer Management menu, 46

    Control Panel, 80

    copying objects, 68

    deleting objects, 68

    Desktop Management menu, 66

    Devices charm, 172

    help on Desktop, 19

    launching Desktop, 60–61

    Lock screen, 22

    pasting copies of objects, 68

    Print bar, 172

    Print command, 168

    Registry, 91

    Run dialog box, 80, 88, 107

    Search for Settings, 82

    Settings bar, 85

    shutting down Windows, 16–17

    snapped applications, 110

    Tab order, 77

    Task Manager, 106, 199

    Task Switcher, 77

    Windows Explorer, 89, 148

keyboards. *See* touch keyboard

Krogh, Peter, 299

# L

legacy programs. *See also* programs

    Exit command, 111

    removing, 104

libraries

    adding folders to, 149

    customizing, 149

    opening, 148

    organization of, 142

    searching, 149

    viewing, 148

Libraries tile, creating, 149

Live Tiles, 39–41

Local Group Policy Editor, 92–93

Lock screen, 22–23

logging in as user, 296

low-resolution video, enabling, 212

# M

Mail app, downloading from Windows Essentials, 334. *See also* emails

Mail tile-based app, 113

    adding accounts, 122–123

    creating emails, 124

    requirements, 122

    viewing emails, 123

Malicious Software Removal tool, 305

Maps tile-based app, 114

    getting directions, 139

    My Location button, 139

    viewing maps, 138–139

Maximize command, 75

MBR (master boot record), 223

media types, 143–144

menus, displaying, 50

Messaging tile-based app, 113, 123

Messenger app, downloading from Windows Essentials, 334

metadata, 191

Microsoft account validation service, 326–330

Microsoft Azure, 320

Microsoft Safety Scanner, 305

Microsoft Security Essentials, downloading, 336

Minimize button, 74

minimizing windows, 48

Mirror option, using with volumes, 225

mobile broadband, 289

mobile computing, 279–280. *See also* Windows Phone 8

    connection priority order, 288

    data synchronization, 285–287

    Hibernate option on Power menu, 293

    `netshell` command, 289

    Power button action, 293

    power consumption, 290

    smart network switching, 288–289

    Sync Your Settings features, 287

    Windows Mobility Center, 284

    Windows Phone 8, 281–283

Mobility Center. *See* Windows Mobility Center

mouse. *See also* touch mice

    snapping with, 109

    using, 46

mouse actions, corresponding gestures for, 45

Move command, 74

move operation, ending and pausing, 190

Movie Maker app, downloading from Windows Essentials, 334

movies, viewing with Video app, 135

program icons, dragging and dropping, 99
programs. *See also* applications; legacy programs
    closing, 111
    installing from web, 102
    installing in tile-based interfaces, 102
    launching with custom keystrokes, 101
properties
    modifying in file system, 191
    sorting on, 192
    viewing, 144
    viewing in Details view of folder, 192
    viewing in file system, 191
    viewing in Windows Explorer, 142
Properties dialog box
    Acronis Recovery tab, 227
    General tab, 227–228
    Hardware tab, 227
    opening, 101
    Quota tab, 227
    Security tab, 227
    Sharing tab, 227, 256
    Tools tab, 227
    viewing, 228

## Q

QWERTY keyboard, 51–52

## R

RAID (redundant array of independent disks), 225–226
RAID 1, using with Storage Spaces, 234
RAID 3, using with Storage Spaces, 234
RAM requirements, 6
Reader tile-based app, 113, 136–137
ReadyBoost feature, using with flash drives, 239
**recimg** command, 215
Recovery control panel, 213
refreshing PCs, 208–210
Registry, 90–91
Repair Your Computer option, 212
resetting PCs, 208–210
Restart option, accessing, 17
Restore command, 68, 74–75
ribbon
    Clipboard group, 188
    Copy To button, 188
    Delete button, 188
    Home tab, 188
    Move To button, 188
    navigating with keyboard, 190
    new folder button, 188
    New group, 188
    Open group, 188
    Organize group, 188
    Properties button, 188
    Redo button, 188
    Rename button, 188
    Search Tools tab, 193
    Select group, 188
    Undo button, 188
ROM (read-only memory), 236
Run As Administrator command, 296
Run dialog box, opening, 80, 88, 107

## S

Safe Mode, enabling, 212
Safety & Security Center, 300
Save dialog box, 76
scroll bars, 75
Search app, using, 153–154
Search for Settings, opening, 82
Search function, 141
Search Tools tab of ribbon, 193
searches, performing, 194–195
security, 295
    Action Center, 306–308
    antivirus program, 297
    backing up, 299
    BitLocker Drive Encryption, 309–312
    EFS (Encrypting File System), 313–315
    IE10 (Internet Explorer 10), 316–317
    logging in as user, 296
    Run As Administrator command, 296
    safe computing, 296–300
    strong passwords, 298
    unknown sources, 297
    Windows Defender, 297, 304–305
    Windows Firewall, 297, 301–303
    Windows Update, 296
Security Essentials, downloading, 336
semantic zoom, 45
services
    disabling, 88
    verifying, 88–89
Settings bar, 16, 84–85
Share charm, using, 157.
        *See also* Network and Sharing Center
Share feature, 142
sharing files and folders, 256
sharing settings, 254–256
shortcuts, tiles as, 36
Show Administrative Tools, 84
shutting down Windows, 16–17, 85
Sign In screen, 24–25
Size command, 74

# WATCH READ CREATE

Unlimited online access to all Peachpit, Adobe Press, Apple Training and New Riders videos and books, as well as content from other leading publishers including: O'Reilly Media, Focal Press, Sams, Que, Total Training, John Wiley & Sons, Course Technology PTR, Class on Demand, VTC and more.

No time commitment or contract required!
Sign up for one month or a year.
All for $19.99 a month

## SIGN UP TODAY
**peachpit.com/creativeedge**